The Widdrington Women
AND THEIR EMINENT MEN

In memory of my mother, Cynthia.

The Widdrington Women
AND THEIR EMINENT MEN

CECILIA CHANCE

PHILLIMORE

2010
Published by
PHILLIMORE & CO. LTD
Andover, Hampshire, England
www.phillimore.co.uk

© Cecilia Chance, 2010

ISBN 978-1-86077-628-1

Printed and bound in Malta
Manufacturing managed by Jellyfish Print Solutions Ltd.

Contents

List of Illustrations vii
Acknowledgements viii
Family Trees ix
Preface xiii

1. Early Days 1
2. The Great Will Case 9
3. Growing up 14
4. Cecilia 'Comes Out' 20
5. Courtship and Marriage. 24
6. Early Married Life 31
7. The Great Adventure 37
8. Exemplary Wife, Troubled Mother 45
9. A Little Princess. 51
10. The Brothers. 55
11. The Governess Years 59
12. Mandell Creighton 65
13. 'A Little Turbulent Piece' 68
14. All Change 73
15. Hyères 77
16. 'I Hate all the Men I Meet' 83
17. 'The Supreme Good Effect of Love' 89
18. Edward Grey 94
19. Marriage. 100
20. An Election 103
21. 17 Hereford Square 107
22. The 'Tin House' 113

23.	'A Very Strange Little Soul'	118
24.	Two Friends	125
25.	A Fateful Encounter	128
26.	'Dear Mr Fry'	133
27.	'A Friendship tinged with Romance'	140
28.	Sir Edward in Office	147
29.	Gerard as Go-Between	154
30.	Between Two Loves	161
31.	May	168
32.	A Question without an Answer	175
33.	A Providential Illness?	179
34.	Two Inauspicious Marriages	187
35.	'O the Misery the Tears the trouble'	192
36.	A Horse that Shied	199
37.	Broken Lives	204
38.	A Fresh Start	211
39.	At War	214
40.	The Death of Fitz	221
41.	Peace at a Price	226
42.	A Time for Reconciliation	231
	Endpiece	238
	Notes	242
	Bibliography	244

List of Illustrations

Frontispiece: The author's mother, Cynthia.

1. Francis Widdrington and dogs, with the author looking on xii
2. Hopwood Hall in the 1940s. 3
3. Cecilia Widdrington 26
4. Shalcross Fitzherbert Widdrington.. 26
5. Newton Hall. 33
6. Dorothy (Dolly) Widdrington, a shy and troubled child................. 52
7. Gerard Widdrington did not fulfil the criteria for 'manliness'....... 58
8. Idonea (Ida) Widdrington, 'wild as a hawk and true as steel'. 70
9. Sir Edward Grey 95
10. Dorothy Grey 101
11. Dorothy Grey, *c.*1887 108
12. Roger Fry 131
13. The conservatory at Newton Hall. 134
14. Ida in full bloom. 145
15. Dorothy Grey, Edward's 'country wife' (photographed 1890) 150
16. Evelyn (Evie) Lloyd Price.. 156
17. May 172
18. Margaret Norman and Cecilia Widdrington: is there a likeness? 173
19. Addison Baker-Cresswell.. 188
20. Addy, Master of the Percy Foxhounds 189
21. Rosemary Cresswell, aged five 197
22. Cynthia Baker-Cresswell 198
23. Edward Grey, 'awakened from his dream of happiness' 203
24. Ida before the deluge, with John, Joe, Cynthia and Diana 207
25. Cynthia and Diana at Hyères, oil sketch by Roger Fry. 209
26. Aline Cresswell, Addy's daughter by his housekeeper 213

27. Roger Fry 218
28. Fitz. 222
29. Bertram Widdrington..223
30. John Baker-Cresswell as a cadet with his half-sister, Rosemary 228
31. Ida Cresswell, oil sketch by Roger Fry 230
32. Cecilia Widdrington in old age.. 232
33. Chance House, Grange Road, Sidmouth. 232

Acknowledgements

First, my thanks go to the late Francis Widdrington, who died in 2009. He allowed me to borrow the diaries kept by his grandmother, Cecilia Widdrington, and by his aunt, Idonea (Ida) Cresswell. Also a special thank you to Pam McLaughlin, both for her encouragement and for undertaking the chore of re-typing my manuscript onto a computer.

In addition, the following people have provided invaluable help and advice:

Mr Charles Baker-Cresswell, Mrs Cinna Belloc-Lowndes, Mr Peter Bridgeman, Mr Derek and Mrs Pat Brockway, the Hon. Adrian Bullock, Mrs Alison Crowdy, Mrs Doreen El-Ahwamy, Mr Bengy Carey-Evans, Dr Gwenda Evans, Mr Robert and Mrs Mia van Gestel, Mr D.D. Green, Mr Anthony Heaton-Armstrong, Mr Peter Lowden, Mrs Margaret Norman, Mr Robin Price, Mr John and Mrs Mair Rees, Professor Keith Robbins, Mr Michael Waterhouse, Mr David Yale.

I would also like to acknowledge the assistance I received from Kings College Library, Cambridge, and the Middleton Library, Greater Manchester.

Last, but by no means least, I wish to thank my husband, Jeremy, for his encouragement and support at all times.

The Gregge-Hopwoods of Hopwood Hall, Lancashire

Dr Robert Hopwood, who died in 1762 without issue, bequeathed Hopwood Hall and the Hopwood Estate to his cousin and friend Edward Gregge, who assumed the name of Gregge-Hopwood.

```
                    Edward Gregge-Hopwood = Judith Sutherland
                              (d. 1798)
                                 |
          ┌──────────────────────┴──────────────────────┐
Robert Gregge-Hopwood = the Hon. Cecilia Byng, dau. of Lord Torrington    Catherine = General Heron of Moore Hall
    1773-1854         & Lady-in-Waiting to Queen Charlotte
                              d. 1836
                                                                              ┌───────┴───────┐
                                                                             Kate       the Rev. George (no issue)
          ┌──────────────────────┬──────────────────────┐
Edward = Susan Fanny Baskeryle Glegg    the Rev. Frank = Lady Eleanor Stanley    Lt Col Harvey    Mary Augusta = Earl of Sefton
1810-91         d. 1906                     b. 1812       dau. of Earl of Derby

   ┌──────┬──────────┬──────────┬──────────┐
Cecilia  Lucy = Henry Crossley  Rose = Sir James   Edward = Mary Cole   Evelyn = Richard Lloyd
1840-1936  b. 1842              b. 1844  Pender    b. 1846                       Price of Rhiwlas
                                                                                 b. 1850
   =
Shallcross
Fitzherbert Widdrington                                    ┌─────────────┴─────────────┐
(see Widdrington family tree)                           Edward                       Robert
                                                       1881-1917                    1885-1916
                                                       (no issue)                   (no issue)
```

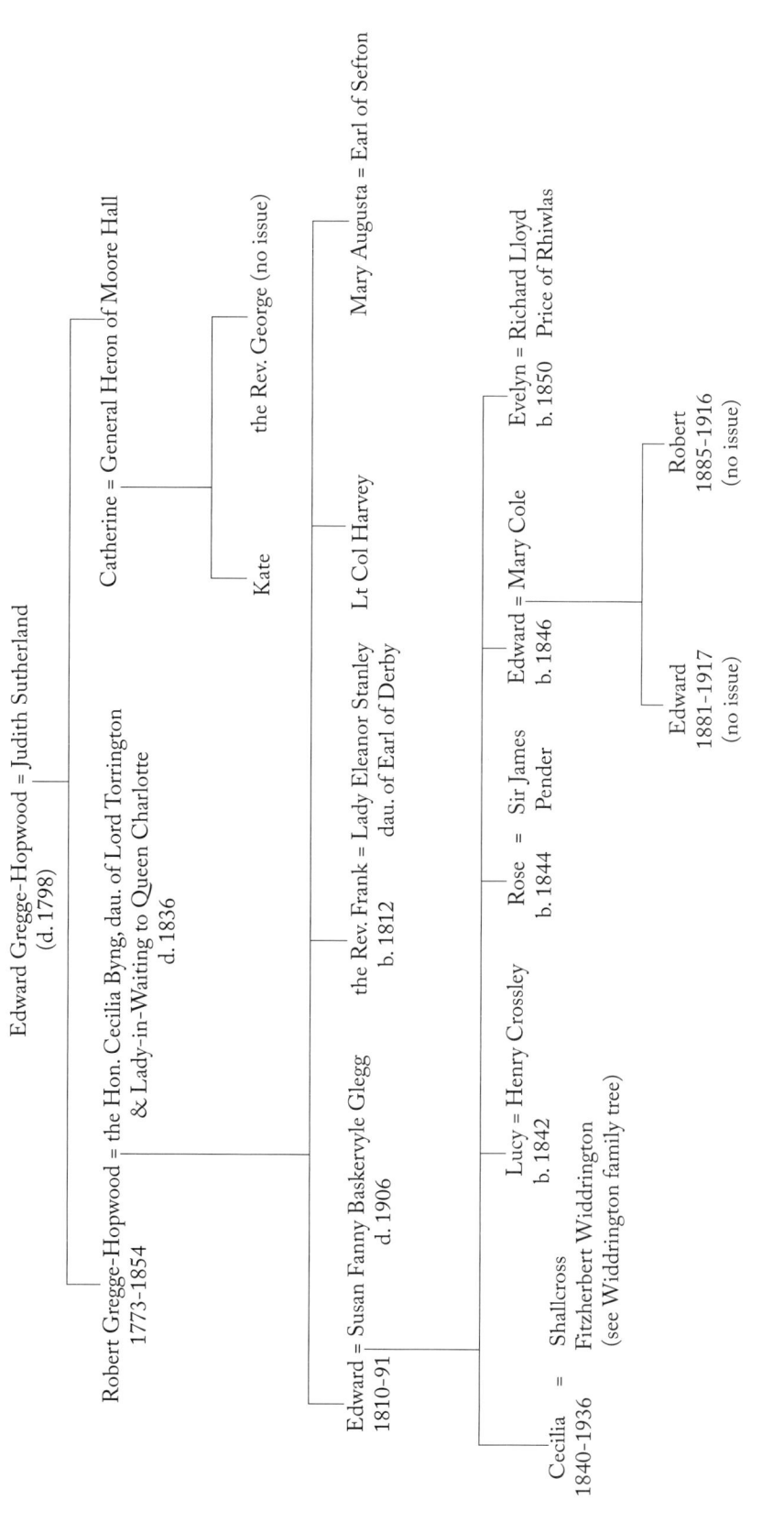

With the death of Edward Hopwood, killed in action in 1917, and the death of his younger brother Robert, killed in action a year earlier, the Hopwood line came to an end.

The Widdringtons of Newton and Hauxley

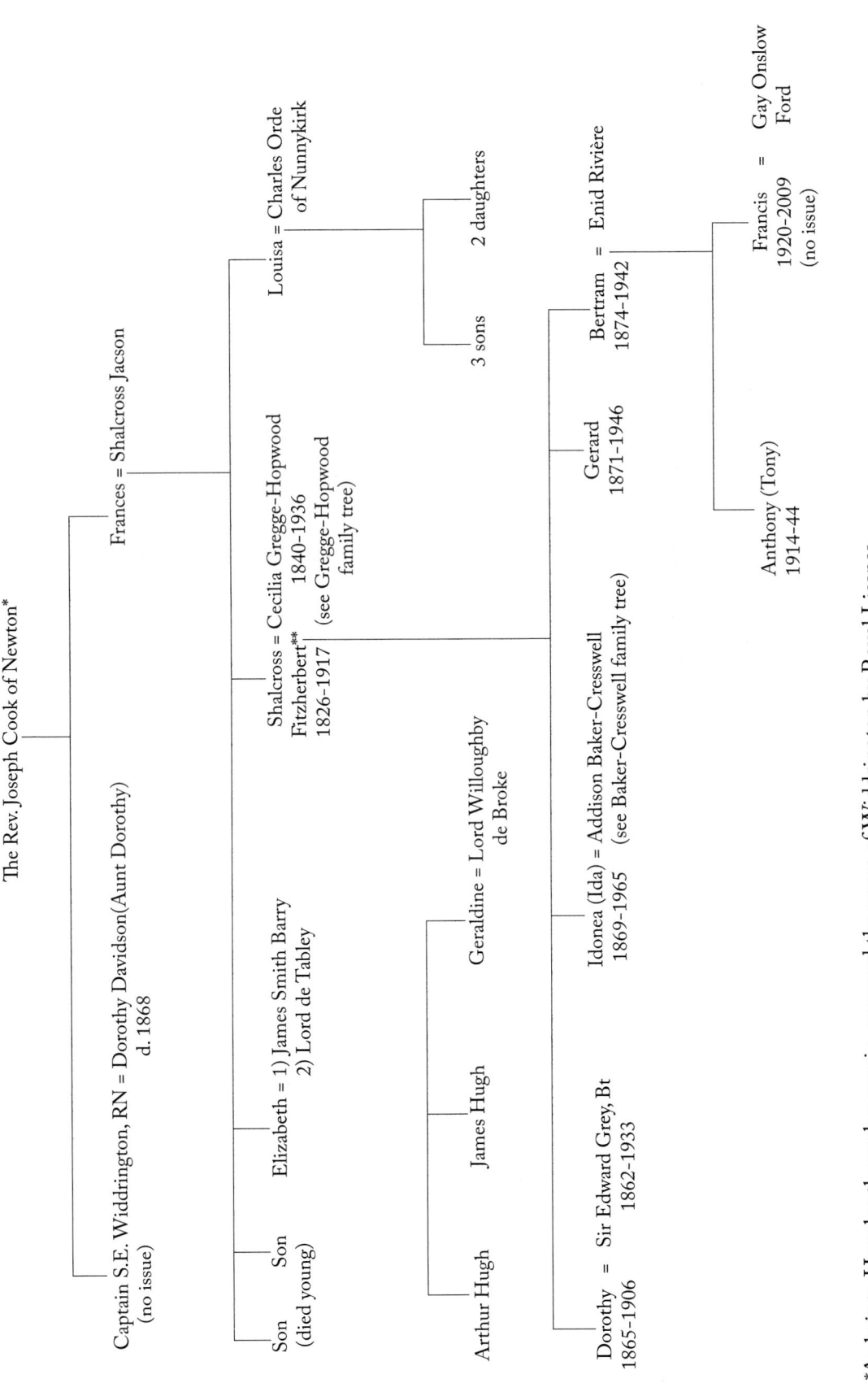

The Rev. Joseph Cook of Newton*

Captain S.E. Widdrington, RN = Dorothy Davidson (Aunt Dorothy)
(no issue)   d. 1868

Frances = Shalcross Jacson

┌─────────────┬──────────────────────────┬──────────────┐
Son   Elizabeth = 1) James Smith Barry   Shalcross = Cecilia Gregge-Hopwood   Louisa = Charles Orde
(died young)   2) Lord de Tabley   Fitzherbert**   1840-1936   of Nunnykirk
                                                   1826-1917   (see Gregge-Hopwood
                                                               family tree)

Arthur Hugh   James Hugh   Geraldine = Lord Willoughby
                                          de Broke

Dorothy = Sir Edward Grey, Bt   Idonea (Ida) = Addison Baker-Cresswell   Gerard   Bertram = Enid Rivière   3 sons   2 daughters
1865-1906   1862-1933   1869-1965   (see Baker-Cresswell family tree)   1871-1946   1874-1942

Anthony (Tony)   Francis = Gay Onslow
1914-44   1920-2009   Ford
                  (no issue)

*As heir to Hauxley through a cousin, assumed the name of Widdrington by Royal Licence.
**As heir to Hauxley and Newton through his cousin Captain S.E. Widdrington, assumed the name of Widdrington by Royal Licence.

The Baker-Cresswells of Cresswell and Harehope

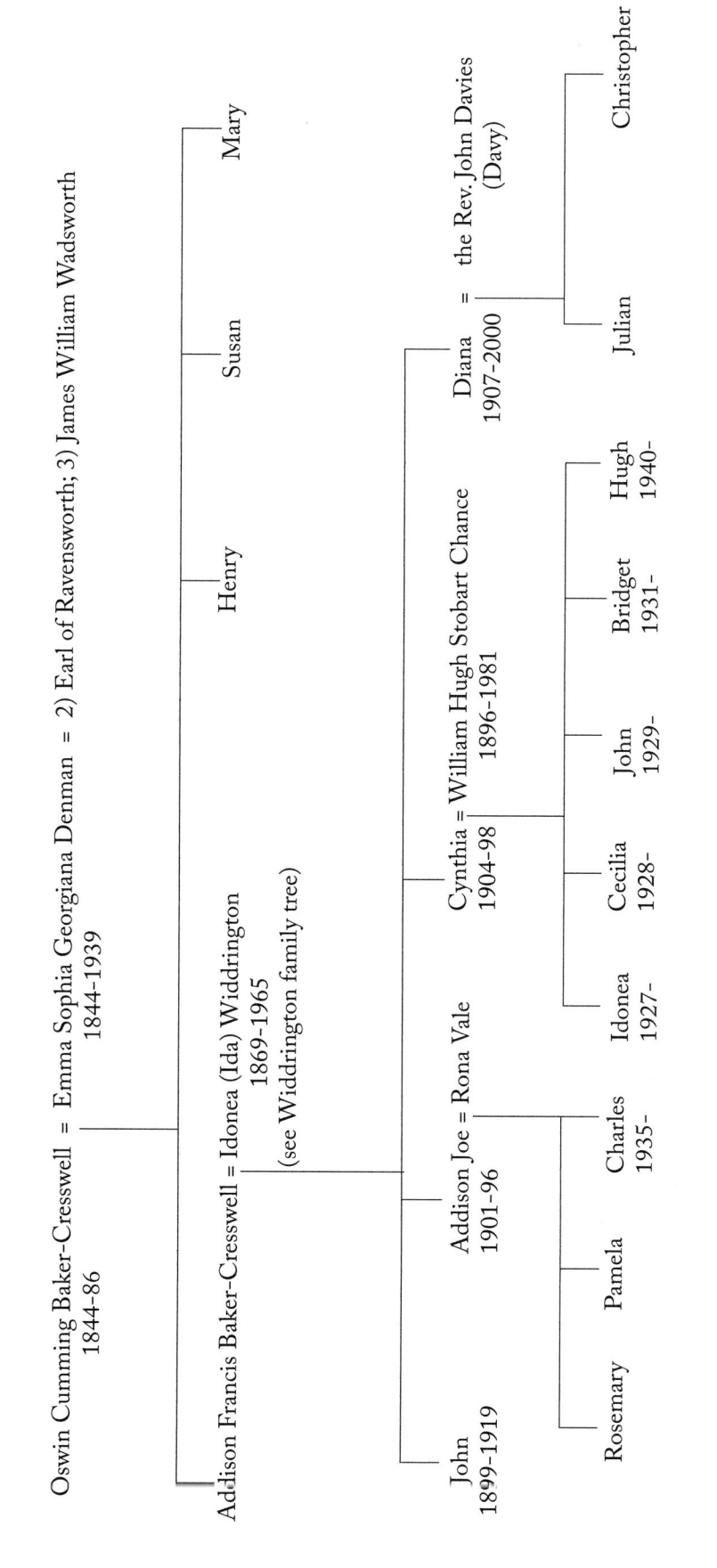

Oswin Cumming Baker-Cresswell = Emma Sophia Georgiana Denman = 2) Earl of Ravensworth; 3) James William Wadsworth
1844-86   1844-1939

├── Addison Francis Baker-Cresswell = Idonea (Ida) Widdrington
│   1869-1965
│   (see Widdrington family tree)
├── Henry
├── Susan
└── Mary

Children of Addison Francis and Idonea:

- John 1899-1919
- Addison Joe = Rona Vale
  1901-96
- Cynthia = William Hugh Stobart Chance
  1904-98   1896-1981
- Diana = the Rev. John Davies
  1907-2000   (Davy)

Children of Addison Joe and Rona Vale:
- Rosemary
- Pamela
- Charles 1935-

Children of Cynthia and William Hugh Stobart Chance:
- Idonea 1927-
- Cecilia 1928-
- John 1929-
- Bridget 1931-
- Hugh 1940-

Children of Diana and the Rev. John Davies:
- Julian
- Christopher

1 *Francis Widdrington and dogs, with the author looking on.*

Preface

It has been said that a woman never grows up until she loses her mother; that once you have ceased to be somebody's daughter you feel fundamentally different. Now there is no one to stand between you and the abyss. What is more, time will have a disconcerting way of speeding up. Where once life seemed infinite, now you are aware that the sands are running out and that what you did not do today you are less likely to do tomorrow – if ever. Worst of all, you realise that a priceless link with the past has been irrevocably severed, and it is now that you begin to brood on all those questions you never found time to ask.

When my mother Cynthia was approaching her 90th year and beginning to feel bored and resentful at the frustrations of old age, I suggested that she should write an account of her life as a legacy for her descendants. Taking up my suggestion she bought a couple of lined exercise books and sitting in her dining-room where the light was good she set to work. Quite properly she began at the beginning: 'I was born on 29th of May, 1904, at 7.00 p.m. at Newton Hall, Newton-on-the Moor, Felton, Northumberland, the home of my mother's parents, the Widdringtons.'[1] Writing steadily in her bold sloping hand, she completed her autobiography within a matter of weeks and after a friend had made a typed copy of her manuscript she had extra copies made and gave one to each of her five children.

As I had anticipated, my mother's account of her childhood and youth gave a picture of a fractured and unhappy time. This had led to a severing of relations with most of her family, whom consequently we children seldom saw. And it was not until after my mother's death at the age of 94 that I began to feel any curiosity about her antecedents. From the little I knew it seemed obvious that they had been a pretty eccentric bunch, with more than an average number of skeletons rattling around in their family cupboards.

Yet how much of what was said about them was true and how much fiction?

Though my mother had hotly denied it, her mother (my grandmother Idonea, always known as Ida) had charged her husband with being a rake and a scoundrel. A man of immense wealth, Addison Baker-Creswell had died long before I was born, apparently leaving his wife almost penniless. Be that as it may, by the time she entered my life my grandmother seemed to be living comfortably enough at Hauxley Hall near Alnwick in Northumberland, with her companion of many years, Dora Waller. From a child's perspective she had been rather a daunting figure, greeting us on our rare visits in her gravelly voice and inspecting us with a witchy smile and a face that creased up like a medlar. She had lived to be 96 and though she mellowed she was never anything less than formidable, flaunting her rouged cheeks and fiery henna-ed hair as she stumped over her stone-flagged floors, supported by her zimmer.

Since she and her daughter Cynthia had never got on it seemed fitting that my mother should have been born at her grandparents' house, for Newton had always been more of a home to her than her parental home and her grandmother Cecilia more of a mother to her than her birth mother. Newton, my mother told me, had been the only place where she felt protected and cherished. Yet after she grew up and married she never revisited this much-loved house, depicted by Pevsner as 'rambling but picturesque'[2] and famous for its eccentric conservatory. I knew there had been quarrels but I never asked for details. I myself had never set eyes on the place, which for the past 55 years had been the home of my mother's first cousin Francis Widdrington and his wife Gay.

Francis, who was now 80, was the last male survivor of a family that could trace its descent to Saxon times. I knew he had fallen on hard times and that at his death Newton Hall and its estate were likely to become the property of the bank, leaving its contents to be dispersed and a unique family record to pass into limbo. If I was ever to get to see the place that had played such an important part in my mother's early life it was high time to pay Francis Widdrington a visit. I had only met him once and doubted he would remember me, and so I wrote to him explaining who I was and asking if I might call. The following day he telephoned, launching without preamble into a flood of family reminiscences.

'What was all that about?' My husband Jeremy asked when finally I replaced the receiver.

'Everything. He obviously longs to talk.'

'Did you fix a date?'

'Next week. We can drive up. He sounded quite chirpy – at least his wits seem to be in good shape.'

'No hope, then, of making off with the family silver?'

I replied that I didn't suppose there was much of it left.

Yet somewhere in that house were things infinitely more precious. I had been told there were a number of diaries and these I was anxious to see. I had learned of their existence from my sister Idonea (named after our grandmother) and of their whereabouts from our cousin, Charles Baker-Creswell, the son of my mother's brother Joe. Charles' home was not far from Newton and after the death of both his parents he had discovered the diaries among their effects, stored in a cardboard box. 'Not to put too fine a point upon it I am pretty sure my mother nicked them from Newton-on-the-Moor,' he explained to me in a letter.

> When – I do not know. She was a collector of everything, pictures, books, objects silver, etc. and none too scrupulous how she acquired them … I decided (rightly or wrongly – I am sure rightly) that the Widdrington diaries should go back to Francis. I made a careful list of them and took them back.

From a copy of the list which he enclosed I saw there were seven diaries in all, two of which had been kept by Ida and the remaining five by Cecilia, my great-grandmother. One of these, I noticed, was not strictly speaking a diary but an account of Cecilia's life put together in old age and not completed until she was over ninety.

What's in a name? When I was a very small child, in token of having been called after her, my great-grandmother had made me a present of a miniature silver coffee set. Too precious for the nursery, the tiny coffee pot with its ivory handle and matching cream jug and sugar basin were kept in their box in the drawing room, where I would inspect them from time to time with a feeling of pride. The bestowal of the gift had made me feel special. And the disclosure of the existence of Cecilia's diaries had fired my resolve to find out more about this almost mythical great-grandmama. One way or another I was going to have to persuade Francis to let me borrow them. I was determined to unlock the door to my great-grandmother's past.

Intriguingly, four of Cecilia's diaries appeared to be records she had kept of the lives of her four children, charting each one's progress from birth. These were likely to prove a godsend, for they would enable me to check her contemporaneous records against the legends that had accrued over the intervening century. Time and frequent retelling often distort the truth and for all I knew the stark polarity and sheer peculiarity of her children's personalities might well turn out to have been exaggerated.

Legend had it, for example, that Gerard, the elder of Cecilia's two sons, had been conceived as a result of an adulterous liaison, this being the reason why he had been disinherited in favour of his younger brother, Bertram (the father of Francis), who had been made his father's heir. An alternative version had it that Gerard, after becoming a socialist, had voluntarily relinquished his inheritance for life in a miner's cottage. Both versions agreed that he was a dimwit: not quite twenty shillings to the pound as the saying went. My heart had always gone out to this family oddball and I was curious to know what Cecilia would have to say about him.

When first I set out on my quest I had known next to nothing about Cecilia's eldest child, my great-aunt Dorothy. Widely acknowledged to have been a beauty, Dorothy's marriage to the Liberal politician Sir Edward Grey was reported to have been *un mariage blanc*, meaning that it was never consummated.

Was this fact or fiction? Dorothy had died following an accident at the age of 42 and, at the request of her grieving husband, a close friend, Louise Creighton, had written a brief biography, a copy of which I had managed to obtain. Printed privately and issued at a time when the grief of those who had loved her must still have been raw, Mrs Creighton had painted a very flattering picture of the departed. Yet as I was to discover she had not told the whole story, for apparently not everyone had admired Dorothy. A popular novelist of the day, Mrs Belloc Lowndes, had described her as 'extremely self-absorbed';[3] while to Grey's fellow Liberal Parliamentarian, David Lloyd George, she gave an impression of being 'insufferably proud'.[4] I wondered if any member of Dorothy's family had shared these poor opinions? If they had, I would not have learned of it from Mrs Creighton, who for some reason had chosen to wipe Dorothy's three siblings clean off the slate. This curious omission (which must have been deliberate) had set me thinking. If there had been a quarrel then it must have been a serious one. For I had also discovered that not one single member of Dorothy's family had attended her funeral. What was the explanation for this apparent heartlessness? It was my hope that Cecilia's diaries would shed some light on the mystery.

Then there was Ida, my grandmother, who by all accounts had been a 'raver' in her youth. Wild and ungovernable, she had broken many hearts, the most noteworthy of her conquests being the young Roger Fry, who afterwards became an influential art historian and critic, much celebrated during his lifetime and still remembered today.

Shortly after my mother's death my sister Idonea (who had always been our grandmother's favourite) had telephoned me with some startling information. She had been corresponding with a Mrs Margaret Norman who claimed that her late mother, May, was the illegitimate daughter of Ida Widdrington and Roger Fry. The circumstantial evidence Mrs Norman had been able to produce in support of her extraordinary claim was impressive enough to have persuaded Francis and Gay Widdrington (whom she had been to visit on a number of occasions) that her claim was genuine. If true, this threw a new and startling light onto the early life of our grandmother – and surely some reference (however oblique) to such a scandalous event must have found its way into one or other of the diaries, no matter how successfully it had been concealed at the time.

'This is likely to be a now-or-never trip,' I observed to my husband as we set off one fine October morning on the 260-mile journey from our home in North Wales to Newton-on-the-Moor, Northumberland. It was plain that Francis Widdrington was eager to talk. But whether he could be persuaded to lend me the diaries was another question altogether.

And if he refused? I decided to close my eyes to such a possibility; though I had to accept that if my mission were to fail it was most unlikely I would be given a second chance.

The Newton drive led through fenced-off parkland dotted with trees and grazed by black-faced ewes. The gates had gone, with only a pair of moss-covered stone gateposts to mark their passing. Bumping over a speed ramp, a right-hand turn brought us within sight of the Hall, a grey stone house facing west towards the Cheviot hills. Jeremy drew up on the raked gravel before a pedimented side door surmounted by what we presumed must be the Widdrington coat of arms carved in stone, and flanked by two saucy stone lions with their noses in the air.

A tug on the bellrope was answered almost immediately. Francis Widdrington had evidently been on the lookout, having been told to expect us at around eleven. He waved us into the famous Newton conservatory which wound its way around the south side of the house enclosing the original front entrance. Now glazed over and filled with a profusion of Mediterranean and tropical plants, its walls lined with Italianate niches and painted panels, it was furnished with oriental rugs and a couch piled high with cushions. The effect was magical, like some Cocteau film set. Trailing creepers brushed our faces as we followed out host into the front hall and thence into the drawing-room where we were introduced to Francis's wife, Gay. Petite and still pretty, she appeared frail. A year or two older than her husband, her failing heart, we were told, was kept going by a pacemaker.

Francis was a large man, through shrunk, so he said, from his original six-foot-six. His face was smooth and bland, his manner courteous. He was perfectly fit, he assured us, apart from a little deafness, 'So you'll both have to bellow.' His most serious complaint, he confessed, was sheer and utter boredom.

The Newton drawing-room had the feel of a room seldom used. Though a log fire was beginning to take hold we guessed there was a 'snug' elsewhere. From comfortable chintzy chairs we admired the six framed wall panels depicting arcadian scenes of rural life. We were told they were the work of an 18th-century Dutch artist, Isaac de Boucheron. 'Five of them bought by my grandfather, Fitz Widdrington', Francis explained. 'When he had them hung he found he needed a sixth – so he painted one himself, with Ida, your revered grandmother, in the foreground.' He chuckled. 'Unfortunately Enid – that's my mother – couldn't stand her sister-in-law. Called her the "black bitch". So when we came to live at Newton she had Ida painted out.'

Francis gave us coffee before taking us on a tour of the principal rooms – much altered by Fitz in the classical style, he explained, his grandfather having had a passion for all things Venetian. It was Fitz who had painted the architectural capriccios in the hall, where St Paul's Cathedral sat alongside a gossiping group of Venetian fishermen, the ochre sails of their fishing boats catching the late afternoon sun. Likewise on the stairwell you seemed about to step into an arcade with St Maria de la Salute, bathed in evening light, standing proud over the waters of the Lagoon.

'As a young man Fitz used to go sketching on the Continent with Edward Lear – picked up something of his style, though I'd say he was better.'

Impressed by the quality of Fitz Widdrington's work we were in no mood to disagree.

The Newton library boasted first editions of Charles Darwin's *On the Origin of Species* and *The Descent of Man*, together with the collected works of all the major 19th-century novelists and poets. But there was no time to linger. I asked Francis if he would mind if I took notes.

'Go ahead – do what you like.' While I scribbled away (regretting my long-forgotten Pitman's shorthand) we were treated to an unstoppable flow:

'I was out of the country when Father died in 1942 and two years later, in '44, my elder brother Tony was killed in Italy. So called "friendly fire", I believe. He'd made what was known as a "soldier's will" – back of an envelope – lodged in a Cairo bank. Left all his possessions to his three godchildren.' Francis laughed mirthlessly. 'The Widdringtons owned a lot of property in those days. On top of the Newton estate there was Hauxley and on top of Hauxley there was Moore Hall in Cheshire – left to my grandmother by a cousin. Tony's will was contested on the grounds that by "possessions" he'd meant only his personal effects. He and I had always got on famously – never had a quarrel. You'd have thought any sane judge would have seen it that way.'

'But your judge didn't?'

'Unfortunately he thought otherwise. Luckily this house and the village were entailed, but the contents weren't included. A more sympathetic judge helped me out with a nod and a wink by "suggesting" that much of the contents were the property of my mother. But times were very different then. When decisions needed to be taken I was serving in Palestine and I made a lot of mistakes – sold off the cottages to the sitting tenants. They were estate cottages then, very primitive affairs, no indoor sanitation. Then a brewery offered me two thousand pounds for the *Cock and Barker* inn … When I said no they offered me five. And when I said no again they raised it to ten.'

'A fortune in those days.'

'I thought I'd be mad to refuse it. Place was a hovel – sawdust on the floor. Must be worth a million today – and every one of those cottages has fancy paving and extensions at the back.'

Francis shrugged at the poor hand fortune has dealt him. I ask him to tell us about his father.

'A splendid man. Brigadier-General Bertram Widdrington C.M.G., D.S.O. and Bar, to give him his full title. We got on famously. But Father was very conservative in his views. Wouldn't permit beer-drinking in the house – and if a male guest turned up for dinner improperly dressed he was made to eat in a separate room.'

'You mean he had to be wearing a dinner jacket?'

'Quite so. Seems odd now, but in those days that was the way of it.'

'How did you get on in the war?'

'I survived it. I was destined for the Coldstream Guards, but in the scramble for commissions at the outbreak of hostilities there wasn't a place in the regiment. So I joined the Welsh Guards because of the family connection. The Prices of Rhiwlas – Dick Price was married to a Hopwood.'

I was lost now. 'And who were the Hopwoods?'

'Grandma's family. A rum lot. Dick Price married Evie Hopwood, Cecilia's youngest sister.' Francis chuckled. 'Dick was a rum character. Wrote a book once – *Rabbits for Profit and Pleasure*. Used to be a copy in the library. Reduced the size of the Rhiwlas estate from eighty thousand acres to ten thousand. Gambling on slow horses with very long odds that lost! Extraordinary chap. Had a suit made with four-inch checks and Welsh dragons woven into the cloth. Led poor Evie a dance.'

I asked Francis to tell me about his grandmother, the Cecilia Widdrington of the diaries.

'She was a Hopwood. Daughter of Captain Edward Gregge-Hopwood – Lancashire family. A very quarrelsome lot. The cause of all the trouble in the family was the Hopwoods. Cecilia was the eldest. A great disappointment to her family because she wasn't a boy. Brought up in a cottage on the Hopwood Estate. Received no education. Wore shepherd's boots with steel toecaps, even for London. If she wanted to get to Alnwick she'd walk there. A great shopper – bought everything by the dozen. When she bought a hat she'd buy twelve. Ditto boots. Everybody loved her. She ended her days in Exmouth – 7 Grange Terrace. With just the cook and a maid. And Gerard, of course.'

'Her son?'

'Quite so. Gerard lived with her. The elder boy. He was quite loopy. A Winchester scholar but he hated grandeur – detested the aristocracy. Went off to live with a pitman's family. Extraordinary chap. Of course he wasn't Fitz's son at all. His father was Jim Smith-Barry. An Irishman – brother of Lord Barrymore. The family had a wonderful place called Fota Island in Cork Harbour. Terrible fuss made about handing the estate over to my father – of course it all came out, then.'

'You mean that Gerard was illegitimate?'

'Quite so.'

By this time my head was spinning and I saw that Jeremy was equally bemused. Thus far there had been no mention of my great-aunt Dorothy so I asked him …

'Aunt Dolly? Never knew her. Dead long before I came on the scene. Never got on with her mother, so I'm told. Or with Ida – your grandmother. Edward Grey, Dolly's husband, wouldn't have Ida in the house. Two wild by half! In his position, who could blame him?'

Since that seemed to dispose of Dorothy I decided to move on. What could Francis tell me about my grandmother?

'Ida? A terror in her youth. Terrible reputation among the gentry. As a young woman she would pitch her tent on Harehope Moor and all the shepherds were welcome. Married Addy Creswell – Addison Baker-Creswell of Creswell and Harehope – your grandfather of course. By all accounts a bad hat. Got kicked out of the Scots Guards …'

'My mother tended to put him on a pedestal. But then she hardly knew him.'

'Addy was a phenomenally rich man, but Ida's mother had grave doubts about the match … All recorded in her diary, or so I believe.'

'Oh yes,' I said, glancing at Jeremy. 'That's what I had heard …' But Francis was in full flow and not to be deflected.

'Naturally the marriage didn't last and Addy left everything to the daughter of his mistress, Dolly Winkworth, a distant cousin. Got some doctor to sign a letter saying he was of sound mind when he made the will. Ida got three hundred a year. Properly speaking she ought to have kicked up a fuss, but her lawyers advised against it. Too much dirty linen.'

'You mean, on her side?'

'Too right. Addy might have claimed custody of the children if it had all come out.'

'What did the rest of the family think?'

'As youngsters Bertram and Ida had been very close. But Enid – that's my mother – couldn't stand her. Jealousy of course. If we children had to drive past Hauxley, where Ida lived, we were ordered to look the other way.' Francis laughed uproariously at the memory. 'Still, she was a brave woman – in later life very go-ahead. Of course when I left the army and came to live at Newton I had to meet her, feud or no feud. Both of us on the Rural District council and so forth. We hit it off all right. She was the Queen Bee of the Women's Institute, the locals thought the world of her. Worked very hard for the R.S.P.C.A. She'd do anything for the animals – marched into slaughter houses campaigning for the humane killer. Went on driving her car into her nineties. Then she had an accident – put her car into a ditch driving to one of her meetings. An ambulance was sent for. "Are you all right Madam? You must be suffering from shock." Your grandmother drew herself up. "People like us don't suffer from shock," she told him. Put him firmly in his place. When they'd pulled her car out of the ditch she got in and drove off to her meeting.' There was more laughter. 'She and Dora – her companion – became vegetarians after what they'd seen in the slaughter houses.'

xix

By now it was close on one o'clock and we asked the Widdringtons if they would care to join us for a pub lunch at the *Cock and Barker* inn. They accepted. The place was humming. Back in 1947 we were told, it had been a primitive hostelry adjacent to the smithy. Over mixed fish platters I tried to steer the conversation in the direction of the diaries but Francis, intent on his own narrative, appeared not to be listening.

When we got back we asked to see the garden. Francis insisted on escorting us, but first he must fetch the dogs – pedigree Schih-Tzus, Gay's pride and joy. 'She was a world class breeder in her day.' It appeared there were eight dogs, odd little creatures with squashed-up faces and feathery tails, kennelled in Fitz Widdrington's former studio. One which was lame looked ready to meet its maker so we took the other seven. The garden, which was well laid out with smooth lawns and 19th-century balustrading, looked remarkably well kept, its formal beds planted up with thousands of bedding wallflowers.

'Fitz used to set up his easel here. When he was painting the butler was instructed to say he was "not at home". Trouble was, he could be spotted by visitors pulling up outside his front door. So he built the new entrance on the east side.'

'Linking the two with his splendid conservatory. Very ingenious.'

'Pretty eccentric if you ask me. But the master's wish was his command in those days.'

Preceded by his miniature pack, we followed Francis down a broad path flanked by overgrown yews. 'In former days,' we were told, 'they were kept regularly clipped by six gardeners using hand-shears. But they got away in the last war when the army took over Newton.' Now they formed a tunnel over the unmown path. Francis explained that the walled garden that was our destination was leased to a lady gardener who grew organic vegetables, caring for the conservatory in lieu of rent. It seemed like a good bargain. The garden was vast, two or three acres at a guess. Apparently its double-skinned walls were built of Dutch brick 'brought over as ballast by ships carrying coal from Tyneside to the Netherlands.' In the past they were warmed internally by iron water pipes heated by coke furnaces. 'Coke was cheap in those days – they practically gave it away. And of course the family were the pit owners.' Now no trace remained of the peaches and apricots that must formerly have thrived on this outdoor central-heating system. Only a few apples, broken loose from their cordons, were providing nourishment for the blackbirds. An old summer house built into the west-facing wall and choked with garden clutter had a forlorn air.

While looking around I decided to raise the subject of Margaret Norman. Did Francis believe her claim to be Ida's granddaughter was genuine?

'Very likely – wouldn't put anything past Ida. Nice little woman – used to see quite a lot of her. Set great store on being a member of this benighted family. God knows why!'

We took a different route back through a spinney and past a small sawmill producing fence posts and firewood, of which Francis was plainly proud. Semi-tame pheasants 'cork-corked' among the trees. Admiring his pheasant coops we were astonished to learn that in spite of his straitened circumstances Francis still employed two keepers.

Once the dogs had been fed and returned to their quarters it seemed the polite time to leave. Gay was dozing beside the dying embers of the drawing room fire. I drew a deep breath, sat down, and attacked the subject of the diaries. Was it true that Francis had some records kept by his grandmother and aunt? If so I would dearly love to see them.

I saw his face closing up. He said he wouldn't begin to know where to find them. The library? I suggested. He hurrumped. 'They're pretty illegible you know. Neither Gay nor I could make head or tail of them.' Lying, I said I was something of an expert on old documents. 'I could make typed transcripts – much easier for you to read. And naturally I would return them straight away.' Francis still demurred – he was not sure he still had them. 'Charles had them, you know – perhaps you'd better ask him.' I was tempted to tell him that I already had – and that I was sure Francis had them stashed away somewhere. But I knew I must tread carefully. If Francis chose not to let me see them that was his affair. I pointed out that some of the diaries were likely to be over a hundred years old and that the longer they were left the more illegible they would become. 'Meaning, the loss of a hundred years of family history!'

'Have a look in your study, Francis dear.' Gay had woken up. 'I expect you'll find they're there somewhere.' With a show of reluctance Francis did as he was bidden. 'He's getting very forgetful – I'm sure I've seen them about,' Gay observed. 'They're probably under something.'

Tension mounted as we waited for Francis, who was gone some time. When finally he returned I was relieved to see that he had not come back empty-handed.

'I seem to have got these – heaven knows what you'll be able to make of them.' He passed me two exercise books both with black covers. 'Be sure to return them,' he growled. 'Better make it registered post.'

Overcome with relief I glanced at the title pages. The first one read: *Gerard Widdrington by his mother – 1871-1894*. I saw that roughly three-quarters of the book's lined pages had been filled and that there were several glued-in snapshots, presumably Gerard as a child. The title on the front of the second book (which has a soft cover and red marbled endpapers) read: *The Events, Experiences etc. of Idonea Widdrington*. I saw that it broke off after 14 pages and must, I guessed, have been written when my grandmother was still a child or a young woman. I wondered if Francis has picked the two which were of least value to him personally? Maybe he was submitting them as a test … I thanked him profusely and promised to look after them and shortly afterwards we took our leave.

'That was quite an outing,' Jeremy remarked as we started down the drive.

'It was. Pity he didn't come up with the whole collection.'

'I dare say with your persuasive powers you'll get hold of them in time.'

I said, 'If I succeed in deciphering these two and producing a legible transcript I hope I shall win his confidence.'

As we left the pretty village of Newton-on-the-Moor and edged the car onto the A1 (one of the most dangerous stretches of road in Britain), I said 'Interesting – that Dorothy didn't get on with her mother.'

'And that your grandmother was barred from her sister's house.'

'I'm itching to know why.'

'If half of Francis's stories are genuine you'll find yourself with enough copy to fill half a dozen books.'

As things turned out it was to take a second visit to Newton plus an 18-month-long exchange of letters and telephone calls before Francis could be persuaded to lend me all seven diaries. Deciphering them brought its own problems, the most basic of which was that neither mother nor daughter had been taught to divide their work into paragraphs, or to use margins. Consequently their writing filled the pages edge to edge, making it hard for the reader to keep her place. Another difficulty was that in places the ink had faded to a pale sepia, rendering the writing barely legible. Fortunately by the late 1920s, when Cecilia embarked on her autobiography, better ink was available and she had acquired a fountain pen.

Finally there was the element of time. In permitting me the loan of the diaries Francis had made it plain that he did not intend me to hang on to them for more than a month or two. This allowed me very little time to check the doubtful bits – especially names, both of people and places. Thus, when in doubt, the choice lay between making a guess or leaving a particular passage out.

Taken altogether and at face value the diaries told a fascinating story. Yet as I pored over their pages, attempting to rekindle the life of the great-grandmother whose name I bore, one question kept repeating itself: when Cecilia sat down to write the story of her life, had her narrative been entirely honest? Because as I discovered, family legend and her version of events did not always agree.

As the eldest child in a disfunctional family of six, from her earliest years Cecilia had seen her role as that of 'carer'. As her long life drew to a close, did concern for her family's reputation (as well as for her own) sometimes guide her pen, overriding her obligation to tell the truth? This without doubt had been the case on at least one occasion – when her well-authenticated love affair with a much younger man was skated over in her diary without comment. Is it possible that there had been others? Her son Gerard's parentage, for example, must always remain in doubt, since Cecilia kept the truth to herself. Other episodes in her life she preferred to remain hidden have since become common knowledge. Some particulars will probably never be known.

In order to recreate the life of my great-grandmother, which began before the age of steam trains and ran almost up to the outbreak of the Second World War, I found it necessary to look beyond the diaries – to newspapers, letters, biographies, historical and sociological evidence and, finally, hearsay – in what was to become a fascinating quest. And the further I went the more it was borne in upon me that two eminent men had important roles to play in Cecilia's story and that of her two daughters – the reckless, flamboyant Ida and her adored elder sister Dorothy, the ice maiden whom her family completely failed to understand. Though some parts of their story will never be known, what finally emerged seems unusual enough to be worth setting down.

CHAPTER 1

Early Days

Cecilia's parents, Edward and Susan Gregge-Hopwood, were not well pleased when their daughter was born on 5 September 1840. She was their firstborn and they had hoped for a boy. She was named Cecilia after her late grandmother. Their displeasure was compounded when a second daughter, Lucy, was born 17 months later. And after her came the unfortunate Rose. 'The parents were much disappointed that 3 girls came … and poor Rose especially was disliked and neglected from the first.'*

At that time Edward's father, Robert Gregge-Hopwood, was still alive. When his eldest son had announced his intention to marry Susan Baskervyle-Glegg, a sparky and attractive girl and an outstanding horsewoman, the widower had been only too pleased to invite the young couple to share his home. (There was certainly no shortage of rooms in the ancient manor house of Hopwood, a rather gloomy mansion built on Tudor foundations and retaining some fine oak-panelled rooms dating from that time and an impressive oak staircase.) Edward and Susan had been happy enough to be spared the expense of housekeeping, though it had been made plain to them from the start that no children of theirs would be welcome at the Hall. Thus out of respect for the old man's wishes the couple's three girls had all been born at Hopwood Cottage – a modest house standing some half-mile from the main house – and it was there that they were to spend the greater part of their childhood, cared for by servants.

In 1846 Susan had finally given birth to a boy, the longed for son and heir who, God willing, would one day inherit the extensive Hopwood landholdings in and around the market town of Middleton in Lancashire. Cecilia could just remember the 'awful fuss' that was made of her brother's birth: 'the great servants hall dinner at the Hall that was given at his Christening and my mother's splendid purple brocade gown (of which I was given long after a piece to bind a small book with) and being sent to bed out of the way!'

The child was named Edward, after his father. He, too, had been born at the Cottage, which remained his home. 'My mother would walk up and see us now and again,' Cecilia

---

* Unless otherwise stated all quotations are taken from *My Diary: The Diary of Cecilia Widdrington 1840 – 1928, 1929-1930.*

recalled, 'and we also used to go down to see our mother and grandfather, in our best clothes and best manners … but our lives were lived at the cottage until I was quite fifteen – no doubt that helped in making us "strangers" of our parents.'

Even by Victorian standards, when the children of the gentry were routinely confined to their own quarters, this was an unusual arrangement. 'But indeed our parents – married lovers as they were – had very little love left to give to us.' Cecilia's abiding memory of her earliest years was the whippings she and her siblings endured at the hands of their bad-tempered nurse, Rachel. 'Of course I daren't tell, but when 2 or 3 years after she began to whip my precious brother – with a rod – my mother saw the marks on his little body and Rachel was sent off that same day.'

Fortunately for the young Hopwoods the nurse-governess Susan engaged to replace this ogre of a nurse was of an altogether different calibre. Emma Williams, 'a little half-educated girl the daughter of a ruined Manchester merchant', proved to be a resourceful young woman of great moral strength, who 'though she knew very little even for those ignorant days, would read up the lessons to teach us'.

More to the point, Miss Emmy, as the children learned to call her, 'impressed on our very beings the far more important lessons of unselfishness, bravery, humour and pity and we always have said <u>I know</u> that any good there is in us … we owe entirely to her, who also taught us Love.'

The young woman proved to be 'the one being who loved us, the one joy in our very dreary lives'. For so far as the outside world was concerned, the Gregge-Hopwood children might have been living on a desert island. With the exception of their father's youngest brother Harvey who paid them occasional visits, and some Heron cousins, also on their father's side, the children 'never knew aunt or uncle or cousin or any of our very aristocratic relations – or even a neighbour.' Harvey, according to Cecilia, was a warm-hearted creature, though she knew their father had never liked him. 'Indeed,' she maintained 'except for my mother he liked no one.'

By all accounts Edward Gregge-Hopwood seems to have been a rather disagreeable man. Or if that is too hard he was certainly an awkward character; a misanthrope who made little effort to ingratiate himself with family or neighbours and an open admirer of the heretic Voltaire. His twin passions were his wife (whom he adored) and field sports. Among the small number who counted themselves his friends he was valued for his refusal to conform. But then the history of his family was a curious one.

There had been Hopwoods at Hopwood Hall 'with its messuages, lands, woods and other property'[1] since the time of King John. But in 1762 the squire, Dr Robert Hopwood, had died without issue, bequeathing his estate to his wife, and on her death to a certain Edward Gregge of Chester, who was a lawyer. Some authorities have it that Gregge was a cousin of the doctor's. Others maintain that he was purely a friend. What is not in dispute is that Dr Robert Hopwood was greatly indebted to the young lawyer. For at the time of the Jacobite rebellion of 1745, Edward Gregge, who was Hopwood's junior by twenty years, had enabled the doctor to avoid service in the local militia by volunteering to take his place. The young man's offer had been generously rewarded when, on the death of Dr Robert's widow in 1773 he duly succeeded to the Hopwood estate, having annexed the name of Hopwood to his own by special Act of Parliament.

2   Hopwood Hall in the 1940s when it was used as a Catholic teacher training college.

However, the character and lifestyle of Dr Hopwood and the man who succeeded to his name and estate could not have been in greater contrast. Dr Hopwood was a man of wide scholarship and sober habits. He had been awarded a Fellowship by the Royal College of Physicians and had built an impressive new library onto the west side of his house. A conscientious squire, he cared passionately for the upkeep of his land and the welfare of his tenants. Edward Gregge's antecedents were of an altogether different stamp. Military men, they were quick-tempered, hedonistic and quarrelsome. Hunting was more to their taste than scholarship, and they cared little for the stewardship of their lands.

'My grandfather', Cecilia recalled, 'kept a pack of harriers and hunted hares, galloping wildly along the lanes and fields of his estate … drinking his glass of port after dinner and toddy at bedtime.' In his youth he had been a friend of the notorious Lord Byron, who was said to have completed the final draft of *Childe Harold's Pilgrimage* while staying at Hopwood Hall. He had married the Hon. Cecilia Byng, one of the three beautiful daughters of Lord Torrington and a former lady-in-waiting to Queen Charlotte. 'A good wife,' according to her granddaughter and namesake, 'though she cannot have been a judicious mother, since she had made a favourite of her eldest son far above all the rest, and so causing jealousy and distrust from their earliest years.'

To discover where this sibling jealousy had led we need to take a look at two of the younger members of Robert Gregge-Hopwood's family. Frank, the son who was next in line to Edward, had immeasurably bettered his prospects in life by marrying the Lady Elinor Stanley, a daughter of the 15th Earl of Derby, the largest landowner in the county. Having followed the time-honoured route of second sons by entering the Ministry, he had high hopes of preferment through the patronage of his father-in-law. Mary Augusta,

Robert's only daughter, had made an equally advantageous match, having married the Earl of Sefton, another local grandee.

From their lofty positions in society these two looked down on their eldest brother with a jaundiced eye. For Edward had married unwisely, taking for his bride one of the notorious Baskervyle-Gleggs.* By affiliating himself to a family who were no longer received by the county he had lowered his own position in society – and by implication, theirs. This in itself was bad enough. But in the eyes of the Rev. Frank, Edward's cavalier attitude towards his inheritance was worse; it infuriated his younger brother. In common with their father, field sports had always been Edward's passion; and providing his allowance was sufficient to pay for his horses, dogs, guns and fishing paraphernalia, it was plain he was not bothered by rotting fences or sour, waterlogged pastures.

His wife Susan was no better. An irresponsible mother, she cared nothing for her children, content, so it seemed, to see them raised like savages. Trading on her looks, she had bamboozled her father-in-law; the old man was putty in her hands. Why, the Rev. Frank asked himself, should this profligate pair – through a mere accident of birth – inherit the whole of the Hopwood estates while he and his siblings got nothing? The injustice of his lot built up in him and began to fester, until fate put a weapon into the Rev. Frank's hands …

In 1850 Susan had given birth to her fifth child – another girl, baptised Evelyn. 'It was a deep disappointment that she wasn't a boy but she was never made to feel it as we were,' Cecilia recalled. She worshipped her baby sister, a 'cheeky little thing' and a charmer. 'Evie' was the only one of the five with enough courage to stand up to their formidable father.

At around this time their parents' decision to rent a house in North Wales where the whole family could spend the summer months was to provide a welcome break in the monotony of the children's lives. Aberhirnant, a sporting estate a few miles from the market town of Bala in Merioneth, was close by the River Dee, one of the best salmon rivers in the Principality. It was a perfect bolt hole for Edward and Susan, where sport was plentiful and the living cheap. To the young Hopwoods, accustomed as they were to the boredom and deadly routines of life at the Cottage, the annual trek to their mountain home was like being transported to Paradise.

Before the railway age the journey from Middleton was an adventure in itself.

> We children and the nurse and Miss Emmy travelled the whole way in a big yellow chariot drawn by 4 horses ridden by 2 postboys in short coloured jackets and white breeches, the horses changed about every 10 miles. The chariot was fitted with 2 large flat trunks on its roof carrying the family garments and under the seat in front another containing the family hats (or rather bonnets it was then) and on this, outside, were seated 2 of the children. Inside wd be Miss Emmy, a nurse with the baby and usually me, as I was never sick travelling inside as the others were, and 2 maidservants on the seat behind, called the Rumble. These journeys were a great, delight to us young ones, as delicious suppers and breakfasts were allowed.

---

* In the *Diary* Cecilia states that the Baskervyle-Gleggs had a tarnished reputation. Why, I have been unable to discover.

I have been to Aberhirnant. Part of the Plas, a rich man's folly built in the Gothic style, has been pulled down, but otherwise it does not appear to have changed much in the century and a half that has elapsed since the young Hopwoods were there. Planted at the head of a narrow boulder-strewn valley, overhung by beech trees and twisted lichen-covered oaks and threaded by one of the tributaries of the Dee, one peers through its arched windows onto a vivid green patch of mountain meadow. Holding on tight as the family 'chariot' bumped and pitched its way up the narrow track, how the children's hearts must have raced as they surveyed this enchanted place – a veritable fairyland.

At Aberhirnant there was an easing of petty restraints, though lessons still had to go on. And although they all lived under the same roof, their parents were seldom seen. 'My mother was a clever fisher and sometimes we were allowed to see her catch a pike or big trout … We were in great awe of the beautiful lady, who we sometimes saw going down to dinner in lovely clothes – but she seldom spoke to us.'

Their father's favourite sport was Foulmart* hunting. 'A strange sport', as Cecilia tells us, 'carried on in a strange manner':

> The beast sleeps all day and at night starts out to find his food, travelling quite long distances among the hills, till at daybreak he stops and finds shelter among the rocks, under large stones, for his day's rest and sleep. The hounds were taken at daybreak, 3 or 4 in the morning, to the spot marked down the day before as his sleeping place, but which he had now left – and taking up the scent followed it along where he had gone in the night, until they reached the place where he lay snugly asleep until the next nightfall, my father and his huntsman following on foot – for the whole course being up and down great mountains the pace was of course slow – and then the place was marked and the hounds taken home which they would reach in time for my father to breakfast with my mother. So the hounds were always running after nothing but a scent, and as this disappointment could not go on always, the Foulmart was from time to time dug cut of his bed under the boulders and given to them to tear to pieces and eat.

By this time steam locomotives were beginning to replace the old 'coach and four' in providing passenger services between Great Britain's major towns and cities. By the late 1840s many private entrepreneurs, seeing that there was profit to be made out of linking Britain's smaller towns to the burgeoning rail network, were laying tracks all over Britain. The small market town of Bala was an early beneficiary of the Age of Steam, bringing the Hopwood children a fresh cause for delight:

> Now the chief part of the journey could be done, and far quicker, on the wonderful new steam train of carriages, our Chariot at first being put onto a truck, children, nurses and all – and firmly secured. Great care had to be taken in measuring the height of the boxes: always hoisted onto the tops of the carriages, carried up on ladders by the Porters – for fear of being too high to pass under the bridges.

Several years were to pass before the Gregge-Hopwoods 'condescended to travel in the public carriages', en route for their summer home!

* An old name for a polecat.

The arrival of the railways led to the transformation of many unregarded fishing villages into flourishing seaside resorts. Sea-bathing as a promoter of health was becoming fashionable, and hotels and boarding-houses were springing up along the new promenades of former villages such as Blackpool and New Brighton. Barmouth in North Wales, with its mild climate and long sandy beaches, was only a few miles from Bala and sometimes the children would be sent there for their health, accompanied by Miss Emmy and a nursemaid. Cecilia recollected those times as 'golden days – holidays spent digging and pond-making and sometimes dear Miss Emmy out of her scanty salary used to give us pennies and take us to the awe-inspiring joy of a shop and let us buy our own sweets – green pink or white. There was no chocolate in those days.'

The downside to those magical holidays was the sea bathing. The Victorians had developed an almost mystical faith in the health-giving properties of salt water and Cecilia's recollections of being dunked in the Irish Sea would horrify the modern parent.

> We were quite tiny at Barmouth and were taken in to huge houses on wheels. When the door was shut it was quite dark save for a tiny hole at the back thro which orders to the bathing man were shouted to go on or stop. Our poor little clothes were stripped off by the nursery maid and hung on pegs – making us feel so naked and helpless, then the horse jolted us into the sea, the house was turned round and the door opened letting in the sight only of the boundless ocean with its angry waves roaring and rolling. At the bottom of the few steps appeared the fat bathing woman waist deep in water, whose 'Come on my pretty dears, the water is quite warm' we knew to be a lie. Into her arms we were placed, one by one, stiff with fear. She dipped us into an oncoming wave, she dipped us again in the next wave and again into a third, without waiting for us to get our breath. The formula then was 'three dips and out' and this accomplished we were handed to our maid, blind, terrified and outraged, rubbed till we were sore and smacked if we cried.

Miss Emmy used to bribe the children to be brave with promises of bread and jam – a rare treat in those days, when the standard fare offered to children of all classes was abysmally monotonous.

> For breakfast bread and milk or porridge and treacle – Miss Emmy's was tea and bread and butter, never bacon or eggs, we never even heard of them … Dinner meat and potatoes and a milk pudding or apples and rice, in summer other fruits and rice – tea at 5 consisting of bread and a measured piece of butter and mugs of milk.

Treats were rare and even those could sometimes backfire – as when the children were given syllabub:

> an awful dish consisting of currents, raspberries and strawberries put into a large basin together with crumbled cake and some wine all mixed up with sugar and a cow was driven up and milked into it, and then ladled into small basins and eaten out of doors. I don't think we liked it very much!

Between them Miss Emmy and the nursemaid made all the children's clothes:

> which were very uncomfortable in those days, thick harsh flannel next the skin cotton frocks with starched collars at the neck making the skin red and sore – but we were not to

complain – cotton drawers down to our ankles got dirty on our walks and we were scolded and took to turning them up, and bad sights we must have looked in our crumpled things! But looks had no part in our education.

Nor for that matter, did books.

> We had a few of the Jack the Giant Killer order ... and Lazy Lawrence, Simple Simon, Waste Not Want Not and such, all of which I remember to this day, and well I may, for later we were given no more advanced ones, so we read and re-read what we had, and from 10 to 15 I was panting for knowledge.

However, upper-class girls were supposed to have a reasonable command of French and in 1850 or thereabouts a French governess, Mlle Gerand, was added to the children's entourage:

> and we were well drilled in that – we had to write out on our slates every English word we spoke in lesson hours 10 times each in French so we took great care not to! They mercifully kept Miss Emmy too for English and to overlook our clothes, and she made a lot for us and tho' quite strict she was always our joy and comfort.

According to Cecilia, Lucy and Rose, the sisters next to her in age, were 'great pals with much imagination in their games with dolls and shells wch they magnified into people with histories and talk.' She on the other hand 'was always of a very serious nature and hated play and games.' Craving knowledge, she was for ever asking questions – a most unladylike fault according to her mother, who was heard to observe: 'Cecilia is clever – she must not be given books.' In desperation she contrived to steal some of the leather-bound volumes from her father's library, 'many of course far too advanced for me such as "Locke on the Human Understanding" and others, but they gave me a glance of what was thought and written about in the outside world.'

While Edward was idling away his days at Aberhirnant his brother Frank had seen his opportunity and seized it. Bending their father's ear the parson began to poison the old man's mind against his eldest son, pointing to the poor condition of the Hopwood lands for which he claimed that Edward, as his father's heir, must be held chiefly responsible.

At that time new and improved methods of agriculture, plus a willingness by landowners to diversify, were resulting in greatly increased yields from the land. Filled with bitterness, Frank had observed what neighbouring landowners were doing to improve their estates. At length, with the support of his wife Lady Elinor and his brother-in-law the noble Earl Sefton, he obtained his father's permission to embark on an ambitious programme of his own. Availing himself of the best advice that could be obtained, in just a few short years the return on his father's investment was remarkable. A Report on the Agriculture of Lancashire stated that between 1846 and 1849:

> Robert Gregge-Hopwood laid 32 miles of field drains using 120,000 tiles and 600 tons of stone; levelled 20 miles of old fences and used 66.5 tons of oak poles to make new fences. He applied to the land 1,312 tons of lime; 5,200 tons of manure (consisting of horse and cow dung, butchers' garbage and night soil); 1,900 cubic yards of bogsoil (peat) and 12

tons of bonemeal ... Robert Gregge-Hopwood also instigated the development of coal mining in the lower Hopwood Clough. These collieries were linked to the canal basin at Heywood by a horse-drawn tramway, and by a short canal to the bridge on the main drive to the Hall ... As a result, receipts from the produce of the lands of the Hopwood estate increased by six times.[2]

Edward's response to what he saw as his brother's interference – and in particular to the great quantity of money that was being spent – was to complain bitterly to his father. A quarrel erupted between the old squire and his eldest son. When Susan attempted to intervene she saw she had lost her ascendancy over her father-in-law, whose mind had been poisoned against her. She and Edward were forced to move out of the Hall and to take refuge in Hopwood Cottage. 'My father built several larger rooms onto one end of it so that ... the cottage idea was lost and it became an ugly straggling house.'

Obliged to live under the same roof as his children, Edward still managed to see as little of them as he was able. (Quite possibly they alarmed him almost as much as he alarmed them!) Since the family's life was less set about with problems in Wales he continued to escape there as often as he could.

Yet although he and his father had fallen out, Edward did not lose sight of the fact that he was Robert Gregge-Hopwood's heir. And as time went on he could hardly have failed to notice the growing influence Frank wielded over the old man. Aware that his father's health had been failing for sometime, Edward began to be suspicious of his brother's motives, and to insist that all bank statements from the Hopwood bank account be sent to Aberhirnant for his inspection. His suspicions were further aroused when news was brought to him that his brother and the Lady Elinor had taken up permanent residence at the Hall; and that they had recently been joined by his sister Mary, together with the noble earl, her husband; and furthermore that a large contingent of their household servants were encamped there too – all living at his father's expense.

A day came when on opening a bank statement Edward discovered a large overdraft in the Hopwood account. He decided it was time to take action. Beating a hasty retreat from Aberhirnant he headed straight for Hopwood Hall to confront his relations.

Chapter II

The Great Will Case

Upon arriving at Hopwood Hall Edward had intended to confront his father with the damning bank statement and persuade him to sign a document which he had prepared, stating that no cheques should be cashed on the Hopwood account that did not include his signature. Since stealth was of the essence he had arrived unannounced, entering the library by the French windows. He found his father sitting in his usual chair and seizing his chance laid the form in front of him and asked him to sign it.

But as bad luck would have it the old man was not alone. His youngest son, Colonel Harvey Hopwood, had recently married and unbeknown to Edward he and his young wife Lucy were also ensconced at the Hall. It was Lucy – set to keep watch over her father-in-law – who now stepped forward, laying a hand on the old man's arm to prevent him from signing. Calling out in a loud voice to summon help she brought other family members hurrying to the scene and, seeing himself outnumbered, Edward was forced to withdraw.

However, his suspicion that his brother Frank was plotting to deprive him of his inheritance was well founded. And in justice it has to be said that the parson deserved some sympathy. Was it not he who had toiled in the fields while his prodigal brother 'took his journey into a far country' – wasting his substance by chasing after foulmarts?

Indeed worse accusations could be levelled at Edward, a professed Freethinker who neglected to attend divine service and was an admirer of Voltaire, the scourge of the church. The example set by such a man was bound to be injurious to his tenants. Was it not therefore the parson's plain duty to block his brother's path to becoming squire?

Under the terms of their father's will Edward stood to inherit the whole of the Hopwood estates. But the will had been drawn up 20 years earlier and, since then, circumstances had changed. It was to deal in a practical manner with these changed circumstances that the parson had summoned his sister and younger brother and their spouses to Hopwood Hall. They were all agreed that the old man must be persuaded to make a new will – and this without delay. For by the time Edward arrived on the scene it was all too apparent that the squire, who was behaving very oddly, was not in perfect command of his wits.

> He would start to undress in the library, imagining it was his bedroom, to the consternation of the Victorian ladies. He also imagined that he saw a company of soldiers outside the window when dining. Gold coins were dropped from his pockets about the house and he would dress for imaginary train journeys late at night.[1]

Since the plotters had a very good reason for not wanting the extent of the old man's mental deterioration to be known, they were guarding him closely, providing a physical barrier against reports by eye-witnesses and endeavouring to prevent Edward gaining access to his father. When Edward burst in and saw what they were up to he issued a pamphlet giving details of their activities, which he circulated among the Lancashire gentry. It was a tactical blunder. The county families turned on him for causing the ancient name of Hopwood to be dragged through the mire, while the Rev. Frank informed his father that Edward was spreading rumours that he was insane. 'By this means the parson persuaded the old squire to write a letter forbidding his eldest son to enter the house?'[2]

From that moment the family quarrel became public property and through the medium of the press rapidly descended into farce, as may be seen from the account given below.

> [Edward Hopwood] on receiving the letter, sent his wife with her seven-year-old son to plead with the old squire. This lady, Susan Fanny Hopwood … told the squire, in front of the parson, that he was surrounded by 'base – very base people'.

Later the same day the parson looked, through the dining room window and saw Edward Hopwood arriving with a magistrate. As he 'came in through the French windows of the library, the parson hustled the doddering squire down the passage and up the Jacobean stairs to his room. Lady Elinor went in with him and locked the door while Frank guarded the landing.

> The crafty parson then told Edward that he could only see his father if he wrote a note stating that his father was perfectly fit to manage his affairs. Edward refused, realising that they would use this note to disinherit him. He then left the house.[3]

Ignoring this set-back the Rev. Frank went ahead with his plan to disinherit his brother. With the connivance of his brother-in-law Lord Sefton he persuaded two doctors to examine his father and afterwards to sign a document declaring the octogenarian to be 'of sound mind'. With a certain show of reluctance the doctors complied. The parson then instructed a solicitor, Mr Slater, to prepare a new will which substantially increased his own portion and that of his brother Harvey, leaving Edward with only a small annual allowance. By the terms of this new will the residue of the estate was to be held in trust for Edward's seven-year-old son, another Edward, who was to be placed under the guardianship of his uncle, the parson. In the event of the boy's premature death (a common occurrence in those days) the estate was to pass to the Rev. Frank and to his heirs in perpetuity. This new will was placed before the old man who duly signed it. After its completion, the Earl of Sefton carried the will to his home.[4]

During the months that were left to him Robert Gregge-Hopwood remained virtually a prisoner in his own home. New bolts had been put on the downstairs passage doors and White, the butler, had been instructed to sleep with his master. During the day the old man was obliged to listen to psalms read out by the parson. He never saw his eldest son again. When he died early in 1854 his son-in-law, the Earl of Sefton, acting on behalf of the Rev. Frank, brought a case for possession of the estate against Edward, thereby forcing the unfortunate man to have recourse to the law. Gripped between rage and fear Edward saw that his whole family had turned against him and that he was trapped. In defending a lawsuit the plaintiff needs to have deep pockets, but having always lived up to the limits of his allowance Edward was virtually penniless. His brother, on the other hand, having the advantage of the support of my lords Sefton and Derby, had access to virtually unlimited funds and so could anticipate an easy victory.

But when all seemed lost hope was rekindled in the person of a certain Mr Harrup of Manchester. A successful businessman with valuable colliery interests, Harrup was also a keen sportsman and a good friend of Edward's, having enjoyed a day's shooting with him from time to time on the Hopwood estate. Learning of his friend's distress, Harrup now came forward with a generous offer. He would be willing to finance Edward's defence on a 'no win no fee' basis. Mightily relieved, Edward was only too grateful to accept.

Both sides now went into action, mobilising their forces for the forthcoming fight. Acting on behalf of the parson, Lord Sefton instructed no less a person than the Solicitor General, the respected and greatly feared barrister Sir Frederick Thessiger. Not to be outdone, Edward's response was to instruct the Attorney General, Sir Alexander Cowburn. His chief lawyer was a Mr Earle, whose first piece of advice was that Edward should make every effort to get possession of the Hall. Possession, as he explained, being nine-tenths of the law, this would greatly strengthen his position. Cecilia's diary gives a graphic account of how this was achieved:

> (My uncle) made the mistake of leaving the Hall empty with orders to the servants not to admit my father – so he went to the house late one evening and paced round and round – but the servants had instructions to lock and bar every window – and so he found it – but as he was passing the billiard room he saw that one very small window had been forgotten and was open! One of those small latticed windows in the oldest part of the house. He was a man 6 feet in height but thin to emaciation and he was determined to try it and he got in! (That window was often shown to people as a marvel – how any grown man could have squeezed thro.) He at once showed himself to the servants, throwing the Butler into a panic and the Housekeeper into hysterics, and ordered tea to be brought into the library, and there he remained all night – the old keeper Bill Taylor his great friend paraded in front of the window … for they felt sure 'the enemy' would kill or do him an injury if they could – In the morning a Bus came and took all the servants away, and my mother was sent for and all of us and our servants.

Having gained possession of the Hall, Edward now found himself a prisoner, since he dared not venture out for fear of being intercepted. Instructed by Earle he spent all that winter 'making himself acquainted with the intricacies of the law', and in particular gathering evidence of his father's state of mind at the time of the signing of the new will. This 'unusual and distasteful business' began to unsettle his nerves, leaving him morbidly depressed. He developed a growing dislike for the oversized rabbit-warren of a house with its dark panelling and ornately carved Jacobean furniture. As a sensitive and observant teenager, Cecilia was never to forget those uneasy months, or their unfortunate legacy.

The case was to be heard in Liverpool at St George's Hall during the April Assizes. Sir Alexander was planning to call Cecilia as one of the witnesses 'to give evidence of how we sisters were often put by my grandfather's chair to scratch his head quite hard with a quill pen', which the old man believed relieved the pressure on his brain. She was thrilled at being treated like a grown-up and wildly excited at the thought of accompanying her parents to Liverpool. Her cousin Kate Heron (always a good friend to the Hopwood girls) had presented her with a new frock and mantle to wear in the witness box and a pretty new bonnet.

Cecilia and her parents travelled up to Liverpool the day before the trial was due to open and ensconced themselves at the *Adelphi*, the best hotel in town. That afternoon Sir Alexander called on Susan to overlook the costume she was intending to wear in the witness box. He pronounced that 'the light grey silk gown and bonnet were all right, only he insisted on her taking out the feather which trimmed it – 'so as to look very quiet.' Then, to Cecilia's bitter disappointment, she was told that she was not to be called to give evidence after all, since on reflection Sir Alexander 'considered it would have a bad effect to call in so young a girl – I was barely fifteen'. However, she was to be allowed 'to sit through it all in court which was a great comfort'.

The trial was spread over 10 days and with so many notable people due to be called to give evidence the proceedings were widely reported in the national press. The summing-up by both sides kept the nation on tenterhooks.

> Cowburn gave a splendid resume of the whole case, bearing very hardly on the brothers and sister — very crestfallen as they sat there being discussed so seriously ... Then came Thessiger's reply, but he did nothing new, and we didn't mind him, but dire was our dismay when the judge – Cresswell – summed up dead against us! His speech took the whole day, until about 4 – when the jury were locked up and we went to our hotel to tea.

Cecilia was never to forget the stricken looks on her parents' faces, confronted with the possibility that their case might fail.

> My father was nervous but silent, my mother very pale – Cowburn called and was in consultation with the lawyers, I suppose as to the next step to be taken if we lost – but nothing could be done and we went to our rooms, as the jury were said not to be likely to decide that night.

However, after 10 days spent listening to the arguments put forward by both sides, the jury must have decided that enough was enough for they took less time than had been anticipated in reaching their verdict. 'How can I describe what happened', Cecilia recalled:

> about 10 – I had only just curled my hair – a low distant sort of murmer could be heard, away down the street, in the direction of St. George's Hall – this became louder and was like the growl of wild Tigers and Lions, and as it came it resolved itself into the shouts of

> Hurrahs of a multitude – On they came, an irresistible crowd, past the hotel porters, up the stairs, into the lobby where our rooms were – Shall I ever forget the sounds and sight of my mother at her room door in her white dressing gown and with her beautiful fair hair falling around her, shaking hands with one after another of that crowd, till she near fainted with the emotion and fatigue, and had to retire – We had all come outside our rooms in whatever costume we could hastily catch up – Miss Emmy, the Herons and others and we all had to shake hands violently with everybody and the crowd was at last persuaded to depart, and we heard at last that the jury had given an unqualified verdict in our favour, completely disregarding the judge! I suppose we slept, I can't remember, but we went back home next morning amid the shouts as we passed through Middleton, and of the tenants assembled to greet us – where the news had flown that Hopwood was once more ours – the rightful owners.

To the surprise of most of the county families of Lancashire and the discomfiture of his siblings, Edward had won the day. But it was a pyrrhic victory. For most of his erstwhile friends, who had supported the parson on account of his distinguished backers, now turned against him; and since the unsympathetic judge had ruled that each side must bear its own costs, the trial had left him very short of money.

However, the new squire of Hopwood Hall was resolved on making a public show of gratitude towards the men who had fought so valiantly on his behalf, and he and Susan hosted a great celebratory dinner at the Hall, at which presentations were made to Sir Alexander Cowburn and Mr Earle, who were the guests of honour.

In those days the preparation and serving up of a formal banquet was a rare event in the provinces, requiring the services of the whole household and most of the outdoor staff. As a youthful observer there was little that escaped Cecilia's keen eye and she left a colourful account of the evening and of the conventions prevailing at that time.

> They gave a grand dinner … but only men – and my mother at the head of the table. We were allowed to see it set out and what impressed us most was the great gilded Epergne in the centre of the table holding all the sweets and bonbons. In those days all was placed on the table, my father helping the soup and then one kind of fish which replaced it, my mother at the other end another kind and all handed round by footmen in grand liveries – sometimes the coachman and grooms were all dressed up and helped. There were always 4 entrées – 6 at a big dinner – and all placed on the table and removed and carried round – endless fuss and fidget – then top and bottom roast and boiled meat replaced by poultry ditto – and always carried on the table — then numberless sweets and game and cheese ending with dessert and the wines and liqueurs – an army of women washing up the plates and handing them back at each course. Then all the time there was champagne, the butler's charge – I wonder they ever got through!

The modern reader may share the same thought.

Chapter III

Growing Up

That never-to-be-forgotten homecoming was a pivotal moment for Edward Gregge-Hopwood. He was now the acknowledged squire of Hopwood Hall, and though not in the same league as such aristocratic county magnets as my lords Derby and Sefton he was the greatest landowner in the parish of Middleton, where the bearers of his name had held sway for over five hundred years. He and Susan moved directly into the Hall, taking young Edward, the precious heir, to live with them. The four girls, attended by Miss Emmy and the French governess, returned to the Cottage.

Edward's triumph, however, proved to be a hollow victory. For though he had won his case he was encumbered by crippling debts – the judge, Mr Justice Cresswell (irked, no doubt, by what he considered to be the perverse verdict of the jury) had ruled that each side must bear its own costs. These had been heavy. And while it was true that the obliging Mr Harrup seemed in no hurry to be reimbursed, Edward knew that the substantial loan he had accepted would eventually have to be repaid.

Bearing this in mind he instigated a regime of the most stringent economy, with warnings to Susan that social life was to be put on indefinite hold. Their Spartan lifestyle was made easier by the fact that the trial had left them with very few friends, for while it was in progress the best county families (revelling in a scandal of such epic proportions right on their doorstep) had been quick to take sides. And since the Rev. Frank, with his aristocratic supporters, was believed to hold the high ground, most of the local gentry had been backing him to win. When Edward was found to have triumphed, his unlooked for victory had left the county feeling cheated and they resolved to ostracise the new squire and his wife. This was no hardship to Edward (who in any case preferred the company of his dogs) but it bore hard on his wife and children. And scratching around for ways in which money could be saved, Edward's eye fell on his daughters. The three older girls, now in their teens, could go on much as before, he decided – with the addition of an extra governess who would cost no more than her board and could teach them a little German. For what was the point of throwing away money on the education of girls who would never have occasion to use it? Thus, starved of books, Cecilia and her sisters grew up in total ignorance of history, geography or mathematics – or indeed of how other folks lived – cocooned in their circumscribed world. Worst of all, they were starved of the company of young people of their own age. Left to their own devices they grew up with no social skills and continued to be painfully shy.

For their brother of course, the position was entirely different. As the only son Edward Junior was the sole bulwark standing between his father and the hated parsonical brother. He had never been robust (a circumstance not lost on his uncle) and his parents' first concern was to keep the boy alive.

In those days the survival of children could never be taken for granted. Setting aside misadventure, there was a quartet of childhood infections – diphtheria, scarlet fever, measles and whooping cough – waiting to carry children off; while those dreaded killers tuberculosis and typhoid fever were by no means confined to the poor. Book-learning was considered taxing and must be kept to a minimum, and in the early days Edward Senior felt competent enough to set his son a little Latin, though most of the boy's time must be given to healthy outdoor pursuits. When he was eight Edward had been given a gun and taught how to handle it but his main occupations were playing with his rabbits or making dens in the woods.

Eventually, however, his parents, having decided on health grounds that school must be ruled out, began to look about for a tutor. As luck would have it they did not need to look far. For it transpired that dear Miss Emmy had a brother-in-law who was seeking a post. The Rev. J. Williams, a married man with two daughters, being to hand and possessed of the necessary qualifications, was forthwith engaged and installed in a house near Middleton. Edward, now rising nine, was presented with a horse and twice a day, accompanied by a groom, he would ride over for lessons with his tutor.

The arrival of the Rev. Williams's two teenage daughters was welcomed by Edward's sisters, who were sometimes allowed to invite them over for tea. At 15 Cecilia was desperate for mental stimulation. Her two weeks' stay at the *Adelphi Hotel* in Liverpool and her daily attendance at the law court had provided her with a taste of that vast, crowded, clamorous place where men went about their business and well-dressed women leapt in and out of handsome cabs without a care; while ship's hooters blared and the poor from half the nations of Europe could be seen humping their scanty possessions towards the docks – rich and poor alike seemingly quite free of the terror and longing which gripped her at the thought of one day having to join the mysterious adult world. At Hopwood Cottage that day seemed tantalisingly out of reach for she was given no privileges or occupations suitable to her age and was still treated like a child.

For Lucy and Rose it was easier since they formed a pair, using their vivid imagination to furnish an alternative world where they could amuse each other for hours on end by playing at being other people. Their foolery bored Cecilia, who wanted facts. Her head had the feel of an empty cupboard. Nevertheless, for want of anything better she continued to enter into her siblings' childish games.

> We used to dig a pretty deep space in the woods near the cottage, the soil of which was all sand, and roofed it over with branches, so making quite a hut, and we dug an oven inside, which we cooked potatoes and bread and whatever we could coax out of cook stealing sometimes quite in the dark, while the governesses were at supper, and lighting it up with lanthorns from the stables and I wonder it was not found out and stopped.

The fact was that Miss Emmy was always on the side of the children, seeing they had little enough in the way of entertainment. And why should the two governesses care?

Then for reasons that were not disclosed the Rev. Williams fell into disfavour and was 'given his congée' as the saying went. In other words he was dismissed. He and his family departed under a cloud and were never seen again, leaving poor Miss Emmy visibly distressed. 'We knew she cried about it, but she never said anything to us.' Worse was to follow. The parents' quarrel with the tutor had set them against Miss Emmy and 'they were never the same to her – one little thing after another went wrong and she was scolded and cried and kissed us and said nothing.'

Eventually the blow fell. After many years of devoted service Miss Emmy was obliged to tell her charges that she had been asked to leave. The reason the parents gave was that their nurse was 'too ignorant' to be in charge of girls on the verge of entering society. A 'finishing governess' was needed and such a one would shortly be arriving to replace her.

To the young Gregge-Hopwoods the departure of Miss Emmy was nothing short of a calamity. For as long as most of them could remember she had been the loving fulcrum of their little world. Without her 'we all felt very desolate and forlorn,' Cecilia recalled. Now just turned 17, she was still agonisingly shy, and on the verge of womanhood felt desperately in need of the counsel of a sympathetic older woman. As things stood she found herself cast in the role of carer, her siblings looking to her to supply the love and practical help formerly furnished by Miss Emmy. It was she who must brush the tangles from her sisters' hair, patch and darn their clothes, apply salve to grazed knees and consult with cook over their exceedingly plain fare. It was her apprenticeship in caring for others: a vocation she was destined to follow for the rest of her long life.

But she was only an inexperienced girl and eventually even her mother, Susan, was forced to acknowledge that in the absence of Miss Emmy life at Hopwood Cottage was in danger of breaking down. The Hopwood girls were shipped up to the Hall to join Edward and their parents. It was not a happy time. The two governesses, having grown accustomed to the lax regime at the Cottage, rebelled. They soon melted away, while the promised 'finishing governess' failed to materialise. The girls got no schooling at all and while Edward continued to pick up some Latin from his father most of the time he and Evie were allowed to run wild.

Feeling lonely and frustrated, Cecilia, who loved music, eventually persuaded her mother to let her to have piano lessons and for a while she was driven into Manchester twice a week to be instructed by a Mr Hecht. Passionately anxious to succeed she would wake herself up at two or three in the morning to practise her scales and finger exercises and to memorise the pieces Mr Hecht had set. But she never mastered sight-reading and after a few frustrating months she was forced to accept that though she had a 'fierce and turbulent love of music' she had little aptitude. Even when she had succeeded in mastering a piece, 'I couldn't play a note if anyone was by me, for shyness.'

Cecilia had a sweet voice, but she fared no better when in a rare burst of maternal benevolence Susan arranged for her to have a voice test with the highly respected Signor Garcia, a maestro who had coached several operatic stars. Her mother accompanied her to Manchester for the audition, which proved a disaster. The great man struck a few chords and asked Cecilia to sing a note: 'And I burst into tears!' Then taking his hands from the piano Signor Garcia turned to observe his pupil. He shrugged, she remembered. 'Dis young girl is far too timeed,' he declared to Susan, who was looking mortified. Praying for the ground to open under her, Cecilia was taken home 'and the singing was given up for ever'.

Then one day with alarming suddenness Susan was taken seriously ill. A high fever and internal pains were followed rapidly by delirium. The family doctor was summoned but was unable to provide a diagnosis. 'Keep her warm and quiet' was the best advice he could offer. Distraught, Edward sent for Dr Ferguson, an eminent London physician. The great man (whose charge was two guineas a mile) merely confirmed the family doctor's advice. 'Let her sleep as much as possible,' he pronounced, and having partaken of some refreshment left after a couple of hours. Nevertheless, 'it was a relief to have had him' Cecilia commented, voicing a common belief in the superiority of expert opinion.*

In view of the severity of his wife's illness it seems odd that Edward did not consider engaging a nurse. Instead he put his faith in Cecilia, who was given the charge of nursing the invalid. At first the responsibility terrified her. ' I ... a girl of seventeen, knowing nothing and never having seen an illness of any kind.' She was asked to sleep in her mother's room so as to be on call at any hour of the day or night, when she might have to apply gentle massage if Susan showed signs of pain – or heat soup.

> Mother was very weak and I had to prop her up and feed her and my father was called in to lift her when the bed was made, but being so strong and anxious he hurt her and could only swear to himself and let me do it. [My father] was almost mad with anxiety and could speak to no one, quite violent if anything went wrong ... but as she got stronger she liked to be read to and he could do that well and it comforted him and gradually her perfect health triumphed.

To Cecilia's private grief the intimacy that had existed between herself and her mother during those anxious weeks was not destined to last. As Susan gained in strength the memory of her helplessness, when her daughter had been obliged to attend to her most private needs, made her cringe. To her mind the whole business of her illness was best forgotten – and the sooner the better.

However, though Susan's chilly manner soon returned, her illness served to melt the ice between Edward and his eldest daughter and this thaw would continue. 'I often think', she confided to her diary, 'that my being able to help so was the cause of him liking me more than the rest.'

But Edward at this time was far from being a happy man, for he took no pleasure in living under the ancestral roof he had fought so hard to gain. He could not rid himself of the mental torment he had suffered during that nightmare winter spent under siege – a prisoner in his own house. Truth to tell he had never much cared for the place anyway. The wealth of elaborately carved oak, blackened with age, oppressed him, while he declared that the mansion's low ceilings were bad for his health.

---

* It seems likely that Susan was suffering from typhoid fever.

The long evenings were the worst. Sitting in his library (which reeked of damp) Edward would begin to fancy he was not alone. Why did his candle flicker? Was it merely a draught from the ill-fitting leaded panes that was causing a curtain to twitch? He began to be obsessed by all those generations of Hopwoods who were no relations of his, though he bore their ancient name. Their ghosts were all about him. Did they bear him a grudge?

Finally he was forced to confess to Susan that he had reached the end of his tether – that though he found the Hall supportable by day, nothing would induce him to spend one night more under its roof and that in consequence they must return to the cottage. Susan was aghast. She knew full well that if they left the Hall the news would spread like wildfire and the Rev. Frank would be round in a flash, sniffing out trouble. To abandon their home was unthinkable: Susan was quite firm about that. But seeing that her husband was equally firm in his refusal to sleep at Hopwood, a compromise had to be found. Susan's solution, though bizarre in the extreme, was, by her determination and Edward's stubbornness, somehow made to work, as Cecilia explains:

> Breakfast lunch and dinner we had at the Hall and dinner over we changed our (low-necked) gowns and carrying them under our arms we all set off to walk to the Cottage – where a footman had preceded us and lighted lamps and made tea – we went in procession – my father first with a lanthorn, then Mother, then us girls and last Brother with also a lanthorn – arriving there we changed into our low gowns and sat round the big drawing room table sewing and one of us always reading aloud (this made us all good readers). At ten we went to bed and in the morning we dressed for the day and shouldering our evening gowns marched down to the Hall for breakfast. How we hated it all – that ½ mile trudge in all weathers summer and winter.

Yet no one dared to complain. Their father's wishes were paramount, and despite the inconvenience their mother had made it her business to see that they were carried out. On the rare occasions when guests were invited to stay overnight a complicated procedure had to be followed. First the brougham was sent over to Moore Hall to collect their obliging cousin Kate Heron:

> And on those few occasions we all slept at the Hall, but my father still at the Cottage, and Mother had to excuse his absence as well as she could, and now and then leave them at cards and drive to him at the Cottage, deputing Cousin Kate as hostess, and to be back next morning at breakfast, going and coming in the brougham.

As time passed Edward's eccentricities became more pronounced. A lean man by nature,

> he had a perfect mania for starving himself and his meals were thin bread and butter and tea, always eaten alone, lunch one chop or wing of a chicken and water (never wine) also alone, then more tea and bread and butter at six. He never dined with us at that time.

Their father began also to develop a pathological suspicion of the men in his employ. Convinced that his grooms were stealing his oats he would get up at cockcrow and insist on overseeing the feeding of his dogs and horses. Where formerly he had not taken the slightest interest in the management of the estate he now made it his business to overlook his book keeper's accounts on a daily basis, his suspicious mind driving the poor man close to distraction.

As a matter of fact, with no effort on his part, by the mid-1850s Edward Gregge-Hopwood was well on the way to becoming an exceedingly rich man. For as the dark Satanic mills of Manchester crept closer to the small town of Middleton, land-hungry factory-owners were casting covetous eyes on the outlying fields and woods of the Hopwood estate. Edward was being offered ridiculously high sums in exchange for their 99 leases. And here and there, little by little, he was persuaded to sell.

Forty years later Susan Gregge-Hopwood, by that time a widow, was to hold a great gala at Hopwood Hall on behalf of the Smoke Abatement Society. Resulting from her efforts the mill-owners were obliged to install expensive new furnaces to mitigate the black smoke nuisance. But her campaign came too late, for by the end of the 19th century the damage had already been done.

CHAPTER IV

Cecilia 'Comes Out'

'By now I was eighteen and had to "come out" – a dreadful moment', Cecilia recorded in her diary, recalling her torment at having to be taken to London to meet young men, and to attend her first balls. For a girl of her class, 'coming out' was a rite of passage that could not be avoided. In those days marriage was the only career option open to well-bred young women. Taking up paid work was unthinkable, even if a girl was qualified to attempt it, which in the vast majority of cases she was not. Thus, unless parents were content to make lifelong provision for their daughters, they must be thrown upon the marriage market in the hope of attracting a husband.

The marketplace was fashionable London, an exclusive area encompassing Mayfair and Belgravia in the West End of that teeming metropolis. 'The Season', as it was known, began in April, when the city's choking fogs had ceased to be a menace, the winter mud had been swept from the streets and the daffodils in the Royal parks trumpeted spring. It was then that the upper echelons of British society – the 'ton', as they called themselves – brought their unmarried daughters to town and for the next four hectic months applied themselves to the serious business of finding them husbands.

The previous winter, in preparation for the coming ordeal, Susan had engaged a dancing master, Monsieur Paris, who had come to the Hall once a week to teach Cecilia and her sisters dancing and to instruct them in the etiquette of the ballroom. His lessons proved to be a welcome diversion in their dull lives. Cecilia, who was tall, graceful and bursting with pent-up energy, had no difficulty in mastering the steps of the polka, the valse and the gallop and with Lucy and Rose soon mastered the rules governing the minuet and other old-fashioned dances. Monsieur Paris made them practise low curtsies 'and how to shake hands and how to sit down and get up on a low chair and how to come into a room gracefully,' which made them all very self-conscious and shy, Cecilia recalled, 'though perhaps necessary'. So it was to prove.

At that stage in their lives Edward Gregge-Hopwood's land-dealings were beginning to bring in substantial sums of money. This was fortunate, for the launch of a daughter did not come cheap. 'I was taken to London and dressed in the height of fashion and most expensively by the best dressmakers,' Cecilia recalled. Astounded by the fact that her mother seemed to know her way about in this vast and bewildering city she submitted to being prodded and squeezed by alarming women who talked over her head with their mouths full of pins as though she was invisible. In the past Susan had not cared a fig how her daughters were turned out, which made it all the more remarkable that now she insisted that her child would need four – or possibly five – ball gowns, in addition to a walking habit and several tea gowns for the afternoon. Cecilia began to wonder how she would ever survive.

Since her parents did not own a townhouse and were still not on speaking terms with their titled relations (who did), Edward and Susan had to make do with a rented house for the duration of the Season. As soon as they were installed (not without a good deal of grumbling on Edward's part) Susan began sending out cards to other mothers of that year's crop of débutantes, whose names, like Cecilia's, appeared on a mysterious 'List' said to be compiled by the Lord Chancellor. Then began a merry-go-round of tea parties that were sheer agony to Cecilia.

> I had one stupid defect, wch will last till I die and wch greatly handicapped me. I could never remember faces even if I was a week in a house with people, I never knew them again – men or women – and even my own children have played tricks on me and I have passed them in the street – I think that has been mostly the cause of my having made so few friends and shrinking from meeting my fellow humans … I have often thought that defect of mine not being able to read music came from the same want of quick message from brain to eye, a defect of brain power in fact! For this reason I dreaded going anywhere, it seemed so rude to stare at people and ask their names while shaking hands and no doubt I have lost many friends through that.

Her handicap was thrown into sharp relief when she discovered that most of the young women she was introduced to seemed to be among friends. Girls they had known since childhood or had met on visits to one another's houses were greeted with shrieks of delight. And how they chattered! She for her part knew not a mortal living soul. With the exception of the two Williams girls (who were gone almost as soon as they came) she had never had a friend outside her own family. How curious, how restricted her life seemed!

The gown she wore for her first ball was a blue tulle confection, its silver-speckled overskirt looped up with pink roses. A high wreath of pink roses crowned her upswept hair. Stealing a look at herself in her mother's cheval glass she found it hard to believe that the oval face staring back at her – with the deep-set eyes she had inherited from her father – was truly her. Even her mother felt bound to admit she looked 'very handsome'.

'Those were the days of crinolines and stays had to be cruelly tight, most painful after a long valse or gallop,' Cecilia recalled. Yet though the balls were every bit as terrifying as she had anticipated, thanks to her good looks Cecilia was never reduced to the ignominy of having to dance with her father, for she never lacked partners. At the end of each dance the form was for her partner to conduct her to a seat and engage her in conversation. 'Then one was expected to flirt, but I was much too shy and frightened, even if I had known how to begin!' After a suitable interval the partner would give her his arm and conduct her back to her mother, who would be seated among her kind, keeping an eagle eye on her daughter and expecting to be introduced . 'A very shy performance,' Cecilia commented. Fortunately 'men did not expect much of young girls in those days' and she confessed she had been 'much admired'.

But if finding a husband was the principal objective of the Season (and no bones were made about that) Cecilia's summer-long spell of junketing could hardly have been called a success. However:

> one benighted man even ventured to ask to come and pay his addresses. We were all at the Cottage and he never saw me alone, and my shyness and utter dumbness wasn't helped by one being put at a table with 2 candles in a corner of the room — all the rest rather watching us and pretending not to – I don't know what we talked of but I must have been impossibly heavy in hand and I don't know which was the more relieved when 10 o'clock came and we disappeared – He left before breakfast, having <u>I suppose</u> told my father nothing more could be said. It was a Mr Cunliffe and we never saw him again.

The following year Lucy was brought out and 'the balls were not so painful with the two of us to talk things over'. Lucy, though, was no more successful than her sister had been in attracting a mate. By the time it was Rose's turn Susan must have considered it a mark of shame to be seen parading three unmarried daughters. Consequently the girls 'never went all three to balls, but took turns'.

At some point during their first London Season Cecilia and each of her sisters in turn would have been obliged to attend one of Queen Victoria's 'Drawing Rooms' at which they had to make a deep curtsey before the monarch wearing white silk or satin gowns with sweeping trains and carrying white ostrich-feather fans. This ritual signalled their entry into Society and with its potential for disaster was guaranteed to cause panic. However the ceremony cannot have made much impression on Cecilia since there is no mention of it in her diary.

By this time both Edward and Susan had grown thoroughly disillusioned with London, where Edward's graceless disposition had made them few friends and where they were regularly snubbed by the likes of the Derbys and the Seftons. Since their girls had made no effort to ingratiate themselves with any of the young men on offer they must either do without husbands or else find them closer to home. In succeeding years:

> We went a few times to London but only for a week or two to Hotels but no balls or parties, they knew nobody, all our relations being tabu owing to the Trial, but they took us to plays – I saw Charles Keen in Hamlet, a great revelation – we knew nothing of Shakespeare or even the names of poets except Walter Scott and some of Byron he read aloud sometimes – one year we even took 3 horses up to ride in the Park – just rode – spoke to no one – we were not shown the sights, as Westminster, St. Paul's and so on, but we walked in the street, always on my father's arm – it must have bored him badly – he used to take us to the chief confectioner of the day and give us ices. An unimaginable treat!

Every winter there were three great Cheshire balls held at Knutsford 'to which all the county magnates came'. And Knutsford being not far from Withington, the home of Susan's parents the Baskervyle-Gleggs, she and Edward regularly based themselves there when attending these balls with their girls.

[Withington] was very grand, but my grandfather was a very alarming old gentleman and keeping up the custom of drinking to coming out girls' health at dessert down a long table of 18 or 20 guests he would rap for silence and call out "Miss Hopwood may I have the honour of drinking your health?" "With much pleasure" I had been told to say, with scarlet cheeks and almost crying. "Fill Miss Hopwood's glass" he would say after asking if I would have port or sherry – we bowed to each other and the ordeal was over. But it's hard to believe what pain and misery it was all thro dinner expecting it – I hated the whole thing – balls and all.' [A further problem was that] Withington was much tabu in the county in those days (owing to family events I will not go into) and my grandmother had to pick up partners where she could – none of the county society visited there and an odd set they mostly were.

It was nevertheless while staying at Withington for one of these hated balls that Cecilia was to meet her future husband. A man 17 years older than herself, when Cecilia and he exchanged looks she must have guessed that Mr Widdrington was disliking the rather vulgar company he found himself in as much as she was. He gave a glimmer of a smile, she remembered, 'and we at once converged'.

CHAPTER V

Courtship and Marriage

Shalcross Fitzherbert Widdrington, who in due course would inherit his aunt Dorothy Widdrington's Northumbrian estate, had been on the lookout for a wife for sometime. The Widdringtons, an old Northumbrian family who could trace their forebears to Saxon times, had a curious history. Ennobled by the Stuarts, the 3rd Lord Widdrington was impeached and charged with high treason for his part in the abortive Jacobite rebellion of 1715. The ill-fated lord, lucky to have escaped execution, had been forced to forfeit both his title and his estates. Thereafter, though his descendants had gone some way towards replenishing the family coffers and regaining land and influence, the Widdringtons seemed to be dogged by misfortune. For over one hundred years no male heir had been vouchsafed to them, and on three separate occasions the ancient name and the lands that went with it had been passed down through the female line by special Act of Parliament. Thus it was that Fitz (his mother, Mrs Jacson, having been born Widdrington and her late brother and his wife Dorothy being childless) had become heir, after taking the old family name.

Fitz might have found a wife sooner if he had not been in love for many years with his niece, the beautiful Geraldine Smith-Barry. Though the laws of consanguinity barred him from any thought of marriage, Geraldine commanded his heart and he could not put her out of his head. But time was passing, he was already close on 40 and his relations were urging him to find a wife. When he met Cecilia he believed he might have found a woman who would suit him.

She, of course, knew nothing of this. What she saw at once was that Mr Widdrington was a cut above any of the loud-mouthed young men she was accustomed to meeting. For a start, when they were introduced, it was evident he did not expect her to flirt. He for his part saw a healthy and well-set-up young woman who he discovered was one of five, making it likely she would be capable of providing him with an heir. There was, moreover, a refinement about her, a beauty that he guessed was more than skin deep. Seeing that she was ill at ease Fitz motioned her to one side and began to question her, attempting to draw her out. Was she fond of music? Did she hunt? When visiting London, had she been taken to the National Gallery?

Looking up at this singular man (for Mr Widdrington was exceptionally tall – well over six foot), Cecilia felt hopelessly ignorant. Yet his kind eyes reassured her and for once her lack of schooling did not seem to matter. After replying to his questions she felt brave enough to question him and learned that he lived close by their cousins, the Herons at Moore Hall, with his widowed mother; that he had travelled a good deal; and that if he could do exactly as he pleased he would sail up the Nile and paint the pyramids.

'The pyramids?' Cecilia echoed – not altogether sure what they were, or where the Nile was. 'Would that be difficult?'

'A challenge – certainly,' Mr Widdrington replied. 'You see, the colours – all that tawny sand. One would need to mix a completely fresh palette!'

'I suppose so,' she said, doubtfully.

'As a matter of fact,' he said, stroking his luxuriant beard, 'I have had the very good fortune to receive some instruction from a master of watercolour by the name of Edward Lear.'

'Oh, I'm so glad – for you, I mean,' Cecilia replied. And though she guessed that it must be perfectly obvious to her new acquaintance that she had never heard of this 'masterly painter', Cecilia discovered to her surprise that she was smiling.

The Gregge-Hopwoods seldom entertained, but an exception was always made for the Manchester Races.

> We had parties always – rather terrible parties, usually two young men of the de Trafford family and their very vulgar sister, wife of Revd. Sparling – she used to sing comic songs – the sort often whose only attraction is to be bordering on the indecent. Fitz came once and was so bored and disgusted that he nearly swore to have no more to do with me!

Witnessing her new friend's obvious distaste for the company her parents kept, Cecilia felt as if she was drowning. For in a short space of time Mr Widdrington had become her lifeline and she felt it was slipping away.

> It was all mist and chaos to me, a blind groping in darkness. It was that helpless groping for 'Light, more Light' that attracted him first to me and (as he has often told me) intense pity – he <u>could not</u> leave me drowning when he had once put out a hand.

But Fitz was no moon-struck youth and he took some time before coming to a decision.

> He had much to get over and many heart searchings – our family were not well thought of in the county, my father being an agnostic and almost a recluse, my mother one of the very doubtful Gleggs. Fitz's best friends did all they could to dissuade him from me.

Another annual event on the Gregge-Hopwood calendar was the Infirmary Ball at Warrington and for this occasion Cecilia and one or other of her sisters (never both) always stayed with their Heron cousins, the Reverend George and his sister Kate, at Moore Hall.

> My father went also, he liked George and still more his brother Harry, they used mysteriously to go together to Prize Fights which were illegal then and had to be arranged with great secrecy for fear of a raid of the police – and also both liked and went to cock-fighting. Harry and his wife always drove over to Moore to lunch and talk shop.

3   *Cecilia Widdrington.*

Cousin Kate was in the habit of inviting a couple of partners for the girls 'and always Fitz was one of them'. And it was at Moore that Fitz finally made up his mind.

> So he asked me to be his wife and in an agony of shyness I said 'ask Mama'. I couldn't show him I cared – cared with a great and intense admiration and gratitude and an affection which increased thro our long union of 53 years together, tho we were never I think what is called 'in love' – but it was brave of him to take so much on trust, which I was far too shy to be able to let him see.

The following day Cecilia returned to Hopwood, where her news received a lukewarm response from her parents.

> He was accepted, tho not with enthusiasm, for it was only little of worldly goods he could offer me at that time, his aunt Mrs Widdrington had the Northumberland place, Newton, for her life and he had only a small allowance from his mother.

Nevertheless her parents' consent was grudgingly obtained and Cecilia, at the age of 24, was permitted to tell Lucy and Rose that she was to be married. She spent her last winter at Hopwood virtually in purdah, for her mother had the old-fashioned idea that it wasn't 'proper' for a girl to go about when engaged.

For two months she saw nothing of Fitz, who was, as she discovered, a very busy man. As trustee to his widowed elder sister Eliza Smith-Barry and guardian to her son Arthur, he had many obligations, for when Arthur came of age he would inherit extensive properties in England and Southern Ireland. In his role as trustee Fitz was obliged to pay frequent visits to his nephew's Irish estates, where skirmishes had broken out between a militant group of

4   *Shalcross Fitzherbert Widdrington.*

Catholic nationalists calling themselves Fenians,* and their Anglo-Irish landlords. He had appointed an old friend of his, Leopold Cust, as agent to the Irish estates, but because of the unsettled state of the country he had felt it necessary to spend a good deal of time there himself.

In February the monotonous round at Hopwood was interrupted when Edward decided to take a month's lease on a house near Windermere in the Lake District and Fitz was invited to stay . Though the intention was good it was to prove a difficult time for the engaged couple.

> We girls had a sitting room and Fitz was to sit with us, with strict orders from my mother that we were never to be left alone, one sister at least had to be with us, and the same when we went for walks. [Fitz read to us] chiefly Tennyson who we had never heard of, and he talked of people and things quite unknown – I wonder he had the patience!

In the evenings after dinner when the family sat down all together there were 'dreadful silences', since Fitz and their parents had no tastes whatever in common.

The wedding had been fixed for 20 April and on their return home Susan whirled into action. In those days upper-class brides were expected to shed their entire wardrobe on marriage (like a snake shedding its skin). Everything they took to their new home must be new, down to the smallest article of underclothing. This custom called for a deep pocket, as well as for close attention to the future needs of the bride. Susan, however, was not interested in the mundane and a shopping trip to London was made 'very disagreeable' to Cecilia, her mother seeing fit to provide her with a heap of beautiful under linen 'all trimmed with real lace', two handsome silk morning gowns and three or four low-cut evening dresses, and very little else. There was nothing that was remotely suitable for a country wife in chilly Northumberland. Cecilia was glad to get back to her sisters 'who were very fond of me and couldn't conceal their despair at my leaving them'.

Wedding presents began to trickle in, but owing to the family quarrel they were few in number. 'I believe I had thirteen all told.' Despite their father's considerable wealth, his three elder girls had an annual allowance amounting to one pound apiece, 'so my dear sisters gave me only small trifles – sleeve and blouse buttons – by saving up their pennies and buying nothing for themselves, and no one helped them. The parents gave me <u>nothing</u> except the trousseau.'

However, a generous gift from Fitz's Aunt Widdrington 'overshadowed everything'. The old lady adored her nephew and was determined to do all she could for his bride. She had inherited some fine diamonds from her mother, which she packed into a large case and despatched to Hopwood Hall. When Cecilia opened this treasure chest she was astonished to find it contained a beautiful Spanish diamond cross on many little gold chains, a splendid Sévigné brooch with pendants and long earrings and a large rivière diamond necklace of single stones. Susan was astonished.

> They made a sparkling show and really went far towards reconciling my mother to the marriage which she had always thought a paltry one - she not having a great knowledge

---

* They took their name from the ancient Irish legendary warrior band of the Fianna.

of English history, wasn't at all aware that the Widdringtons were the descendents of one of the oldest families in the kingdom and the heroes of the old Chevy Chase ballad, 'For Widdrington my heart is woe, As one in doleful dumps, For when his legs were smitten off, He fought upon his stumps.' She was much more human and kind to me from that time.

Cecilia was attended on her wedding day by her three sisters and two Smith-Barry cousins. Her wedding gown, chosen by her mother, was, she declared, 'very handsome'.

> White satin and a deep Brussels lace flounce looped with wreaths of orange blossom and all held out by a huge crinoline – the larger the more fashionable in that day – a high wreath of orange flowers supporting a very large Brussels lace shawl, thrown over the whole head – face and all! … My mother and I drove to church in the large yellow chariot and post horses and post boys – we could hardly squeeze in, with our crinolines. There was much cheering and staring as after the service (read by Cousin George Heron who nearly broke down) I took my husband's arm and we were driven home in our humble Brougham …

Like young brides before and since Cecilia passed the wedding breakfast in a daze.

> I don't remember any more except the parting – it was rather hurried, we had to catch a train at Manchester, my father pressing a £10 note into my hand as he helped me into the carriage and kissed me! The first and last time he ever kissed me in his life. Intense relief that it was all over I chiefly remember and we two alone at long last.

The couple's first night as man and wife was spent at Conway in North Wales, en route for the port of Holyhead, the gateway to Ireland. Fitz had planned to honeymoon on one of his nephew's Irish estates, thus enabling him to combine pleasure with a certain amount of business; and on the following day they were joined by his Irish agent, Leopold Cust, accompanied by his young wife and their infant son, Charley.

'We walked a lot that sunny day – over the wire-like suspension bridge, then a world's wonder, and after dinner took train to Holyhead as the boat crossed by night – my first sea voyage!' After a day and a night spent in Dublin the party boarded the train for Cork. To Cecilia every sight that met her eyes was a fresh cause for wonder: 'Ireland was at its best that year, green and purple and brown was my impression of it as we travelled through miles and miles of gorse in splendid flower. I never see gorse without thinking of that day.'

At Cork they bade goodbye to the Custs and took the new branch line to Queenstown, a busy port that was the last stopping place for ships crossing to North America. Arrived at the little station with its waft of the open sea they were met by a liveried coachman who saluted Fitz and doffed his hat to Cecilia, staring at her with unabashed curiosity. The short drive to Fota Island, which sat snugly in the inner harbour and was linked to the mainland by a causeway, was sheer delight to Cecilia, who gazed about her at carpets of bluebells and trees already in full leaf, as if it were summer.

Fota House, which was their destination, might have been designed for honeymooners. Originally built as a hunting lodge, it had been enlarged in the classical style in the early

19th century, given a fine Greek Doric portico on the entrance front and elegant shallow bows overlooking the garden. In contrast to Hopwood Hall with its low ceilings and profusion of dark Tudor oak the entrance hall, supported by pairs of yellow marble columns, seemed always to be flooded with light. Running from room to room Cecilia was enchanted to find how light and airy a place it was, and how romantic – the elaborate plasterwork on its high ceiling depicting swags of bay and pairs of cooing doves. Upstairs, in the charming boudoir that had been made ready for them, overlooking the garden, she found more swags and more doves. 'Oh – it is the prettiest place I have ever seen!' she exclaimed to Fitz, delighted both by the house and by its romantic island setting.

Fitz's late brother-in-law James Smith-Barry (who had been married to Fitz's elder sister Elizabeth and had died tragically at the age of 40) had devoted the last years of his short life to the creation of the Fota arboretum. It was the age of the great plant-gathering expeditions, when intrepid botanists were bringing back to Britain specimens from all the corners of the globe. Many rarities had found their way to Fota Island where trees and shrubs native to the New World as well as to South Africa, China and Japan were now to be seen flourishing in the island's exceptionally mild climate.

'We sauntered about in the most beautiful garden in the world,' Cecilia remembered some 65 years later:

> and revelled in the sunshine of the loveliest summer that had been known there for years – and watched the oyster fishing – a great feature there – and drove into Cork. We were obliged to go there the very first day to get me a couple of muslin gowns (I had nothing but silk in my trousseau!) and a garden hat – I had nothing but smart bonnets.

Part of Fitz's time had to be spent on estate business, but when he had time to spare he would bring out his sketch book or set up his easel in some picturesque spot. 'A great pleasure it was to me to sit by him watching and talking', Cecilia recalled.

> O how we talked! And there my entire ignorance of everything and everybody came to him I fear as a revelation, he did not think anyone could be so ignorant ... I have often wondered since how he could have endured it, I suppose my intense desire to know and the pains I took helped him.

In the early years of their married life Cecilia had been more than a little in awe of this walking encyclopaedia whom she had had the good fortune to marry and it was her habit to defer to him, trying hard to make up for her ignorance by keeping lists of names and facts and studying the newspapers. Later, when her failure to obey her own instincts had led to a gross injustice, she would learn that no single person can be the fount of all knowledge, and time and experience would teach her to place more trust her own judgement.

In the evenings they began the habit of reading aloud to each other – a custom that was kept up throughout their married life. 'Fennimore Cooper's tales, Dick Turpin and his wonderful ride on Black Bess ... but mostly Walter Scott's novels – I think we read out Ivanhoe three times over!'

When Fitz was obliged to visit one of his nephew's outlying properties he would often take Cecilia with him.

> After a while we made a little visit to Killarney, quite a new experience to me, living in tiny Irish hotels and driving in their queer one-sided cars – but I was always a good travelling companion – helpful and taking a great interest in what I saw and heard … We made an expedition to the wild south west of Ireland and right to the extreme south point Valencia – where they were making experiments with under sea Cables and other scientific work – it was a real tough time – the Poorest of inns and the plainest of foods – but I liked it all.

Cecilia's enthusiasm for everything that was new, however uncomfortable or outlandish, and her cheerful disregard for rutted roads, thin stews and flea-infested beds, endeared her to her husband, always an enthusiastic traveller who seldom had enough money to throw away on such luxuries as first-class hotels.

Then the Custs with their infant son Charley paid them a visit. 'Our first guests', Cecilia remembered, recalling that Amelia Cust was:

> a very handsome rather fine lady, and quite out of place in the lonely places one has to live in, often left for days quite alone when he went on his rounds, the country then being in a very unsettled state and there had been several agents shot from behind hedges and she was very plucky we thought and very pleased to come and be with us as she saw next to no one.

In view of the dangers he faced from the Fenians, Leopold Cust had already entrusted Fitz with the care of his wife and the guardianship of young Charley and of any other children who might be born to them: though neither could have guessed how soon Fitz would be called upon to stand by his word.

After three happy months getting to know one another and enjoying the luxury of being mostly on their own, 'the time came when our honeymoon had to end, and with great regret and some foreboding on my part. For the world now had to be faced and those in-law relations which as yet I did not know.'

Chapter VI

Early Married Life

Meeting the in-laws can be a daunting prospect for any young bride. For Cecilia, whose crippling shyness was compounded by the knowledge that her family was ostracised by half the county, it was a major ordeal. She quailed at the thought of having to meet her mother-in-law, to whom she had only been briefly introduced on the day of her wedding. Rumour had it that Mrs Jacson had a 'hot and haughty' temper and Cecilia was in terror of being snubbed.

Yet she need not have worried. For by the time she and Fitz returned from their honeymoon it had been confirmed that she was three months pregnant – a happy circumstance which guaranteed her popularity. She recalled that Mrs Jacson had been 'very kind', driving her about and introducing her to nice neighbours, 'her manners always stately as became the old Widdrington stock'. They drove over to Hopwood where they were 'well received, my 3 sisters with great love and interest'. All this was a great relief to Cecilia for she knew that for the foreseeable future she and Fitz were going to have to make their home with the old lady 'and my marriage made her kinder to Fitz'.

Though her husband would never have admitted it, Cecilia had guessed that Fitz was not over fond of his mother; nor in the past had Mrs Jacson particularly cared for him. It is possible that she had expended her store of love on his two older brothers, neither of whom had survived. He had always preferred his Aunt Dorothy and would gladly have made his home with her at Newton Hall if it could have been done without giving offence. As things stood, Fitz's marriage to the beautiful Miss Hopwood (who had lost no time in fulfilling his family's hopes by becoming pregnant) had greatly improved Fitz's relations with his mother 'and so we lived very peacefully together for some months'.

There was, however, one potentially awkward encounter that could not be avoided. Whether or not it had been wise, Fitz had felt it his duty to made a clean breast to his wife of his attachment to his niece Geraldine Smith-Barry, and though Cecilia respected him for his honesty she could not help feeling alarmed at the thought of having to meet this paragon. She knew, moreover, that the Smith-Barrys had been 'much prejudiced against me' and that Fitz's sister Elizabeth had heartily disapproved of her brother's marriage. Nevertheless the meeting could not be delayed indefinitely, for Fitz had business to do on his nephew's behalf. In September they drove to the Smith-Barry's Cheshire seat at Marbury, where they spent several weeks. Happily Cecilia's sweet nature and her willingness to please saw to it that they 'soon got reconciled'. She and Geraldine 'got to love each other and had much in common'. The two young women were to remain friends for the rest of their lives.

Cecilia's diary has little to say about the Smith-Barry's eldest son, Arthur, merely noting that he was 'great at cricket'. It was the younger son, 19-year-old Jem, 'at that time and for long after the handsomest man I have ever seen', who had impressed her. (In view of what was to happen later we may guess that the young man's fine physique, together with his full-lipped, rather sensual, mouth and deep-set brown eyes, may have awakened feelings in Fitz's young bride which possibly surprised her.)

'Their mother I never could really like', Cecilia confessed.

> She had been very lovely and still had her beautiful and refined features and graceful carriage and manners, but she was deeply in love and had been for some years with Lord de Tabley (a Lord in Waiting to the Queen) and he had made her too worldly and self-conscious for my taste, but always nice and pleasant to me.

What had struck Cecilia most forcibly was the critical nature of the whole Smith-Barry family. 'All – even their dearest came under it and to me – who had none of it – it seemed unkind and I was long in getting to understand it better.'

Cecilia had been six months married before Fitz took her to Newton Hall, the plain stone house with its view of the Cheviot hills where his Aunt Dorothy had lived quite alone for the 12 years of her widowhood. Having no children of her own, all the affection of this 'quite uncritical, loving and prosaic woman' was centred on her nephew Fitz 'and now for him and for his wife nothing was too good.'

That November Cecilia's sisters Lucy and Rose were invited to pay her a visit. They were delighted to have the opportunity of seeing her future home, though they could not help remarking privately that Fitz's aunt appeared to be 'quite hearty and healthful and full of fun' and by no means ready to relinquish her hold on her property. They felt sorry for their sister who was having to wait for a dead woman's shoes.

Cecilia's baby was expected at the end of January and Fitz was determined that the child should be born in the old family home. His mother had taken it upon herself to find them a suitable nurse. After interviewing a number of applicants she had chosen a woman with impeccable references whose previous employers had expressed themselves as being entirely satisfied with her management of their nurseries. Fitz was grateful to his mother for engaging such a paragon on their behalf. But when Ward arrived the young mother-to-be had her own reservations. She found the older woman's attitude intimidating.

'Ward speaks of our baby as if he will belong to her,' she said to Fitz, trying to make a joke of it.

'She will have the care of him, won't she? So she's right in a way. Rest assured my dear – Ward knows all about babies.'

'Whereas I know nothing?'

'Just so. But you mustn't worry. You must watch how she goes about things and you'll soon learn.'

After a trouble-free labour the baby was born at 3.00 a.m. on Thursday 19 January 1865. Cecilia felt a stab of disappointment when the midwife told her the infant was a girl, though fortunately Fitz did not seem to mind. They named her Frances Dorothy. Cecilia was pleased to find she was able to breastfeed her daughter and all seemed to be going on splendidly for the first 10 days. But then she was seized with puerperal fever, an infection of the uterus which in those days all too often proved fatal. For six weeks she inhabited a no man's land midway between the living and the dead. Fitz, distraught at the possibility of losing his wife, summoned 'the great Edinbro Dr Simpson of chloroform fame'. But without recourse to modern drugs there was little he could recommend beyond what their own Dr Wilson was doing and in the end it was Cecilia's strong constitution which pulled her through.

It was not until half way through March that the young mother was considered well enough to have her child carried into the sick-room and placed in her arms. Cecilia did not recognise Dorothy. Fed on sweetened cow's milk by her devoted nurse, her baby had grown fat and dimpled and gave off an unpleasantly sour smell. She screamed loudly at the strange face bent over hers and Cecilia hastily handed her back to Ward, whose practised jigging and clucking calmed her instantly. Cecilia was mortified to see her baby's face break into a smile.

It was not an auspicious beginning and matters failed to improve. In April, with Cecilia scarcely recovered, Dorothy was taken to Hopwood to be shown off to her grandparents. 'Great Grandma Glegg was there and they all admired Dorothy very much,' Cecilia

5   *Newton Hall.*

recalled, remembering how all the womenfolk would troop up to the nursery to see her baby being washed. She herself felt no particular warmth towards this alien creature, and failed to understand what all the fuss was about. She made Dorothy wear caps when anyone saw her, 'as I hated the sight of a little bare head.'

Their daughter's itinerant lifestyle and Fitz's inability to provide his wife with a proper home rankled with her parents and more so with her grandmother. Old Mrs Glegg (always happy to stir the pot) 'influenced my mother to be bitter and to dislike Fitz'. Mortified by their sharp tongues, Cecilia felt her confidence ebbing away and the 'old shy feeling' came over her, rendering her powerless to defend her husband. She accepted that it was awkward – having to make do on Fitz's small allowance from his mother – but what was the good in complaining? She was thankful when it was time for them to take their leave.

Their next visit was to Mrs Jacson, where Dolly (as they had taken to calling her) proved a tremendous hit, and more praise was heaped on Ward. At that time the nurse was having to double as Cecilia's personal maid and she recalled how Dolly used to be placed on her lap while Ward did her hair. 'I didn't see much of you, or care,' she admitted, addressing her daughter in the diary she began to keep for her some years later.

> I remember when Ward went to church I thought it a bore to sit and rock you. But I was young and thoughtless and many a time since have I wished I had not left you so entirely to Ward – she was very good and careful, but peculiar and got her own way with me entirely, and I daren't say over Ward for years after what you should wear or what I wished you to do and her influence over you came to be anything but good after a while, as she adored you and made you think far too much of yrself.

However, she accepted that the past could not be undone. 'One can live but once and everyone thought you were clean and well cared for and pretty and nice and so you were.'

During the following year Fitz and Cecilia continued their peripatetic life which made it convenient to leave Dolly and Ward with Mrs Jacson, 'who was delighted with you and always did love you dearly to the last hour of her life, more than anyone in the world we used to think.'

By the spring of 1866 Cecilia was pregnant again. In October of that year while staying at Marbury, she went into premature labour after rowing a heavy boat out on an ornamental lake to pull up water lilies which she wanted to take back to Newton. A little son was born, hastily christened Hugh, who died after only 24 hours. Fitz was greatly saddened. Cecilia's attitude was more robust: 'I was glad he didn't live – I didn't like the idea of a puny eldest son', she admitted. She was soon back on her feet, her rapid recovery probably hastened by the agreeable company of Jem. Now close to manhood, the younger of the two Smith-Barry boys seemed better looking than ever. And when he grinned at her the message his eyes conveyed was unambiguous, even to her inexperienced gaze.

That year Geraldine Smith-Barry was married to Lord Willoughby de Broke of Compton Verney in Warwickshire, a great landowner and renowned sportsman. Then at Hopwood a great ball was held to mark Edward's coming of age and in the same year Rose announced her engagement to James Pender, the son of a wealthy baronet. It was not until Christmas that Fitz and Cecilia returned to Newton and were reunited with their daughter. Then early in the New Year Aunt Dorothy was taken seriously ill. Cancer was diagnosed and it soon became clear she had not long to live. Faced with this emergency Fitz's first care was for his aunt and fearing she might be disturbed by little Dolly he arranged for his wife and child to go into lodgings at Alnmouth, a nearby fishing village, 'while Fitz remained at Newton with his aunt who was comforted by his presence'. Cecilia does not appear to have found anything unusual in this arrangement. 'All thro' those months I used to meet him on the road, each walking half way 2 or 3 times a week.' Aunt Dorothy lingered on until September and when her death came it was 'a most poignant sorrow to Fitz, they were the dearest of friends'.

With the exception of a few small legacies Dorothy Widdrington had left everything to her nephew. At the age of 41 Fitz therefore became the owner of a sizeable country house with its appurtenances of stables, kennels and the home farmery, its park and woodlands, the two estate villages of Newton-on-the-Moor and Hauxley, the Hauxley colliery, various estate houses and cottages and a number of tenanted farms, which in total covered some thousand acres. There was in addition some money in the bank. By the standards of his neighbours in the coal-rich county of Northumberland Fitz would have considered himself reasonably comfortably off, though by no means rich. Yet as soon as he had settled his family into their new home he embarked on an ambitious programme of improvements, making a start with the garden which was 'very badly arranged and nowhere on the level'. He decided it must have a proper terrace with formal beds set into it. Very probably his plans had been incubating for some time, and when he came to draft them it is likely he had been influenced by Fota House, with its classical lines and airy interior, for he settled that the old house must be opened out, its inner hall approached through an archway supported by Doric columns.

Encamped in the thick of it, Cecilia provides us with her own account:

> So he set to work to cut away the ground near the house and pile the earth up in a high ramp at the park sides and so get his level – and a big work it was, but a bigger was to build and add nurseries and servants' rooms to the old part of the house wch was very dilapidated and in a horrid state according to modern sanitary ideas – This involved his pulling down half the house – all the old part in fact leaving only the library drawing room dining room and bedrooms over them – I don't know how he dared begin it! He employed no architect having himself a good knowledge of architecture, so he made his own plans and employed a very good builder at Felton who could carry out his ideas.

Fitz was not by nature a driven man. His guiding principle was always to do what was right and after coming into his inheritance he took on the duties encumbent upon a conscientious squire of his time. Thus he was a regular church attender, took his seat on the Alnwick Bench and played his part in training the county yeomanry. Yet occasionally he could turn obstinate and settle on pleasing himself. Fitz was an accomplished artist and with his painters eye for a striking landscape he had a passionate love of travel. Hitherto his explorations had been confined to Europe. Yet he longed to venture further afield: to sail up the Nile, visit the Holy Land, see for himself the ancient city of Baghdad. Thus when the work on his house was nearing completion, and he judged that the excellent

Felton builder, plus his agent, could be trusted to complete the work in accordance with his designs, he resolved to fulfil his dream.

In the future (God willing) Cecilia would bear him more children. However – whether by accident or design – there was at that moment no baby on the way, and confident that his sister Elizabeth would take Dolly for six months (supervised by the excellent Ward) he suggested to his wife that they should seize the moment.

As she listened to Fitz outlining his plans, Cecilia could not at first believe he was in earnest, for her husband was proposing to take her to places that seemed as remote as the moon. She asked him for time to think it over (though she knew she would say yes). When such a great adventure beckoned, what was the sense in delay?

Chapter VII

The Great Adventure

A few days after Christmas Fitz took Dolly and Ward to Holyhead to catch the Dublin ferry. They were en route for Fota House, where his sister Elizabeth and her family were spending the winter. Elizabeth had raised no objection when Fitz asked her to take her niece under her wing while he and Cecilia took a holiday. The three-year-old was attractive and amusing – full of quaint sayings – and Elizabeth knew she could trust Ward, who was a thoroughly reliable nurse.

All the same, six months seemed a long time for a young wife to be roughing it in outlandish places. 'Supposing Cecilia falls pregnant?' she said to her brother.

'I shall take the obvious steps to see that she does not,' Fitz replied, looking fixedly out upon the garden.

'Ah, yes,' said Elizabeth, reflecting that her brother's ardour for pyramids and paint must rank superior to his animal passions. 'Go off and enjoy yourselves then', she said, making herself comfortable in a patch of winter sunshine that had invaded her drawing room. 'While you still can!' she added, suppressing a smile at the memory of her former overflowing nurseries.

With Fitz's mission accomplished he and Cecilia were ready to set off. Early in January 1868 they took the train for Liverpool where they embarked on the trading steamer *Orinoco* with a mountain of luggage (though Fitz insisted he had cut it to the bone). Though their cabin was cramped and far from luxurious it was no matter and Cecilia delayed the unpacking to lean over the rail watching two little tugboats, belching smoke from their coal-fired boilers, guide their ship into the leaden waters of the Mersey; from whence the *Orinoco* made her cumbrous way into the choppy Irish Sea.

They were bound, Fitz had explained to his wife, for the Egyptian port of Alexandria, where he planned to hire a boat to take them up the Nile as far as his purse – and the trustworthiness of the crew – would allow. He had long yearned to see the Egyptian antiquities, still more to paint them. Cecilia's imagination was stretched to its limits as she attempted to keep pace with her husband's intended itinerary. Her graphic account of their trip, set down 50 years after the events it describes, must have been written at a time when she had access to earlier diaries, which unfortunately have not survived. 'I was always a good traveller,' she began, 'and very companionable.'

> I was only sick for 3 days lying in my bunk all that time without food and getting up on the 3rd day quite well and able to eat. We mercifully only had one storm off the coast of Portugal. We called at Gibraltar and Algiers but didn't land till Malta, where our one other passenger left us. It was the first time I had seen a foreign town and the hot sun shining on the varied colours of the dresses of the different nations there filled me with wonder and delight and I had to be told not to stare so!

In those days travellers bent on pleasure seldom ventured further than Italy or Greece. Those few that did were either desperadoes or aristocrats with deep purses and abundant leisure, who carried introductions to local big-wigs and were accompanied by a retinue of servants. Fitz was not in their league. He knew that in North Africa and regions beyond he and Cecilia were likely to encounter fleas and bug-ridden beds combined with the most primitive sanitary arrangements. Almost certainly they would suffer bouts of diarrhoea, if nothing worse; for serious illness stemming from a variety of causes was always on the cards. Also banditry was rife throughout the region. However, Cecilia's display of hardihood on their Irish honeymoon had persuaded Fitz of his wife's thirst for adventure and indifference to discomfort. Otherwise he could not have risked taking her on a trip which he knew could only be accomplished by practising the strictest economy.*

Malta had been annexed by Britain in 1814 at the conclusion of the Napoleonic wars and was rapidly to become an important naval base. Fitz knew the Governor, 'a Cheshire Leigh' and they called at Government House. A grand ball was to be given on the following night for the officers of the ships stationed in Valetta harbour, which the Governor insisted they should attend. 'I was much dismayed,' Cecilia recalled, 'for I hadn't an evening gown.' She made do by altering a blouse 'and with a silk skirt and some flowers it wasn't so bad.' Cut adrift from the restrictive mores of home and always an acute observer, she had gained enough confidence to slough off her inhibiting shyness and to her gratification attracted any number of partners.

The *Orinoco* remained several days in port, giving the Widdringtons time to explore the island. Fitz took the opportunity of engaging a Maltese whom he hoped would serve as courier-servant on the Nile. He also engaged a cook. The party now numbering four embarked for the port of Alexandria, where the beauty of the colours in the hot sun struck Cecilia 'dumb with surprise'.

At that time Egypt was still part of the tottering Ottoman Empire. Governed under the Sultan by a subordinate with the title of 'Pasha', the envious eyes of the British and the French were focused on its strategic harbour and when the country was seen to be heading for financial collapse an Anglo-French commission had been set up to supervise its finances. Funding from this source had provided Alexandria with an efficient rail-link to the capital, enabling the Widdringtons to make the trip to Cairo on a comfortable, thoroughly European, train. Putting up for a few days at *Shepherds Hotel,* they set out to explore the 'strange beauty' of the numerous mosques and threaded their way through

---

* Though neither he nor Cecilia could have known it, the following year was to see the birth of mass tourism, when a certain Mr Thomas Cook was personally to escort a party of sixty, paying 50 guineas a head, to the opening of the Suez Canal.

the darkened bazaars, where men sat smoking and sipping their sweet black coffee 'amid their wondrous wares'. Then they hired donkeys to take them to the Great Pyramid. Conducted along a narrow passage to its interior chamber with its great stone coffers, Cecilia (though 'awestruck') felt claustrophobic.

Fitz could keep his pharaohs and his tombs, she decided. She herself preferred live Egyptians to dead ones and was happier marvelling at the ever-changing scene in the hot, crystal-clear African air. Fitz began enquiring for a boat and crew to take them up the Nile as far as the First Cataract and back. The sailing boats used on the Nile were called Dahabeeyahs and the ones hired by Europeans were mostly large and luxurious and came complete with a guide-interpreter known as a Dragoman. Fitz, deciding that they could not afford one of these, settled for a smaller boat carrying a crew of 10, to whom would be added his two Maltese servants. Cecilia commented that it was 'no light venture to start away with 10 men who knew no language but their own and servants almost as ignorant and he told me afterwards that he had many misgivings and sleepless nights as to the responsibility and the wisdom of his undertaking.' Her keenness, however, and 'intense wish to go, overbore everything' and eventually they set off.

The design of their boat, with its rows of oars and huge lanteen sail, had not altered much from the days of antiquity. Though Cecilia made no mention of their sleeping quarters there must have been some sort of cabin. Their crew proved to be a cheerful lot, 'whiling away their time with their monotonous chants'. But unfortunately both Fitz's Maltese servants turned out to be pretty useless. 'The courier knew neither English nor Arabic but a sort of patois French and the cook knew very little cooking.' Luckily their captain – or Reis, as he was called – was an intelligent fellow and Cecilia soon began 'by signs and smiles' to make friends with him:

> and when he found it was the language I wanted to beat, he began to teach me word by word and by signs. With that and the short list of words in Murray's *Guide to Egypt* I soon got on and having at that time a very powerful memory I was able to converse in a way.

Cecilia was thrilled to discover she had an unsuspected gift for languages and, Fitz being no linguist, it fell to her to act as his mouthpiece – giving a further boost to her growing self-confidence. As her fluency increased their Reis began to confide in her:

> In time, I learnt many curious details of the Captain's home life for they will talk to a woman of the most intimate details they wd be ashamed to mention to a man! – the reverse of our Christian way – I found too on my solitary walks into the desert while F. was painting - when I met a man and saluted in Arabic, the moment he found I could speak and understand he became my humble servant and admirer at once and with no thought of robbing me (as people said they would).

They sailed all day from sunrise to sunset, hoisting the huge lanteen sail and tying up at night at some village where the sailors, who slept on shore, had friends or wanted to buy provisions. They used to go ashore in the evening light:

> But there is nothing to see in their villages except the women preparing their evening meals in their blue cotton gowns straight down like our bathing dresses and their yashmak

– a piece of triangular black stuff covering their nose and mouth – or washing clothes in a shallow bit of the river, keeping a sharp lookout for Temsak! – crocodiles! Or a man naked except for a loincloth working his 'shadoof' with which he pumps water from the river – a long pole with a little basket or pail at one end and a lump of clay at the other to balance – to irrigate his little patch of pulse or corn.

They ate the flat yeastless bread of the country: 'very good when hot and fresh' and by dint of encouragement from Cecilia eventually persuaded their inexperienced cook to prepare their simple meals. 'We bought the rancid butter called Lemm – only fit to fry with – and we had rice to boil and eat with jam – and eggs – and had coffee and milk, and sometimes a kippered herring! (come from dear knows where!) and very seldom a very thin chicken.'

With no choice but to drink the water of the Nile, the Widdringtons copied their crew by filtering it in the porous earthenware bottles of the country and came to no harm. They must both have had iron constitutions!

The N.W. wind was our best and if it turned against us or was too strong to dare to hoist the big sail, and always at curves in the river, all the crew wd harness themselves to a long rope and going ashore wd pull us along – the Nile was going down then and there were many unexpected sandbanks, and 3 or 4 times we got stuck on one and the men wd strip and plunge in and hoist or haul us off – always with a sharp lookout for the Temsak!

Cecilia had had the foresight to pack a first-aid kit suitable for minor accidents or upsets and after she had successfully treated one or two members of the crew who had been complaining of stomach pains with a few drops of Chlorodyne in hot water laced with brandy, she gained a reputation as a doctor.

One evening after supper when she and Fitz were sitting on deck enjoying the cool breeze, they were interrupted by a servant from another boat tied up close by. He said his master was close to death and learning that they had a doctor on board had come to ask help. Fitz went to investigate. Finding the man feverish and in great pain he guessed he was suffering from peritonitis. In those days the surgical removal of an inflamed appendix was not practised and the sufferer usually died; though providing the appendix had not burst the application of very hot compresses was sometimes known to work. Having heard of this treatment Fitz sat up all night with the unfortunate man 'fomenting with very hot water, nearly scalding his own hands doing it'. By morning his patient seemed a little better. Fitz continued with the treatment for three or four more days 'and with that and with help from my little case he got quite well doubtless saving his life'.

They learned that the man was a Mr Goldie Taubman, 'a Manx man quite young and quite alone'. Plainly he was of some substance, for his boat was much smarter and better equipped than theirs. After his recovery he and the Widdringtons travelled up river together and in the cool of the evening, while Fitz was setting up his easel and getting out his paints, Mr Taubman would accompany Cecilia on her walks into the desert. Soon he was spilling out his hopes and his ambitions.

> His one interest was wild men and he told me he meant after his Nile trip to go to West Africa, learn their language and try to influence them for good ... and he was very enthusiastic and looked very wild and mad, but I believed in him and sympathised.

Cecilia became quite taken with this interesting fellow traveller, while he – full of admiration for her adventurous spirit and those bright, sympathetic eyes looking up at him from under her sun bonnet – completely lost his heart. When they parted at Aswan 'probably never to meet again', Cecilia confessed that they had become 'very sentimental'.*

While they were resting at Aswan the Widdringtons made the acquaintance of one of the great English eccentrics of those days: Lady Duff Gordon. Assuring them that she could only live in the climate of Upper Egypt, this 'strange lady' had purchased a large sailing boat known as a dahabeeyah 'and made it most luxurious with servants and her faithful Dragoman Ahmed.' The couple were invited to dine with her on board to meet her son, Sir Marcus, who evidently took no interest in ruins, but in true patrician style had come out to shoot sand grouse!

The Widdringtons determined to continue up river as far as Philae, passing through the First Cataract. It was there that they encountered three more scions of the British aristocracy, all drenched to the skin and looking helplessly at their upturned boat, which was stuck fast on the rocks. 'Much exertion and more chattering from an army of men' was required before it could be got off and taken ashore to be repaired. The Widdringtons invited the three young men to dine on their boat. When they learned of Fitz's plan to visit the Holy Land, one of them, Lord Ruthven – 'a most amusing man' – asked if he could travel some of the way with them. It was agreed that they should meet again in Cairo, for to the Widdrington's regret their funds did not allow them to continue upriver to the Second and Third Cataracts. 'We took down our big sail going downstream and our sailors took to their oars – the whole way back.' On the return journey they stopped off to visit the great temples, the mile-long avenue of Sphinxes and the painted rock tombs. Cecilia, however, continued to be 'more interested in living Arabs than dead Egyptians, and I would remain outside improving my Arabic while Fitz explored the dark interiors'.

Back in Cairo, after paying off the crew and the two Maltese, the Widdringtons found it was cheaper to remain on board rather than return to the hotel. So retaining the services of their obliging Reis as guide and cook they went off to explore more bazaars

---

* Some twenty years later Cecilia and Fitz saw in the paper 'that thro the exertions of a certain Mr Taubman the English were going to take or 'protect' the country of the Niger, and we later saw he was to be knighted and to take the name of Sir Taubman Goldie.' And by a curious coincidence he and Cecilia were to have one more meeting. Shortly after Sir Goldie's knighthood had been conferred he was invited to a royal dinner party at which the young woman sitting opposite him bore such a striking resemblance to Cecilia that he stared rudely and after dinner asked her whether she was the daughter of a Mrs Widdrington whom he had met in Egypt and 'who she so wonderfully resembled'. The young woman was Dorothy, by that time married to a rising politician, Sir Edward Grey.

> They talked ... and she told me and I went to call and he was married and they asked me to tea, but it was not a success, she didn't like me – he had talked too much about me! He walked down the street with me and we parted and I never saw him again.

and mosques 'and with him saw many curious parts of the town and he interpreted for us when my Arabic failed and we bought a few silk things for those at home.'

On the advice of this admirable man (who had become fond of them and was to weep bitterly when they boarded the train for Alexandria), Fitz engaged a Nubian servant who undertook to guide them through Palestine and on to Damascus. 'And so we ended our Nile tour,' Cecilia concluded, convinced that they did it 'cheaper than it had ever been done before owing to our doing without a Dragoman and also my Arabic'.

Coming from Cecilia this was a rare note of self-congratulation. And she had every right to be pleased with herself. As his self-taught interpreter she had given valuable service to her husband, allowing Fitz to concentrate on his painting undisturbed. Her earnest desire to communicate with the crew in their own language and to learn about their lives had gained her their lasting respect.

It was during their Nile trip that Cecilia's power over men's hearts had begun to manifest itself. She was never to master the art of flirtation. But blessed by nature with a pretty face and an unaffected manner she had always been a first-rate listener and her sympathetic interest in the doings of men (those demanding, complicated creatures who believed they controlled the universe) was to last throughout her long life. Consequently men continued to be attracted to her, and she to them, long after she had left youth and beauty behind.

After meeting up with the agreeable Lord Ruthven the three took ship for the Palestinian port of Jaffa, where Fitz's Nubian servant was dispatched with orders to hire four quiet horses, plus an unspecified number of mules (with their attendant muleteers) to carry the baggage. They were now bound for Jerusalem – a tortuous ride of some fifty miles over hilly terrain. Their first day's ride brought them to a monastery which was known to take in pilgrims. The monks had been sworn by their strict order never to look at a woman. But since female pilgrims arriving on horseback were unheard of, Cecilia was inadvertently allowed to enter and to get a good look at the place. When eventually their mistake was discovered 'the poor old monks hastened after us, shading their eyes and gesticulating and shouting at me to get out – which of course I did at once!'

Late in the afternoon of the following day, after an exhausting ride along stony tracks on hard, unfamiliar saddles, the travellers reached the walls of Jerusalem and pitched their tents just outside the Damascus Gate. But as night fell, as if by a signal every dog in the city, joined by more prowling around its walls, set up a barking and howling which continued throughout the night, making sleep impossible. The following morning by general consent the tents were packed up and the party moved bag and baggage into the one decent hotel, leaving the Nubian in charges of the horses and mules. Making the hotel their base they succeeded in visiting most of the principal sites, several of which (such as the three 'sockets' of the crosses of Christ and the robbers) were patently false.

> We were shown ... the site of the synagogue and so on, which of course are now on a lower level, the level of the whole town being raised by the stones and earth of the ruined walls ... Some ruins are still *in situ* and Solomon's temple and the Mount of Olives are also as they were in Christ's time, but inside the present walls are many feet above it. We also rode down to Jericho and the Dead Sea – Fitz bathed in it and found its strong saltiness

prevented his body from sinking enough to be able to swim in it- we bought a small flask of the water of the Jordan to baptise a future son!

After a couple of weeks of sight-seeing they rode on to Galilee 'and the Sea thereof'. By this time Cecilia's boredom threshold for antiquities had been breached and the Biblical significance of the site failed to impress her. In common with her father she had never had much time for orthodox Christian teaching. Besides, the weather had turned cold and the long rides, 'taken at a foot's pace so as to let the baggage mules get before us' and necessitating long halts whenever water and a few trees were to be found, were becoming monotonous. Also she found that her Nile Arabic was not well understood in Palestine and she had to start all over again 'making shift with signs' until she had mastered enough of the dialect to talk with the local people and their Nubian guide. However, their amusing companion Lord Ruthven succeeded in keeping her pretty well entertained and both she and Fitz were sorry when home commitments obliged him to take his leave.

At Galilee Fitz caused consternation to their guide when he proposed that they should abandon the well-trodden road to Damascus and make a detour of some fifty miles in order to visit the ruined city of Baalbek. The Nubian protested violently, but Fitz was adamant. He produced a map of sorts, showing the way, and Cecilia recalled that 'I had to take the lead with it open before me on the saddle, and there was almost a revolt when one night we had to camp at a place where we could not get much of either food or fodder.' However, they persevered, and after three fraught days picking their way over the ill-marked tracks, the magnificent ruins of the ancient city appeared over the horizon.

In Biblical times Baalbek had been the centre of the worship of Baal – the title given by the Canaanites to their chief male god who was worshipped as the deity of fertility. (As the Bible reveals, the orgiastic nature of their ceremonies was strongly denounced by the Hebrew prophets.) When the conquering Greeks arrived Baal was identified as being one and the same as their sun god Helios and city was renamed Heliopolis. Later it fell to Rome, but with the break-up of the Empire the once-great city's remote situation spared it, for the place was seldom visited. Thus many of its ruins, including the almost intact Roman temple of Bacchus built in the second century, still survive to this day. Rendered almost speechless with awe, Fitz and Cecilia threaded their way between the city's ancient walls, 'all huge pillars and huge stones', Cecilia recalled:

> so large that it's a mystery how they can have been transported there from the quarries they were dug out of, in days when there was no mechanical help of steam hawsers and so on, it must have been done by human strength in huge numbers – slaves no doubt and captives, no regard of course to whether they lived or died of it.

They stood amazed before the source of the River Abana 'which issues from its rock strewn spring, at one bound a large river … It was a weird place and well worth a visit,' Cecilia concluded, adding inconsequentially that they had missed out Bethlehem and Nazareth, Tyre and Sidon as being of no particular interest, 'one Arab village being very like another.' Baalbek proved to be 'by far the most interesting sight of our Palestine tour.'

By this time, however, Cecilia had had more than enough of roughing it. Saddle-sore and weary, she was mightily relieved when on reaching Damascus Fitz headed for the best hotel, an Arabian Nights-like edifice, its quiet inner court filled with orange and lemon trees and oleanders. 'Very sweet and clean,' she noted approvingly. Their mules were relieved of what by this time had become a mountain of baggage and the muleteers paid off, together with their Nubian guide.

Cecilia recalled Damascus 'with its street called "straight"' as 'being a city of cool-looking courts with low houses built round them and numerous minarets with their Mussins calling the faithful to prayer'. At which point honesty compelled her to add: 'and I can't say I was sorry the journey was over, the long hours of riding tired me, and nothing of interest to reward it, unless one was a devout Christian.'

Fitz was keen to go on to Palmyra, to explore the real desert. But by now low on funds he knew it was time to be heading for home. After travelling by diligence to Beirut they took ship for the Turkish port of Smyrna (the modern Ismir), where they had hoped to pick up a passage to Constantinople. Sadly, the only ship for many days had just left. Pressed for time they took ship for Athens.

During the whole five-and-a-half months of their travels, the Widdringtons had not encountered a living soul who wished them harm. But on this last leg of their journey they had a narrow escape. Early one morning after viewing the Acropolis they set off to climb Mount Parnassus and when nearing the summit were accosted by a fierce-looking ruffian who seemed intent on robbing them. However, they were

> rather untidy and shabby at this time … so when we greeted him with smiles and sat down to our scanty fare he must have seen we were not worth robbing and he sold us his crook for a few pence and let us pass on.

By now they were into the middle of June and it was time to complete their journey. A ship took them to Corinth and on up the Dalmatian coast and across to the Italian port of Bari, 'where we took train day and night to Venice, that most wondrous city on earth or rather on the water'.

They were only able to stay a few days 'in wonder and delight', but they vowed to return. A long and tiring train journey took them by stages over the Brenner Pass and on to Munich, Nuremburg and Frankfurt 'and so by Antwerp to London and then home.'

Cecilia recalled that they were ' sad and sorrowful' that the greatest journey they were ever to undertake had finally drawn to a close.

CHAPTER VIII

Exemplary Wife,
Troubled Mother

Little Dolly could barely recognise her parents after their six months' absence. She had thrived as the centre of attention while staying with her aunt, first at Fota and afterwards at 26 Chesham Place, the Smith-Barry's comfortable London establishment, which the family had returned to for the Season.

'Do we have to go home with mama? We both prefer it here,' she whispered urgently to Ward. Her aunt had just bought her a lovely little blue and white coachman's coat and a straw hat decorated with daisies.

'Of course we do. Newton is your home, isn't it?'

The nurse, who had enjoyed her light duties in the absence of her mistress, did not sound noticeably encouraging.

When the Widdringtons returned to Newton at the end of July they found the house transformed. Passing from room to room Cecilia exclaimed delightedly at her home's new stylishness. The elaborate plaster ceilings wrought by the Italian team of plasterers, the arches leading to the inner hall, with its paired Doric columns, the elegant new staircase, filled her with wonder. Upstairs she and Fitz admired the spacious day and night nurseries and the miracle of their new state-of-the-art plumbing.

'Our new baths and flushing lavatories will save the servants a deal of work,' she observed.

'Indeed they will,' Fitz agreed, justifiably proud that the design and layout of the house had been mostly his own creation. Above all, he was delighted with his new conservatory. Though others might scoff at the queer way it wrapped itself round the south front of his house to the 'oddly detached pedimented porch on the east side',[1] it satisfied his love of the picturesque and his nostalgia for more sunny climes. In time it was his intention to add niches for statues and fix trellises for climbing plants. He could not wait to see it filling up with exotic blooms.

'We have been married five years and three months,' Cecilia observed, 'and now at last have the happiness of our own place.'

'And its responsibilities,' her husband reminded her.

For much still remained to be done. But before they could begin, Fitz's first duty was to help his mother move house. For now that he and his family were permanently installed at Newton there was no point in the old lady remaining in Cheshire. A new home, Orde House, had been found for her, close by the home of her younger daughter, Louisa Orde, at Nunnykirk. Though near enough to Newton for visiting, it was far enough away (such was Cecilia's hope) to discourage her mother-in-law from daily interference.

With his mother satisfactorily settled, Fitz was free to turn his mind to the important question of soft furnishings. In common with home improvers before and since he was painfully aware that he had exceeded his budget; and in order to save money he invested in a wonderful new device that had recently made its way onto the British market, having been invented by an American, a Mr Isaac Singer. With the aid of this marvel of technology he and Cecilia set work to making curtains and loose covers: 'Fitz working the useful new sewing machine and I cutting out.' This saved them a deal of expense.

Around Christmas Cecilia knew that she was pregnant again. The happy news soon got out. Burdened with advice by all Fitz's relations and cautioned to take care of herself, Cecilia, who felt perfectly well, insisted on continuing to lead an active life.

That spring they went to London and 'had a little "Season" of dinner parties and teas and plays wch I liked better than anything'. Henry Irvine and Ellen Terry were giving a season of Shakespeare at the Lyceum. Cecilia, intent on seeing every play, found that they could only afford the cheaper seats. And as her husband 'didn't care to go unless to better places' she went by herself 'and many is the time I have waited hours in the queues at the doors for a seat – sometimes one in the gallery.' Class differences and aching feet were of small consideration when set against performances of Shakespeare by the greatest actors of their day.

The baby was due in September and everyone seemed to assume that it would be a boy. As the time for her confinement drew near Cecilia was disconcerted to learn that both her mother-in-law and Elizabeth Smith-Barry were proposing to stay at Newton for the event.

'Cannot you persuade them to stay away until it's over?' she said plaintively to Fitz. 'You know how I can't abide to be watched.'

Fitz, however, could think of no tactful formula for dissuading the women from coming without causing offence and, greatly to his wife's dismay, both of them came.

On the morning of 12 September, a Sunday, Cecilia went into labour and at three o'clock in the afternoon the doctor, inspecting the new-born infant which he had hold of by the feet, exclaimed: 'Congratulations Mrs Widdrington! You have a fine daughter!'

At which point the midwife, observing with compassion the look of consternation on Cecilia's face, added by way of encouragement: 'And a healthy bairn by the look of her. She has a fine pair of lungs!'

Which was true – for the child (who was red as a turkey cock and could not be said to be pretty) had entered the world screaming her head off. Indeed, the din she made was so loud that, as Cecilia had not asked to see her, she was parked in an adjacent room to be out of hearing, and later moved to the nursery. By some misunderstanding Ward had been given the impression that the infant was not to be touched. So, hungry and abandoned, she screamed 'the live long night'; until Ward could bear the noise no longer and gave her a bottle.

'What a horrid little thing,' said Dolly, who had been kept awake by the noise and was looking on with distaste. 'Can't we give her away?'

'No we can't,' Ward snapped. 'She's your sister, isn't she?'

'But I never asked to have a sister, did I?', the four-year-old pointed out reasonably. She was to resent the new baby's presence in the nursery from that very first day.

After a cursory look at the squalling infant Mrs Jacson and Elizabeth had packed up their bags and left, not troubling to hide their disappointment.

The birth of this second girl had badly shaken Cecilia's morale, threatening to destroy her hard-gained self-confidence and to plunge her back into the 'old feeling' that whatever she did must be wrong. No one knew better than she the disgrace of failing to have been born a boy. She nursed the infant for three months 'and should have longer, but Ward always hated me doing it and put all sorts of difficulties in the way'. Although the nurse had taken against the new baby, she was so jealous and set against interference that she took every opportunity to keep Cecilia out of the nursery.

The baby was my grandmother, who as a very old lady gave the following account of her christening:

> When I was christened … I was of course handed over to the parson in the usual way, and he said Name this child. He had been for long years out in the East and Colonies and had hardly got used to England yet. Mother had been allowed to choose my name because I did not matter and any name would do … [She] had found my name in some old annals and discovered that Idonea had been a family name for some centuries so she chose it for me, and answered the parson very clearly. He asked for it to be repeated and when he heard it again he said "Well I've heard a lot of queer names among the black people but never one as queer as this" and he reluctantly christened me with my unusual name. So I started off 'queer' and I think a little whiff of it has remained with me all my life.

The child's name was soon shortened to Ida; and Ida she remained for the rest of her long and turbulent life.

At some point – just as she had done for Dolly – Cecilia began to keep a diary in which to record Ida's development. On the inside front cover she transcribed an old rhyme: 'The bairn that is born on the Sabbath day, Is merry and bonny and wise and gay.' Then, addressing her child directly (for she meant Ida to be given the diary eventually), she began: 'Such a fat little baby – rolls and wads of fat – you would hardly open yr eyes for fat at first.' In contrast to Dolly, Ida was an ugly baby, with a flat wide nose, a small mouth and smaller eyes. Her only redeeming features being her 'Lovely little hands and feet and pretty bright curly hair.' Cecilia remembered Ida 'looking through Ward's arm to her back as she walked you about to sleep.' The nurse, however, soon gave up that trouble 'and many a time I found you put to cry yrself to sleep in yr bassinet. But I never felt I could interfere, I wish I had.' Backed up by Fitz and Mrs Jacson, Ward would insist that the baby was 'naughty' and needed discipline; and though Cecilia always had 'an uncomfortable, strained sort of feeling' she was cowed by her elders into acknowledging her own ignorance, and she did nothing. 'I kept you once,' she remembered, 'while Ward and Dolly went to church, but I always got scolded for something or other … so there was little pleasure I ever had in having you to myself'.

However, Cecilia's life did not begin or end in her children's nursery. In those days, when domestic service came second only to agriculture in providing employment for the working classes, Fitz (who did not consider himself rich) kept a staff of 10 or 12 indoor servants.* Of these the most senior member – the butler – was answerable to him, as were the footman and his personal valet. The rest – comprising housekeeper, cook, lady's maid and nurse, plus parlour, nursery, kitchen and laundry maids – looked to his wife and were her responsibility. She it was who must set the tone of the house: seeing to it that her maids went about their duties with cheerful faces; that meals were well chosen and well prepared and arrived on time; that flowers did not droop and were regularly replenished; that staff were notified in good time of the arrival and departure of guests; and that the housekeeper's monthly accounts were in good order, avoiding extravagance and waste. She must also interview new staff, deal with their personal problems, keep a check on their health and oversee their moral welfare. Young girls straight from elementary school, who had never before left home, would frequently apply to old Mrs Widdrington when seeking a post, for Fitz's kindly aunt had given Newton a good reputation which Cecilia was at pains to keep up.

However, a fine line had always to be drawn between fair dealing and any form of mateyness. Hobnobbing with the 'lower orders' was strictly off limits. In her autobiography Ida recalled how she

> secretly liked and would willingly have played with a very subservient and suppressed nurserymaid, but no such familiarity was allowed … The only exception would be the lady's maid or the housekeeper or occasionally the cook, as these head servants had a station and a position over the lower ones which equalled and excelled that of the master and mistress over themselves.

The custom below stairs, Ida went on to explain:

> was for the whole household including the Butler to have dinner together in the Servants' Hall as far as the first course, which consisted of large quantities of meat, legs of mutton, rounds of beef, ribs of pork etc. and when that was eaten the head servants all arose and clasping their plates and glasses in their hands, processed through the Hall, down the long passage, into the Housekeeper's room, always known as 'The Room' as if it was the only one in the house. Here the sweet course was served by one of the kitchen maids and duly eaten in state and seclusion.

Ida remembered meeting this procession once. 'I was late for lunch and was running to the dining room by the back way. I was much impressed and mystified.'

In those days it was taken for granted that the wife of a country squire must be prepared to entertain a host of relatives and friends, whose comings and goings were dictated by the season. At Newton the New Year was always celebrated by a large family gathering, the older children being permitted to stay up to greet the "dark man" (chosen from among the guests) who, on the stroke of midnight, would be heard knocking at the front door to be admitted. To shouts and cheers he would come in bearing the traditional lump of coal which signified good luck for the coming year. Auld Lang Syne was then sung, before the younger members of the household trooped off to bed.

---

*   Charles Darwin's total wages bill for a similar number of servants worked out at around £100 per annum, 'a sum that was about half his butcher's bill for any single year'.

In the winter months hunting was the dominant sport of the Northumbrian gentry. Living close to the Scottish border they had only been weaned off cattle-raiding a few generations back and the thrill of the chase was in their blood. On the first day of the year a substantial breakfast was traditionally served at Newton to the family and their guests, all bent on attending the New Year's Day meet. Fitz hunted regularly, accompanied by Cecilia – herself an accomplished horsewoman – when she could spare the time.

But the exposed Northumbrian coast was frequently battered by bitter winds, blowing straight off the Arctic, often accompanied by heavy falls of snow. With the ground frozen solid and snowdrifts clogging the lanes, hunting had to be abandoned and it was then that skates were retrieved from attics, and ponds and lakes were swept clear of snow. At Newton, which had its own small lake (always referred to as 'the pond'), ice-skating was popular, particularly among the young – happy to stay out practising their figure-of-eights until failing light forced them indoors.

For the *bon ton* the coming of spring spelled the opening of the London Season. The Widdringtons, however, who had never aspired to be smart, had neither the money nor the inclination to join in the social merry-go-round. They were content to pay visits to family and friends, or simply to stay at home where there was always plenty to be done. Cecilia was conscientious in visiting the poor and the sick among Fitz's tenants and generous in contributing to their needs. She was also a regular visitor to the wretched souls who were no longer able to support themselves and had been consigned to the local workhouse. Appalled at the callousness which demanded the separation of husbands from wives, she would take books and read to the women 'which I think brought them some small comfort'. Although she viewed the Anglican church and what she saw as the self-satisfied hypocrisy of its ministers with a jaundiced eye, she was happy to teach the children in the local Sunday School, and for Fitz's sake always took her place beside him in church.

The 12 August (the 'glorious twelfth', as it was known) was a red letter day in the sporting calendar, for it marked the opening of the grouse shooting season. Fashionable London had already been deserted by the *ton*, for by mid-July, even in Mayfair and Belgravia, the stench emanating from the streets and the mews could no longer be borne by sensitive nostrils and the morning milk was frequently delivered sour. Fitz with his 1,000 acres could not rival the sport offered by the great Scottish estates. Newton, however, possessed its own charms; rough shooting on the moors with ponies and dogs and Cecilia's elaborate picnics, boating and swimming on the 'pond', tennis parties and excursions to the beach at Alnmouth. While Fitz played host to a succession of friends and relations throughout the summer months, Cecilia was always on call, leaving no part of the day she could legitimately call her own.

In time Fitz gained the command of the local militia, with the rank of major, and every August saw his regiment encamped in the grounds of Alnwick Castle for military training. Ida recalled how

> Father always drilled the regiment on his big bay mare. She was called the Taily Mare, she had no other name and it was because she had a habit of swishing her tail round and round incessantly the whole time she was out, not wagging it up and down the usual way a horse does, but round and round in a circle.

Every year a great tea party was held at the camp for the wives and children of officers and Ida recalled her mother 'looking very lovely in a smart summer dress', driving them in the barouche with a pair of horses.

Though Cecilia enjoyed these summer outings, not all the events that made up their social calendar were to her liking. She particularly disliked the tedium of the typical country house visit, usually made during the autumn and winter.

> We made many visits in the county – we drove to them in our own carriage and horses and they and our coachman, Shotton, always were put up for the three night's duration of them … I can't say I much enjoyed them. The men were out all day and took their lunch with them and we poor ladies were left to employ the time as best we could. We brought down our fancy work (which at that time was ugly crewel work)* and talked over our children or servants, or drove out – which I hated most – to call on neighbours, or walked in the garden and got through the day somehow.

Though she would have been loathe to admit it, Cecilia did not particularly enjoy the company of women of her own class. In general they were as poorly educated as she herself had been before Fitz took her in hand, and she found their chatter jaw-achingly tedious. With their prejudices set in stone, they saw no injustice in the pampered position in society which they enjoyed; their grasp of the realities of the wider world being almost totally lacking.

Around Christmas time the Widdringtons gave regular 'school feasts' for the children attending the two elementary schools at Hauxley and Newton-on-the-Moor. A lavish tea was followed by competitive games and a 'bran pie' in which the children would dig for presents.

Then it was time to prepare for their own family Christmas. This was always celebrated jointly with their Orde cousins, either at Nunnykirk or Newton. A few years earlier Queen Victoria's late consort Prince Albert had imported the German tradition of bringing a fir tree into the house, decorating it with baubles and lighted candles, and piling the Christmas presents beneath its boughs. The custom had caught on rapidly and by the late 1860s no Christmas gathering was complete without 'the Tree'. After presents had been exchanged and a gargantuan meal consumed there would be 'games played for parcels' – small prizes chosen and wrapped by Cecilia. Finally a sheet would be suspended from one of the picture rails, the lights dimmed, and the 'magic lanthorn show' would begin, with Fitz, as the magician, making pictures appear on his white screen, to gasps from the audience. The precursor of the cinema projector, the magic lanthorn – a simple optical device using slides to display a magnified image – was one of the marvels of the mid-Victorian age.

Thus each year would draw to a close, the long winter evenings enlivened by reading aloud, the family warmed by the extravagant use of those vast seams of coal which had enriched so many of the Northumbrian gentry – including the Widdringtons.

---

* A type of embroidery using a loosely twisted yarn on a ground of linen or cotton, following a pattern.

Chapter IX

A Little Princess

Cecilia's *Dorothy Diary* in which she gave an account of her elder daughter's life up till the time of her marriage, is a very frank affair, often painfully so. She was proud of her daughter, with her golden locks and large blue eyes and the quaint sayings that her aunts and grandparents and cousins found so clever and diverting. Yet Cecilia admitted that there had never been much warmth between mother and child. This she regretted, laying the blame squarely on Dolly's nurse. She believed that Ward had stolen her child's love in the weeks immediately following her birth, having taken advantage of Cecilia's illness in order to supplant her.

She also blamed Ward for the part she had played in shaping Dolly's character. The child had been shamefully indulged, teaching her to be hard and selfish. Her rooted dislike of her sister Ida had been picked up from Ward. It was the nurse who had planted the idea in Dolly's head that Ida was an interloper. And worse – that her sister was bad.

While there was some truth in Cecilia's allegations, they did not tell the whole story. For the art of successful mothering is best learned by example and Cecilia's early life had provided her with very poor training. Up until the arrival of Miss Emmy she had been reared without a shred of affection. Never having known the comfort of a mothers arms, who was there to serve as a model? If she had not been taken ill, if she had been able to nurse her baby for those vital first weeks, the outcome might have been different. As matters stood, when six-week-old Dolly was placed in her arms by the reluctant nurse it was already too late. A mother only in name, she felt she had no role in relation to this child. She was looking at a stranger. How, then, was she supposed to begin?

Yet after making allowance for this rocky introduction to motherhood, we may guess that even under the best conditions Dolly and her mother would have had difficulty in getting on. Their temperaments were too different. Though Cecilia's upbringing had made her shy, she was never prickly or difficult or self-obsessed, she reached out to people, had a welcome for everyone, was at pains to put the world at its ease. Dolly preferred to keep her distance. Acutely observant and deeply introspective, she reserved her warmest feelings for wild things, in particular for birds. From her earliest childhood she had an aversion to physical intimacy and always loathed to be touched. She loved order and seemliness, which Ward was able to provide, and disliked anything or anybody

6 Dorothy (Dolly) Widdrington, a shy and troubled child.

who ventured to violate her private space. Like the poet W.H. Davies, she loved to 'stand and stare'. Thus the disruption Ida had brought into Dolly's life had come as a profound shock. Her fastidiousness rendered her incapable of empathising with a malodorous infant with red cracked skin in the folds of its fat little legs who screamed the live-long day and half the night. Taking note of Ward's hostility towards the new arrival, it was natural for Dolly to take her cue from the nurse.

However, there was one characteristic which mother and daughter shared, which was physical courage. An early example of Dolly's *sang-froid* in the face of danger was recorded by her mother, who had watched Dolly, when still an infant, crawl naked out of the nursery into the passage 'and at the turn a great tortoiseshell cat met you, and you stopped and it stopped, and it arched its back and spat'. Showing no sign of fear, the baby had returned the cat's inspection for some moments before turning and making a dignified retreat. Cecilia had been impressed by Dolly's self-possession, which from an early age had been formidable. Nothing ever seemed to faze her.

From babyhood Dolly had been universally admired. 'You were beautifully dressed in those days,' Cecilia recalled. 'Too well – lovely white frocks, embroidered, wch Ward used to let you crawl on the dirty floor in and wear every day with lovely sashes till they were torn to rags – but I durst not complain.' Taken to Hopwood to be shown off, Cecilia's brother Edward said that his niece was like a small fairy 'In yr lace frocks and silk stockings and smug curls.' At 10 months the child was already walking and by the age of two she was able to express herself fluently and was soon prattling away. She had a prodigious memory. She 'knew the end of all the poetry and the names of all the flowers'. Her Hopwood grandma was surprised 'because you remembered cineraria and other difficult flower names from one telling'.

Grandma Jacson doted on her, showering the child with presents and showing her more adulation than can have been good for any small child. The Smith-Barrys were likewise devoted to their precocious niece. When she was placed in their care at Fota during the months when Fitz and Cecilia were exploring the Eastern Mediterranean, Dolly amused them all with her funny ways. 'You were full of facts and odd speeches, you certainly were a little maiden wise beyond yr years,' Cecilia commented. When teased by her cousin Arthur, who insisted that little girls were made of sugar and spice and that she would melt if she went out in the rain, the three-year-old replied tartly: 'No I shouldn't, because it's under my skin.' Even His Grace the Duke of Northumberland had been put in his place by Dolly. On a visit to Alnwick Castle with Fitz the child had greatly amused the Duke, who had offered to take her up with her father to inspect the roof. 'Well, you're a very pretty little girl,' he told her as they got out onto the leads. 'Handsome is as handsome does,' Dolly replied, 'and I have heard that he is not my friend who flatters me.' The words of course had been put into her mouth by Ward. It was she who set the standards, she who was responsible for shaping the impressionable child's mind. Her influence was omnipresent. She was like an immovable rock, set between mother and child.

In those days the daily routine of upper-class children followed a strict pattern. This called for frequent changes of clothes. Once past babyhood, Dolly's morning outfit consisted of a plain frock over which she wore a pinafore. Nursery lunch (which was of very plain fare) would be followed by a rest on her bed (the only time she was alone) prior to the obligatory afternoon walk. For this daily outing Ward would lace her into stout leather boots, and (if it was winter) button her into a tight-waisted coat, and place a hat (very likely adorned with a feather) upon her head, which was tied under her chin with ribbons. Back from the walk there would be nursery tea, prepared by the nursemaid. Then it was time for the protesting child to have her silk stockings and satin pumps put on and to be helped into one of her best frocks. And after her hair had received a vigorous brushing she would be declared ready for the daily descent to the drawing room. Even then she must needs be accompanied by Ward, who kept hold of her hand as far as the drawing room door, which marked the limit of her territory.

Since the hour between tea and bedtime which Dolly spent with her parents was as likely as not the only time she saw them, inevitably the atmosphere was somewhat strained. If it could have been spent in light-hearted games things might have gone better. But Cecilia, who was acutely aware of the failings of her own parents in the matter of education, was determined to see that her time with Dolly was put to good use. Thus, after reading aloud some simple tale to her child, Cecilia would give Dolly the book and encourage her to pick out the letters. This well-meaning ploy met with stubborn resistance, for the little girl, who had her pride, believed that she was being picked on. Though Cecilia was disappointed she determined to persevere. Perhaps Dolly would do better with arithmetic. She introduced counting games and was nonplussed when no amount of coaxing and repetition would persuade Dolly to count up to a hundred. Was it possible that against all the evidence her child was stupid?

What Cecilia failed to see was that her badgering was wounding Dolly to her innermost core. The little girl could not abide to be shown up – in particular by her mother. Though her mind was sharp as a needle, she had been encouraged by Ward and others to believe she was well-nigh perfect. Interpreting formal instruction as criticism she resolutely closed her mind to it. Fitz, who perceived what was happening, attempted to discourage his wife from persisting with Dolly's lessons. Would it not be better to employ a nursery governess for the reading and arithmetic – freeing the time with Dolly for some occupation which the child enjoyed? Dolly sewed beautifully for her age. Perhaps Cecilia could show her some new stitches? Yet his wife remained blind, incapable of seeing that she was building a wall of resistance between herself and Dolly, and that a pattern was being set which would persist.

When Dolly was five Cecilia engaged a French nurserymaid, Josephine, hoping that she would encourage Dolly to learn a little French. This ploy was soon nipped in the bud by Ward. Fearful that the new arrival was impinging on her territory, the nurse would not permit the girl 'to do one single thing except work and sew, or ever have a thing to do with the children'. Unsurprisingly Josephine soon left, to be replaced by Georgiana, 'a slow, dull creature' who was not considered by Ward to be a threat.

That summer the Widdringtons spent a few weeks in London, taking Dolly and baby Ida with them. Ward, of course, came too. Here Cecilia's relationship with Dolly took a more favourable turn. As Ward was tied up with the baby, Cecilia was able to enjoy the rare pleasure of having Dolly to herself. Every morning mother and daughter would walk in Hyde Park and every afternoon they paid visits. 'I used to take you everywhere,' Cecilia recalled. Determined that Dolly should have all the opportunities that she had missed, Cecilia took her to the London Zoo, the Royal Academy and the famous gardens at Kew. Dolly was invited to tea parties with other children and 'seemed very sociable'. The five-year-old was always beautifully turned out. Cecilia bought her a white fur jacket and had her dressmaker design Dolly's party frocks to match her own. One of these, 'of blue silk with white muslin over', was 'just like me' and so was another – 'pink with a white lace tunic looped up with bows'. At 30 Cecilia was still a very attractive woman and mother and daughter must have made a striking pair.

Dolly seemed to thrive on all the attention she was getting. Yet it is hard to guess what was passing through the mind of this oddly precocious child. One Sunday Cecilia remembered dozing off in church during the sermon and being nudged awake by Dolly 'in a great fright'. 'Wake mother,' the child hissed. 'I saw a picture once of the Devil flying away with a woman who slept in church!' Had Ward drawn the child's attention to the picture? Who can say?

The following May the longed-for son, Gerard, was added to the family and two years later Bertram arrived. The younger boy's boisterous ways soon made him an easy favourite and Ida adored him. Once he had grown beyond babyhood the two teamed up and sister and brother remained the best of friends throughout their childhood.

Dolly, meanwhile, did her best to ignore 'the three little ones' who between them had turned her nursery, once a quiet haven, into a zoo. A succession of nursemaids engaged by Cecilia to ease Ward's workload came and went, seldom staying long. Overworked, yet stubbornly determined not to delegate one jot of her authority, the nurse's temper deteriorated, leaving Dolly with a growing sense of isolation. Where did she belong?

All this while a stream of visitors flowed through the house: grandparents, aunts, cousins, friends of her parents; arriving with children, pets and servants and frequently staying for weeks at a time. Caught up in this busy whirl, it did not occur to anyone that Dolly might be lonely. It certainly never entered the head of her mother, charged with keeping the show on the road.

As it happened, most of the visiting child guests were boys, whose loud voices, greedy appetites and thoughtless exuberance greatly displeased the fastidious Dolly. She responded by retreating into her shell and having fits of the sulks, profoundly irritating Fitz. Thus father and daughter drew apart, which was unfortunate because Fitz – a wise and considerate man – might have succeeded in coaxing Dolly out of her shell if it had ever occurred to him to try.

CHAPTER X

The Brothers

Barring the emergence of new evidence, at this distance in time it is impossible to say with any certainty who fathered Gerard, Cecilia's first surviving son. Indeed it is possible that Cecilia herself was not absolutely certain. Family legend has pointed the finger at Fitz's handsome young nephew, Jem Smith-Barry. And Cecilia's own diary gives this theory some support, for the opportunity almost certainly existed.

Nine months before Gerard's birth Cecilia and Fitz had been staying at Fota, the Smith-Barry's summer home, where Jem is likely to have been one of the family party. Had Fitz's young wife under the spell of that enchanted island thrown caution to the winds and taken the handsome young man as her lover? If she had, Fitz may have found her indiscretion easy to forgive. His was not a jealous nature. He had been close on 40 when he and Cecilia married and neither of them had been in love. The laws of consanguinity had denied him the right to marry his niece Geraldine, the one great love of his life; and if his wife had been indiscreet with Geraldine's younger brother, who was he to cast a stone?

In any case Fitz had been preoccupied that summer with graver concerns than a possible flutter between his nephew and his wife. Two years previously the Fenians had staged an armed uprising aimed at throwing off the British yoke and establishing an independent Irish republic. British troops had been called out and the revolt was put down. But both sides had been guilty of brutality and a sense of injustice still festered among the native Irish. Though Fota was a haven of tranquillity large parts of the province were still in turmoil, governed not by law but by the gun. During his stay at Fota Fitz had volunteered to accompany the agent (his old friend Lionel Cust) on some of his trips to outlying parts of the Smith-Barry estate. He observed that Cust's nervousness was causing him to take an unnecessarily harsh line with some of the tenants, which he believed could only make a bad situation worse. Cust's response made it plain that he believed the iron fist was the only way to deal with an ignorant and villainous peasantry and Fitz was distressed to see that his friend had made himself very unpopular.

While enjoying their holiday at Fota the Widdringtons had left five-year-old Dolly and baby Ida at Newton, under the care of Ward. Halfway through their stay they received a telegram from the nurse informing them that Dolly had scarlet fever. Cecilia wanted to return at once, for this was a serious illness. But Fitz succeeded in dissuading her, arguing that Ward, with the help of their excellent Dr Wilson, was perfectly competent to pull the child through and that there was no point in putting her own health at risk.

When they returned home they discovered to their consternation that Dolly had been very ill indeed, close to death in fact. Nursed night and day by the devoted Ward, who had read to her for hours at a time, they found the convalescent working a kettle-holder, still so weak she could barely stand.

Meanwhile, to keep baby Ida clear of the sickroom, she had been banished to the care of one of the housemaids, who had neglected her badly. 'Poor baby ... ate a whole doll at that time – of wax!' Cecilia recalled. Whether this curious meal had been dictated by hunger or eaten out of sheer boredom can only be guessed at, but fortunately Ida managed to survive it. A degree of neglect that might have broken a weaker child had created in Ida a tough little creature; her hale digestion matched by a sturdy spirit.

The following May Cecilia gave birth to a boy. His arrival was greeted with jubilation and he was given the name Gerard. 'You were very welcome my son.' Cecilia began her *Gerard Diary*. 'I thought your little brother born at Marbury in 1866 was to be my only boy. I would hardly believe it and asked the nurse if she was *quite* sure. "Put on your spectacles Mrs Green if you aren't" said Dr Wilson to the midwife.' Held up for inspection, the newborn was shown to be 'a great big strong boy – plump and with a fine head, large eyes and full red mouth, well made all over'.

Cecilia was jubilant. And if Fitz had any reason to suspect that Gerard was not his son he may have decided he would do best to keep his suspicions to himself. His wife's first three pregnancies had not provided him with an heir and in a family notorious for failing to produce healthy males he may have feared that there would not be another candidate for the Widdrington succession. And Jem, after all, as his sister's son, had the Widdrington blood in his veins. 'A bird in the hand ... ' However, some credence may be given to Fitz's doubts over Gerard's paternity by the fact that the boy was not given his fathers baptismal name but was christened plain Gerard Widdrington.

Cecilia adored her son. 'The mother instinct awoke in me then for the first time truly,' she recalled. The baby's bassinette was brought to her bed and 'I used to walk up and down with you if you were restless, and oddly enough, Father was never disturbed by my doings, bad sleeper as he was.'

She kept Gerard with her, breast-feeding him 'night and day' for six months. 'It was summer, and many a time you have been sent to sleep staring at the bright cracks of sunshine in the closed shutters. I never drank beer nor wine, for fear you might imbibe a taste for drinks – nor ate anything that would hurt you'.

Unfortunately Cecilia's unalloyed pleasure in her son was not destined to last. Once Gerard was weaned his mother had no excuse for keeping him out of the nursery, shielded from the possessive nurse, and the boy was obliged to join his sisters.

By then it was an established fact that Dolly did not care for babies. They mewled and puked and made extra work for her nurse, upsetting the calm orderliness that had previously prevailed in the nursery. Ward treated the newcomer reasonably enough: at least he was a boy. While two-year-old Ida positively welcomed the appearance of her brother, despite being upset by poor Gerard's evident distress. For the child was missing the day and night comfort of his mother's arms and set up a great bawling. He could not be made to settle. Matters became worse when he started to cut his teeth. Before long his screaming came to dominate nursery life, while every passing week seemed to throw up fresh troubles. At 17 months he went down with a mysterious illness. Ward thought it must be foot and mouth as a number of cows at the Home Farm had it. 'Yr mouth was sore inside and yr feet blue and sore.' Whatever the correct diagnosis, Gerard's illness pulled him down. He was slow in learning to walk and refused to speak 'or even to try', Cecilia noted despairingly, beginning to fear that her son might have been born dumb. A persistent dribbler, when eventually he began to form words his 'queer pronunciation' could only be understood by Ida, who was obliged to be her brother's interpreter.

In those days, when the British Empire was close to its zenith, the ambition of every mother was to produce sons who were 'manly'. Unfortunately Gerard did not fulfil any of the criteria for manliness. Painfully shy and excessively timid, at five he was still dribbling and his speech was far from clear. In an age when courage was demanded of boys and stoicism much prized, he shrank from contact with other children and screamed when sat on the donkey. Then he began to suffer from nightmares. He would wake in the night bathed in sweat but could not explain what had frightened him. 'I used to listen outside yr door,' Cecilia recalled, 'and was so relieved if I heard no crying … We never dared scold you much, to make you cry after.'

Two years and four months after Gerard's arrival, Cecilia gave birth to a second boy. 'We never hoped for TWO boys,' she wrote joyfully, opening a new diary. 'And what a big one you were! The biggest of them all.'

This time there can have been no lingering doubt in Fitz's mind concerning the boy's paternity, for the child was given his father's name. He was baptised Bertram Fitzherbert Widdrington. Gerard's rights as his father's legal heir, however, were not called into question.

From the start the younger boy's manliness was never in doubt. A passionate headstrong baby, at two months old he 'refused to have anything to say' to his mother, 'and I was forced to wean.' By 10 months he was refusing his bottle 'if he saw the others eating anything else.' He soon caught up with his brother, who invariably gave in to him when the younger boy snatched his toys. 'The selfish always get the best of it and he couldn't bear to hear you cry,' Cecilia observed wryly. 'It was even now that [Gerard's] unselfish character began to be seen.'

However, unselfishness, though admirable in a girl, was not prized in the young Victorian male. The contrast between the two boys was very painful to Fitz, who 'spent sleepless nights' worrying about Gerard. Everything was a difficulty to him, 'even swinging on the new trapeze we had put up in the passage'.

Fitz was proud of Bertram, who whenever he caught sight of his Papa would pester him with 'Mup, mup' – 'wch meant climbing till your feet were on his shoulders, then being walked about with and finally with a great jump landed on the floor'. At Christmas, when they had the magic lanthorn show, Bertram would be brought down and was not the least bit frightened. The child had sharp intelligent eyes, a small mouth and curly fair hair verging on red. Cecilia considered him 'a very ugly vulgar boy' and did not take him about much because she considered him 'too hideous'. She thought he looked prettiest when he was naughty. At one-and-a-half he was wearing Gerard's clothes 'of when he

7 *Gerard Widdrington did not fulfil the criteria for 'manliness'.*

was 3 yrs old'. In those days little boys were dressed in frocks and his mother recalled him wearing his brother's hand-me-down blue poplin frock with '3 pleats down the front and gold buttons' under a blue pelisse, with a black velvet hat trimmed with turkey feathers. Strutting about in this finery Bertram must have looked an odd little fellow!

Gerard had been blessed with a head of glossy brown hair of which his doting mother was inordinately proud. Even when it fell upon his shoulders she could not bring herself to have it cut. Before wise Dr Wilson, hoping to boost the child's vitality, finally persuaded Cecilia to reach for the shears, she had Gerard's photograph taken 'to remind me'. The three-year-old was lifted onto a chair where he sat with his legs sticking out, dressed in a short velvet frock with puffed sleeves, his lion's mane of hair spreading over his lace collar.

The picture is preposterous! Looking every inch the girl Gerard scowls into the camera, 'very cross indeed'. And no wonder. He was 'delighted to see in the glass all the hair coming off', his mother was obliged to admit. Always her favourite, Cecilia seemed to dread the thought of his having to grow up and face what she feared he would discover to be a hostile world.

In those days at around five years old the sons of the English gentry would discard their pretty frocks, to be kitted out as British Jack Tars – their sailor suits, complete with lanyard, providing evidence of their manliness and future competence to run the Empire. But clothes do not make the man. Despite Gerard's change of apparel, the boy was still languid and easily fatigued, taking as little exercise as he could get away with.

In the summer of '76 Cecilia took all four children to Scarborough for a seaside holiday. Geraldine (now Lady Willoughby de Broke) joined them and the two young families enjoyed themselves famously; two-and-a-half-year-old Bertram 'strutting around with the rest and feeling so big.' Everyone had fun except Gerard, who hated the sea. 'You bathed twice but didn't like it – you were an odd boy – you seemed to like nothing very much,' Cecilia observed rather sadly. Back home, Bertram lorded it over his brother, getting more attention than was good for him in his mother's opinion.

The winter that followed was unusually harsh and one day after a heavy snowfall Gerard's siblings dashed out to make a snowman. He, however, could only watch them from an upstairs window: 'Your chilblains were too bad to let you be in the snow', Cecilia recalled.

So it went on throughout the brothers' childhood; Bertram 'cheeky and cheery' and attention-grabbing invariably succeeding in getting his own way, putting Gerard in the shade. And although the two played together happily enough when no other child was by, feeding their pets and making camps in the woods, it would have been perfectly clear to an onlooker that it was the younger boy who always took the lead.

Chapter XI

The Governess Years

Miss Yate was 19 when she arrived at Newton Hall in January 1875 to be governess to Dolly, who had just passed her 10th birthday. She came with excellent references and was described by Cecilia as 'a high-spirited girl very clever and very sharp with her tongue and would stand no sort of nonsense'. It did not take Miss Yate long to discover that she would have a difficult path to tread between the schoolroom and the nursery. Fortunately she had been blessed with a good measure of tact and common sense, for she succeeded in establishing a mutually satisfactory *modus vivendi* with the jealous and possessive Ward. 'How she and Ward kept free of quarrels I never knew,' Cecilia commented. Thankfully they did.

Governesses have always occupied an invidious position in their employers' households: too grand to mix with the servants and not grand enough (though frequently better educated) to be treated as one of the family. However, since the Widdringtons put a high value on their children's education they made it their business to keep a close eye on the governesses they employed. 'They breakfasted and dined with us … and sat in the evening till 10 if they liked, so we got to see if they were suitable.'

The arrival of Miss Yate aroused mixed feelings in Dolly. The good side was her promotion to the dining room for breakfast and lunch, enabling her to escape the tedious company of her siblings. The bad side was her continuing mistrust of formal education. 'I fear you were a mass of conceit and self-complacence which Miss Yate had to knock gradually out of you', Cecilia wrote of that time. 'You have told me since that you go quite hot to remember the pert conceited things you said to her.' She failed to see that Dolly was bent on defending herself from the taunt of being thought ignorant and stupid in the only way she knew – by making use of her sharp tongue.

And indeed in the early days the child had cause for complaint, for Miss Yate's regime proved to be alarmingly rigorous. Disconcerted by the backwardness of this plainly intelligent child, and determined to help her young pupil to catch up, she forced Dolly to rise at six for an hour's tuition before breakfast. This was followed by two sessions before lunch and a further one between Dolly's afternoon walk and tea. In addition she obliged Dolly to sit half-yearly written examinations, reducing the child to tears and eventually making her ill. Old Dr Wilson was called in and diagnosed her malaise as overwork. The child was 'too much pressed with study … and had not the brain power to stand it'. He advised that the pace should be slackened. It was, and in a more relaxed atmosphere Dolly began to respect her governess and in time even to love her. For her part Miss Yate came to appreciate that her pupil's 'cleverness' (which no one denied her) had little to do with book-learning, but was of that intuitive order so well understood by Dickens and immortalised in the character of Cissy Jupe in *Hard Times*. Asked to record her impressions of her former pupil after Dolly's untimely death, Miss Yate described her as 'a beautiful child with an unusual dignity of manner … Even as a child,' she recalled, 'she knew how to keep anyone she chose at a distance.'[1] Miss Yate was one of the few individuals able to penetrate Dolly's defensive veneer and to appreciate the unusual child within.

For in order to understand Dolly (which Cecilia never did) it was necessary to accept her complete lack of interest in what were then considered to be the ladylike accomplishments. She struggled at the piano, but soon gave it up, having no ear for music, especially of the emotional kind. She had no wish to be 'swept off her feet'. Opera she loathed; its artificiality and display of raw adult emotion serving only to disturb and embarrass her. Foreign languages were another anathema. Nor did she share her parents' passion for the decorative arts. She had no aptitude for drawing or painting; and though her father was recognised as an accomplished artist and Newton was famous for its fine Italian and Dutch paintings and as a treasure house of rare and beautiful artefacts, many collected by her parents, Dolly seemed blind to the beauty of the environment in which she was privileged to grow up. A healthy, vigorous child, she liked best to spend her time out of doors, delighting in riding, swimming, tree-climbing and, above all, studying the wild creatures that made their homes on her father's estate.

In particular, she loved to watch the birds and was clever and patient at taming them. First there was Sonny, a bullfinch which came at her call and would perch on her head. Later there was a young starling she rescued, feeding it with chopped worms and meat. 'We all hated the dirty thing,' Cecilia recalled, 'but I must say you deserve animals, you take such care of them.' There was a special corner of the garden which Dolly visited daily to accustom the wild birds to her presence, so that eventually they would feed from her hand.

Cecilia was indulgent over her children's fluctuating menagerie of pets, prepared to tolerate the mess they made providing they were properly looked after. At one time or another Dolly loved and cherished an assortment of creatures, from Brandy the dachshund ('a brown thing a yard long and always in everyone's way') to rabbits and guinea pigs. The child hated to see any small creature neglected and would rescue her siblings' pets once they tired of them. She maddened her father and the gamekeepers by pulling the rabbit snares tight to prevent the victims getting their heads through.

Until she was 12 years old Dolly slept in the same room as her nurse. Eventually, while Ward was away on holiday, the thought of the nurse's overbearing ways spurred Cecilia into making some long-overdue changes. She decided to sacrifice her own spacious airy bedroom in order to make a much-enlarged schoolroom. Dolly was to be moved into the old schoolroom, for the first time in her life acquiring a space she could call her own. The room looked out over treetops to the distant line of the sea and Dolly was told she could furnish it just as she chose. 'You ought to have had it long ago,' her mother admitted 'but Ward disliked it, so I didn't move you out of pity to her.' The effect the move had on Dolly was gratifying: 'You were a much nicer little girl now and got to be fond of me and tried to be nice to Ida – though you never could be congenial spirits.'

Cecilia had chalked up her first victory and when Ward returned the nurse knew it. Yet two more years were to pass before she could find the courage to dismiss this troublesome woman. In the meantime Fitz's mother, old Mrs Jacson, died. Fitz felt her death badly. The family were obliged to go into mourning, at considerable expense. Dolly, always her grandmother's favourite, kitted out in a black serge Norfolk jacket from Jays of Newcastle, began to think about death. What did it feel like, being dead? Did you feel anything or nothing?

A couple of months later one of the Newton footmen, a good-looking youth called William, died rather suddenly from consumption, which was still a common complaint in those days. Dolly asked her mother if she could go and see his body. After thinking about it, Cecilia said that she could. "It was the first dead person you saw,' she recalled. 'He was a nice pretty lad.'

Death was in the air. For some years Fitz's friend Leopold Cust, who was still employed by the Smith-Barrys as their Irish agent, had been living virtually under siege, with Fenian atrocities reported almost daily. His wife, Charlotte, by this time the mother of six children, had quite gone to pieces, living in mortal terror of Leopold being ambushed, or of their whole family being murdered in their beds. At Fitz's invitation the Cust family had got into the habit of spending the long summer holiday at Newton, bringing them much-needed relief. Their children and the young Widdringtons were much of an age and though inevitably there were squabbles, by and large the two families got on famously.

In March 1878 shocking news was received from Ireland. Leopold Cust (who the previous year had inherited his father's baronetcy) had died very suddenly in the presence of his wife, after having trouble with the veins in his leg. Fitz at once set off for Cork, leaving Cecilia to ponder the implications of the tragedy. Suddenly her family had more than doubled, for as co-trustee with Cust's widow, Fitz was now responsible for Sir Leopold's six under-age children, the youngest still a babe in arms, the eldest a lad of fourteen.

When Cecilia had first met Charlotte Cust, on the first, shy, day of her Irish honeymoon, the inexperienced bride had been grateful to have a married woman on call who could advise her on intimate matters which her mother had never seen fit to discuss. Though she had found Charlotte's manner rather stiff the two young women had become friends.

But the intervening years had not been kind to Charlotte. Repeated child-bearing and a chronic shortage of funds, coupled with the ever-present threat posed by the Fenians, had combined to wear her down. She had become nervous and irritable, endlessly fault-finding and picking on her children for the smallest fault, and though Cecilia would have been loathe to admit it, she found the company of the unhappy woman rather a pain. She suspected that Fitz's kindly nature and innate sense of duty would prompt him to make all sorts of commitments which were bound to impinge on her own life; and few would blame her for anticipating the burden of caring for the widow and six bereaved young Custs with decidedly mixed feelings.

Arrived in Ireland, Fitz found Charlotte Cust in a state of collapse, 'too broken in body and mind' to be capable of taking decisions. Shattered by her husband's sudden and unexpected death, the tragedy had gained her very little sympathy. For Sir Leopold, as agent to a member of the hated Ascendancy, had ruled by the rod and succeeded in making himself very unpopular.

Matters were made worse by a disturbing story that was being put about. It transpired that the Mother Superior of a convent sited on Smith-Barry property had enclosed an adjacent piece of land in order to make a graveyard, where her nuns could be buried with the appropriate Catholic rites. This had been done without obtaining the landlord's permission and when Cust learned of it – and that the first burial had already taken place – 'he gave the officiating priest a severe dressing down'.[2] However, the priest had stood his ground and looking the agent in the eye, he motioned to him to put his foot on the grave. Without thinking, Sir Leopold had complied. Immediately (according to rumour) he had felt a sharp pain all down his leg. And by the next morning he was dead. When this news – soon destined to pass into legend – got about, the neighbourhood was thrown into turmoil, causing what the *Tipperary Free Press* described as 'a very unseemly demonstration in Tipperary Town'.[3] Under these distressing circumstances Fitz thought it wise for the widow and her children to leave her isolated home without delay. But where were they to go?

On inheriting the baronetcy Leopold had discovered that the money that came with it did not amount to very much. Now that he was dead, what little there was could not be spent, since it must be held in trust for his heir, 14-year-old Charley – now Sir Charles, who was a cadet on the training ship *Britannia*. Leasowes Castle, the Cust family seat (lying in an exposed position on the coast south of Birkenhead), had been let and was in any case quite unsuitable as home to an impoverished family. A great rambling pile with mock Tudor turrets, it needed an army to keep it in repair and was fiendishly expensive to heat. It looked to Fitz as if the family would have to take refuge at Newton. And for a while that is what they did.

For the next few years the unfortunate Custs were shuttled back and forth between Charlotte's high-born relations and the Widdringtons, with Newton, where they continued to spend the long summer holiday, proving to be the one constant in their nomadic lives. It was 'Heaven upon Earth' to those children, Cecilia recalled, 'For Lady Cust was persuaded by Fitz to relax from her constant fault-finding and let them amuse themselves, even at the expense of dirty clothes, as ours did.' The children fished and made dens in the woods and there were picnics up on the moors and trips to the beach at Alnmouth, the whole gang setting off in the Widdrington's large open carriage 'which now was needed for so many'. Charlotte Cust, who was 'very feeble', was always glad to leave the 'doings' in her hostess's capable hands.

But all was not sweetness and light. For Dolly hated to be one of a crowd and was given to sulks, her discontented face infuriating her father. Worse, though, was the behaviour of Ward. Though she would always insist on making up one of the party she made sure it was appreciated that she was being 'put upon'; her carping and criticising a sour reminder to her mistress that the nursery was still a battlefield in a war offering no prospect of a truce. Her attitude ground Cecilia down and played on her nerves, until one day, 'after an unusual flouting of my authority', she snapped. Taking her courage in both hands she confronted Ward and gave her notice to leave. It was a defining moment and both of them knew it. In the heat of a righteous anger, and without consulting Fitz, she claimed a mother's right to have control of her own children 'and my long bondage was at an end'.

The departure of the nurse was to mark the emergence of the confident personality recognisable in Cecilia throughout her middle years. She had won her first major battle. No longer feeling herself to be the junior partner in the marriage, she had gained herself the right to stand up and be heard.

Dolly gave her nurse 'a capital fitted up travelling bag' as a leaving present and was permitted to accompany her as far as Alnmouth, where after a tearful farewell Ward boarded a train. Following her departure Ward's position was filled by a succession of nurserymaids, none of whom stayed long. By this time, however, Dolly, now rising 14, was virtually free of the nursery and could look after herself, though she still needed help in controlling her thick mane of fair hair. The repercussions of Ward's departure on the teenager are hard to gauge. It is possible that Dolly's loss of trust in her parents stemmed from that day. Nevertheless her moroseness abated under her young governess's firm but benign rule. 'Yr disposition is far nicer', her mother commented. 'Indeed there is no fault to find, you are getting unselfish more and very fond of sewing . . I am in hopes you will grow up nice.'

Then a blow fell. Miss Yate announced that she was leaving. She was now 23 and had decided to try her luck in the rapidly expanding colony of Australia. Cecilia was shocked. She knew the admirable Miss Yate would not be easy to replace and sure enough she was succeeded by 'a few useless governesses', one of whom was dismissed within a month. The elderly Miss Marshall, 'a perfect French scholar', fared slightly better. On account of her age she was considered responsible enough to be left in charge of all four children while Fitz and Cecilia went off to Algeria. Did they worry about their children during their two-month-long holiday? Very likely not. Those were more fatalistic days. They should not have been surprised, however, when Miss Marshall gave in her notice the minute they returned. It appeared that the two boys had been obstinately resistant to the governess's superior French. She had also fallen foul of Ida. The child had run away for a whole day 'till she was found in the woods and coaxed back.'

'I am very tired of this education and governesses!' Cecilia wrote despairingly after engaging a Mademoiselle Poulson who was 'most excitable and highly strung' and 'knew five languages perfectly' but could not get on with the climate. She could not cope with Dolly either. 'I am sure you will not like to look back on this part of your life' Cecilia addressed her daughter via the *Dorothy Diary*. 'Its as though you were mad … (Miss Poulson) was very romantic and rather silly its true, but you were most rude and cruel.' The poor woman soon left, to be replaced by Miss Duke: another abject failure. 'She knew nothing, wouldn't walk, wouldn't talk except about her grandmother – and off she went in three weeks.'

Finally Miss Herbert was engaged: a parson's daughter from Devon. Cecilia's first impression – that the girl was 'a good little nothing' – could not have been more wrong. Constance Herbert, one of a large and exceptionally gifted family, was to give loyal and loving service to the Widdrington family over many decades. A steadfast friend to both the Widdrington girls, in time she grew also to be devoted to Fitz, and in his old age was to help Cecilia to care for him.

That was in the future. Meanwhile Dolly had sunk into a state of well-nigh impenetrable gloom and Cecilia decided to move her out of the schoolroom, where she learned nothing and was disrupting the education of the little ones. Shortly after Dolly's sixteenth birthday Cecilia took her off to London, hoping that the metropolis would supply her daughter with a little of that 'finishing education' that she and her two sisters had been promised, but which had never materialised. Piano and singing lessons were taken up, only to be abandoned when Dolly refused to practise, and she also went a few times to Queen's College to be coached in French and Italian. But her aversion to formal education seemed as strong as ever, while the rules, and the press of strange girls, bewildered her. Cecilia was forced to admit that her expensive experiment had proved a disaster. Her only recourse, she decided, was to try to teach Dolly herself. Predictably that did not work out either. 'I think you want something more – or anyway *someone* with a stronger character than yourself ... there is a sad lot of imperiousness and selfishness I notice, come on since Miss Yate left.'

The truth was that Dolly, confused and miserable, stood desperately in need of a wise counsellor. All unknown to her mother, that person was already waiting in the wings. Three years previously, when Dolly was 13, her parents had taken her on a visit to Fallodon, a pretty red brick house lying to the north-east of Alnwick and famous for its gardens, which was the home of an elderly couple, Sir George and Lady Grey. The Grey's late-born only son, another George, had died young, leaving a widow, Harriet, and seven dependent children with little means of support. Though far from wealthy themselves Sir George and his wife had invited Harriet and her fatherless children to share their home. Dolly was introduced to the young Greys, but did not meet the eldest, 14-year-old Edward, who was away at school – a pupil at Winchester College.

However, it is likely that Dolly's first meeting with the vicar of Embleton would have taken place while she and her parents were guests of the Greys. The Rev. Mandell Creighton, a man of vast scholarship and a mercurial personality, was a close friend to Sir George as well as being the Grey's parish priest. The Creightons and the Widdringtons struck up a friendship and it was not long before the parson and his rather formidable wife Louise were being invited to Newton, to 'dine and sleep' as the custom went. For a while the two families were on terms of considerable intimacy. But their friendship was not destined to last – for reasons that will become apparent.

CHAPTER XII

Mandell Creighton

That Mandell Creighton, a charismatic churchman, was destined for a bishopric, had never been in doubt since the day of his ordination. Even as a young man he had the gift of seeming to fill any room he entered with a special vibrancy. Though he could not strictly be called handsome, his high domed forehead, piercing blue eyes, tall stature and luxuriant beard (in which Edward Lear's family of wrens could have nested without undue discomfort) undoubtedly gave him a presence. And though in later life his commitment to Christian orthodoxy was sometimes questioned by people to whom these things mattered, this 'versatile and pleasant ecclesiastic' was much in demand socially, his inclusion in any gathering guaranteed to lift the level of conversation above the trivial, without rendering it either ponderous or dull.

Born in 1843, Creighton had no 'side' and never tried to hide the fact that he had been 'born above the shop', his father Robert having been the owner of a successful furniture retailer's in Carlisle. A self-confident, rather pushy child, he was sent to the cathedral school, where his superior intellect was soon spotted by the headmaster, who encouraged him to sit for a scholarship to Durham Grammar. Passing with flying colours, he eventually became Head Boy and on being asked by the headmaster's wife what he was aiming for in life he replied that he intended to be a bishop. Some cousins on his mother's side had taken holy orders and the high church aura of the school along with the beauty of the magnificent Norman cathedral nearby had no doubt encouraged him to follow the same path. After failing to win a much-prized Balliol scholarship he applied to Merton and was successful. One of the smaller Oxford colleges, Merton had a reputation for attracting the 'nobs'. Yet although most of his fellow undergraduates were public schoolboys, Creighton had no difficulty in holding his own and making friends. By the time he had gained a tutor fellowship from his college and been elected President of the Oxford Union, few would have challenged his right to be called a gentleman.

Oxford in the 1860s was liberal in outlook and bubbling with controversy, both on account of its antediluvian syllabus (which the great classicist Benjamin Jowett declared to be in urgent need of reform) and the conflicting views of scientists and theologians. Its atmosphere of lively debate suited young Creighton perfectly. In 1870 at the age of 27 he was ordained deacon by the Bishop of Oxford. The following year, catching sight of a feisty young woman while attending a lecture given by John Ruskin at the Sheldonian Theatre, he managed to cadge an introduction. Her name was Louise von Glehn. Of half-German, half-Scottish extraction, her prosperous home in the new London suburb of Sydenham was within walking distance of the relocated Crystal Palace, where a few forward-looking academics had inaugurated what they called 'enrichment classes' for young women. Louise had attended these classes, which changed her life: she was one of only six students to pass the first 'Higher Examination' for women set by London University. She was just 21 and on a visit to Oxford, meeting all sorts of interesting people, when she met Creighton. It did not take her long to decide that the dashing young Fellow of Merton was by far the most interesting and within a short time the couple had settled that they were to be married.

For the newly-weds married life in Oxford was as close to perfection as it was possible to be. They were living in the Banbury Road, not far from the city centre, surrounded by like-minded friends – young, ambitious, high-spirited and with confidence bred in the belief that they were 'going places', as part of the nation's intellectual elite. It therefore came as a shock to Louise when her husband told her that the Northumbrian parish of Embleton, which was in the gift of Merton College, had been offered to him, and that he had a mind to accept. Creighton's ambition was to gain a professorship and to achieve this he needed to be published. By now there were two young children in the house, and with the duties of a father (which he took seriously) added to his tutorial obligations, he had little time left for serious study – let alone writing. 'You had better go up there and see what the vicarage is like,' Louise advised him, her heart sinking and her mind racing ahead. Creighton went and liked what he saw. The vicarage was most impressive – virtually a fortified mansion. It included a peel tower built in the 13th century to protect the village from marauding Scots across the border. 'The people are very friendly,' he wrote to his wife. 'I find the villagers very kindly and a general desire to be hospitable.'[1] Knowing where her wifely duties lay Louise agreed that it was right for them to go.

She had come prepared to find Northumberland a cultural desert of muddy lanes and uneducated cottagers. Yet it would be good for her, she conceded, 'to be obliged to make friends with people whom in Oxford I should have dismissed as hopelessly uncongenial'. In the event the couple were fortunate to find themselves close neighbours of two of the wisest and most respected grandees in the county: the elderly Lord Grey of Howick, son of the liberal earl who had taken the Great Reform Bill through the Commons in 1832, and his cousin, Sir George, a former Under Secretary for the Colonies and three times Home Secretary. Both the Greys and their wives welcomed the Creightons into their circle and they all became friends. Louise had a great admiration for Sir George's wife, Lady Sophia, who had taken her widowed daughter-in-law and seven children into her home with generosity and forbearance; the three generations appearing to live happily under one room without any sign of friction. (Privately Louise regarded Harriet Grey as 'a rather dull and commonplace woman', yet she was grateful for the young woman's companionship during the trying months of her frequent pregnancies.)

Though Creighton was happily married, he still had an eye for a pretty woman – though there had never been any question of impropriety. Unlike most clever men (with their tendency to regard women as a captive audience waiting to be impressed) he was genuinely interested in the feminine point of view and was an excellent listener. He was also very fond of children: happy to join in their rumbustious games when opportunity offered and to hear their opinions, which he treated seriously. When he first met Dorothy Widdrington it was already plain that she would grow up to be a beauty. However, he found her a silent, rather moody, child and, sensing that she was unhappy, he set about trying to coax her out of her shell.

Ever since she could remember Dolly had been plagued by sycophantic male flattery. Unfailingly, if men noticed her at all, it was because they found her pretty. But what did this 'prettiness' amount to? To the child it seemed a very undesirable attribute, since it caused men to behave in a stupidly embarrassing way which made her cringe and made them look silly.

Mr Creighton was different. Though he seemed quite old, he was talking to her without the slightest sign of condescension. At first she was at a loss how to respond. Then he drew her to one side and by degrees she relaxed and found herself telling him of her delight in wild creatures: how she liked to stand quite still and watch the squirrels when they didn't know she was there, or baby rabbits peeping out of their burrows at sunset. There was a special place in the garden at Newton, where she brought crumbs and worms to feed the wild birds. 'If you come every day they get used to you and seem to expect you,' she told him shyly. 'They fly down when they see me coming – they don't seem to be a bit afraid.'

'I believe you are the kind of person who rather likes to be alone sometimes,' Mr Creighton said gravely.

Dolly nodded.

'But people always think you have got to be doing something.'

'The Devil finds work for idle hands – is that it?'

'Mama seems to think so.'

When the Creightons came over to Newton, Mr Creighton would always make time to seek Dolly out. As he came to know her better he saw that she was sorely lacking in self-confidence. The child seemed to be convinced that she was going to grow up to be a failure.

'I don't know why I am often so horrid, or why I hate lessons so,' she confided to him one day. 'I suppose I must just be very stupid.'

'Well, I don't believe you are,' he replied. 'I think you just have the kind of cleverness that makes you want to find out things for yourself.'

Once he had asked Dolly what it was she wanted most in the whole world. The child had been silent for a while. Then she replied quietly, 'To be good.'[2]

It was the Creightons who had suggested to Constance Herbert that she should apply for the position of governess to the Widdrington children. It is likely that they knew her father, the Somerset parson. Before she took up her post, Mandell Creighton had provided her with a thumbnail sketch of her charges. Finally he came to Dolly. 'She is going to be a very interesting person,' he said. 'Just now she seems to find life difficult and very serious and she does not find anyone of much use to her. She is quite dutiful, but she has evidently come to the conclusion that those around her are on the wrong tack in most things.' Unfortunately for Dolly the 'wrong tack' was set to continue for some time.

CHAPTER 13

'A Little Turbulent Piece'

When Ida was 20 she bought a notebook with lined pages and a red marbled cover, intending to record the story of her life. *The Events, Adventures, Experiences (and remarks thereon) in the Life of Idonea Widdrington, Younger Daughter of S.F Widdrington, Newton-on-the-Moor, Northumberland*, she began with a flourish, writing with a broad-nibbed pen in her bold, sloping hand. At some later date she added in pencil: *'Wild as a hawk and true as steel'*.

After this promising start she must have stared at the page, wondering how to proceed. At length she began:

> This is the evening of the 1st Sunday in July 1890. I have been sitting in front of this book for ever so long, wondering how I should begin it, and I don't know yet. Perhaps I had better say how old I am and what I'm like for fear I might forget in the long years to come when I am old and out of shape. Well, I'm twenty, nearly 21 … but it doesn't feel like it a bit. As to what I'm like you might say It doesn't matter but it matters a great deal to everybody I mean their faces and figures and things. It would be very dreadful to go through life so ugly that people either stare at you very hard or else 'kindly' don't look your way at all … My photograph shows me a not altogether ugly girl, but certainly not a pretty one … Its features are rather mashed up one into the other, the nose spreads itself over the cheeks, the cheeks into the eyes and the mouth well its large and capable of looking coarse.

Ida's self-portrait does not flatter. She knew she was no classical beauty, like her sister Dorothy – 'one of those Goddesses who walk the earth'. Her bright hazel eyes were small and set too close together, her nose a trifle flattened. Yet honesty forced her to admit that she was admired. And what was beauty after all? Dolly was an ice maiden who loathed to be praised. Ida, on the contrary, lapped up compliments like a kitten lapping cream. Nothing pleased her more than to be told that her thick auburn mane of hair was 'the most lovely colour in the world', or that she had 'the most pearl like skin and the brightest eyes' and so on and so forth. 'I suppose the plainest woman has found flatterers, but still it always struck me as odd that anyone should take the trouble to flatter me', she wrote, with her tongue in her cheek. For well before she was 20 Ida had discovered her power to attract; her vivacity acting as a magnet to both sexes, but especially to men, who buzzed round her like bees round a honey pot. 'This is going to be an absolutely truthful book', she continued. 'For I have a curious detestation and hatred of lies … Nurses, governesses, everybody has fallen foul of me about lying, nothing made me more furious than to be disbelieved when I knew I had not uttered a word except what was true in my short life.'

This outburst reminded Ida that she had intended to begin at the beginning 'so that there may be some order in this book if nowhere else that has to do with me and my doings.' She continued:

> I think I was rather a miserable child on the whole. I was always in a state of being frightened at something – and such deadly fright! The nurse did not like me and that was the source of most of my evils. A child does not reason and say to itself 'So and so does not like me and that's why I'm unhappy' but no living creature feels it more quickly or keenly than a child. And there is no escape, because there are no powers to invent means. No child ever said to itself 'if I tell about this or that … they will see what my case is'. It does not even know it has got a 'case'. It has never seen anything different … I must have been a very sensitive child, everything in my nature was in violent extremes.

As a small child Ida admitted that she had been very gullible. 'Every mortal thing anybody chose to tell me, stories and people in them were as real as my own life.' Thus she was easy prey for her sister Dolly, who despised her and 'took a cruel pleasure' in frightening her. Even her own mother (that passionately-loved apparition who, when Ida was young, was seldom seen except for one magical hour in the drawing room after tea) could sometimes be heedlessly unkind.

Ida recalled that she had a terror of traction engines, which had started when she was teased into believing that they were alive and 'more or less ferocious'. She could never forget 'one dreadful day' when she was driving in the pony carriage with Mother and Dolly:

> There is a place on the road where there is a dip and a lonely cottage and tall trees on either side. It was always more or less dark there and darkness was a thing I could not stand. Lo and behold when we came to this place what should be there but two traction engines! … Well there those horrible Beasts were and had got to be passed — but one had got two of its wheels into the ditch and was half upset and making a most frantic puffing and snorting … Dolly and Mother said 'Oh *poor* thing, look how dreadful, they'll never get it out and it'll die there' … and then 'Look at the other one! They've left it all alone … look, its coming after us, its going to eat us!'
>
> Is it really coming after us?' I asked, very terrified but trying to be brave. Sure enough it was creeping along the road all by its dreadful self … I was speechless, but these ruthless tormenters went on.
>
> 'Its sure to come at you first because you're the littlest and can't run very fast.' … I remember yelling and screaming for sheer fright, and trying to hide myself under the apron of the carriage, crying bitter tears and firmly believing my last hour had come.

At that point Dolly and their mother must have realised that the teasing had gone too far and put an end to it, but not before terrifying Ida almost out of her wits. Yet it seems

8 *Idonea (Ida) Widdrington,
'wild as a hawk and true as steel'.*

this tormenting of Ida was not an isolated incident, as the 20-year-old vividly recalled.

> Another fertile source of amusement to anyone who chose to arouse it was my terror of wolves ... Driving home in the dark – oh it was horrible!! Mother and Dolly would go on inventing long stories and always with the fearful culmination – 'Wolves pursuing us'!!
>
> 'Hark', Mother would say, 'Do you hear? They are after us already. And she and Dolly would begin to make a peculiarly dreadful sound like a pack of wolves in the distance, and although I *saw* them doing it I still thought it was really the noise the pursuing pack were making as they tore after us ... The noise used to go on gently for some time and then got much louder and there would be a snort and a snarl and I could hear their panting breaths and see them not so very far distant – yes I declare I could see them ...
>
> Then there would be a consultation. 'Well you know somebody must be thrown out and then the wolves will eat them and that delays them and allows the carriage to get on' ... I knew what was coming quite well and sat with terror in my heart.

It is hard to credit Cecilia's obtuseness in failing to recognise the thin borderline between fact and fancy in the mind of a young child. It is unlikely she had intended to be cruel, though Dolly must have seen that her sister's terror was genuine. Yet, having, as it were, been given *carte blanche* to torment Ida – and by no less a person than their mother – how was Dolly to resist?

Fitz also could be guilty of unthinkingly cruel teasing, as Ida remembered.

> Bears were a great source of terror to me ... they always inhabited dark corners of any room, I could see a big brown bear sitting with his head up sniffing the air and one paw raised and now and then opening a great red mouth and making his eyes shine in the darkness. I think 'bear fright' if I may call it so was Father's great amusement. Once at Nunnykirk* they dressed Father up in fur rugs and made him look like a great big bear with some animal's head on his, and he crawled growling into the saloon. I knew it was Father and rugs, but I also *knew* it was a bear, and it was much more a bear to me than it was rugs and father, and do what I could I couldn't get over this feeling ... I can't explain, even to myself, this nameless terror, but I think I should have been really less afraid of a *real* bear ... [Father's] whole nature changed for me, he was no longer recognisable, he was only a medium for fright. And so with everything throughout my childish life, a thing was to me what they

---

*   The home of Fitz's youngest sister, Isabel.

told me it was, against the evidence of all the senses, and I still think that a thing exists …
for each soul differently – who is to determine what the reality is? Music, painting, a distant
scene, colour, a poem, down to animals and even persons, a different atmosphere surrounds
them for each one of us: who is right, who is wrong?'

Philosophising on the nature of reality had most likely led Ida into deeper waters than she cared to explore. Or else this latest project, so enthusiastically begun, had soon left her bored. In any event, after covering 13 closely-packed pages the diary was abandoned – probably stuffed into a drawer, where, miraculously, it survived.

Ida's account of her personal appearance leaves her reader in no doubt that she was a young woman who liked to be noticed. Yet she failed to mention her most striking feature, which was her vitality: her inexhaustible lust for life. Even as a baby – when her neglect at the hands of her nurse might have broken the spirit of a weaker child – her screams indicated her passionate will to be attended to – to be heard. Ida was always pressing forward, seeking the limelight. And when at last she was freed from Ward's yoke she began to assert herself. Her showing off infuriated Dolly; her irrepressible flirtatiousness sickened her older sister. Ida was always making a spectacle of herself – she couldn't go near the stables without rolling those bright little eyes of hers at the stable lads.

Nevertheless Dolly had to admit, along with everyone else, that Ida had an affinity with horses, coupled with a complete absence of fear. The beasts instinctively trusted her and she in turn trusted them. As a young child she had possessed the ability to calm a nervous horse simply by approaching it with a few soft words and extending a hand.

Yet she could not leave creatures alone to be themselves, she was always wanting to control them – to teach them to do tricks. At one time she kept a family of black and white rats. She made harnesses for them and taught them to draw a little cart, and she would put the young ones in the cart to give them a ride. She made them race, ordering her brother Bertram to keep hold of them at one end of a long upstairs passage while she went to the other. When she gave the word Bertram was told to let them loose and they would race to get at her 'as hard as ever they could'. Then she would 'cuddle them up' with a titbit.

If Dolly was the born naturalist, never seeking to interfere with the natural order but searching for ways to study birds and animals in their natural environment, then Ida was her opposite: the inveterate circus trainer. All creatures great and small must be bent to her will. As her brothers emerged from the petticoat government of the nursery they too must be made to understand who held the whip hand; it was not long before they fell under their sister's spell. Ida was the ringleader in all their mad pranks. 'The boys were quiet enough until you came in like a whirlwind and then all was strife – you were a little turbulent piece', their mother recalled.

Like that of her sister, Ida's education suffered from the rapid turnover of governesses. The arrival of Constance Herbert was to change all that. Ida loved Miss Herbert from the first day and began to apply herself to her books in order to please her. The boys, too, showed pleasing signs of settling down and attending to their lessons with a better grace.

So they went on, with Ida and her brothers sharing the schoolroom until Gerard was almost nine. However, this gentle regime, while perfectly acceptable for girls, was not thought to provide an adequate training for the sons of the ruling class. Boys needed to be taught by men, they must learn Latin and Greek and mathematics and be taught to be 'manly': toughened up in preparation for their adult role, in which by virtue of their birth they would find themselves occupying positions of authority over lesser mortals.

An essential step in this toughening-up process was to banish boys from the familiar comforts of home and hand them over to strangers; men who, it was supposed, were equipped to supply them with the appropriate training. Virtually all mothers would have agreed that this was a barbarous system. Yet they lived in a man's world, and as the practice was universally followed, few questioned it.

On account of Gerard's slowness and his unusual sensitivity, the boy's banishment had been deferred. But it could not be postponed indefinitely. Eventually it was agreed that the child would begin school in September, shortly before his ninth birthday.

Chapter XIV

All Change

Cecilia would not have it that Gerard was dim. It was rather the case that her son was disturbingly different. True, he was behind with his lessons. Their parson, Mr Golightly, had been coaching him in mathematics, while Fitz had started him on Latin, though it had to be admitted that his progress had been lamentably slow. But then he would take up the queerest things. Once Cecilia had discovered him star-gazing through Fitz's precious telescope and she could not get him to come away. He loved to peer at insects through a microscope he had somehow got hold of. Also mechanics, or anything in that line, seemed to hold his interest. Yet there could be no doubt about it: something was seriously amiss with the boy.

Though rising nine, Gerard's speech was still slurred. And he was woefully nervous – especially with animals. Fitz had bought him a pony, but he could not be persuaded to ride it, or even to be taken to see the hunt. He was always on the side of the victim, could not abide to see a fox being chased to its death. Even at a distance, the sound of the huntsman's horn would reduce him to screams of distress. He refused also to try his hand at fishing because he hated to hurt the fishes so.

'Fitz is quite low and spends sleepless nights thinking about you and how difficult everything comes to you', Cecilia recorded sadly. 'Even swinging on the new trapeze we have put up in the passage! I can't help hoping age will improve you.'

Whether or not Fitz had his suspicions over Gerard's paternity, at this stage in the boy's life he seems to have accepted him as his heir and was thus in 'a constant fret' over him. The boy was tall for his age and growing fast, yet he did not seem to want to grow up and was still content to be dressed in his sailor suits. His greatest joy was in catching newts and water beetles, 'fishing them out from the putrid ponds far and near' and keeping them in glass jars in the old nursery.

However, the dreaded day was fast approaching when Gerard must be sent from home to attend a proper boys' school, where the masters would prepare him for the entrance examination to his father's old school, Winchester College. Fitz had been several times to London to inspect schools in the south of England – he and his wife having agreed that the boy 'had best not go among northerners and most likely learn the dialect'. Two of the Cust boys, Leo and Percy, were pupils at the Dene, a preparatory school near Caterham, which according to Lady Cust was proving satisfactory. Fitz went down to run his eye over the place and judging it to be up to the mark and Mr Fenton, the headmaster, to be quite a decent fellow, it was decided that Gerard should join the young Custs the following September. 'That way the boy will not be thrown entirely among strangers', Cecilia attempted to console herself.

As a distraction from the coming ordeal Cecilia gathered up the three younger children and took them off to Blackpool, at that time a small seaside village north of Liverpool, for a short summer holiday. And what a joy it was – having her children all to herself with not even a nursemaid in attendance, and 16-year-old Dolly, who considered herself too old for buckets and spades, packed off to her Hopwood grandparents. The children built sandcastles and shrimped and swam from the long sandy beach, and Ida enjoyed a moment of triumph after catching a hysterical woman's runaway horse and being showered with praise by its owner.

Like all happy times it was soon over and it was time to have Gerard's hair cut 'short as short', his new school uniform packed in Fitz's old school trunk and his new tuckbox filled with cakes, chocolates, sardines, jam and Newton's finest apples and pears. Cecilia could not face the final parting, so it was Fitz who escorted the boy from Newcastle station to Paddington and thence by cab to Victoria and the stopping train to Brighton. Caterham was the third stop. To the nervous child the day-long journey must have seemed like travelling to the ends of the earth.

Some weeks later Cecilia poured out her agony in her *Gerard Diary*:

> It is over and you are gone. I feel as if I had died – the house was desolate and I could settle to nothing or smile or anything for weeks after. What an unhappy creature is the mother of sons – they are wrenched from her when they are dearest and never really return … You were very philosophic about it all – you knew it had to be done, that 'all boys went' so it just had to be borne and you bore it.

Gerard's weekly letters were short and told his parents nothing. Cecilia travelled to Caterham for his first half-term exeat, carrying him off to London and a steamer trip to Woolwich, which Gerard appeared to enjoy, though she noticed he was very subdued. The Christmas holidays found him 'shyer than ever and speaking in such a small voice when speaking of school'. His first school report, however, was satisfactory and much to his mother's relief he soon 'rubbed into home ways again and had great games and romps'.

By this time, though, a new and quite unlooked-for calamity had overtaken the Widdrington family; one that was about to turn their lives upside down. The previous winter seven-year-old Bertram had developed a cough that would not clear. He was feverish and sweating a good deal at night; Cecilia's 'great fine boy who ate porridge and bacon for breakfast' was becoming pale and starting to cry over his lessons. When the spring weather came he seemed to recover. Yet once winter started to bite his symptoms returned. By this time Cecilia was alarmed enough to take him to London for a consultation with Dr Jenner (the leading specialist in children's ailments and a grandson of the physician who pioneered vaccination). The eminent physician's diagnosis served to confirm her worst fears. Dr Jenner suspected that Bertram had developed what he described as 'a tuberculosis of the bowels' and advised that the child should be moved to a warmer climate without delay. 'Shut up your books and take him into the sun' were the doctor's words, which when reported to Fitz caused him to make an uncharacteristically snap decision. He proposed that the whole family should spend the winter in the South of France, with the exception of Gerard, who would join them at Easter for his school holidays. Friends of theirs had brought back good reports of a small resort midway between Nice and Marseilles which still had reasonably priced hotels and had lately become popular with English families. The place was Hyères. Fitz suggested that Newton be put under wraps, enabling them to leave early in the New Year, with no fixed date set for their return. (If Bertram's health demanded it he saw no reason why they should not prolong their visit.)

He was not unmindful of the fact that living abroad would save him a small fortune in household bills. 'So you the smallest of us will have the power to move the whole house,' Cecilia recorded in her *Bertram Diary*. Anticipating a lengthy absence she had given 10 of the indoor servants notice to quit, leaving only Pell, their housekeeper, to keep an eye on things.

Fitz's pruning of the outdoor staff was less drastic. Since he could not face up to getting rid of his horses, Shotton, the coachman, was kept on, with one stable lad to help him. All the chickens were sold. But as it would not do to allow his estate to go to wrack and ruin, two of the gardeners were retained together with his gamekeepers and woodsmen.

The thought of the impending move filled Cecilia with a fierce joy. Though she loved Newton, she sometimes felt she was slave to the place, with its winters spun out for half the year and its endless commitments. At Hyères she would be able to relax and to enjoy the company of Fitz and the children. Or so she thought. She had not reckoned with Dolly, whose response to the move was one of utter dismay.

"How long are we supposed to be staying in this horrid place?' she asked her mother suspiciously.

'For as long as it takes Bertram to get better,' her mother replied. 'And there's no need to pull such a long face. Once we get ourselves settled you'll find you enjoy it.'

Dolly, on the brink of her 17th birthday, was quite certain she would not. She had not the slightest wish to see the wonderful centuries-old buildings her mother kept extolling, nor to view the sea through the umbrella pines (whatever they were) nor to bury her nose in the wild thyme … Nor did she particularly wish to improve her French, since she had no desire to travel.

That winter she had been allowed to attend the meet with her father; and though she loathed the unwelcome attentions of some of the men (fending off their compliments with a frosty hauteur) she loved the sensation of galloping side-saddle over pasture and ploughland. She had even dared to venture the occasional jump – finding her horse respond to the touch of her heels in a manner which fed her confidence. Now, just as she was beginning to enjoy herself, the hunting would have to be given up.

Nor was that all. She knew she would sorely miss the company of her friend and mentor the Rev. Mandell Creighton. Though she did not see him often, whenever he and Mrs Creighton came to Newton he would seek her out and they would talk about the books she had been reading, or some item of news she had read about in the *Northumbrian Gazette*. Mr Creighton had an uncanny knack of being able to read her mind. He was the only person who recognised the depth of her unhappiness and her profound dissatisfaction with herself.

'You are at a difficult time in your life, for you do not yet know who you are,' he told Dolly. 'That not knowing makes you feel ill at ease – in particular with your family. You must try to be patient, then in time you will discover the people who are right for you. Or perhaps there will be *just one other person*.'

His eyes had twinkled at the vehemence with which Dolly shook her head. She had already made up her mind that she would never marry. Yet somehow Mr Creighton would succeed in making her feel better about herself, as if her life was not after all destined to be a complete failure.

It went without saying that Cecilia had been keeping a watchful eye on the friendship she saw developing between Mr Creighton and her daughter. It was unusual for an intelligent man to show such an interest in a mere child. However, though she had a marked distrust of parsons, she had to admit that Mr Creighton's influence over her daughter appeared to be entirely benign. No doubt it was good for Dolly (who ignored her own father, unless it was to make some hurtful and cutting remark) to have an older man she could confide in, and who would advise her. To cheer Dolly up, the parson had promised to write to her while she was away – if her mother would allow it. Dolly was not at all sure that her mother would, and had not the courage to ask her.

When news of the impending upheaval had been broken to Ida she was found by her mother 'weeping bitterly behind a screen'. Asked what was the matter, 'I sobbed out that we were leaving the ponies and I just couldn't bear it, I loved them so.' Once she had been reassured that the ponies would still be there when the family got back she cheered up. With her mercurial personality she was always ready to take a leap at life, constantly seeking out new sensations, fresh sources of pleasure. She would be crossing the English Channel for the very first time, bound for a country where oranges and lemons could be picked straight off the trees! Bursting with excitement, she helped her mother to pack up the mountains of books and summer clothes due to be sent off in advance and to decide on the indispensables that must travel with them: 'those dreadful bundles of rugs and sticks and umbrellas and mackintoshes which could not be got into trunks'. It was like living in a story book you made up as you went along – and what could be more exciting than that?

Gerard, the one who was being left behind, received the news stoically. The tide of destiny was carrying them all along and he knew there was nothing he could do about it; though he looked imploringly at his mother when bidding her goodbye at the end of the Christmas holidays. Bertram, feeling his importance, strutted about like a little soldier, until his exertions would bring on a fit of coughing and he would be gathered up by his mother and taken to bed.

'At last all was ready,' Ida recalled, 'goodbyes were said, horses and ponies were all kissed on their warm soft noses, tears were choked back, the carriages were laden, Shotton was on the box and away we went … I had always wanted to see the Mediterranean, it seemed to me a land of beauty and romance.'

The child was not to be disappointed. In common with her mother, Ida was to fall instantly in love with the Mediterranean, responding to its warmth, colour, exuberant vegetation and the fabled panorama of its coastline, where wild figs and umbrella pines grew almost down to the beaches and fishing boats bobbed on an azure blue sea. In the future she would always be drawn back to the South of France, returning again and again, until the First World War and her subsequent lack of funds put foreign travel beyond her reach.

CHAPTER XV
Hyères

After a journey of a day and a half by coach and train the Widdringtons arrived at Hyères. Known for its mild winter climate – the air smelling healthfully of pine and wild thyme and a whiff of the sea – it was a simple fishing village in those days, only recently discovered by the English. A few hotels had sprung up and a scatter of villas was starting to appear in the hills above the village, among the olive groves and pines.

A horse-drawn omnibus met them at the station and conveyed them to the *Hôtel de l'Hermitage*, which had been recommended by friends. It was kept by a French chef and his English wife, and after a swift inspection of the rooms by Cecilia proved satisfactory, the family tumbled out of the coach and began the business of settling in.

It was the children's first trip abroad and everything was new and strange. For the first few weeks lessons were suspended and Ida and Bertram were free to do as they pleased, as Ida recalled:

> We had complete liberty to play in the woods and the rugged paths down to the sea, through the oak groves and olive trees and the wonderful fairyland of umbrella pines with their strange shapes and immense shady branches, it was all very cheerful and full of surprises – like the trap-door spiders and processional caterpillars.

Bertram's doctors had prescribed him a rich diet of beaten eggs and cream, to be taken every three hours, in order to build up his health. However, the diet did not seem to be working. Bertram felt queasy for much of the time and he tired easily. Ida, who had a morbid fear of her brother getting worse, had appointed herself his nurse. Whenever she saw that he was running out of steam she would hoist him up and give him a piggy-back. All the guests in the hotel were agreed that she was a little heroine for the way she looked after her brother.

Their mother held herself rather aloof at first. Though Cecilia would have protested if anyone had accused her of being a snob, she was aware that it would be fatal to fall into the wrong set, with Dolly at such a vulnerable age. Dolly in any case was being incredibly tiresome. Pining for home, she was making not the slightest effort to interest herself in her novel surroundings. And she missed the companionship of Miss Herbert, whom Cecilia had decided to leave behind. As a replacement she had engaged a French nursery maid, Eva Trosset, hoping that she would help the younger ones with their French. She was of no use to Dolly, however, who treated her with the utmost disdain. Haughty and intractable, she took herself off on long solitary walks or wrote pages-long letters to Mr Creighton, which she hid from her mother, as she also did his replies.

Fitz on the other hand was most wonderfully cheerful. Freed from his public commitments and untroubled by the daily cares of overseeing the management of his estate, he now had ample leisure in which to paint. He soon became very attached to Hyères, where the light was so lucent, the people so friendly and the living so cheap. It would be good, he said to his wife, to have a place there which they could call their own, and to which they could return the following winter. When she agreed they began to look out for a villa. A short distance from the hotel they had already noticed a charming place. Close by it was a second, still in the process of being built. They decided to track down the builder. When it was finished, would he agree to let? It appeared that he would, and they swiftly settled on a price. 'A handshake and it was done.' An Englishman's word was his bond in those days.

Then just as Cecilia was beginning to feel she could relax, news came from home that her sister Lucy was dead and that the funeral had already taken place. Lucy had married a Mr Crossley of Aldburgh Hall, Masham in Yorkshire and though she and Cecilia had never been particularly close their common memories formed a bond and they had kept in touch. Lucy had died from diphtheria contracted from her eight-year-old son who had died a week earlier. She was just thirty-nine. Some said that the true cause of her death was a broken heart caused by the loss of her much-beloved child and Cecilia was inclined to believe it. However, though her sister's death cast a shadow and Dolly's tiresome behaviour was a continuing irritation, by and large the move to the sun was proving itself: there could be no doubt, Cecilia attested, that she and Fitz had taken the right decision.

When Gerard came out for his Easter holiday there was the usual period of shyness to be got over before he could relax and enter into the fun. A favourite occupation of the Widdrington children which had never lost its charm had been making their own tree house. Hyères provided them with ample scope for house-building in the woods behind the hotel. Blissfully unsupervised by the adults, the three younger ones built themselves a splendid house, where they could bake potatoes on a campfire and cook hard little cakes on a griddle. Fitz put up a sign: 'The Smugglers Rest'. The Bishop of Gibraltar, who had called on their parents, was offered a cake, which he ate – blessing the children. 'We would all be so happy', Cecilia wrote plaintively, 'were it not for Dolly's poisonous moods.'

The days were lengthening, however, the temperature was creeping up, sun-bonnets were coming out. And the English were leaving. In those days no Englishman worth his salt would have dreamed of being seen on the Mediterranean coast during the sweltering summer months.

'Shall we be going home soon, then?' Dolly asked her mother.

She was told that they would not. For Bertram, though brown as a native and coughing less, had still to be coaxed to eat and would tire after the least exertion. By teatime he had no more energy left than a sparrow. The doctors advised that he should spend the summer in Switzerland, to gain the benefit of the pure mountain air. As matters stood, his parents had needed little persuading. After paying the deposit on a villa they had every intention of spending a second winter at Hyères. Returning to Newton for the summer, they reasoned, would mean engaging new staff and setting the social ball rolling again; a thankless expense which had little to recommend it, since Dolly was not yet 'out'. The following spring their daughter would be obliged to make her London debut, involving Fitz in considerable expense. By allowing Newton to remain under dust covers large sums could be saved.

They went first to Montreux, a popular resort on the eastern shore of Lake Geneva, intending to go further into the high Alps and make their summer base at Davos. While taking a steamer trip on the lake, however, Cecilia got into conversation with a school mistress, who after learning of Bertram's illness offered the following advice. 'Madame … why not try Morgins les Bains for your boy, close to, up on the hills by the Dents du Midi, with the same high air as Davos and the same iron waters but as yet unknown to strangers and quite cheap.'

Cecilia and Fitz decided to go and investigate. There was only one hotel, built of wood like all the Alpine houses and very primitive, but scrupulously clean and airy. They settled at once to stay there for the summer. Ida was never to forget the excitement of the journey.

> Our train in those days went as far as the foot of the mountains and from there up the long seven-mile climb you took the diligence, which very seldom ran, or hired a carriage of some sort – which we did. We all packed in and began the climb and on our way up we got our first sight of the Dents du Midi. It must have been the sunset as the whole mountain with its four great peaks glowed a rosy red, one could not believe it was real. Rocks, snow, even the grass lower down was a vivid pink and we travelled on and got a wider view of Mont Blanc and the range of the Jungfrau and the Eiger … At last with jingling bells and a great whacking of whips we reached the hotel.

As soon as she was unpacked Cecilia took Bertram to see the local medic, Dr Edoeur. The long journey had exhausted the boy, who had 'lost all appetite and was very pale and feeble'. It was plain to the good doctor that the rich creamy diet he had been prescribed, supplemented by frequent snacks, was not suiting him. He advised that it should be dropped forthwith and the child given ordinary fare and sat down at table with the others. 'From that time Bertram began to improve wonderfully quick, he gained flesh and appetite and strength – he was soon out in the pine woods all day long and could enjoy life once more – grateful I was to the Dr and we soon became great friends.'

The Widdringtons were the only English family staying at the hotel, which was a veritable United Nations – children from France, Russia, Sweden, Norway, Denmark and Italy all mixing happily together and soon making themselves understood by signs and grimaces. 'And many were the pranks they played', Cecilia recorded:

> frightening the French mothers terribly roasting potatoes and eggs on fires they made outside in the wood, climbing all the trees near, wading in the roaring torrent … but no

harm happened and they were happy as the days were long – Bertram joining in it all and gaining strength with every hour.

Dolly, however, too old to join in these romps, was close to despair, writing despondently to dear Mr Creighton: 'We shan't go home till about this time next year which I perfectly hate and am longing to go home with all my heart and am dreadfully homesick sometimes. I don't think anybody can be quite happy out of their own country.'

Thankfully after a week or two her spirits began to revive in the sharp mountain air. Like her mother, Dolly was a keen walker and now her self-absorption – her conviction that she was a humbug, that her life had no meaning, no inner value – found relief in vigorous physical activity. But Cecilia saw that she needed a companion and wrote to Miss Herbert, inviting her to come out and join them. The invitation was accepted. To Dolly's great joy it was fixed that the governess would accompany Gerard when he came out in July. Cecilia travelled to Geneva to meet them and on the way back she decided to give Miss Herbert a taste of the country by approaching the village on foot, taking the zig-zag path used by the peasants and leaving the diligence to take up the luggage. The Devon parson's daughter had never been abroad before and was as excited as a child. Her addition to the party proved a success 'and well she did and was a comfort to us all,' Cecilia noted approvingly.

In August Fitz was obliged to return to England on business matters relating to Lady Cust. Taking advantage of her husband's absence Cecilia approached Dolly with a daring proposal. What would she say to accompanying her mother in an attempt to scale the great mountain that rose behind the village and was known as the Dents du Midi? It would be a stiff climb of some 10,000ft, taking them beyond the snow line. Did Dolly feel up to giving it a try? Her daughter replied that she did. After climbing boots had been purchased and other necessary arrangements made, the pair set off with two guides, leaving Miss Herbert in charge of the younger members of the family.

In the days before women were permitted to wear breeches few of their number would have attempted such a punishing climb and after successfully making it to the summit mother and daughter returned to the hotel in a glow of triumph. 'You were a different creature then,' Cecilia remembered. Perhaps she had guessed that what Dolly needed was a challenge that would force her out of herself. In any event the climb had acted as a tonic. 'You got nice to me then and more chatty, we were great friends, walking and scrambling together.'

In truth, strenuous exercise spiced with danger appealed to both their natures and before long Cecilia came up with an even more ambitious proposal. Few climbers other than professionals had attempted the ascent of Mont Blanc, at 15,000ft the highest peak in the Alps and one which had claimed many lives. The number of women who had reached the summit could be counted on one hand. Yet with Fitz (who certainly would have forbidden it) safely out of the way, the challenge presented by the mountain was to prove irresistible to Cecilia. When she proposed a joint attempt on the summit to Dolly her daughter was equally smitten. Preparations were made, guides hired and, leaving the younger children in the care of Miss Herbert and Dr Ecoeur (whose plea to be allowed to accompany the women 'in case of accident' had been turned down), mother and daughter set off. Dolly was 17, Cecilia 42; here is her account of the adventure:

On September 3rd we started for Chamonix and there hiring 2 guides and 2 porters we started and went as far as the Grands Mulets where we slept for a few hours – I felt very ill and sick – the excitement I suppose, but got better tho' I didn't sleep and at abt 2 in the morning we started by moonlight and as we began to climb we were all roped together, abt 6 feet between us – and a climb it was! Hour by hour steadily, stopping for breath every three or four minutes. In normal times there are only 2 dangers in the crossing, the 6 foot wide crevasses, on a ladder carried up by the men. One by one we went, the head guide first, then me, then a guide, then Dolly and at last the 2 porters – THAT required nerves and then the almost precipitous Dome de Dromadaire, where the guide in front cut footsteps in the ice into which we coming after had carefully to fit our feet – and glad I was when that was over – the top was reached at abt 11 am – a round flat space – and we rested there an hour. The guides had brought food but we weren't hungry and felt better without, but with now and then a mouthful of snow as we came along. We were too high over every hill for it to look beautiful or to see far. We went down another way and often sliding on the ice slopes, all sitting one behind the other touching – the first one guiding the procession with his alpenstock – and arrived at our Hotel at abt 7.

Wisely, no doubt, Cecilia had said nothing to Fitz, who remained in ignorance of his wife's rash enterprise until it was safely accomplished. She had, however, left a letter with Dr Ecoeur which she had asked him to post to her husband if she and Dolly did not return. 'Dear Fitz', it began, 'I am dead – and I will tell you how it came about.'

Her insouciance in the face of the very real danger that she and Dolly might both have been killed (leaving Fitz bereft of a daughter and a wife and his three remaining children motherless) speaks of the bona fide mountaineer. Once the climbing bug had bitten, Cecilia felt bound to accept the challenge presented by Europe's highest mountain, no matter how dire the possible consequences.

It was not until she and Dolly were safely back that the foolhardiness of the venture hit her. 'I worked myself up into pain and fever with excitement, was horribly tired, couldn't sleep and didn't recover … for many weeks after.'

Not so Dolly. 'Our great feat didn't tire you out one bit, you walked well up and down and slept with no fever.' What was more, the joint physical challenge represented by those two strenuous climbs brought mother and daughter together in a rare interlude of peaceful coexistence. Sadly it was not destined to last.

The Widdringtons stayed on at Morgins until September, when the snows came. Then it was time to return to Hyères, to find that the builder had been as good as his word and their villa was finished. Cecilia set about buying furniture and within a week they were able to move in. They named the villa 'La Boccherini' after the composer of a popular minuet. Two French servants and a chef were engaged and quite soon they were settled enough to begin entertaining, giving little parties, sometimes with music.

By this time Dolly was already halfway to becoming an acknowledged beauty. At five foot eight, with her shapely figure and large clear blue eyes, her thick fair hair now fashionably dressed by her mother's maid, Cecilia could not fail to notice she was a show-stopper wherever she went; all that was lacking, she thought ruefully, was the slightest hint of animation. Still, with the encouragement of Miss Herbert she was at least learning to be polite in society. 'All yr bad manners were kept for home', Cecilia confided to her diary. 'At this time you were never very nice to me – I won't complain, I suppose all mothers go through a bad time – and I did.'

On 18 January Dolly celebrated her 18th birthday. The day was fast approaching when she would have to make her entry into Society. Cecilia knew how much Dolly was dreading what lay ahead, and recalling the agonies of shyness she herself had suffered, she felt nothing but pity for her daughter. Yet it had to be done. For in the quarter century that had elapsed since she herself had 'come out', nothing had changed. Girls of their class, brought up with little education, in the confines of their homes, still needed to find husbands if they were to have any life at all. In that respect Dolly was no different from the rest. If only she could learn to relax!

Chapter XVI

'I Hate all the Men I Meet'

In April 1883 the Widdringtons closed up La Boccherini and headed back to England. Gerard was packed off to The Dene and, as Newton was still under dust covers, Ida and Bertram were sent as paying guests to Miss Herbert's home, a rambling old Devonshire Rectory.*

Dolly's first London Season was a disaster, as her mother's account of it makes plain. Within the rarefied milieu of the landed class time seemed to have stood still in the 25 years that had elapsed since Cecilia's own debut. The same queen was on the throne, albeit without her consort. Now the diminutive First Lady, 22 years a widow and still in her widow's weeds, spread an aura of gloom through the royal palaces, making her 'drawing rooms' occasions to be dreaded rather than to be enjoyed. Orders of precedence were still inflexibly in place and while ladies' fashions may have altered (the unwieldy crinoline having given place to the curiously unflattering bustle) the dress code for both sexes was still rigid – and woe betide anyone who stepped out of line.†

Cecilia's first duty was to see that her daughter was kitted out with suitable clothes. And now it was impossible to fathom Dolly. For the girl who loathed to be noticed, who cringed when anyone attempted to flatter her, had all of a sudden become 'terribly keen on all being very perfect'. Trailing her daughter round dressmakers, tailors and milliners, it now seemed that only the best would satisfy Dolly and Cecilia found she

---

* In later years Ida wrote the following account of Constance Herbert's family:

> Mr Herbert, a converted Jew, was a very clever and remarkable man, and Mrs Herbert was one of the most wonderful women I have ever known. She brought up a family of 11, on a small stipend, with practically no help, and at the same time ran a little school, doing most of the teaching herself. She was never put out, nothing ruffled or upset her, she always had time for everything, especially being kind to everyone she met, whether child or adult. She always had a smile on her face and found everything in the world was lovely and everybody charming and good.'

Two of the Herbert's grown-up daughters, Doris and Flo, kept a girls school in Tynemouth. Ida 'begged hard' to be sent there. 'But it was not allowed in those days for girls of my class to go to school.'

† The great Lord Rosebery was said never to have got over his mortification after turning up for a dinner at Windsor Castle in a dinner jacket, when all the other men were wearing white tie and tails.

was spending far more than she had bargained for. Which might have been money well spent on a daughter who meant to enjoy herself, but was wasted on Dolly, who had no such intention. 'O but it was dry work young lady!' her mother recalled, exasperated by Dolly's refusal to play her part.

Most mornings she would go riding with her father in Hyde Park, wearing her fetching new riding habit. But Fitz had to admit that there was no pleasure in taking her about, since she was such a disagreeable companion, with never a word to say (let alone a smile) for her poor long-suffering father.

Still, he and Cecilia were both determined that Dolly must see the Season out. Resolute in their belief that marriage was the only viable option for a girl of their class, they seemed blind to the very real distress they were inflicting on their daughter. Yet was there in fact no other way?

By this time Constance Herbert had established herself as an influence for good in the Widdrington family. Dolly and Ida had both become very fond of her, the former admitting that the governess's presence was a check that prevented her from saying disagreeable things. She was aware that two of Miss Herbert's sisters had taken up nursing and had thought long and hard about this. Could nursing provide the escape route she was looking for? Everyone knew of Florence Nightingale (a young woman of similar background) who had found the courage to take up nursing – breaking the accustomed mould and forging her own destiny. Why should she not do the same? She asked Miss Herbert to find out whether it would be possible for her to train as a nurse. 'I feel pretty sure I shall never marry,' she confessed to the governess. 'I hate all the men I meet and the thought of living at home for ever as Miss Widdrington makes me so wretched I could scream.' It is not known whether Miss Herbert took any action on Dolly's behalf, but for whatever reason Dolly's suggestion appears to have been dropped.

Meanwhile the Season dragged relentlessly on. In those days, when the gossip columnists of the London daily newspapers took a keen interest in the current crop of debutantes, Dolly's parents were gratified to learn that their daughter had been picked as one of the Season's reigning beauties. Following the publicity a famous artist came forward with an offer to paint Dolly's portrait 'and made a very bad one of you in a bonnet', Cecilia recalled. Invitations to all the most coveted balls began to pour in. With her mind see-sawing between pride and despair Cecilia noted in her *Dorothy Diary:*

> You were very handsome, tall, fine figure, whitest of skins with a faint pale pink in yr cheeks wch never deepened with dancing, nor you never got hot nor panted, none could tire you – you could dance through the longest valse ... but you were as cold as ice and almost repellent to men in yr manners, never seeming to care for one of them save as things to dance with – but they admired you and I think were piqued for they came back and hovered about but got less than nothing for their pains.

'Oh dear, I do wish the time was come to leave this horrid London. I do long to go back to Newton so.' Dolly wrote to a friend.[1]

Even her friend Dr Creighton seemed to have taken her parents' side over the matter of her London Season. In response to her complaint that she was being taken to London against her will the cleric had replied:

> I want you to think about your parents and their views. What are your parents to do? They want to do for you all that they can … Are they wrong in that, even if you do not care about it? I do not think so. No parent likes to believe that their children in after life may say or think 'you kept me in ignorance: you kept me shut up: you did not show me the world … Your parents wish you to see the world and to see what you think of it.[2]

Well – if that was the world, she did not think very much of it.

But even the most trying times must eventually have an end and after three exhausting months the Season ground to a halt in mid-July. Yet for Dolly the torments were by no means over. To bridge the gap before the grouse-shooting season opened on the 'glorious twelfth' of August, it was customary for the *haut monde* to engage in a round of country house visiting. With Dolly in tow, the Widdringtons trailed round friends and relations in the Shires, finally coming to rest at Hopwood Hall, where Dolly was quizzed mercilessly by her grandmother.

Then at last she thought it must be over, with the family all gathered up and assembled at Newton for the long summer holiday. Nineteen months had passed since Dolly had last seen her home. Surely, now, she would be permitted to relax – freed from being constantly on parade and under the eye of her mother? Alone at last, she sought out that quiet corner of the garden where in former days she had fed her wild birds, wondering if they would still remember her. Of course they did not. There were different birds there now. Nothing stayed the same, she reflected sorrowfully. She herself had changed. She was no longer the young girl who had fed the rabbits and paddled about in the pond in old frocks and gone with her siblings to play in the hay. She was 'out' now, a young lady.

Then to her dismay she found that her mother had been arranging tennis parties; and that despite Newton 'not being properly set up' there was to be another round of balls, for which her parents were planning to get up house parties and give dinners. Conscious that all this effort was being expended for her benefit, Dolly continued to resist it. Still desperately shy, she resented having to put on a mask and play the charming young girl. For what was the point of parading herself before all these men if she did not intend to marry? Physical affection repelled her and the horrifying intimacy marriage implied was impossible even to contemplate. Besides, marriage meant having to bear children and Dolly knew in her bones that motherhood was not for her.

Out of tune with her parents' world, rebellious and discouraged and desperately seeking to find some purpose around which to build her life, Dolly was anxious to see her friend and mentor, the Rev. Dr Creighton. The two had corresponded regularly during the long months of her exile, when she had often sought the older man's advice, pouring out her heart over her shortcomings: her failure to be 'true to herself' and her recurring difficulties with her parents.

Creighton had a deal of sympathy for Dolly, believing (quite correctly) that her parents did not understand her. Failing to recognise the unusually perceptive and thoughtful young woman hiding behind the supercilious mask, he saw that they were set on forcing her into a mould for which she was entirely unfitted. His wife, Louise, a gifted and well-educated woman of the upper middle class who in addition to bearing him six children wrote popular and highly lucrative history books, was his model for what women could do and be. By birth and by persuasion Creighton was a Liberal. He knew there were many 'worlds', and that the one being offered to Dolly was never going to satisfy her. In one of his letters he wrote:

> What you do, what you make of your experience, that is left to yourself. Everyone has to judge for themselves … One has to learn that one's soul is one's own, that one's life is in one's own hands. Don't do like other people if that won't satisfy you. Be true to yourself. I would not say that to everybody: but you have a self which is precious. I wish that more people knew as well as I do what a precious self it is. I know it and I love it dearly. Believe me that I follow you always with the deepest possible interest and with many prayers.[3]

This was heady stuff to be read by a young and impressionable girl. When asked in later years how Creighton had helped her, Dolly replied: 'He made me believe that I mattered.' And at another time: 'He helped me to believe in myself. He talked to me like an equal about real things. He taught me to think.'[4]

Though Cecilia had not asked to see Creighton's letters she was becoming uneasy over the correspondence. Never a lover of parsons, she felt that Creighton's interest in her daughter was overstepping the bounds of propriety and she had resolved that she and Fitz should moderate their hitherto friendly relations with the Creightons when they returned to Newton. Thus to Dolly's disappointment she saw very little of her friend during the months she spent at home, though they continued to correspond.

Though Bertram's health was much improved his parents were advised that he was not yet strong enough to withstand a Northumbrian winter. Consequently, once Gerard had been sent back to school Cecilia returned to Hyères, taking Ida and Bertram with her. Dolly stayed on at Newton with her father where the pressure on her was unrelenting. Balls were being held all over the county which Dolly was obliged to attend, escorted by her father. Always beautifully turned out, she exasperated Fitz by continuing to play the ice maiden.

Her spirits picked up with the start of the hunting season, for she enjoyed the thrill of riding to hounds. With her good seat and striking looks she was not long in collecting a string of admirers, one of whom was the 21-year-old baronet Edward Grey, who had succeeded to the title the previous year on the death of his grandfather. But when he attempted to engage her in conversation he got short shrift from Dolly, who fearing that she was expected to flirt, stared him haughtily out of countenance.

The family were reunited for Christmas at La Boccherini and 'on the whole this year closed more happily than it began', Cecilia recorded – no doubt with some measure of relief. Dolly had been given the best and sunniest room 'and left it rather tidier than the year before', her mother reported. With the exception of Gerard they stayed on at the villa until the following spring. Visitors came and went. There was plenty of tennis and reading aloud to fill in the dark evenings. Dolly was persuaded to persevere with her French and was even learning a little Italian. She 'stuck well to it', and was noticeably 'more kind and gracious' to her siblings. To her profound relief she learned that her parents had decided they could not afford the expense of giving her a second Season. The first had proved more costly than they had anticipated, and short of money (and in no hurry to return home) they had resolved to spend the summer on the Continent, taking Bertram and the girls (with Miss Herbert in attendance) on a tour of Northern Italy and Switzerland.

Just like her mother, Ida turned out to be an enthusiastic traveller, never seeming to tire or mind the heat or the constant flurry of packing and unpacking. Boarding the train at Hyères, she was sent into raptures as they followed the breathtaking route along the French and then the Italian Riviera, thrilled by the beauty and the novelty of all they saw. In contrast Dolly was inclined to droop. The heat did not suit her and though in Venice she was gratified to have her halting Italian understood, she had no particular wish to trail round museums and churches, each and all displaying some grisly representation of Christ's agony on the Cross, which she found distasteful.

The fact was that foreign travel did not suit Dolly. She had no eye for art, nor any taste for the dramatic, and by the time they got to Zermatt in the Swiss Alps she had begun to feel unwell. She became pale and listless, responding when spoken to with monosyllabic grunts, in the old, familiar, maddenly irritating way. She was putting a blight on the rest of the party and her parents decided she had best return to England with Miss Herbert, which she did. She was never to venture onto the shores of continental Europe again.

That autumn the Duke and Duchess of Northumberland held a great ball at Alnwick Castle. The Widdrington parents, home by then, got a house party together and gave a dinner, and it was at Alnwick that Dolly was first formally introduced to Sir Edward Grey. The young scion of a distinguished Liberal family, who seemed likely to go into politics and make a name for himself, was considered a 'catch' and Cecilia looked on with interest as he asked Dolly for a dance. 'But you rather criticised him', she noted, adding with a touch of regret: 'I thought he looked rather nice.'

To add to her chagrin she noticed that Dolly seemed to have plenty of time for the Rev. Dr Creighton, who was also attending the ball with his wife, Louise. Urbane, witty, and oozing benevolence, he cut a very fine figure in the ballroom, with his slim build, his high domed forehead, his twinkly smiling eyes and that splendid bushy beard beautifully combed. Cecilia was furious when she saw her daughter disappearing with the parson – no doubt in search of some secluded corner where they could talk unheard and unobserved. Afterwards she picked up her pen to give free rein to her feelings:

> There is a terrible intimacy between you and him I don't half like – he is distinctly rude to me and takes every opportunity of talking to you – alone – these Priests! He writes to you and has for months – every month – wch letters you never show me but I distinctly – and so does everyone – notice a change for the worse in your rude and rough manner to us for some time after you have got one – especially he seems to inspire a contempt for Father – wch grows rather than decreases – so much so that he never addresses you if he can help it in public – not liking people to notice your rough reply – this is very sad – of course I considered it my mother's duty to get hold of one or two of Creighton's letters and although their tone was of fulsome flattery and not such as any gentleman would have written to a girl – yet I saw there was nothing worse – at present. Still, I would have stopped them with any girl but you – having such perfect trust in your rectitude – but even so I don't think they ought to go on long – there is no knowing when other feelings creep in on one side or the other and I shall watch and see – you are very handsome – and he by no means elderly – I will forgive him his insolence against the parents and the disagreeable manner and the remarks he makes because I think you get some good from him – and certainly much pleasure – but O how it intensifies my mistrust of priests!

Aware that Dolly's intimacy with the priest was getting her talked about, Cecilia and Fitz bottled up their feelings sufficiently to pay the Creightons a visit – 'more for the sake of countenancing them abt a nasty scandal anent him – than for any pleasure'. Though she gives no details of the rumours that were circulating Cecilia evidently thought they were unjust and for the sake of their daughter's reputation she and Fitz made a show of supporting the troublesome priest.

What with one thing and another that autumn and winter were not a happy time. Dolly hunted a few times with her father, 'but it is always a pill to him to take you – never a pleasant word – only sour looks if not done your way'. Her moods cast a gloom over the whole household.

In December she and her parents were invited to stay at Fallodon – where Edward Grey seemed rather inclined to be nice to her. But Dolly was in a dark mood, full of criticism, and did not seem in the least inclined to be nice to him. 'I feel fearful for your future if you make no friends', Cecilia wrote forlornly in the *Dorothy Diary* as she brought it up to date at the end of 1884. Yet, however unpromising the outlook, the mother in her must always continue to hope. As a postscript she added: 'we shall see'.

CHAPTER XVII

'The Supreme Good Effect of Love'

Cecilia's contention that Dolly made no friends was true only in the sense that her daughter tended to turn up her nose at the young women she encountered at balls: those frivolous, single-minded butterflies with their perpetual air of astonishment at the brilliance of any young man who condescended to lead them onto the dance floor; their fixed belief that they themselves were valueless until they had been claimed by some man.

But in the autumn of 1884 Dolly was introduced to a young woman a few years older than herself with whom she felt immediately at ease. Her name was Ella Pease. She was the daughter of a prosperous Newcastle business man, and her parents, who were Quakers, lived at Alnmouth and were friends of the Creightons. The Widdringtons had met them at Embleton Vicarage and, though the two families tended to move in different circles, they found they had many interests in common and had become friends.

One day, a year or two before Dolly was 'out', Ella had been brought over to Newton by her parents. It was her first dinner party and she was painfully shy. After dinner she saw a beautiful young girl enter the drawing-room. She sat quietly in a corner, saying nothing. 'From her own corner in the drawing-room room Miss Pease had gazed across at her, too shy to get up and cross the room to her, and they had never spoken.'[1] But in 1884 the two met again and they soon became friends. Ella, bookish and direct, seemed to be entirely lacking in what Dolly considered to be the false, worldly values of the young women she was in the habit of meeting. She was instinctively drawn to Ella's Quaker ethic of plain living and plain speaking. Now at last she had found someone with whom she could share her private thoughts and aspirations. She confessed to Ella that she hated her life and that when she was younger she had thought about becoming a nurse. 'Why not do it?' Ella said. With her friend's encouragement the idea began to glow like a lamp inside her head, or a light at the end of a long, very dark tunnel.

During the winter of 1884-5 Ella was often invited to stay at Newton. Yet when Dolly asked if she could stay with the Peases for a day or two, her request was refused: the rules of etiquette decreed that she might not stay anywhere without a chaperone.

Occasionally the two friends would go hunting together, Dolly mounted on her new horse, Qui Vive, a present from her father. Ella's recollections of Dolly at that time testify to the fact that away from her parents Dolly was just as capable of enjoying herself as any other healthy, energetic young woman.

One particular memory stayed with Ella. She had set out from Alnmouth with some friends to go hunting with Dolly, but the ground, which had been soft by the sea, grew hard as they approached Newton and the roads became sheets of ice. 'At Newton they found Dorothy skating, and she insisted that they should join her. She fastened skates onto their riding boots and pinned up their riding habits and they skated till it was dark.'[2] Dolly had a passion for skating and when Ella came to stay the two friends 'would begin directly after breakfast and go on absolutely happy till it was dark, never pausing to sit down or come in for a meal'.[3]

Yet those days of self-forgetfulness – the 'absolutely happy' times when Dolly was able to lose herself in challenging physical exercise – were to be few in number. For with the coming of spring Fitz and Cecilia looked towards London, steadfast in their belief that they would be failing in their duty as parents if they did not bestir themselves to give Dolly that second Season which she had missed.

For what was a woman without marriage? The unmarried daughter living at home was a miserable creature. Everything was denied her – she might as well be dead. 'I believe you have as much energy as I have', Cecilia addressed Dolly in the *Diary*. 'And no field for it – no girl can have really with an active mother – they must always feel secondary and not really needed – for this reason I feel sure you would be happier married.'

After the economies of the previous summer Fitz reckoned he was in funds. So turning a deaf ear to Dolly's vehement protests, on 7 May she was dragged off to London, to a house her parents had taken in fashionable Mayfair. And from 6 Lower Berkeley Street the battle commenced, as they 'engaged in the eternal round of balls, dinners, plays' and so forth. Dolly, however, was refusing to cooperate. She was determined to 'like nothing very much' and after six fruitless weeks of partying her parents were ready to admit that

> it would not be necessary to wear ourselves out with another season for your pleasure – you merely went through the treadmill but never cared … you never came near liking anyone – or even approving and not disliking – I began to feel rather in despair – we had done our very best for you – with seasons, lovely dresses, nothing spared – that you might not feel out of things – hunters so that you were a capital rider – lessons so that you were a first rate dancer – a taste of all frivolities - nothing left out and serious things as much as you would take in.

It was all very disheartening.

But among the 'serious things' offered to Dolly had been a visit to the Visitors' Gallery in the House of Commons. And here their efforts had met with a modicum of success. Fitz, like most of his class, was a staunch supporter of the Tory Party, and it is possible that an element of cussedness may have provoked Dolly into taking the Liberal side. Alternatively she may have been persuaded by listening to Dr Creighton, a firm upholder of Liberalism. Or to give Dolly her due, she may have worked the matter out for herself. She had always taken an interest in politics, and a sense of the injustice of an electoral system which denied a vote to the majority of the population may well have drawn her into the Liberal fold.

In any event, in the early days of June of that year William Gladstone's third Liberal Government had found itself in trouble, and Parliament had been dissolved. As a consequence the young baronet Edward Grey, who for the previous six months had been employed as unpaid private secretary to an official in the Treasury, now found himself without a job and, having time on his hands, began to attend some of the summer balls.

Cecilia's watchful eye was not slow to take in the fact that Edward always 'went to balls where we were', and he began to show a marked tendency to gravitate towards her daughter. 'I soon began to see he had set his heart on you – but I couldn't the least tell what you felt except you had plenty to say to each other.' This was true. To her mother's astonished relief Dolly seemed to have thrown off her haughty manner and to be behaving for once like a normal girl who was enjoying herself. As the month of June advanced it became a regular habit for Sir Edward to make up one of their party for lunches and dinners; and when they made a trip to the British Museum he was all the while beside Dolly, and joined with her in laughing disrespectfully at the poor dead mummies!

Cecilia was holding her breath.

> Finally July 8th we all went to a ball at the New Club and Ed Grey asked you to be his wife and told me at supper he had done so and that you had said yes – my heart gave a great throb of relief and surprise too – I never expected it – anyway so soon as that you would give an answer at once – but I feel entirely satisfied about your fate – it is the very life I would have chosen for you if I could – one of activity and intellect and usefulness, with plenty of society but not of the frivolous sort.'

If Cecilia was overwhelmed by the rapidity with which Dolly had made up her mind to accept Edward Grey's proposal, so too was her daughter. 'Poor child you cried all the way home and all night too I believe – I think you feel somehow broken down out of your cold reserve and that you are surprised to find you care.' Yet there was to be no hesitation, no turning back. 'She had now got what she called "one clear and luminous fact" in her life. She could take refuge from herself in another.'[4] Edward spoke to Fitz the next day and it was settled. 'Then he dined with us and gave you a frank kiss before us all at parting – I liked him for that.'

Dolly replied to the many letters of congratulation that flooded in with a touching mix of wonder and humility. From Lower Berkeley Street she wrote to her friend Ella Pease:

> You know I can't help feeling that everyone must be quite as surprised as I am myself, and that they must think just as I do, that he is much too young to marry and ought to have 'done better'. However people are so wonderfully nice to me that I am quite dazed by it ... One thing I feel strongly is that my capabilities of friendship have been somehow increased hugely and I think of you with still greater pleasure than I have ever done before.

Once the news of the engagement was out there was nothing to keep the Widdringtons in London and they packed up and left. Accompanied by Edward they went first to Hopwood Hall to introduce their prize to Cecilia's masterful old mother.

Meanwhile a General Election had been called and to Edward's surprise and gratification the 23-year-old learned he had been adopted by the newly-created division of Berwick-on-Tweed to stand as their Liberal candidate. Voting being due to take place early in November, there was no time to lose if he was going to make himself known to his constituents, and he hurried home.

Back at Newton it was learned that Bertram had carried mumps home from school and, not wishing Ida or the bride-to-be to become infected, it was decided that their father should take both girls for a spell to Leasowes Castle, the Cust's family home, where Fitz's former ward, young Sir Charles, had finally taken up residence.

The castle (a higgledy-piggledy pile of eccentric build, having had bits and pieces tagged on at various times with no thought given to achieving a pleasing whole) lay just behind the dunes near Birkenhead. While it was a nightmare of a house to own (as Sir Charles was soon to discover), with the quaint arrangement of its rooms and its long sandy beach it seemed quite cut off from the everyday world and was a perfect place for the young to forget themselves in. From Leasowes Dolly wrote a long letter to Constance Herbert which gave convincing evidence of her new and hopeful state of mind:

> I am lost in gratitude and happiness which it is ridiculous even to try and write down or speak about, and yet I am awfully depressed at times when I think what a life of tremendous possibilities mine will be. I don't feel anything in me likely to turn into what I feel I require, but I suppose something always comes of trying to do one's best, and I am so changed for the better, even in this short time I think I must respond to the developing influences I am sure to meet with ... I reflect I shall probably never be here as a girl again, and I make the best of it and tear about the sands with an apology for a frock and no shoes and stockings on, and we spend most of our time on the roof, where we transport rugs, dogs, cushions, books, rats and doves and have foolish conversations and many obscure jokes. Occasionally I forget where I am and get dreaming and then they call me a lop-eared donkey and throw things at me.

Quite gone was the disaffected young woman who formerly had to be coaxed into being agreeable. For Dolly knew with no shadow of doubt that by some miracle she had found her heart's companion. She had been born anew. With Edward's love, every aspect of her life had changed.

With Bertram still quarantined, Fitz next took his girls to Blairgowrie in Perthshire, where Grandma Hopwood had got up a house-party for the fishing. And it was there, amid the wild Highland hills and splashing streams that suited Dolly so well, that she sat down to write a long-overdue letter to her friend and mentor Dr Creighton:

> Corryfourly, Bridge of Cally, Blairgowrie, 30 August 1885.
>
> Dear Mr Creighton
>
> You must think I am going to follow the advice you so kindly gave me, and drop your acquaintance suddenly and for always. This is not likely to come to pass, however, only each time I have tried to write to you I felt there was such a huge amount of feeling in me that I should have liked to talk to you about, and gave it up in despair. But after all, why should I

hope to be able to show you any more of myself, when I am convinced you know more than I do? It is comfortable to feel that the greatest in oneself has never been expressed and yet is understood by a true friend. I find out every day more what a much greater thing this love is than I had ever pictured it. I think I had always despised it a little in the bottom of my heart, and thought that it must be blinding and lowering to some parts of one's nature; instead of this I feel sure now there is not one little scrap of good in me, or one cranny of character, that has not got its capabilities of good increased a thousand fold. I am sorry to have to say though that I have not yet risen above vagueness and I believe no more now than I did before in my power of influencing for good. Edward assures me to the contrary, but how can it be called influence when every thought and feeling I have originates in him? It seems to me that men have the power of taking back to themselves the good or evil that they have created in women. I don't believe we have much control over ourselves one way or the other, but the direction of our lives entirely depends on whether the man we are forced to love is good or bad. I feel wildly rebellious sometimes at the thought of my lost freedom. I had got to think latterly that I could make a life for myself and direct it well, and took such pleasure in the thought of being a nurse as I shall never take in anything again. Now I shall have to combat with my happiness if I am to do any good in the world, instead of being driven to do good as a means of getting it: the motive power, however, has been increased in proportion to the difficulty, which is the supreme good effect of love that I had never suspected.

Your loving Dorothy.

It is a remarkable letter to have been written by a 20-year-old, who had received little in the way of formal education, but who had learned through times of great personal unhappiness to know herself.

Dolly would never overcome her habit of often morbid introspection. Yet now her nature had been flooded by the healing power of love, and she felt she had been transformed. Formerly she had believed that love between the sexes was mere passion, which (to her fastidious mind) lowered mankind to the level of the beasts. That side of love had never been discussed between herself and Edward and she sensed that, like her, he felt unsure about it. It was an aspect of marriage from which both had shied away.

True to her generation she believed that a man must always be master in his own house; even though, for a woman, it meant the loss of her personal freedom. The gain was that through Edward she had learned that what she believed to be a better – a purer – kind of love was possible between a man and a woman – a spiritual force which could be a powerhouse for good. Dolly clung to that.

Chapter XVIII

Edward Grey

In a fragment of autobiography which Edward Grey dictated in the last year of his life he began: 'I was born on 25 April 1862 in London, and I have always felt that my six brothers and sisters had the advantage of me in that they were all not only brought up but born at Fallodon.'

In common with Dorothy, Edward had a profound sense of place and throughout his life his roots remained firmly bedded in the Northumbrian soil; the place where he grew up and where he died. G.M. Trevelyan, his first biographer and a fellow Northumbrian, gave this account of Edward's home:

> Fallodon has no rare and peculiar beauty. It is merely a piece of unspoilt English countryside – wood, field and running stream. But there is a tang of the North about it. The west wind blows through it straight off the neighbouring moors, and the sea is visible from the garden, through a much-loved gap in the trees. The whole region gains dignity from the great presence of the Cheviots and the Ocean. Eastward, beyond two miles of level fields across which he so often strode, lie the tufted dunes, the reefs of tide-washed rock and the bays of hard sand; on that lonely shore he would lie, by the hour, watching the oyster-catchers, turnstones and dunlin, or the woodcock immigrants landing tired from their voyage.[1]

Built in Cromwellian times by a Puritan merchant and much altered since, Fallodon Hall was a medium-sized country house, the climbing shrubs covering its walls up to the first-floor windows giving the place a homely feel. Its walled garden was famous in the locality for the quality and variety of its fruit. The Fallodon estate of around eight hundred acres provided the Greys, who had lived there since 1755, with a pleasant way of life and a reasonable income.

As soldiers and later as politicians, the Greys were a distinguished family. The first Earl had had been ennobled by George III after fighting with distinction in the American War of Independence. His eldest son, another George, entering politics on the Whig side, eventually became Prime Minister. He was the great Earl Grey of the Reform Bill (also giving his name to a famous brand of tea). His heir moved from Fallodon to a more imposing house at Howick, close by. It was Edward's great-grandfather, descended from a younger branch of the family and created a baronet for his services to the Crown, who inherited Fallodon. George, Edward's grandfather, had a distinguished career in politics, being appointed Home Secretary in the Whig Government of 1846. A fervent Evangelical, he served on the committees of the Church Missionary Society and the British and Foreign Bible Society for many years.

This second Sir George and his wife Anna Sophia had been blessed with only one child. Naturally they had high expectations of young Georgy, trusting that he would follow the family tradition and make a name for himself in politics. However, Georgy – a lively, handsome and thoroughly engaging youngster – did not care much for his school books, having set his heart from an early age on becoming a soldier. At first his father refused to give his consent, believing peacetime soldiering to be an idle profession, leading only to vice and debauchery. But when the Crimean War broke out, giving the military a chance to serve their country, he felt honour-bound to change his mind, even though it meant risking the life of his only child. So Georgy joined the Rifle Brigade, serving in the Crimea and later in India, where he saw service during the Indian Mutiny.

Upon returning to England on home duties in the Midlands Georgy fell in love with an attractive young woman called Harriet Pearson. She came from the lower gentry and was not notably bright or possessed of any special talents. She was, however, a placid good-natured girl who seems to have entirely suited Georgy. They married, Georgy gave up his commission and they moved to London, where in 1862 Harriet bore him a son, whom they named Edward.

9 *Sir Edward Grey.*

At that point old Sir George proposed that his son should come home and take over the management of the Home Farm. There was plenty of room for them at Fallodon Hall, if Georgy's wife was agreeable to sharing the house with her in-laws. Harriet, not having much choice in the matter, indicated that she was.

'My mother was one of the gentlest of human beings,' Edward recalled. 'This made it possible for the arrangement for a joint home between my grandparents and parents to work smoothly, and my early recollections are of an uneventful and exceedingly happy home. What we know first in childhood we imagine to be typical and the usual way of the world, and I was brought up assuming that the world was a happy place, in which no grown-up people did anything which was wrong.'[2]

In rapid succession Harriet gave birth to six more children, three boys and three girls; while her husband, in his happy-go-lucky way, went hunting, shooting and fishing; and when time could be spared from these pleasant pursuits, oversaw the management of the Home Farm.

When he was nine Edward was sent away to a preparatory school, where he did well, his parents receiving excellent reports. But when he had just turned 12, tragedy struck. His father had been appointed to be an equerry, on a part-time basis, to the young Prince of Wales, who was thought to be running wild. It was hoped by his tutors that Georgy's equable nature, grounded as it was in a solidly Christian home, might serve to rein in the wayward Prince without alienating him. In 1874, however, while carrying out his duties at Sandringham, Georgy became seriously ill with what was diagnosed as 'septic pneumonia'. Edward and his mother were hastily summoned to his bedside, but he died that same night.

This calamity profoundly shocked the 12-year-old boy. In an instant his happy childhood had been terminated. 'My mother was in deep grief, and I stunned with that sense of catastrophe which in a child produced continual outbursts of tears,' he recalled. Yet as his father's eldest son he made a heroic effort to conquer his own grief. Years later one of his sisters wrote:

> After father's death Edward looked on himself as my mother's chief protector. I well remember ... his collecting us younger children together and telling us that she was to be our first consideration, that we must be very quiet and thoughtful and do everything we possibly could to help her and be a comfort to her. He was very stern with us. His thoughtfulness and consideration for my mother were remarkable in so young a boy, and he took his position and responsibility as head of the family very seriously.[3]

Perhaps too seriously. The death of his father and his mother's evident helplessness had forced Edward, prematurely, to play the man. Meanwhile the duties of his fun-loving father (always ready for a romp and happy to join in his children's games) passed to his grandfather. From that time everything changed. In later life Edward had nothing but praise for old Sir George, who with his wife responded heroically to the challenge of bringing up seven young children and attending to the well-being of their mother. However, as a role model for an already over-conscientious boy, this kindly and pious man was far from ideal.

Edward was sent to Winchester College, where he became known among his fellows as a loner. Much admired for his sharp intelligence and brilliance at ball games, he made no close friends. 'He seemed rather solitary,' a contemporary recalled. 'He went his own way and thought his own thoughts'.[4]

It was during his schooldays at Winchester that Edward developed a passion for fly fishing. Lord Northbrook, a kinsman of his who lived nearby, owned the fishing rights on a reach of the River Itchen, which was famous for its brown trout. He permitted Edward to fish there, and whenever occasion offered the boy would abandon his studies and take up his rod. Like many adolescents he was intensely introspective and the chuckling flow of the water through the rich meadowlands (the sound only broken by birdsong) perfectly suited his mood. His school holidays were spent at Fallodon where, surrounded by his siblings, he had little contact with young people of his own age.

In 1880 Edward went up to Balliol College, Oxford, and it was during his long summer vacation that he first came under the influence of the vicar of Embleton, Dr Mandell Creighton. Old Sir George suspected (quite correctly) that his grandson had not been applying himself to his studies with due diligence. Fearing that Edward was in danger of failing his first year's examinations (known as 'Mods') he had asked Creighton to give the boy some coaching. The parson agreed. He already had some pupils staying at the vicarage, and for two months Edward joined them. The young man was impressed by Creighton's wide scholarship and worked hard to please him. He passed his exams, happy to know that in the older man he had found a true friend.

For his part Creighton had been greatly impressed by his pupil, sensing that Edward had the potential to achieve great things – though the direction he would take was as yet unclear. As a fan of the young man, it is likely that Creighton decided to try his hand at a little matchmaking, because it was after his repeated references to the 'uncommonness and character of Dorothy Widdrington' that Edward, 'stirred by what I heard of her' made his first (unsuccessful) approach to Dorothy on the hunting field.

During his second year at Oxford a spirit of rebellion took hold of Edward. 'The time passed pleasantly, but as far as work was concerned, quite unprofitably', he recalled. He excelled at 'real' tennis,* playing for Oxford against Cambridge, and went trout-fishing, and took long rambles in the Oxfordshire countryside, passing his evenings in carousing with his fellow undergraduates. In that all-male society the high jinks Edward and his friends got up to were comparatively mild. Yet it was as if he had a premonition that he was enjoying his one and only taste of freedom. He knew his grandfather was failing; and during Edward's last year at Oxford old Sir George died.

Now the head of his family and a baronet, Edward, who had just passed his 21st birthday, knew he was in grave danger of failing his final exams. After a sticky interview with Benjamin Jowett, the Master of Balliol, he was 'rusticated' (sent home for a term) with a clear directive from the great man to start working.† Back at Fallodon in disgrace, Edward bestirred himself sufficiently to scrape by with a third-class degree in Jurisprudence. However, it was during his banishment that he made a purchase which was to have a major impact on his future life. He bought his first five pairs of waterfowl.

Most of us can dream of lives we never lived, paths we never explored. Edward, always a keen naturalist, was to pass his happiest hours in quiet observation of the natural world and its creatures: Wordsworth's 'types and symbols of eternity'. Freedom to stand and stare was always to mean more to him than any prize that worldly ambition could afford him. If his father had lived – if Edward had not been destined to pass his most formative years under the influence of his grandfather, with its emphasis on duty and public service – he might have been content to lead the pleasant life of a Northumbrian country gentleman. As things turned out, returning home after a somewhat ignominious departure from Oxford with no clear idea of what he should do next, he sought the advice of his former tutor.

The vicar of Embleton (who had never made any secret of his rather advanced Liberal views) was in no doubt over the path Edward should follow. Politics, he assured Edward,

---

* The precursor of lawn tennis; real tennis is played with racquets in a covered court.

† The record in the Balliol minute-book, signed by Jowett, reads: 'Sir Edward Grey, having been repeatedly admonished for idleness, and having shown himself entirely ignorant of the work set him in vacation as a condition of residence, was sent down, but allowed to come up to pass his examination in June.[5]

was in the young man's blood. Was not the life of a Liberal politician, with all the opportunities it offered for doing good in the world, the obvious route to take? Only half-convinced, Edward was persuaded to give politics a try. On Creighton's advice he wrote to his kinsman Lord Northbrook, at that time a member of Gladstone's Cabinet, asking to be given some 'serious and unpaid employment'.[6] Northbrook obliged by finding him a temporary position as secretary to the chairman of a conference convened to discuss Egyptian affairs.

That July the House of Lords rejected a government bill which aimed to extend the county franchise. Their Lordships' rejection caused uproar throughout the country and Edward was asked to chair a meeting of protest to be held in Alnwick. Still only 22, he had never made a speech in his life. But encouraged by Creighton he agreed, on condition that his mentor would look over his speech before he delivered it. Drawing on his experience in the pulpit, Creighton replied with the following letter, which Edward preserved:

> Dear Edward,
>
> I am very glad that you are coming on Saturday. It is quite the right thing to do. Use every opportunity that may offer itself of making yourself a political personage with a direct line ... I should say that a speech of a quarter of an hour was about the right thing. If you aim at a quarter of an hour you will perhaps hit twenty minutes which will do very well. It does not much matter what you say; you are sure to say what is right and proper ... Have before you some point which you are going to lead up to and with which you are going to finish, and have the strength of mind to sit down when you have reached it, and have fired the shot which you meant to be your last. There is a great temptation not to have an ending definitely prepared. This leads to a speaker to wander about aimlessly at last, and repeat himself and flounder about and do away with the effect of the first part of his speech. He is like a bore who has come to see you, and does not know how or when to say 'good bye' ... Remember it is better people should say 'I am sorry it is over' rather than 'I am glad that it is over'.[7]

It was the best piece of advice that Edward ever had. Taking heed of it he composed his speech, rehearsing it before his mentor on the day of the meeting. Though it may have received a few tweaks from the parson, in substance it was his own. The two then set off for Alnwick in the dog-cart. When Edward got up to speak he was greeted by loud cheers and his speech was rapturously received. Hearing of it, Lord Northbrook asked the Chancellor of the Exchequer to take the young man on as an unpaid assistant private secretary. The Chancellor obliged. Edward was on his way. During the following months he was to make a second political speech and to address several local meetings.

In a private journal he kept at that time he recorded his political progress. In January 1885 he wrote:

> When I came to Fallodon last June I looked forward to idleness till February. Instead of that I have had much political experience ... Official life has given me business habits and I have got some idea of the wheels of the political machine and how they work. Before June I had never opened my lips in public or private in a speech. Last June I had hardly formed one political idea: now ideas have formed and are forming daily. Then I knew no Political

> Economy: now I have even got glimmerings of original ideas on it … I have enjoyed a good deal of sport but it has become a recreation, and the consuming interest I felt in it is now employed in carving my way into Politics, Social Problems, moral philosophy and culture. Oh! If I could progress every year by such strides as this!

Bursting with excitement at the way his life was shaping, Edward began to see himself in the guise of the budding politician. However, if he meant to take that path – following in the footsteps of his grandfather and his great grandfather – it would mean he would have to endure living in the smoke and grime of London for at least half of every year. The consummate countryman, could he ever become reconciled to such a life as that? He did not know. He would have to wait and see. In the meantime politics could be regarded merely as an experiment. Six months later Edward was to become engaged to a young woman who loathed city life with every fibre of her being.

Chapter XIX

Marriage

When Edward Grey learned that he had been selected as Liberal candidate for the new division of Berwick-upon-Tweed, he knew he would have a tough fight on his hands. His Tory opponent was Earl Percy, heir to the Duke of Northumberland. As the sitting Member for the old division of North Northumberland, which he had held for 15 years unopposed, Percy felt confident of hanging on to his seat. His father, the Duke, the largest landowner in Northumberland (at that time being in possession of some 150,000 acres) regarded the constituency as his personal fiefdom. When the news broke that the Earl was to be opposed by young Grey, who was rumoured to support the Radical wing of his Party, it was greeted by the Percy faction with a mixture of amusement and derision. The 'Pinafore Baronet' was the sobriquet they applied to him, in virtue of his youth, anticipating an easy victory.

However, Edward went into the campaign determined to give his opponents a fight. As summer mellowed into autumn and the evenings began to close in, he was to be found night after night taking out the pony trap and heading off to some obscure village hall, more often than not accompanied by his fiancée. Jumping nimbly onto the platform – the lamplight playing on his boyishly handsome face and strikingly tall figure – he would help Dolly up to take her place at his side. The sight of the young girl, fearlessly confronting a crowd made up exclusively of men, many still in their working clothes, astonished his audience and set them stamping and cheering. Without doubt the beautiful Miss Widdrington was proving to be an asset in Edward's campaign, though whether by drawing eyes she could draw votes had yet to be seen. What was evident was Edward's success in addressing his audience's needs, for the men listened intently as he spoke up for radical improvements in their lives, which must include an extension of the franchise to give the rural working class the same voting rights as were presently enjoyed by working men in the towns.

Dolly's and Edward's wedding had been planned to take place early in December 1885, giving the young couple time to draw breath once the furore of the election had died down. But Dolly's repeated visits to Fallodon were beginning to set tongues wagging, and old Lady Grey was not the only one who was 'getting rather scandalised at her being seen there so often without a chaperone'.

Aware of the wagging tongues Cecilia thought it would be politic to have the date of the wedding brought forward. She knew that Edward's mother, Mrs Grey, had been house-hunting – for it was settled that she and her family were to move out of Fallodon before Edward brought home his bride. When she learned that Mrs Grey had found a house she considered suitable, Cecilia hesitated no longer and, speaking to Edward privately, she let him know what was on her mind. Edward, she reported, 'caught at it eagerly', which left only Dolly to be persuaded. At that point Cecilia made it her business to have 'a very amicable talk abt many things' with her daughter 'and you came to see I was right in having it so soon – wch first you naturally started at'.

Whether the facts and duties of the marital bedchamber were spelled out to Dolly during this 'amicable talk' we have no means of knowing. Yet given Cecilia's dislike of beating about the bush we may be sure she would have made time to deal plainly with this delicate subject.

It is unlikely that Cecilia had got much satisfaction from the physical side of her own marriage; though to be fair she would not have expected it. Sexual arousal in men was seen as part of nature's plan, to which

10   *Dorothy Grey.*

wives were expected – if not to respond – then at least to submit. A wife's acquiescence was required for the procreation of children and for many women that was the end of it. Physical passion had little part to play. In view of Dolly's aloofness and the prickly nature of her relationship with her mother we may guess that this dangerous topic would have been bypassed, so as to avoid embarrassing them both.

After discussing with his agent the question of bringing his wedding day forward, Edward fixed on 20 October as being the most convenient date. In the weeks that were left there were many pressing matters that would compete for Cecilia's attention: for a start there was the trousseau.

Cecilia could have been forgiven if she had quailed at the thought of having to 'set to and do clothes' with her fault-finding elder daughter. But there was a sweetness in Dolly at that time which was new and endearing and augured well for the future, and mercifully she had chosen to cooperate.

'It may interest future generations if I tell some details', Cecilia wrote in the *Dorothy Diary* which she had resolved to wind up after giving an account of the wedding. Grandma Hopwood had given Dolly a diamond necklace valued at £150 as well as several other pieces. Her wedding gown was of 'cream satin and brocade with silver and gold old design on it'. Morning outfits included 'a fawn jacket with muff and toque all trimmed with fine beaver fur', a 'nice sealskin mantle and muff' and a 'light tailor-made suit of linen'. For evening there were two white India muslin gowns, another of black lace and other gowns besides, and a 'white plush opera mantle'. 'Not a large trousseau', Cecilia commented, 'but good and very useful – I let you choose your own way everything – a habit you already had.'

Excluding the items of jewellery the cost of Dolly's trousseau came to just over £400 – which represents £16,000 in today's money. In an age when a housemaid might earn £15 a year if she was lucky, and a fully trained butler be had for £50, this appears wildly extravagant, although to Cecilia it would have seemed a reasonably modest outlay.

On the day of the wedding 'poor Newton was never so crammed'. The 54 guests for whom room had to be found in the house included Mrs Grey and her six younger children, Grandma Hopwood, Cecilia's brother Edward and his wife, Fitz's sister Eliza (now 'Auntie de Tabley') and a Mr Beaumont, the best man. 'All went off famously', Cecilia recorded. 'It was a lovely Autumn day, green and red and gold the trees and bright sun – you looked your best and were very calm – only on the way to church when we had a little affectionate talk you cried a little.'

Seventy guests sat down to the wedding breakfast which was held in the Newton dining-room. The huge wedding cake was much admired. When the happy pair drove off in the brougham (Dolly having been persuaded with some difficulty not to ride away on her horse), poor little Bertram broke down terribly and his mother 'had quite a piece of work' to comfort him. 'And so dear child ends your life in your old home', Cecilia concluded the *Dorothy Diary*:

> I wish it had been pleasanter and brighter but one cannot fight against nature and yours is one to make a grand wife and clever woman of society and but a discontented daughter – I did my best – but my nature is too energetic to have gone with yours – still you will come I know to look back with pleasure on the days you spent here, if with somewhat of regret … Here follows your photos and newspaper cuttings and I shall not have much more to write of your future which is now out of my keeping and in your own.

The marriage of Dorothy Widdrington and Sir Edward Grey would have been widely reported in the society pages of the national as well as the local newspapers, but the cuttings which Cecilia must have kept are missing from the *Diary*. On the blank pages which remained she pasted a studio portrait of Dolly and twin photos of the happy pair which must have been taken at the time of their engagement. Edward, dressed informally in a striped blazer worn over a wing-collared shirt, has his arms crossed and his hair smoothed down and wears a vestige of a self-conscious smile. Dolly is shown in profile, her head thrown back, unsmiling, but looking sweet and vulnerable.

On the following page there was a photograph of the wedding cake, captioned: 'Wedding cake made by Riddell of Alnwick given by Grandma – weighed 200lbs – the wonder of the town – 100's came to see it – I decorated it myself with lace and feathers.'

Chapter XX

An Election

> It was known that their marriage was what in France is called *un mariage blanc* ... It gave rise to an impression, perhaps natural under the circumstances, that Grey was not what in the Middle Ages was called 'a full man'. This, however, was not the case. It was, nevertheless, true, that when they returned from their honeymoon Dorothy Grey told her husband she had discovered in herself a strong aversion to the physical side of marriage. As a result of this admission Grey said that henceforth they should live as brother and sister.
>
> Mrs Belloc Lowndes, A Passing World

It had been settled that following his marriage Edward would be granted a fortnight's leave from his election campaign, in order to give him and his bride time for a short honeymoon. It seemed too brief a spell for the leisurely trip to the Continent that was the fashion, and after talking things over the couple decided to pass the time quietly at Fallodon.

It had not been a wise decision. The house which Edward's mother had believed might suit her had subsequently been found wanting and the sale had fallen through. Consequently Mrs Grey, together with Edward's younger siblings, were still installed at Fallodon. Honeymooners need privacy – a time to explore their new relationship away from prying eyes. But with his family all around him and his grandmother, old Lady Grey, still ruling the roost, there was precious little privacy to be had. All meals were still taken *en famille* and although the library (which had been Sir George's favourite room and looked out upon the garden) had been set aside for their exclusive use, this was in fact the couple's only private space apart from their bedroom.

For any young man to have to embark on matrimony under the prying eyes of his relations must be an inhibiting experience to say the least. In Edward's case the situation could hardly have been worse. During his courtship it is doubtful that he had ever ventured further with his bride-to-be than to give her a chaste kiss. Like Dorothy (as we shall now call her) he was almost certainly a virgin. And now, when custom demanded that he should consummate the marriage, Edward seemed almost perversely to have set himself up for failure.

He might have fared better if his wife had given him the least sign of encouragement. But Dorothy was like a shy bird, forever eluding him – and there was no one to whom he could turn for advice. If only his genial and easy-going father had still been alive! Seldom had a young man stood in greater need of a counsellor. Yet no suitable candidate was to be had.

What Edward did not know (and what Dorothy could not at first pluck up courage to admit to him) was that her fastidious nature shrank from the carnality of an act which to her mind lowered men and women to the level of the beasts. It was a side of marriage she had pushed to the back of her mind. Perhaps if the act could have been performed without fear of pregnancy she might have reconciled herself to it. But though she loved her husband to the utmost core of her being, she had a profound horror of childbirth. She had never wanted children of her own and other people's offspring filled her with unease. She wished her relationship with Edward to be exclusive and to remain pure. In other words for it to continue just as it was.

Some seven years earlier the radical atheist Charles Bradlaugh and his co-author the feminist activist Annie Besant had been arrested and charged with obscenity after publishing a sixpenny pamphlet advocating various methods of contraception. Among others, Bradlaugh had appealed to the eminent biologist Charles Darwin to testify in their defence. He received short shrift from the great man, who had replied:

> I have not seen the book in question but for notices in the newspapers. I suppose that it refers to means to prevent conception. If so I should be forced to express in court a very decided opinion in opposition to you and Mrs Besant ... I believe that any such practices would in time lead to unsound women & would destroy chastity, on which the family bond depends; and the weakening of this bond would be the greatest of all possible evils to mankind.

The author of *On the Origin of Species* – himself a father of 10 – was quite fixed in his belief that 'if it were universally known that the birth of children could be prevented, and this was not thought thoroughly immoral by married persons, there would be a great danger of extreme profligacy amongst unmarried women.'[1]

Darwin (who in common with most men of his time believed in the innate superiority of his own sex) was giving voice to an almost universally held opinion. Birth control in marriage was never an option for respectable women, for whom the only certain method of preventing the arrival of children was sexual abstinence. Was this too much to ask of Edward?

In the early days of their regard, when each had been putting out feelers to test the mind of the other, Edward and Dorothy had discovered a mutual admiration for the poems of William Wordsworth. His mystical love of nature – his passion for untamed landscapes and for the 'bliss of solitude' – seemed perfectly to mirror their own feelings, while his lines:

> One impulse from a vernal wood
> May teach you more of man,
> Of moral evil and of good
> Than all the sages can.

might have been written specially for them.

Wordsworth's close companion during his most productive years had been his sister Dorothy. She was the poet's muse. And did not the two Dorothys have much in common? Dorothy Grey was persuaded that they did. Like herself, Dorothy Wordsworth had a strong affection for birds and had made studies of their ways, possessing the patience to sit perfectly still for an hour or more observing the habits of one particular bird, or some other small creature. Both women shared a lack of personal vanity and both preferred to be out of doors rather than in, and were physically hardy. Finally, Dorothy Wordsworth had a deep and steadfast love for one man, which was returned in kind. William was always her dearest friend, her mind perfectly attuned to his. Brother and sister lived in a state of harmony – of completeness – which to Dorothy Grey's thinking was the most perfect relationship possible between a man and a woman. Was there any good reason why she and Edward should not live in the same way?

When eventually she plucked up courage to share her thoughts with her husband, confessing to Edward that the intimate side of their marriage distressed her and that in any case she did not want children, it is possible that Edward may have reacted with relief. Sexually uninformed, his fumbled attempts at love-making (carried on in the bosom of his family) very likely upset him as much as they did Dorothy. Very young and very much in love and painfully ignorant as he was, Dorothy's suggestion that they should live as brother and sister may not have struck him as unreasonable. Nor would her confession that she shrank from motherhood. Children, she pointed out, were selfish and demanding. Would not their intrusion spell the end of a flawless relationship? In his innocence, Edward must have been inclined to go along with his wife; and thus the matter was settled between them.

With the threat to their happiness satisfactorily disposed of, the newly-weds threw themselves into the final hectic weeks of Edward's election campaign, buoyed up by a mixture of youthful spirits and passionate conviction. In a letter to Constance Herbert (who had become and was to remain one of her closest friends) Dorothy graphically conveys the heady mix of excitement and young love which she felt at that time.

> Fallodon, 3 Nov. 1885
>
> I have been a long time writing to you but I knew you would not be angry ... I have quite settled down here now and everything gets nicer and nicer every day, which I suppose can't last, though our happiness does seem to be established on a pretty firm footing. I had more excitement last night than I thought I was capable of feeling. Edward had a meeting at Crookham, quite a small place for which he had made up a speech in preparation and we went by train to Cornhill and dined at a little inn there ... We started in a brougham for Crookham. When we were about half a mile from it we were met by about a thousand people, all roaring and screaming, and part of them with torches, and they took out the horses and pulled us up to the chapel where Edward was to speak. The row was fearful when we got out, and still worse when we got inside. Cheers for Lady Grey and the young Bart kept up for ever so long and I was presented with a bouquet.
>
> They were very pleased with the speech, which Edward had to make more of than he expected and when it was over we were again dragged to a man's house where we had tea and after that we thought it was all over; but no, the horses were not allowed to be put

in and those wretched people dragged us two whole miles on our way to Belford. It was very exciting and nice of them, but there had been a misunderstanding about our horses following us, and we waited about twenty minutes in the road, with the crowd's enthusiasm cooling down, and feeling very uncertain whether we were ever going to get home at all … We got off at last and enjoyed the drive very much, and the one from Belford to Fallodon still more, as it was a perfect night and we were in the dog-cart with a fast horse (and each other) … My face feels quite stiff today with smiling so much and my mouth is certainly several times larger …

Your loving Dorothy.[2]

Edward won the seat for the Liberals, at 23 the youngest member of the House of Commons, and helped to bring to an end an epoch in which the great landlords had exercised almost unlimited power over their countrymen.

For the next 31 years he was to be returned to Parliament by his North Berwickshire constituents – hanging on to his seat against all the odds (and frequently against his own inclination) during the long years when Liberalism was out of fashion, and finally returning to the Front Bench as Britain's Foreign Secretary.

In the words of his first biographer, G.M. Trevelyan: 'He had won the lasting affection of a strong-hearted folk, not easily dragooned, slow indeed to accept new friends, but once they gave their confidence, not quick to change.'

When the battle was won, Edward Grey and his Tory opponent Lord Percy went off fishing together 'to recover from their exertions.'[3] The House of Commons was a more gentlemanly institution in those days.

Chapter 21

17 Hereford Square

> I have got settled down at last in this little house which we both like very much. It is very clean and new, and belongs to an old bachelor who knows how to make himself cosy. I have a little conservatory with ferns, an aviary half of which is full of our bachelor's foreign birds, and the other part occupied by a pair of whistlers* which are very amusing, though they are still rather wild.
>
> Letter from Dorothy to Ella Pease, 6 Feb. 1886

Before Edward took up his duties at Westminster he and Dorothy needed to find somewhere to live. After looking at a few places they settled on a house in South Kensington: 17 Hereford Square. They moved in at the end of January 1886 and while Edward was at the House Dorothy made a start on the novel occupation of housekeeping.

Hereford Square was not the most convenient address for a Member of Parliament, involving Edward in a stiffish walk down to the Chelsea Embankment and a further two-mile hike along the Embankment itself. However, for a man of Edward's exceptional fitness it was a pleasant walk on a fine day and, if wet, he could always summon a cab. When the House was in session he tended to keep unusual hours, leaving home at four in the afternoon, and frequently not returning until two or three the next morning. Dorothy adapted to this curious routine without complaint. 'I find the most convenient plan of living is to sit up till he comes and then breakfast very late next morning, have no lunch and then a good tea before he goes away again', she wrote to Ella Pease. 'My life is a funny mixture just now, I spend a deal of time in the shops buying candles and the like and then come home and hear all about Parliament and its intricacies.'[1]

It was indeed a complete break from her former life and in the early days the novelty of finding herself a married woman in command of her own establishment kept her from missing her beloved Northumberland. But marriage had not altered her habit of introspection – as she had confessed to Dr Creighton all those years ago, Dorothy was still striving to perfect herself – to be *good*.

---

* Ducks, probably goldeneyes, which make a whistling sound in flight.

11   *Dorothy Grey, c.1887.*

She noticed that other women of her class, having time on their hands, tended to involve themselves in 'good works', and following their example she joined the Charity Organisation Committee and the British Women's Temperance Society, and attended some of their meetings. She quickly discovered, however, that she was not a 'committee person'. The well-meaning women set on preaching sobriety to their less fortunate sisters bored her with their rather patronising do-goodery and she soon dropped out. Yet from her privileged position in society her conscience still nagged her. As a young girl she used sometimes to accompany her mother on charitable visits to sick parishioners. But the smells and the stark poverty of their homes had left her so fraught that Cecilia had been obliged to stop taking her. Recalling her younger self Dorothy felt ashamed and, encouraged by a friend, she attempted to become involved with a working-girls' club in the East End. Sometimes she would visit the girls during their dinner hour, taking them flowers. 'She looked beautiful standing among the rough hard-working girls,'[2] the friend recalled. Yet her gift of flowers was entirely inappropriate. By no stretch of the imagination could she identify with a working girl's needs and aspirations. She was too stiff and shy to play the lady bountiful with any hope of success and like the committees the visits were soon given up. For all her good intentions, Dorothy lacked the common touch.

Like her mother a generation earlier she decided to embark on a course of serious reading, determined to make up for the wasted years of her youth so that Edward need not feel ashamed of her. During the long evenings when Edward was kept at the House she battled with Schopenhauer, a German philosopher much in vogue at that time, who possessed a darkly pessimistic world view. 'This philosophy is a world in itself, certainly, and does not seem to me to have many points of contact with the ordinary world,' she wrote to her old friend Dr Creighton, with whom she had never lost touch. 'But I find it a great help in keeping one's inner life fresh', she added bravely, 'and preventing oneself being crushed by the material part of life.'[3]

Going about with Edward she began, tentatively, to make one or two friends, though on the whole she was content with her own company, when she could not have his. For marriage had completely transformed her. Within a few short months the edgy discontented girl had metamorphosed into a young woman who hardly dared to believe in the unfathomable depths of her own happiness.

Yet in essence she had not changed. No power on earth would ever succeed in changing the shy, country-loving Dorothy into the London sophisticate bent on furthering her husband's political career – the type of young woman (it was whispered among the dowagers) whom Edward would have been wiser to have married.

In those days London was deserted from Friday till Monday by most of the *bon monde*, heading (if they were lucky) for one of England's great country houses such as Petworth House in Sussex or Mentmore in Buckinghamshire, where ambitious hostesses vied with each other in attracting the most influential and fashionable guests. It was well known that much of the business of government was conducted at these Friday to Monday*

---

* 'Weekend' was a word never used in upper-class circles, for it implied that the user was a wage-slave tied to a Monday-to-Friday job.

house-parties, where difficult decisions could be thrashed out over a glass of port and friendships were made or lost.

Edward (who, rumour already had it, was heading for great things) received frequent invitations to these gatherings, to which it was assumed that Dorothy would accompany him. But she was at her worst when faced with a room full of people she did not know. Stiff with shyness she would clam up, taking cover under a mask of supercilious disdain. She loathed the brittleness of what passed for 'Society' and after struggling through two or three of these hateful assemblages she resolved to go on strike. Determined to remain 'true to herself' she refused to accompany Edward to any more house parties, confessing to her husband that 'there are so few people I would rather have with me than away'. And since Edward at that period of his life was no great socialite and was in any case very much in love, he was happy to exchange the country house circuit for a couple of days fishing with Dorothy sitting contentedly at his side, or to make a quick dash up to Fallodon on the North-Eastern railway line, where he was planning the construction of a second lake, to contain his expanding collection of waterfowl.

For truth to tell, Edward was not yet fully committed to the life of a politician, which he still regarded as an 'experiment'. He was always looking over his shoulder, wondering whether he had made the right choice when he decided to enter the House of Commons. And yet perhaps it did not matter, for by the spring of 1886 all the signs indicated that his career as a Member of Parliament was destined to be brief. The fact was that Edward had joined the once great Liberal party at a time when many feared it could not survive. For it was split down the middle and the cause of the split was Ireland. William Gladstone, the ageing Prime Minister, now in his third term of office, who had struggled with the 'Irish Question' over half a lifetime, had finally come out firmly on the side of Home Rule. The iniquity of the present system of government – in which all decisions affecting the Irish population were taken in London by a small Protestant minority, while the Catholic majority had no say in how they were governed – was patently unfair. Indeed, Gladstone had come to believe that it was immoral. He had proposed that the Irish people should be granted their own parliament, while still retaining their rights and obligations as part of the United Kingdom. The Tory Party was violently opposed to this proposal and within Gladstone's own ranks opposition was fierce, with the 'Liberal Unionists', as they styled themselves, maintaining that Gladstone's proposal was mere pie-in-the-sky and could never be made to work. While Edward had some doubts of his own about the way Gladstone was leading his party (deliberately setting Liberal against Liberal) he had come out on the side of the Grand Old Man, since he firmly believed that 'coercion was not, under modern conditions, possible as a permanent system of government'.

However, it was beginning to seem that he 'had identified himself with Liberalism at a time when the party seemed on the verge of disintegration.'[4] Commenting on the battle that was raging within the Party, Dorothy wrote to a friend:

> It's very interesting being mixed up in it all, but rather disappointing too, I must say. The Irish bother is so fearfully unsatisfactory, people taking up Home Rule not because they think it will do any good, but because they can't see anything much better to do. Everyone prodding his neighbour to speak out and then dropping on him when he does so. It is really

a most unpropitious time to have gone into Parliament. People seem to me to think a split inevitable, and of course an immense deal depends on how, when and where the split with one's party is made.[5]

The anticipated split was not long in coming. A mere six months after Edward had been elected, his Party was once more obliged to go to the country. And this time he was not opposed by the Percy faction, but by a member of his own Party, the Liberal Unionist and a fellow Northumbrian landowner, the Hon. F.W. Lambton. What was worse, his distinguished cousin, the 84-year-old Earl Grey of Howick, had also come out firmly on the Unionist side. But Edward stuck to his guns and to his own surprise (and that of almost everyone else) he succeeded in hanging onto his seat. In the face of a massive swing to the Tories his remarkable popularity among his stout-hearted fellow Northumbrians had won him the day. He and Dorothy scarcely knew whether to be pleased or sorry.

The disarray within their Party had not only cost the Liberals the election; it had condemned them to spend the next six years on the Opposition benches. Half a century later, when a fellow Liberal, David Lloyd George, came to write his memoirs, he castigated Edward for his lack of commitment to his party during his years in the political wilderness. Fishing meant more to him than politics, the Member for Caernarvon (no friend to the aristocratic Member for Berwick-on-Tweed) scoffed witheringly. Lloyd George had no time for a man who, by his reckoning, was content to be a fair weather politician – willing to do his duty when his Party was in power, but leaving it to others to keep the Liberal flame alight in the dark days of Opposition. Though his words may have been unduly harsh there was more than a grain of truth in what Lloyd George said. Edward had no taste for tramping round provincial town halls firing off speeches, when the alternative offered by simple country pursuits was so much more enticing.

But Edward did not entirely ignore his commitments as a Member of Parliament, for it was during this fallow period on the Opposition benches that 'the great political alliances of his life were founded in personal friendship'.[6] He had begun to associate with a group of like-minded Members a little older than himself who, while sharing Gladstone's belief in the need for Irish independence, recognised 'that all other Liberal reforms could not be postponed until Home Rule had been realised.'[7] Among this group were two brilliant and successful barristers, Herbert Asquith, a man of 35 who had made his way at the Bar without the benefit of any private income, and Richard Haldane, a 28-year-old Scot, who in addition to his considerable earnings as a barrister was in possession of a small country estate at Cloan in Perthshire. Also included in this group were Arthur Acland and Sydney Buxton. Edward, still only 24, found Buxton and Haldane particularly agreeable and they became close personal friends, dining regularly with the Greys. Dorothy was always more at ease in a small intimate gathering and, having decided opinions of her own, was not afraid of airing them, happy to take part in the men's heated discussions over policy and strategies for the future. 'Her downright question "Why?", wrote Sydney Buxton, remembering the Dorothy of that time, 'often startled and almost terrified a careless talker, but was in truth to those who knew her the best proof of her keen attention and interest.'[8] Richard Haldane became her special favourite – he was a bit of a loner like Dorothy herself and socially inept, his decidedly porky presence and mumbled utterances sometimes causing mirth, and he had been disappointed in love – while Francis Buxton's wife Mary was in time to become one of Dorothy's closest friends.

In 1886, uncharacteristically, Dorothy developed an urge to travel. Edward had never been abroad in his life. An indifferent linguist, the attractions of his native land seemed quite good enough for him. Dorothy thought differently. She wrote to a friend: 'My object at present is to get Edward to like travelling and I thought a three months' trip to India would be the best way of achieving it, but now find finances positively forbid.'[9] However, a year later her plan was carried out and they took ship for India, where they were lavishly entertained. It appeared that everyone, from the Viceroy to the local governors and maharajahs, was eager to provide hospitality for the handsome young couple. 'Dorothy's beauty, so uncommon in its stateliness, in its expression of radiant health and strength, was a match for the good looks of her husband; it took people's breath away when they entered a room side by side.'[10]

In the end, however – for all India's breathtaking and exotic beauty – Edward and Dorothy came to the conclusion that it was not for them. From Agra Dorothy wrote to her friend Ella Pease:

> This is the most wonderful place for buildings we have yet been in, and the culmination of all white marble is the Taj Mahal. Every time one sees it again it takes one's breath away more and it becomes more necessary to touch it to make sure it is real; it is purity itself and the perfection of carving and inlay work, but it is quite impossible to say where its beauty lies. The beauty is not good beauty though, and like all these splendid buildings, it might be the work of gods, men or devils and one doesn't quite know which.[11]

She and Edward did not anticipate visiting India again. Or if they changed their minds they promised themselves that their visit would be altogether different: 'Living about in tents in the jungle quite independent of everybody'.[12] As things turned out, a second visit was never to take place. For not very long afterwards Edward and Dorothy discovered the perfect holiday retreat. And it was much closer to home.

Chapter XXII

The 'Tin House'

In spring and early summer, whenever occasion allowed, Edward would take up his cousin Lord Northbrook's open invitation to fish on his waters on the Itchen, the Hampshire river where he had spent so many happy hours as a schoolboy. It was a celebrated chalk stream famous for its brown trout, its limpid waters with their many tributaries meandering through water-meadows. In the early days of their marriage, on Friday afternoons Edward and Dorothy would take the stopping train from Waterloo to Itchen Abbas, a small village near Winchester, putting up for the weekend at the *Plough* inn, a simple hostelry in the village. Saturdays, weather permitting, would find Edward fishing from dawn to dusk, with Dorothy reading beside him, or else wandering off, eyes and ears alert to the unfolding wonders of meadow and riverside as spring advanced into summer. A lover of birds since childhood, when she had her own special place in the garden at Newton for feeding them and observing their ways, those peaceful hours gave Dorothy an ideal opportunity for honing her skills to the point when she felt confident of being able to recognise each bird as its notes broke the otherwise blissful silence. On Sundays, obedient to custom, Edward would put away his rod and, taking a packed lunch he and Dorothy would set off on one of the strenuous country walks which both of them so much enjoyed.

Lord Northbrook (a politician to his finger-tips and a former Governor-General of India) had been a fan of Edward's ever since the young man had sought his help in finding an opening in politics. And seeing the bother his cousin was put to in transporting his tackle back and forth from London, he offered him a small piece of land close to the river, suggesting that Edward might like to build a hut there in which to store his equipment. Edward jumped at the offer. But by the time it was completed in 1890 the 'shed' had turned out to be rather more commodious than a place for storing fishing tackle. Consulting with a local builder, Edward had decided he wanted 'a place in which to get food, sleep and shelter' when he was not fishing. The building that emerged was a sturdy if somewhat primitively constructed cottage. Standing on brick foundations, it was built of wood, its interior divided into four rooms. Its pitched roof – with its single brick chimney stack – and outer walls were clad in corrugated iron sheeting. A glass-panelled door led onto a strip of grass. And that was that. It could hardly have been more simple.

The 'tin house' (as Dorothy was wont to describe it) won the couple's hearts from the first. Their own creation, it was to become their refuge, perfectly fulfilling their need to escape the 'mean and vulgar works of man' for the healing peace of the countryside. Before long, from March until the end of June they were spending most weekends at the cottage. They tried to leave London on Friday afternoon, but if Edward was delayed by work he would let Dorothy go first and follow on the late-night express. Arriving at Winchester around midnight he frequently chose to walk the five miles to the cottage. Long afterwards, recalling those peaceful walks, he wrote:

> Escape from London meant that hurry, noise and bustle had been left behind. I had entered unto leisure, where saving time was no object ... There was a foot-path way on each side of the river. By one of these one entered the cottage without, except for the momentary crossing of one road and of three secluded lanes, having had touch or sight of a road. There were thirty-three stiles on this path. There was much charm in this midnight walk. Traffic had ceased, cottage lights had been put out, the inmates all at rest or asleep. Now and then one heard in passing the song of a nightingale or a sedgewarbler; but in the main there was silence.
>
> It was pleasant after the hardness of London streets and pavements to feel the soft dust under my feet. On a still summer night there were sweet and delicate scents in the air, breathed forth from leaves and herbs and grass, and from the earth itself. It was as if one's own very being was soothed and in some way refined by the stillness, the gentleness and the sweetness of it all.[1]

The days Edward and Dorothy spent at the cottage were undoubtedly some of the happiest of their lives.

In time they would fix trellises against the tin walls which soon became covered in climbers – roses, honeysuckle, clematis, Virginia creeper and ivy – providing nesting sites for robins and tits and other small birds. A flower garden was begun. And a few years later a small worked-out chalk pit was incorporated into their curtilage. Scrambling up its crumbling face with the agility of goats they would insert plants into its crevasses and persuade them to grow and go nest-hunting among the brambles.

Among the small number of friends admitted into this sanctuary was the naturalist W.H. Hudson, who gave an account of a visit he made in 1900, in his book *Hampshire Days:*

> They had told me about their cottage, which serves them all the best purposes of a lodge in the vast wilderness ... it is pretty well hidden by trees and has the reed and sedge and grass green valley and swift river before it, and behind and on each side green fields and old untrimmed hedges with a few oak trees growing both in the hedgerows and the fields. There is also an ancient avenue of lime trees which leads nowhere and whose origin is forgotten. The ground under the trees is over-grown with long grass and nettles and burdock; nobody comes or goes by it, it is only used by the cattle ... that graze in the fields and stand in the shade of the limes on a very hot day. Nor is there any way or path to the cottage, but one must go or come over the green fields, wet or dry ... And no dog nor cat, nor chick, nor child – only the wild birds to keep one company ... they were all about it and built their nests amid the green masses ... which covered the trellis walls with their luxuriant growth.

Back in 1865 the first two-wheeled riding machine had been invented. Known as the velocipede or 'boneshaker' its metal tyres made for an extremely uncomfortable ride and it had never become widely popular. Later experiments in two-wheeled locomotion produced the 'penny farthing', its seat carried atop a high back wheel. Though its solid rubber tyres made for an easier ride, a fall from a penny farthing was not to be taken lightly and as its cost was an average worker's six months pay, it did not achieve wide popularity outside the moneyed classes. The invention in the early 1890s of the pneumatic tyre by an Irish veterinary surgeon named Dunlop, together with improved methods of locomotion by the use of gears – and last but not least, the bicycle becoming progressively more affordable as manufacturing methods improved – the two-wheeler became a practical investment even for the working man and his wife and throughout the length and breadth of Britain everyone clamoured to ride the bicycle.

Some went so far as to assert that the bicycle had done more for the emancipation of women than anything else in the world, and Dorothy tended to agree. For the bicycling craze put paid to the bustle and the corset, instituting 'common sense dressing' for women and increasing their mobility considerably. She and Edward were early converts to this new method of locomotion and after buying bikes for their own use at Fallodon, Dorothy insisted on bicycles being purchased for all the Fallodon staff, believing that the benefits they brought ought to be shared. It was not long before bicycles were despatched from London for use at the cottage. They were to bring many previously inaccessible places within reach, greatly increasing the scope of Edward and Dorothy's Sunday expeditions.

Dorothy had always been fond of reading aloud, a habit she had acquired from her mother. When the weather turned wet the ample supply of books stored at the cottage kept the Greys entertained. The poems of William Wordsworth took pride of place and favourite passages from *The Prelude* would be learned by heart. Like the poet, Edward and Dorothy 'saw God through nature'.[2] Neither possessed any consistent scheme of philosophy or religion. Edward 'fed his spirit on the pantheism … of the early Wordsworth, with a strong Christian tinge … but dogma, whether orthodox or agnostic, was repellent to his intellect and to his character.'[3] Dorothy felt much the same 'but had a touch of greater hostility to the orthodox, particularly to the Church of England because she had been brought up in it, whereas to Grey, old association was no reason for disliking anything.'[4]

In 1894 the couple began to keep a diary which became known as 'The Cottage Book'. Leaving it open on the table in the sitting-room, they used the book to record their impressions of the changing seasons; noting the state of the weather, the first greening of the beeches, the budding of the first rose, as well as the progress of each pair of nesting birds, their triumphs and frequent disasters. Though Edward proved himself the better stylist and was the more frequent contributor, Dorothy's entries retain a freshness and immediacy that is immensely appealing. They show her to have been an ornithologist of a high order and Edward was always quick to acknowledge his wife's superiority in the knowledge of birds and their lore. 'I hardly dare to write anything about birds', he confessed in a May 1902 entry. 'I am so overshadowed by D.' And in another place he testified that 'D.'s exploits overshadow everything else.'

After his wife's sudden and premature death Edward had a few copies made of 'The Cottage Book' for private circulation among their friends. In the 1990s Michael Waterhouse, an admirer of Grey and like him a keen fly fisher and ornithologist, succeeded in tracking down a rare copy and was able to get it reprinted. *The Cottage Book – the Undiscovered Country Diary of an Edwardian Statesman* was published by Victor Gollancz in 1999, edited and with an introduction by Michael Waterhouse.* Below are some of the Grey's entries:

2 July 1894
D. It rained a little now and then in the morning, but was warm, 76 and a south wind. The wren sang nearly all morning. We talked about it while we were at breakfast the first morning, and thought how nice it was and that we knew enough to be able to love it so much, and how many people there were who would not be ware of it, and E. said, 'Fancy if God came in and said, "did you notice my wren?" and they were obliged to say they did not know it was there.' The nest we thought was a reed warbler now has live sedge eggs in it.

20 May 1895
D. The same cold weather, 46. I lit the stove before lunch. Have not succeeded in finding a nightingale's nest and feel very low about it. I was sitting on a tree root in a wet place and watching the wagtails when a stoat put its head out of a hole about two inches off my dress, hissed and made a loud noise like a loud harsh water-hen several times and then got quiet. I saw a blackbird chase a squirrel about twenty yards along the ground and then attack it as it corkscrewed up a large oak. It hit the squirrel several times. I could not see that the squirrel had an egg in its mouth. Three cuckoos flew about me; one of them I am nearly sure had an egg in its mouth and flew down in several places in the long grass, once close to the river. It was followed and worried by six little birds. I watched a robin fight. Two cocks kept at it for a long time and at last seemed to get their feet locked together. A very young thrush evidently thought that something was being fed, as it came rushing up to them as they struggled. They went away laughing.

24 to 27 April 1896
E. We came on Friday and have made much of our time. It has been a fine warm spring, but April has been too dry and there is still no prospect of rain. Chestnut leaves are out and the flower is beginning, blackthorn fading: beeches are brown but with patches of green in them.

Limes cannot be called green at all yet, but some young oaks are in the small yellow stage … A tree in fresh new leaf is like something surprised by a great joy: it catches your eye and asks you to share it … :We went by train to Salisbury and bicycled back† getting foundered and lost in the old Roman road, but finding our way back to the Stockbridge road after much walking and many miles. It was more than I could take in – the town, the cathedral, the great country over which we came, the many places which we passed, pressing on because we were so late, and the light, which we saw looking back towards the evening sun from the tops of the hills.

* A paperback edition was published by Weidenfeld and Nicolson in 2001.
† A distance of some 30 miles.

17 May 1897

D. The wagtails have been fiddling with the old thrush's nest but don't seem serious. Up wren path* I found one chaffinch, one parter,† one sedge and six wren's nests, of which the last three were cock nests, one lined but empty, one with one egg and one with young. There were many wrens to be seen and I watched two who were climbing up trees and going along branches and taking notice of each other all the time. I felt very loving towards them and when I began to read again I did not like the book, Keats' love letters. Keats and Fanny Brawn don't compare well with wrens.

25 June 1899 (Sunday)

E. Could anyone do a more summery thing than to lie in the middle of a mass of yellow lady's slipper and listen to the bees on it? At any rate, that is what I did this afternoon. It wasn't quite perfect because the sun was not out, and the scent of lady's slipper needs the sun to bring it out. For a moment I felt like a senseless field beast for lying down in such flowers and crushing them, but my doing so was a very proper tribute to the profusion of nature. In a garden where flowers are grown by the square foot it would have been a crime, but to the north of Itchen Wood nature gives lady's slipper by the acre. So I lay in it and put my eyes level with the flowers and listened to the bees.

27 June

D. We have taken to sleeping out at last, having always meant to and never bringing it off. I wake up a nice lot and enjoy my night. When a trout jumps and splashes flat it sets all the sedge birds noising. A heron has croaked both nights, and the coots sound are very various. I got the little breeze that says 'the dawn – the dawn' and dies away. The larks are first, you wouldn't think they could see their way up in the dark; then every sedge and reed warbler makes monotonous, ugly noises, then swallow, and last thrush and then you go and sit on the bridge and notice the light. Swallows skim long before you see a swift, but these did not come out of the clouds for me. At this time of year small things drop out of the tops of the limes all night and fall through the leaves. I thought, too, I heard light bat wings in and out. Last night was E.'s first night out, and about 1 … the mattress had to be carried in from the rain, so the night was not very successful.

One point that should not be forgotten is that the 'simple life' at the cottage, so much enjoyed by Edward and Dorothy, would not have been possible without the daily ministrations of their housekeeper and cook, Mrs Susan Drover. How many times a day must that faithful servant have walked up and down through the unmown grass of the Lime Avenue – shopping, cleaning, washing, attending to the stove, keeping the place aired when her employers were absent and seeing to it that Sir Edward and Lady Grey's meals appeared regularly on the table? And yet she is practically invisible in the pages of the *Diary*, only once putting in a brief appearance.‡

---

* The Greys' name for one of their favourite walks.

† A partridge.

‡ On 17 May 1897 Dorothy wrote: 'E having gone up to London I have spoken to no one all day except "dinner at half past five please Susan".'

Chapter XXIII

'A Very Strange Little Soul'

Following her marriage, Dorothy's relations with her parents had taken a turn for the better. Perhaps her radiant happiness was catching, for it appeared to have erased the troubled past. When the Widdringtons came up to town it seemed the natural thing for them to stay with the young Greys at Hereford Square; while Christmases continued to be spent at Newton in the old way, with games played for parcels and the familiar linen sheet suspended from a picture rail for Fitz's magic lanthorn show, always followed by a party for the staff.

And yet the wind of change had begun to blow over Dorothy's old home, now that she was no longer the daughter of the house – that privileged accolade having passed to Ida. Ice and fire, prudence and impudence, retirement and shameless display – in whatever terms you chose to describe it, the character of one sister was so far removed from the character of the other that with Dorothy gone the general tone of the house was bound to have been reshaped.

For whereas Dorothy's icy demeanour tended to freeze people who did not know her well into silence, Ida had only to enter a room to create turbulence. She was like an electric current, jolting people into sitting up and paying her attention: 'In France, in Switzerland, all those years you were the sort of centre of things far more than Dolly, you opened new ideas up, made all the acquaintances, all the interest', her mother recalled. Yes, she had witnessed it all, surveying the antics of her younger daughter with a mixture of pride tempered with apprehension. For it had to be said that Ida had an unfortunate tendency to carry her enthusiasms a little bit too far.

At the time of Dorothy's marriage Ida had been 16 and still in the schoolroom. But shortly afterwards Miss Herbert left and Ida's schooldays finally ceased. 'I could see it was a great joy to you to be quite free and more than counterbalanced the solitude of it', her mother observed. She and Ida got on well. They hardly ever had a quarrel and if one occurred it was 'of the shortest duration'. In her new position as daughter of the house Ida was 'very good and bright and cheerful and quite a comfort … helping me in the village – Sunday school etc. – and knitting socks for the boys'. Her parents had bought her a new horse – Puck. He was an excellent beast, but rather excitable. Even Shotton the coachman found him difficult to handle. But Ida could make him do anything she wanted. She and her father 'got pretty regular 3 or 4 days a fortnight hunting' and on one particularly long ride Ida was 'the only lady at the finish'. Generally she led a free and happy life 'and I must say you quite appreciate it and know how well off you are,' her mother observed. (Such a contrast to Dolly at the same age!)

In the spring of 1887 Cecilia took Ida to London to be 'finished'. She had singing lessons with a Miss Bishop, who said Ida had a fine voice and showed great aptitude. She also took up the guitar. In addition there were dancing lessons, and 'you got an opera, lots of plays, tea at the House of Commons, concerts – pictures …' They visited the boys, both of whom were now at Winchester, and altogether there was 'lots of running about'. Ida 'liked it all and was very amenable and pleasant,' and on 21 May the 17-year-old was allowed to attend her first ball.

In June they returned to Newton to prepare for a garden fête due to take place on the 21st to celebrate Queen Victoria's Golden Jubilee. '300 people to tea and games and presents and medals and dance and supper and fireworks – you are always a help in such things, so cheerful and bright', Cecilia recorded. 'And you often go and take the school bank money all Friday and go among the people a bit.'*

On 12 September Ida celebrated her 18th birthday. She was giving every sign of being a credit to her parents and though her formal presentation to the Queen would not take place until the following Spring, Fitz and Cecilia agreed that she might now consider herself 'out'. But unbeknown to those two good souls, Ida had already embarked on the first of a string of disastrous love affairs.

Looking back, Cecilia concluded that it must have been at the summer ball given at Alnwick by the County Militia that Ida had first made acquaintance with Ronnie Jervis. Following the ball the Militia hosted a week of tea parties and suppers and cricket matches, all of which were attended by Ida – 'which had I known the sequel I wd have kept you from.' For the Honourable Ronnie was also present at these junketings and by the end of the week Ida's world had been turned upside-down, for she was head-over-heels in love. This was unfortunate.

Ida was a beautiful dancer and when the two continued to meet at all the autumn balls, Jervis would always single her out, whirling her round the dance floor and sitting out with her between dances. It was plain that he was much taken by her puppy-like devotion and by the way she would hang on his most banal utterances as though they came hot from the lips of the Prophet Isaiah.

But observing the pair with a keen mother's eye, it became clear to Cecilia that the young man was not in search of a wife (not, that is, unless she happened to be a woman of fortune) and that although he was happy enough to flirt and dance the night away with Ida, his heart was not engaged.

'I am not easy', she confided to the diary, fearing that her daughter was being led up the garden path. Ida was seeing far too much of Ronnie for her own good – for she had love written all over her face and was surely going to be hurt. Worse, she was in danger of making a fool of herself. 'I had to keep you from Alnwick flower show so as not to

---

* Cecilia had inaugurated savings banks in the elementary schools at Newton-on-the-Moor and Hauxley, through which the village children were encouraged to learn the value of thrift.

meet Ronnie – who so obviously doesn't care for you that its a wonder pride doesn't come to yr help.'

But Ida was past caring about pride. Her first love was to become the benchmark against which all future loves were to be measured. A younger brother of the 4th Viscount St Vincent and a distant cousin on the Hopwood side, at 28 Ronnie Jervis had little to offer a wife beside his looks and his charm. And yet Ida – her newly awakened sexuality combining with some quality she believed to be pure and sacred – was convinced that her feeling for Ronnie had been 'true love' and that any attachment which fell short of it must be judged as second rate.

'I believe it will last to a certain degree – perhaps all yr life,' Cecilia observed. Perhaps it did. Eventually Ida was forced to accept that Ronnie did not care for her as much as she cared for him 'and many a wild and windy walk you had to work it off,' her mother recalled. 'But you have to go through it and nothing can help you', she added, commiserating with her daughter in her youthful despair.

The Widdringtons took a 'large house' for Ida's first Season, which was a thundering success. 'You took singing and guitar lessons and all the gaiety I could give you', her mother reported.

> You certainly are a most awful favourite, you dance straight through yr balls, any number of partners, young and old, grave and gay delight in talking to you. You had dinner at Mrs Tennants* and evidently were the chief attraction there, we dined, we lunched, we called, we gave lots of dinners and went to abt a dozen balls – lots of plays – down to Cowes with the boys – to Eton and Winchester cricket – to Lords – Handel opera, concerts, brought various animals ending in a squirrel and thoroughly enjoyed it all.

With the Season accomplished, mother and daughter set off for Hampshire to stay with Cecilia's sister Aunt Rose, taking the squirrel with them. Rose, who was childless, had always been a petulant hostess. She objected to the squirrel and they did not stay long. Rhiwlas, the home of Cecilia's favourite sister Evie, was decidedly more fun. They found her husband Dick enthusiastically crushing ore, a seam of gold having been discovered in the mountains in nearby Dolgellau. Game for anything new, Ida joined in. 'You and Uncle Dick got chums over the gold-finding', Cecilia recorded. That was what she liked about Ida: her lust for life – small wonder she was becoming so popular.

They returned to a 'wet bad summer' at Newton, which put paid to picnics and tennis parties. The squirrel died. Moping at home, it soon became apparent that Ida's triumphant London Season had done little to banish the Honourable Ronnie from her mind. 'Poor little one, you were very sad … but I think steady absence is the only cure', her mother opined.

Hoping to distract Ida, Cecilia encouraged her to keep on with her singing and guitar-playing and Christmas saw mother and daughter 'very busy getting up a concert and plays' with the local schoolchildren, to be put on in the village hall. Then Cecilia and Ida decided to put on a double act, with a one-act play called *Past Friends*. They performed it in the drawing room at Newton 'at our Xmas party of Ordes and Greys' and were roundly applauded. Ida's flamboyance and lack of inhibition made her a natural on stage.

---

*   Wife of Edward Tennant, heir to Lord Glenconner and a close friend of Edward Grey.

'You could get yr living at it no doubt', Cecilia commented – though of course that was unthinkable as in the Victorian era no well-brought-up young lady would contemplate appearing on the professional stage.

The bad summer was followed by a blessedly mild winter, ideal for hunting. But 'the sport of kings' was notorious for encouraging impropriety between the sexes, and sure enough Ida began to be pursued – this time by an older man who was to prove a far graver threat than Ronnie Jervis. For while Ida's first love had come close to breaking her heart, Willie Lawson – 'my other bugbear', as Cecilia called him – if his attentions were not stopped, could very well succeed in ruining Ida's reputation.

Cecilia's diaries have little to say about Lawson's circumstances. He was in fact a man of substance, a Justice of the Peace whose seat at Longhurst Hall – a handsome bow-fronted mansion built by his father, with Grecian pillars and a lofty central hall surmounted by a dome – was situated about ten miles to the south-east of Newton. At 32 he had fallen out of love with his wife and was a philanderer, accustomed to getting his own way. That Christmas he had become involved in Ida's amateur dramatics and they had sung a sentimental duet together, earning considerable applause. Subsequently Cecilia was perturbed to see that Lawson had begun to hover round her daughter, laying on the charm and showering her with extravagant compliments. She was alarmed to see that her daughter was falling under the older man's spell.

And then matters started to get serious. For it was becoming plain that Lawson was genuinely in love with Ida, and whether as wife or mistress he intended to keep his hold over her. 'You aren't in love, but sort of mesmerised by him', Cecilia addressed her daughter in the pages of the diary. 'That horrid Lawson' drew Ida like a magnet, exciting her baser nature in a way that was shameful in a young girl.

Though Longhurst Hall was not visible from Newton, Ida and he had discovered that if she climbed up onto the moors, to a particular spot, and lit a fire, Lawson could see it from his house and signal to her with an answering blaze. When Cecilia found this out she realised that there was a side of Ida's nature that was ungovernable. Though she lacked the classical beauty of her older sister, her bright little eyes, the thick, unruly mop of auburn hair and her lively 'animal spirits' were designed for turning heads. Ida had always been restless – hungry for new experiences. Always the leader, she would plunge headlong into one mad escapade after another, never pausing to count the cost. Cecilia had done her best to warn Ida about the danger of arousing men's 'lower nature', but her daughter refused to take her seriously. Her sexual allure was already formidable. Could she not see that these bonfires she was lighting were shamefully provocative? If news of them got about what were people to think?

She decided that Fitz was not to be told. She did not want to alarm him. What Ida needed was the counsel of someone nearer to her in age – someone whom she admired and who possessed the moral authority to rein her in. Dolly sprang instantly to mind.

Cecilia and Fitz, who had never lost their lust for foreign travel, were planning an ambitious trip to the West Indies for the following spring, possibly extending their stay to include New York. They anticipated being away for at least six months and, not wishing Ida to miss out on her second Season, Cecilia asked Dorothy whether she would be willing to act *in loco parentis* while they were away.

As might have been expected, Dorothy was less than enthusiastic at the prospect of making herself responsible for Ida. She and Edward had created their own private world and there was no place for her sister in it; yet she could see no legitimate way of refusing. Dorothy would never be reconciled to living in London and when obliged to be in town for Edward's sake she always tried to live quietly, avoiding as many functions as she believed she could get away with. 'If you don't go, and say nothing about it, nobody ever finds out', she had persuaded herself.[1] When Parliament was in session the few hours each day she was able to spend with Edward were sacred. While he was at the House she liked to work at improving herself by serious reading, or to keep in touch with a few close friends by making calls and exchanging letters.

Her old friend and mentor Mandell Creighton had recently been made Bishop of Peterborough and the two still corresponded regularly, Dorothy's lack of belief in orthodox religion never having been allowed to stand in the way of their friendship.

'I spent the Season with Dolly and Edward and in consequence met all their friends and was well acquainted with the inside of political life … It was a great experience for me', Ida wrote 70 years later, painting that long-ago summer in rosy hues. The reality had been somewhat different.

When Ida arrived with her trunks and hat-boxes and awkward-shaped parcels of sheet music, music stand and beribboned guitar, Dorothy inwardly groaned. Their house, which was not large, seemed suddenly to have shrunk to the size of a matchbox. Although Ida had come with her own maid she never succeeded in keeping her belongings from spilling all over the house – shawls thrown over the backs of chairs, hair combs pulled out and flung down anywhere, letters, begun and left unfinished, deposited on Dorothy's little escritoire.

And then there was Ida's singing. Everyone seemed to agree that she had developed a fine contralto voice and naturally she would keep up her lessons and her daily practising she trilled happily. 'Mama has insisted!' Dorothy, who freely confessed she had no ear for music, found the sound of her sister practising her scales, accompanied by twanging chords on her guitar, exceedingly trying. The noise seemed to penetrate to every corner of the little house, making it impossible to read, or even to think.

And then there were the interminable dinners and balls, which Dorothy avoided as often as she could by rustling up substitute chaperones. But she could not escape altogether and in any case felt obliged to stay awake until she knew that Ida was safely home.

Ida was forever pestering Dorothy to pass on titbits of political gossip, convinced that the House of Commons was a hotbed of conspiracy and that her clever brother-in-law must be 'in the know'. Her prurient curiosity exasperated Dorothy. Didn't Ida realise that the first duty of a politician's wife was to be discreet? Still, occasionally she would relent and share some tittle-tattle with her sister, if only to get a little peace. One of her stories struck Ida as so comical that she kept an account of it.

Dorothy had grown quite fond of Mrs Gladstone, the ageing Liberal leader's eccentric wife, whose vagueness and failing memory were always leading her into scrapes. At a political reception at which the Gladstones were guests of honour they arrived embarrassingly late and the guests noticed that Mrs Gladstone was 'very oddly dressed – wearing the skirt of one dress and the bodice of another'. Apologising to her hostess the old lady explained that she hadn't been able to find her matching bodice. One of the ladies pointed out that it was hanging down the back of Catherine Gladstone's skirt.

'It had got caught up by what is called the check-strap – a strap with hooks inside the bodice to keep it down', Dorothy explained to her sister. 'And Mrs Gladstone had never noticed it.'

It was no doubt Dorothy's influence which had secured Ida an invitation to one of Pamela Tennant's 'Rosebud Dinner Parties', which she gave to enable débutantes to get to know one another. No chaperones were invited to these much-coveted dinners 'which was very dashing in those days – just us young girls'. It was there that Ida first met Eddie Tennant's younger sister, Margot. This spirited young woman – a tall, rangy girl with sharp features and a long neck – was a year or two older than Ida and 'entirely unconventional'. Margot enjoyed shocking people, caring not a jot if she got talked about. Ida noticed that her daring improprieties made her very popular with the men and decided to model herself on Margot. Herself a natural exhibitionist, she was thrilled to discover how easy it was to seize the limelight, her foolery seeming to draw men to her like a magnet.

Every morning after Ida had dragged herself from her bed Dorothy was obliged to listen to her sister boasting about the latest victim in her long line of conquests. She attempted to remonstrate, berating Ida for cheapening herself. Edward, too, found his sister-in-law's high jinks embarrassing, in particular when he found her flirting with his political friends. But Ida was on a high. What did her ice-cold sister know about enjoying herself? She refused to listen.

When their parents finally got home they were met with loud complaints from Dorothy regarding Ida's objectionable behaviour. 'I can't say it was a great success, leaving you', Cecilia was obliged to admit. 'You were I found rather tiresome to Dolly, not leaving them alone enough and rather tactless.' However, she believed that Dorothy was mostly to blame, having been 'very impatient and not kind, selfish of course, and made you feel you were in the way.'

Always inclined to take her younger daughter's side, Cecilia persuaded herself that Ida's 'silliness', as she called it, was just part of the exuberance of youth. At least she knew how to enjoy herself! Best of all, there had been no contact with 'horrid Lawson' during their six months' absence. With any luck that chapter was closed.

That summer Edward's grandmother, old Lady Grey, finally found a house that she thought would suit her and moved out of Fallodon. His mother's long search for a home proved equally successful and by the autumn Fallodon was empty of his relations. For the first time since his marriage Edward felt the house was truly his own. He and Dorothy decided to celebrate by throwing a party for some of their friends and Ida went over to join them. Her three-day visit was a disaster. 'You went as untidy as you could – behaved oddly and jauntily – disgusted Edward and his quiet friends and D. spoke most seriously to me later and can't have you there till you are quieter.' Even Cecilia was obliged to admit that on this occasion Ida had been mostly to blame. 'There is a sort of coolness between the sisters', she noted. And yet she stuck to her belief that though they were 'both in fault', Dorothy was the chief culprit. 'If D. had more patience and kindness she might influence you and do you far more good than I can, but she won't and I can only wait patiently for better times.'

Unfortunately those 'better times' never came. As Dorothy and her sister drew further apart Cecilia's relationship with her elder daughter also began to deteriorate. Dorothy had become hard. And there was something else. After over four years of marriage there was still no sign of a child. This worried Cecilia. Yet when she had attempted to raise this intimate matter (which surely as Dorothy's mother she had every right to do) her daughter would fend her off, pointedly changing the subject.

On a shopping trip to London Ida had taken a fancy to a scarlet hunting coat and had talked her mother into buying it. 'I didn't like it', Cecilia confessed. 'It's too conspicuous for my taste – but you like bright colours and why not?' Predictably, Ida wore the 'famous red coat' throughout the hunting season and equally predictably Dorothy protested at her sister's eye-catching outfit. Ida's ambition to get herself talked about was proving all too successful and if not checked could impinge on Edward's good name. Though Dorothy chiefly blamed her mother, her father's attitude, too, was open to criticism. Had he not favoured Ida, making it plain she was his favourite from the time they were children?

As time went by, Cecilia saw that Dorothy was attempting to draw a line under her old life; apparently determined to distance herself from her home and her family. This saddened her. Yet though Cecilia was willing to concede that Ida had her faults, her sympathy still lay with her younger daughter, as it always would.

When Ida had just turned 21 the character sketch her mother attempted shows that though she would never understand her elder daughter she knew Ida pretty well. 'You are a very strange little soul', she wrote:

> wild and untameable except through yr affections and it is a great mercy I have been able to get yr love and so can shield you from much harm, and reason and philosophise till all is 'blue'. O the talks we have had! Very strange ones at times ... The poor love you dearly all about, you are very nice to them – especially children – and have a knack of patience wherever you go – nothing ever escapes those sharp small eyes and you have a great memory – you are certainly more alive than most humans ... You are very fond of dress – all bright colours please you – rather extravagant you are to clothe. But you are above all a child of nature – Pan – long solitary walks on the moors you delight in and seem to derive some good and comfort from contact with nature – all creatures love you too and you have a certain power over them . .. You always have heaps of pets about – 2 marvellously tame red squirrels that ran about on the breakfast table nibbling things ... You seem as if you couldn't live without beasts about ... You have a strong, healthy body – and ditto mind – except on one point ...

That 'one point' was the rub: Ida's flagrant sexuality.

A husband would eventually have to be found for her – but 'where is he?' Cecilia saw that he would need to be many-sided:

> Rich – you are by nature luxurious – yet simple – a sportsman yet a man of brain – kind and loving yet strong ... You are capable of being intensely miserable and wd never bear unkindness, I know – better stay as you are – I do hope to see you happily married tho not yet.

When Ida eventually married the man she chose to be her husband could hardly have been a greater disaster. Unfortunately Cecilia had overestimated both her power to influence Ida and her younger daughter's ability to choose wisely and well.

Chapter XXIV

Two Friends

As a young child Ida had been saved from a feeling of worthlessness by an independent spirit and, above all, by her kinship with the natural world. In this respect she could not have chosen to have been born into a more congenial environment. In contrast to modern children whose parents believe they need 24-hour supervision, once past the petticoat stage the young Widdringtons enjoyed a large measure of freedom. After the daily lessons were over they were free to play out of doors, roaming at will over their father's estate. This early taste of liberty perfectly suited Ida:

> I wanted to be out, under the sky, in the grass, among the flowers, in the woods, and in the autumn rustling my feet in the masses of dead leaves gathered at the edges of the paths … I wanted to watch the little beetles and big beetles and the spiders and all the strange shaped insects, climbing and living in their underworld, and sometimes there would be a mouse, and in those days frequently a red squirrel … My love of animals, which has dominated my life, began at a very early age.

Ida's devotion to animals was shared by the great friend of her childhood and youth, Aline Cust. After Sir Leopold's untimely death and his wife's collapse into a pitiful state of ill health (exacerbated no doubt by the siege-like conditions under which she had been forced to live in Ireland and her recurrent pregnancies) Newton had opened its doors to the Cust family, providing them with the nearest approximation to a settled home they would know for many years. Aline and Ida swiftly struck up a friendship. Adventuresome and physically tough, they were birds of a feather for whom danger was a challenge to action and rules were made to be broken. 'The Custs came this year and as usual you and Aline got in more mischief together than apart' is a typical entry in the diary Cecilia kept for Ida. In common with her friend Aline was devoted to animals and both girls were committed to their welfare. In later life Ida's commitment would turn her into a crusader – fighting and eventually winning a campaign for the humane slaughter of farm animals. Aline's commitment was more down-to-earth. She had an enquiring mind that made her want to investigate causes and find solutions to practical problems. She was both clever and obstinate and, not being particularly pretty, had fewer temptations to fritter away her time in ballrooms than her more frivolous and attractive friend. At one time Aline had considered becoming a nurse. But after embarking on her training she soon decided that she was on the wrong tack. She realised that what she really wanted was to train to become a veterinary surgeon.

In those days a handful of brave and determined women had succeeded in entering the medical profession. But these pioneers were looked at askance by a majority of the public, to whom the notion of a woman thrusting herself into what hitherto had been an exclusively male province was deeply shocking. The prospect of women becoming vets – who were obliged to attend not only to domestic dogs and cats but also to farm animals, often having to work in filthy conditions on remote farms – was so unimaginable that it had never entered anyone's head. It entered Aline's head, however, and after discovering that the best training was to be had in Edinburgh she wrote to the principal of that city's veterinary college to make enquiries about registering as a student.

Aline's mother, who was still living in straitened circumstances, had by this time secured an appointment as a Woman of the Bedchamber at Queen Victoria's Court. When she learned of her daughter's intention she was horrified. She was quite adamant that the ageing Queen would not approve of a lady following such an indelicate profession and no more did she. If Aline attempted to enrol at the college Lady Cust would disown her, cutting off her daughter's slender allowance. That seemed to be the end of it. But when shortly afterwards Aline's brother Leo died suddenly after contracting meningitis Aline found she had been left £600 and armed with this unexpected windfall she determined to go ahead.

Lady Cust was as good as her word and following Aline's registration at the veterinary college she never saw her mother again. It therefore fell to Fitz, who had given Aline his full support, to escort his ward to Edinburgh and help her find lodgings; and from that time it was at Newton that she spent her vacations. It became her second home.

Many years later, in a letter to the Veterinary Record, Aline admitted that she had been 'half starving on six shillings and sixpence a week, eating only one solid meal a day at a cost of five pence in company with the newspaper boys of Edinburgh, my only other meal being of raw oatmeal with hot water poured over it.' She was living in an attic with no fire 'and when too cold to work any more I used to go out after dark into the quiet backstreets and run to get warm enough to sleep.'[1] She persevered, however, completing the five-year veterinary training with distinction; although so great was the prejudice against women entering the profession that she was not allowed to sit the examination that would have qualified her as a Fellow of the Royal College of Veterinary Surgeons.

Meanwhile Ida, listening with a mixture of horror and respect to her friend's account of the dissection of dead beasts performed in the company of a roomful of irreverent male students, continued to pursue her frivolous life. Self-indulgent by nature, she did things by fits and starts 'but with enormous time wasted'.

Cecilia's bugbear Willy Lawson still hovered in the wings – a hateful moth attracted to Ida's flame. At one point he came close to persuading her to elope, but fortunately Ida came to her senses in time, narrowly avoiding lifelong disgrace. If her intention was to follow Margot Tennant's example and get herself 'talked about' she was succeeding all too well.

Another family member who was seldom out of trouble was Fitz's nephew Reginald Orde, his younger sister's son. 'A rare little ruffian he had been all his life', Cecilia recorded. After a number of disreputable scrapes his father had used his influence to get Reginald into a crack regiment – the Rifle Brigade. Subsequently the young man married and he and his wife had set off for India. Reports of his conduct while serving the Queen on the sub-continent had been less than reassuring, the young officer apparently having spent most of his money, been unfaithful to his wife and 'all but turned out of the regiment.' Nevertheless when the couple returned on home leave they were invited to Newton 'and we meant to be quite kind to him and forget the past'. But Reginald lost no time in making a pass at his cousin Ida: 'A few songs on the banjo – one or two talks and a fatal hunt when you were left hours with him to come home late – and the same old tale began.' Cecilia looked on with mounting dismay, for Reginald 'seemed to take more hold of you and work more harm than any of them.' For the first time in her life Ida had become deceitful, refusing to look her mother in the face. 'I was quite frightened and knew not what to do … you were odd and unfriendly for weeks and months.' Cecilia was forced to endure many a sleepless night before her daughter could be persuaded to face up to what a fool she had been 'for having taken to such a worthless being'.

Why did Ida fall for such rogues – such unsuitable men? Reckless and highly sexed, she seems to have responded to some feral unprincipled streak in the men she was attracted to – qualities she could recognise in herself. Yet guided by the high moral principles of her parents (for whom she continued to feel the deepest love and respect) and heedful, no doubt, of the ever present threat of pregnancy, it is likely that up to this point Ida had always succeeded in stepping back from the brink, and that her sexual skirmishes had gone no further than heavy petting.

A happier aspect of her impetuous nature was Ida's devotion to the stage. During the long winter months amateur dramatics provided a welcome diversion for the occupants of many a large country house and Newton was no exception. Ida was a talented actress and under her direction her siblings and visiting friends would be roped in (not always willingly) and assigned parts, everyone being obliged to attend rehearsals for the grand performance which traditionally took place after Christmas in the Newton village hall.

There was in addition an amateur dramatic society in Alnwick known as the 'Workmen's Sociables' for which Ida would help to get up concerts and plays. These activities provided a satisfying outlet for her restless energy and she was thrilled when, aged only 18, the 'Sociables' invited her to become their president. Her singing lessons in London had helped to boost her confidence and she was often invited to sing, accompanying herself on the banjo or the guitar. Before long she found herself giving concerts all over the county, raising quite serious sums of money which were donated to charity. There was never any question of Ida taking up singing or acting on the professional stage.

Years later, when Cecilia looked back at the lives of her four children, she regretted that it had not been considered desirable for Ida to receive a proper stage training. Yet given her daughter's mercurial nature it is unlikely that Ida would have had either the guts or the tenacity to survive as a professional actress.

Aline Cust, who had pursued her ambition in the face of fierce family opposition and much physical hardship, eventually forged a successful career for herself to become Great Britain's first female veterinary surgeon. In time Ida too would make a name for herself in the field of animal welfare. But that time was still far off. For the present she was too spoilt, too vain, too butterfly-brained – above all, too engaged in the time-honoured battle between the sexes – to give her mind to emulating Aline's eminently practical crusade for the wellbeing of the animal world.

CHAPTER XXV

A Fateful Encounter

Early in March 1891, Fritz and Cecilia, accompanied by Ida and Ella Pease, set off on a tour of Italy. After spending a week at their beloved Hyères they took a train for Genoa and from there went on to Rome where they remained for six weeks, soaking up the spring sunshine and marvelling at the antiquities. Their next stop was Naples, where wealthy friends of the Widdringtons, the Rendells, owned a villa famous for its gardens. 'Such roses I never saw elsewhere', Cecilia recorded. The two young women soon found themselves caught up in a whirl of social activity, 'lunching, bathing and basking' and taking trips on the Rendell's yacht to places round about. But Fitz and Cecilia did not much care for Naples. Possibly they were worried that Ella and Ida were having too little supervision, for after making the ascent of Vesuvius, ignoring pleas from the girls, they whisked them away.

After a brief stop in Florence for more sight-seeing they went on to Venice – Lord Byron's 'fairy city of the heart' – where they planned to stay for at least six weeks. Fitz could never have enough of Venice, having fallen in love with the city a quarter of a century earlier after he and Cecilia had spent a few days there 'in wonder and delight' at the conclusion of their Middle Eastern odyssey. At Newton he had decorated his walls with capriccios of the city, giving his hall the appearance of an arcade overlooking the Lagoon busy with fishing boats, and further off a two-masted ketch; while his staircase had become a viewing platform from which to look out across the water to the dome of St Maria de la Salute, set in an imaginary landscape of architectural marvels under a sunny Venetian sky.

The Widdringtons found lodgings on the upper floor of a palazzo overlooking the entrance to the Grand Canal. But within a few days of settling themselves in, Ida's proclivity for attracting the attentions of unsuitable young men, and her inability to resist their advances, led to an unfortunate occurrence. Somehow she succeeded in evading her mother's watchful eye for long enough to make friends with a young Sicilian army officer, who had evidently lost no time in declaring his undying love for the beautiful English girl to her astonished father. Fitz was faced with the embarrassing task of seeing him off and Ida was devastated. Inevitably there was a scene, with Ida's hysterical lamentations threatening to put a damper on the holiday. Exasperated, Cecilia gave her daughter a severe dressing down. 'You cried bitterly over it,' she recorded. 'It was a sharp but excellent lesson to you that you can't play with fire – wch you never quite believed before I think.'

But then a chance meeting occurred which was to put everything right. While the Widdringtons and Ella Pease had been on their sightseeing tour of Italy a rather earnest young Englishman had been following a similar route. It was his first visit to Italy and on a six-month pilgrimage he had visited Rome, Sicily, Naples, Florence, Siena and places in between. Setting out with a companion (who had since returned home) he had lived very simply, in order to spin out his money. Much of his travelling had been done on foot.

Everywhere he went he had been taking notes and making sketches, marvelling at artefacts previously known to him only through books and weighing his personal observations against the views of the experts. The young man had a passion for art and had already received some practical training. His ambition was to become a professional painter. His name was Roger Fry.

He had been in Venice for two or three weeks before the Widdringtons arrived and had made one or two friends among the bohemian set. But after six months of travel and concentrated study, Roger was both physically and mentally exhausted. What he needed was a restorative tonic, some gaiety, frivolity – a taste, perhaps, of some feminine high spirits.

He had not spoken to a woman since he left home, unless it was to ask the price of a bed. Then one afternoon as he sat sketching the church of San Gregorio, poised majestically on the opposite side of the Lagoon, his eye was caught by a young woman. 'I was half asleep in our gondola in the sun,' Ida recalled in a letter she wrote to Roger some months later. For it was she – daringly drawing on a cigarette and flirting with Antonio, their gondolier, who had drawn up his craft beneath their palazzo. At that moment Ella emerged and, seeing Roger sketching, she went over to him and struck up a conversation, which concluded in the young man being invited to join them for tea. (On holiday one could afford to drop the formalities and she felt certain the Widdringtons would not mind.) 'The next thing I woke up to', Ida reminded Roger in that same letter, 'was Father in a window above my head holding out a tumbler of tea and saying laughingly "Look here what we've got – you'd better come up."'

Ida was bored and still smarting over the dismissal of her Sicilian officer. She enjoyed relaxing in the sun and was in no mood to be coerced. Then another party wanted to land 'and we had to move our gondola and go further up the canal and when you and the parents and Ella came down … I was introduced to you.'

Discreet questioning had revealed that Mr Fry, like Ella, was a Quaker. Indeed he volunteered that the Frys had Pease connections and he was therefore judged to be perfectly respectable. Cecilia warmed to him at once, forming the opinion that his companionship would prove to be a 'real advantage' to Ida, serving to dampen her exaggerated grief over the banishment of her Sicilian. And his arrival had been a lucky chance, since Ella was on the point of leaving them to go cruising with friends on the Aegean. Was it possible that Mr Fry might fill her place? He was such a gentle soul, with an elevated mind, serious and obviously clever. 'One of those who are not "fire" but can be a real solid friend', she jotted down in the *Diary*.

The following day Mr Fry was invited to dine. Fitz noted with approval that their new friend was remarkably knowledgeable about art. He suggested that they should go sketching together. For the weeks remaining of their stay in Venice, the Widdringtons and Mr Fry were inseparable. 'How we loafed and gondolad [sic] and took our meals out for the day for sketching, and bathed and dined on the Lido,' Cecilia noted, 'and found out wondrous beauties and marvels and queer places to dine in – L'Autica Bura the prime favourite – and heard the bands and fed the Kangaroos.' Blissfully unaware of what the future had up its sleeve Cecilia was willing to declare that one and all had had a capital time.

So who was this delightful Mr Fry? The Frys had been members of the Society of Friends (to give the Quakers their proper title) for seven generations. Like many who shared their belief – with its emphasis on duty and hard work coupled with an austere lifestyle – the family had prospered. Early in the 19th century Roger Fry's great-grandfather, Joseph Storrs Fry, had founded a chocolate-making factory in Bristol. Run on paternalistic lines, it eventually made him a millionaire. One of Roger Fry's uncles was at that time chairman of the company, his father Edward having settled for the law, a profession in which he had prospered, having been awarded a knighthood on becoming a judge and risen in time to become a Lord Justice of Appeal. He and his wife Mariabella had been blessed with nine children – two sons, Portsmouth and Roger, born six years apart, and seven daughters, one of whom had died in infancy.

Roger was deeply devoted to his mother, though in common with his siblings he stood in awe of both his parents, who had raised their family according to strict Quaker principles of self-denial and self-control. Hugging, kissing, ragging and frivolity in any form were taboo at No. 6 The Grove, Highgate, the elegant Georgian house where Roger had spent his early years.

As a child, the boy's awareness of art had been confined to an annual visit to the Royal Academy with his father and drawing lessons taken with his sisters. His mother, herself a competent watercolourist, had given him some encouragement in this medium, and a watercolour sketch he made of their Highgate house and its beloved garden must have pleased him, since he had taken the trouble to sign and date it.

The young Roger's early knowledge of girls had been confined to his sisters, all of whom had been educated at home, and various female cousins. As a mark of the family's status his sisters had been presented at Court, but since their religion forbade them to attend balls, theatres or sporting events, they were never 'brought out' in the usual sense and were given few opportunities for meeting their contemporaries. Suitors were discouraged and, having had it drilled into them from their earliest years that service to others was the object of a woman's life, none of the girls had married.

When Roger was 11, with no prior warning, he was sent away to board at a preparatory school at Ascot, where weekly floggings were regularly administered by the headmaster. After becoming a prefect Roger was obliged to be present at these sadistic ceremonies, leaving him with a horror of violence which stayed with him for the rest of his life. He was deeply attached to his mother and missed her dreadfully throughout his school life.

Ascot was followed by Clifton College, Bristol, a public school which modelled itself on Dr Arnold's more famous Rugby School. The aim of both establishments was to produce Christian gentlemen willing to serve their country either in the Church, the armed services, or the law. Roger's awakening appreciation of the fine arts found little to feed upon in this stifling atmosphere, the school appearing to be determined to stamp out any flicker of originality. It was not until he arrived at King's College, Cambridge – having pleased his father by gaining an Exhibition in the Natural Sciences – that Roger began to open up. Responding to the architectural splendours of the ancient university city, and encouraged by a circle of new friends, the young man embarked on a journey of self-discovery. It was during his time at King's College that Roger first began to question the tenets of his parents' austere faith and to look critically at the restraints laid upon him during his childhood.

His elder brother, Portsmouth, was an invalid, having suffered a crippling accident while climbing in Switzerland which had permanently damaged his brain. Thus all Sir Edward's hopes were vested in his younger son. In his own youth the father's ambition had been to become a scientist. When Roger crowned his time at Cambridge with a First in the Natural Sciences, the path was open to him to try for a Fellowship, in due time becoming the distinguished man of science his father longed to have been. Edward was therefore not well pleased to discover that Roger had other ideas. Cambridge had changed his son, setting his feet on dangerous pathways frequented by atheists and radical politicians. He had been elected to the Apostles, a secret society that was extremely select and which applied itself to 'profound questions concerning social and moral rights'.[1] Most important of all, his eyes had been opened to the splendours of the visual arts. Roger had begun to draw and paint, testing his draughtsmanship by making sketches of his friends and experimenting with water colour. On leaving the university he informed his father that he wished to enrol at an art school. He had resolved to become a professional artist and needed to receive training to discover whether he was good enough. Sir Edward was appalled. His son's choice of a career seemed to him a profitless waste of a first-class intellect. He persuaded his son at least to try for a Fellowship. Grudgingly, Roger agreed. When he failed to obtain one his father gave in, reluctantly agreeing to his son attending a small art school in Hammersmith.

The Fry's charming Highgate house had by this time been exchanged for a large, gloomy and rather pretentious Bayswater mansion that Roger hated. Yet, still financially dependent on his father, he was obliged to live under the parental roof, where he had daily to suffer his mother's reproachful looks and the weight of his father's displeasure. Before very long his uneasy relationship with his father became more than he could bear, and he prevailed upon Sir Edward to advance him enough money to make a cultural tour of Italy, to gain himself some relief. Fortunately the Quaker ethic encouraged foreign travel as a tool for furnishing the mind, and his father agreed. This was how Roger came to be in Venice during that summer of 1891, where he was to meet two women – one young, the other well advanced into middle age – destined to play a major role in the next chapter of his life.

12 *Roger Fry.*

Roger had never met anyone like the Widdrington women. From the first he was astounded by their outspokenness, by the topics they were prepared to discuss, by their refusal to be fazed, even when viewing representations of the nude male body …

And then the places they had visited – Mrs Widdrington had sailed up the Nile, ridden at the head of a mule train into Jerusalem and visited the legendary city of Baalbek, with savage guides who had threatened mutiny. She had even made the ascent of Mont Blanc! Roger could not imagine his own mother doing anything as remotely adventurous as that.

Nor had his sisters and female cousins prepared him for anyone who remotely resembled Miss Widdrington. With her astonishing frankness Mrs Widdrington had confided to Roger that her daughter was getting over a love affair and that she approved of him becoming Ida's friend, since it would take her out of herself. After Miss Pease had left them Roger was delighted to discover that he was being given the privileges of a brother: that he was trusted by her parents to escort Miss Widdrington about the city without the constricting presence of a chaperone.

He could scarcely believe his good fortune. For was not Miss Widdrington the most wondrous creature he had ever met, with the bold swagger of her step, her easy laughter, the unfathomable messages conveyed to him by those twinkling eyes? And then the way she had of sharing with him any topic under the sun which happened to come into her head – from the best way to gut and skin a rabbit to the state of Mrs Gladstone's underwear …

Was there ever a young man (with the July sun beating down upon his head and the dazzle of the Lagoon threatening to turn him giddy) who would not have succumbed to the fascination of such a creature as 21-year-old Ida Widdrington?

When Roger waved off the Widdringtons in the carriage which was to convey them to Asolo, their next destination, Mrs Widdrington made him promise that he would write. For the truth was, that though she was 30 years older than their new friend, she had fallen a little in love with Roger and was loath to lose touch with him. It was plain he was an innocent and might be grateful for some guidance on worldly matters, which with two grown sons of her own she felt confident she would be able to supply.

'What fun we have had!' exclaimed Miss Widdrington. 'Newton will seem so dreadfully dull after Venice.'

Mrs Widdrington insisted that he must come and stay, if he wouldn't be bored.

'Do come,' Miss Widdrington pleaded, 'Though what you'd make of us wild Northumbrians I cannot imagine!'

Nor could Roger imagine what his family would make of the Widdringtons. He found it impossible to picture them against the sober background of his Bayswater home. London was not Venice and the reality was that friendships made on holiday did not necessarily transplant. The Widdringtons were landowners with aristocratic connections. His family, though eminently respectable – distinguished even – belonged to the upper middle class. In the normal course of events the Widdringtons and the Frys would never have met.

Yet they had met, and since the Widdringtons possessed that confidence and disdain for convention that gave members of their class the freedom to make its own rules, it was possible they might even have meant what they said. Roger hoped so. Surprising as it might seem, he appeared to have fallen in love, not simply with Ida, but with her mother. He was in thrall to both the Widdrington women.

CHAPTER XXVI

'Dear Mr Fry'

After bidding goodbye to Venice the Widdringtons passed a few days in the picturesque village of Asolo before taking train to Lucerne, where Gerard and Bertram joined them for 'a lovely ten days tramp altogether'. Fitz, now approaching 70, opted out of the more strenuous walks and took the train. Yet at 51 Cecilia was still an indefatigable walker and it was she who set the pace. Setting out from Andermatt they headed for Interlaken, then made their way down into the Rhine valley, stopping for picnics and plant-collecting on the high mountain passes and putting up at simple hostelries. From Basle they took a steamer down the Rhine, breaking their journey briefly at Cologne (the city's Germanic earnestness did not appeal to Cecilia) before finally disembarking at the Belgian port of Antwerp with its quaint gabled houses and bustling markets.

'And so ended our capital time,' Cecilia recorded. 'Probably I shall never have strength to walk with you all like that again, but it's a nice memory of freshness and green-ness and snows and forests.'

At Newton it was back to a chilly Northumbrian summer: 'The old ways and works and muck and long after we hated it', Cecilia confessed. Nor was the time-honoured exchange of country house visits always a success: 'We went a visit to Sir John Orde in Scotland, mortal dull, no one to meet us and rain,' Cecilia recorded candidly. But life at Newton never stood still and the family 'plunged at once into the Yeomanry Ball and mushroom getting and people entertaining.'

'Roger Fry came in October, nice as ever', she noted; a brief statement that left a good deal unsaid. For since her return, she and Roger had been corresponding regularly, their exchange of letters affording her the keenest pleasure. Condemned by a shortage of funds to return to his Bayswater home, the young man's frustration at his parents' lack of understanding had found relief in an outpouring of feeling to his new friend – his dear Mrs Widdrington. Her replies to his letters, he told her, brimming over with sympathy and encouragement, had restored his belief in himself, giving him the courage to persevere. Cecilia was touched. She was greatly looking forward to Mr Fry's visit.

He had never been as far north as the Border country. As a Londoner, the vast empty spaces of Northumberland, with its untamed moors and stunted trees carved into weird

13 *The conservatory at Newton Hall.*

shapes by the prevailing east wind, must have taken him by surprise. Even more surprising, on entering the house (as everyone did) through the conservatory, Roger would have found himself transported to the lush warmth of a tropical garden. Had it been the subject of a conjuring trick? White jasmine and geraniums scrambled up the walls, brushing his face as a servant escorted him up a flight of stone steps to a kind of bower or anteroom – he did not know how best to describe it – furnished with wicker chairs and oriental rugs and a low couch piled high with cushions. Roger was later to discover it was the place where the younger members of the family congregated, for smoking was allowed.

The warm welcome he received from Mrs Widdrington would have dispelled any anxiety he may have felt at having been so frank in his letters.

Roger was not accustomed to the life of a large country house with its constant comings and goings. He noticed that Mr Widdrington spent a good part of each day in his studio – a north-facing room beyond the green baize door approached by a stone-flagged passage. Tucked away in the servants' wing he could be confident of escaping interruption. The elder son, Gerard, he found difficult to make out. Unfailingly polite, he seemed a queer, shy fellow. Roger learned that he would shortly be leaving for Oxford to begin his university studies. In the meantime Gerard seemed to hang about as if uncertain where he belonged, in a household which, in addition to the family and their friends, included 12 domestic servants and a menagerie of pets. He learned that a younger brother, Bertram (plainly the favourite) was at Sandhurst, hoping to become an officer in the Brigade of Guards. But it did not take Roger long to discover that it was the women around whom everything at Newton revolved.

Mrs Widdrington wore the governance of her household lightly and with a beguiling informality that characterised most aspects of life at Newton Hall. Some part of her busy day was always reserved for Roger; she would find some time to be alone with him, her natural warmth encouraging him to unburden himself. Religion, philosophy, his struggles over his art, difficulties with his father – no subject was barred. Roger found he could talk freely with Mrs Widdrington in a manner that would not have been possible even with the closest of his male friends.

And then there was something more: some mysterious chemistry working between them. At 52, though Mrs Widdrington had lost her girlish figure, she still retained her vitality and charm. And sometimes Roger would have the queerest sensation – that it would be bliss to be gathered up in her arms.

Meanwhile Ida continued to dazzle him, challenging him with her eyes and that disturbingly deep musical voice, to follow where she led: out to the stables to admire the horses; down to feed the ducks on the tree-fringed lake; off for a tramp on the heathery moors, the music of their splashing streams mingling with the cry of curlews …

All the outdoor staff seemed to be in love with Ida. She appeared to have Shotton, the coachman, eating out of her hand. But Roger saw that her life was essentially aimless. Ida was wasting her best years on trivialities and he chided her gently. She reminded him of Catherine Earnshaw, Emily Brontë's gothic heroine. Had she read *Wuthering Heights*? No? Then he must send her a copy.

Mrs Widdrington, imagining Mr Fry to be that rare creature – a man who could be trusted not to get 'silly' with Ida – felt no qualms over leaving the pair to go about together unchaperoned. There had come a day when they had walked on a sunny beach backed by massive dunes and Ida, flattered that such an intelligent being should take an interest in her doings, confided to Mr Fry that there was a man who was *the love of her life*, 'only he happens to be married'. Speaking casually she added that Roger might write to her if he liked, 'but I shan't write back if you're going to scold – and on no account must you tell my mother'.

That same autumn some friends of the family, the Anns, who lived at Blenkinsop Castle in Cumberland, had introduced Ida to hawking. Encouraged by her enthusiasm they had presented her with a merlin, a small fast-flying falcon bred to work over open moorland. The fierce little bird was ideal for hunting rabbits and Ida soon had it trained to return with its catch to the leather perch she wore strapped to her wrist.

Then someone gave her a goshawk, a slate-grey buzzard-like creature with handsome white underparts that could drop like a lightning bolt on to unsuspecting prey.

On a visit to the Anns in November Ida went down with influenza and was forced to extend her stay. Her protracted visit was providential, however, for her maternal grandfather, Edward Gregge-Hopwood, died that same month, obliging Cecilia to drop everything and go to Hopwood Hall to attend her father's funeral and help her mother sort out his affairs.

By this time Ida and Roger Fry had begun to correspond secretly and the convalescent amused herself by dashing off page after page to 'dear Mr Fry' in her bold sloping hand, with scant attention paid either to grammar or punctuation. Probably hoping to provoke her friend she would return again and again to the vexed subject of Willy Lawson. 'He's a kind of outlaw', she explained:

> his wife ran away with somebody else's husband and then he took her back and all the county knows the story and bars him and his bad temper doesn't get him on any better either, it was a kind of pity took me to talk to him and because in old days I had liked his face. I was allowed to talk to him and he abused his privilege and it cost him more than enough to stick to me but he says he can't help it.

While Ida was prepared to admit that Mr Lawson was a bounder, she defended her attachment on the grounds of loyalty: 'one of my biggest goods, which means really loyalty to one's own self,' she endeavoured to explain.

Roger Fry's letters to Ida have not survived, though evidently he had replied that since Lawson was a rotter, surely Miss Widdrington did not expect him to admire the fellow? 'No, I did not mean you to admire him', she wrote back, 'for <u>all</u> his good riding.' Perversely, she added that she did not believe Lawson was in love with her 'more than the man in the moon – and certainly not I with him and that's gospel'.

What was Roger Fry to make of this contrary young woman? He considered Ida to be confused and rudderless and continued to believe that she was capable of better things. Her mercurial personality fascinated him and though he knew he would draw down her wrath by criticising her hedonistic lifestyle, he persisted. It was done always in a spirit of kindness. Ida for her part felt flattered that a young man who seemed to live on a higher plane and to breathe a purer air seemed to care about her.

The fact was that in common with her mother she was beginning to find Mr Fry indispensable. He was her very special friend, not to be confused with ordinary friends (with whom one needed to mind one's tongue). He was her 'soul mate'.

Ida knew (or believed she knew) everything that was to be known about the love between a man and a woman: that overwhelming ache that can gnaw at one's vitals, deeply pleasurable, yet at the same time a kind of purgatory. It bore no relation to her feeling for Mr Fry, which was based on trust and respect. He was the one human being to whom she could bare her heart without fear of being laughed at or betrayed. Yet she knew she could never make a life with him, for his interests and hers were worlds apart. Mr Fry was effete by Ida's robust standards; a typical townie who would recoil from the sheer grossness of some of her favourite pastimes. And how she delighted in teasing him! After a day spent on the moors with her falcons she wrote gleefully:

> Dear Mr Fry,
> I was out with the goshawk yesterday and she killed 3 rabbits and we had ferrets and got 2 more alive. Such dear ferrets. I suppose you would not like me in my sporting frame of mind and according to you made a nasty picture yesterday sitting with a split rabbits head in my hands blood on my coat and hands the merlin feeding on my fist, spattering fresh brains about and a ferret curled up in my lap oh most unsightly woman!

Roger Fry kept all her letters, which may now be found in the Fry archive at King's College Cambridge. Since none is dated it is not always easy to place them in sequence. Reading them we discover a self-absorbed, passionate, ill-educated and rather naive young woman with a natural flair for an expressive phrase; a girl who was prepared to open her heart in an entirely uninhibited manner.

Ignoring her mother's warning to take heed of men's lower nature, Ida would justify their intimate tone on the grounds that Mr Fry – unlike all the other men of her acquaintance (whose offer of friendship was only a mask for their thoroughly boring tendency to fall at her feet) – was essentially 'pure'. '*Addio*', she would end her letters, or else simply 'Yours, Idonea', signing off with her given name, which she must have felt had a more sober ring than the more homely Ida.

Time passed. Cecilia returned from Hopwood and although the family was officially in mourning Ida pestered her parents to be allowed to attend the customary autumn round of balls and house parties. While staying at Cresswell Hall (a grandiose mansion built on the site of an ancient border stronghold by a family enriched by King Coal) Ida, who was worn out by a fortnight's party-going, slipped upstairs to her room to dash off a letter to her 'soul mate'. 'Midnight, Tuesday' she began, before launching forth:

> Oh dear, I feel so sorry about many things, sorry that I'm always finding fault with your really nice letters, sorry that they <u>do</u> vex me in some degree, sorry that I can't put it better now and very sorry that you think we're drifting far away from the spirit of our talk on the yellow sands, with the sound of the 'strife more sweet than peace' in our ears. I hear it now, this is a great grand house near the sea, a house that I love because it's so boldly big and well built and it stands right in the funny flat sort of woods that grow near the coast, everything is big and broad and wind swept and wave beaten.

Though Ida did not know it, a few years later she was to enter into a disastrous marriage with the owner of Cresswell Hall, which at that time was home to his mother, a spoilt beauty who after her husband's early death had married the Earl of Ravensworth. Her letter continued:

> Why have I the impudence to worry you with my narrow little ideas on your character? I feel rather like a little wasp trying to sting through the hair of a big good dog. Your letters all through savour of generosity, of large-mindedness and distinct good heartedness, mine kick, bite and annoy … I <u>know</u> I read things all cross sometimes, and they annoy me and make me think you are laughing at and despising me … I've been thinking so hard lately about yr letters that I think my eyes have got opener about them and I see they are meant more kindly than I thought, but as I said before, the rough side of the tongue of life has not yet licked me and I <u>do</u> call yours a rough tongue … It made me very angry because it hurt my dignity of which I have uncommon little but now and then I find he <u>do</u> [sic] exist.

In a letter covering 12 closely written pages, Ida complained bitterly at the stupidity of men, though she admitted that sometimes 'the Devil will out'. She had, for example, been 'bad and teasing and altogether naughty' that same evening. There speaks the incorrigible flirt. She would not admit that she was playing with fire, provoking Roger Fry to react, refusing to acknowledge that she was doing any such thing.

In the New Year of 1892 news came from Windsor that the Duke of Clarence, eldest son of the Prince of Wales, had died, plunging the whole nation into mourning and putting an end to that winter's festivities. But not for Ida, for she had accepted an invitation from Mrs Clowes, an acquaintance of her parents, to join her party at Hyères. 'She let you go about far more than I had expected.' And before long Ida had made the acquaintance of a family called Corbett. 'Mrs Corbett was most kind and had you to lunch and to sing … and young George [Corbett] as far as I can learn was forever with you.' The young man was apparently bowled over by Ida's singing and 'due to Ida's curious unbelief in men's passion and the rousing of it' the inevitable occurred. Cecilia tended to blame Mrs Clowes, who had failed to spot the way the situation was developing 'so you went on unconscious of the talk around … till one evening he poured out his love at yr feet and offered you his life (poor thing, he had nothing else to offer you, they were miserably poor)'. True to form, Ida professed herself to be 'bewildered and pained'.

What was worse – George Corbett had promised Ida that she could have his St Bernard dog – a huge sentimental beast she had found easier to love than its master. After turning down George's proposal Ida feared she would be obliged to surrender the dog. But the gallant young man insisted his offer must stand and in due course 'Barri' was shipped to England and delivered to Newton, to become Ida's inseparable companion.

While Ida was playing with fire at Hyères, Roger Fry had been furthering his studies by attending an art school in Paris. However, what should have been a liberating experience had disappointed him. Most of his fellow students seemed to no better than mediocre, while 'rampant Bohemianism … with its song-singing and its merciless chaff and its frequent practical jokes'[1] all seemed rather childish. He had made no real friends and spent much of his time at café tables, pondering the direction his life should take and replying to letters from Ida and his dear friend Mrs Widdrington. He could not help comparing his present cheerless state in the bitterly cold French capital with the magical weeks he and the Widdringtons had spent in Venice the previous summer.

One day as he spun out a small glass of cognac he had ordered to stave off the cold, Roger sat re-reading Ida's latest effusion, wondering how much she had meant of what she had written. 'You funny thing' she began,

> I might break loose and go away and never write any more … Only you <u>help</u> so, it would be difficult to cut loose now, and you know too much about me and there are too few people like you in the world … I want to see you quite a lot really.

Was that true? He desperately wanted to believe it. He was planning to return home soon. Could they perhaps meet in London? Roger retrieved his pen and a sheet of notepaper from a battered briefcase and on a wave of hope summoned the waiter and ordered a second cognac. 'Dear Miss Widdrington', he began …

Early in May Roger Fry left Paris and returned to his Bayswater home, and shortly afterwards a somewhat emotionally battered Ida bade farewell to Hyères. On her way home she had arranged to spend a few days in London with Dolly and Edward. She found her sister preoccupied and not particularly welcoming. A general election was in the offing and Dorothy was in no mood to take her sister around and about. However, she did agree to invite Ida's friend Roger Fry to dine and she liked him at once. Her preoccupied state suited Ida. It is not known where she and Roger Fry met, nor how many meetings the pair contrived over the next few days. What is clear is that by the time Ida left London she had received another proposal of marriage. Feeling, as she wrote to Roger afterwards, 'more honoured, flattered, touched and proud than I can express to by what you tell me as regards my most unworldly self', Ida had refused him. She had been completely taken aback and for once was overcome with remorse at her own foolishness. For she knew that her mother would be shocked if she learned that her unmarried daughter had been writing to Roger Fry; and by committing him to secrecy she had involved the poor creature in her deception.

The consequence of that deception was worse than she imagined. For Roger Fry was now in a most unenviable fix. Mrs Widdrington had no idea that he had been corresponding with her daughter, believing that she herself was his sole confidante. He suspected that if she were to learn the truth she would feel betrayed – humiliated even. The thought of Mrs Widdrington being hurt was deeply troubling. He could not bear to think about the pain he might have inflicted; for second only to his love for Ida was his deep attachment to her mother. He begged Ida to say nothing about their correspondence, nor to disclose to her mother what he now saw to have been a futile and rash proposal. For what had he to offer a girl like Ida? Like an idiot, he realised that he had fallen victim to a romantic dream. What a tangle Roger Fry had got himself into!

Chapter XXVII

'A Friendship Tinged with Romance'

When Ida arrived home her mother could see at once that something was troubling her. Questioned, Ida admitted that she had been upset by an unfortunate incident involving a young man while a guest of the Clowes at Hyères. Not for the first time, her friendship had been woefully misunderstood.

Then it all came out in a rush. The young man's name was George Corbett, and his mother had admired her voice and invited her to come and sing and they were very nice people and she was enjoying herself and George had said she might have his dog – a most beautiful St Bernard called Barri. Only then he had got 'silly' … 'But I may keep the dog,' she added lamely.

Cecilia had heard it all before. Ida was obliged to submit to a severe ticking off and after the familiar warning against the dangers of exciting men's passions the matter appeared to be closed. Yet a week later Ida was still mooning about the house, preoccupied and plainly unhappy. Her reaction to the unfortunate George Corbett business seemed to her mother to be unwarrantedly overdone and she became suspicious. She knew that while Ida was in London she had been seeing Roger Fry: 'and I – with a sort of instinct that there was more in those London wanderings that seemed – half guessed, half were told'. Ida and her mother had always been very close and though Ida had been determined to stick to her promise and give nothing away, eventually she 'couldn't go on with it any more' and had come clean.

In a contrite letter to Roger, she explained how it had happened.

> She found me alone at odd time kept saying child, child, aren't you getting any better? And I always said No Mamma … I'm so worried to death and people upset me. And she was always terribly sorry for me, so that I felt a worse brutal humbug each time and at last she said And somehow I can't help thinking you are not easy in yr mind about Mr Fry … And I asked her why she had any notion about it at all. And she said partly through your letters to her, she thought perhaps she was meant to see through and be warned.

Ida confessed that by this time she had worked herself up 'to a pretty desperate state' and when her mother suggested that perhaps it would be best if she and Roger Fry did not meet she realised that deception was 'worse than useless'.

> At last I said 'Oh Mamma what is the good of keeping it from you any more, it <u>has</u> happened' and I burst out crying and felt awful and wondered what you'd say to me. And poor Mamma was so <u>awfully</u> sorry about it and held me tight till I got better.

Clasping Ida to her bosom Cecilia must have been grateful that her daughter could not see her face. For Ida had just delivered a bombshell. Through her tears Ida was insisting that though she did not love him she could not live without her 'soul mate' – that Mamma 'must let him come!' Ida's letter concluded:

> Seriously are you so <u>very</u> vexed with me, it was so hard to lie when closely questioned ... I said how hard it would be for poor you to meet her again with that knowledge between you how <u>brutal</u> of me to have made it so hard for you both but oh Roger what was to be done, I wonder if you know how hard it was for me?

Ida was aware that a close bond had been forged between Roger Fry and her mother. Just how close that bond had become she could not guess.

In truth Cecilia had been devastated by Ida's disclosure. She was surprised to feel the pain ripping through her: it was heartache, pure and simple. And since she knew she must not let it show she unburdened herself by addressing Ida through the pages of the *Diary*.

> All the time you were in France you seem to have been receiving and writing long letters from Roger Fry, who had been in Paris – deeply interesting and intimate letters, written by you on hills in woods on the marsh and by him in cafés late at night instead of sleeping – and worse you told him to meet you in London and he did and Dolly asked him to dine and you and he wandered about London ... and lo! There was another soul had to pour itself at yr feet – this time long pent-up feelings in a self-repressed nature – it was terrible – absolutely unexpected to you – who thought you had a friend in him.

It was equally terrible for Cecilia.

> But when is friendship possible between a man and a woman – especially young! Another sad railway parting and journey ... It was a great shock and a sorrow to me ... for I too had been corresponding with R.F. with infinite pleasure and I feared all must be at an end.

Cecilia marvelled that Ida did not love him. 'As a girl <u>I</u> should how deeply! But no, you always knew your own feelings.'

Now, in the interests of all, her own feelings must be put on hold. She sat down and wrote Roger a sympathetic letter. He took it very well. 'He was so wise and dear about it – never man felt so deeply or so truly and held to what had to be done without pose or pretence.' Knowing, however, that he must be suffering, she felt that action needed to be taken. It was all very well for Ida to insist that she could not do without Roger. She only wanted him on her own terms, which were plainly unfair. Cecilia wrote to Roger again, suggesting that they should meet and talk things over and decide what was best to be done. She thought he would be wise to stay away from Newton. Could he perhaps take a train to Newcastle – where they could meet at the *Station Hotel*?

'Oh what a funny plan of going to Newcastle, in the midst of all this awfulness', Ida wrote to Roger when she learned of her mother's suggestion. 'I cannot help laughing about it. I picture such a dismal meeting between you two in that beastly station (always stations now) and it does seem too funny not to be laughed at.'

It is doubtful whether Cecilia and Roger found much to laugh about as they took dinner together in the sombre palace erected some forty years earlier by the London and North Eastern Railway Company. Tact was called for on both sides to dispel the awkwardness of Roger Fry's deception and Cecilia Widdrington's hurt. Their innate kindliness and the concern each felt for the other must have come to the rescue in covering any embarrassment, for both were anxious that they should remain friends.

Mrs Widdrington (as Roger Fry still called her) suggested a 'cooling off' period to enable both young people to regain their equilibrium. Time must be allowed to do its work. The pain would heal, she assured him, if there were no more meetings and no letters for a while – she suggested the space of a year. That would give him peace of mind to concentrate on his painting. 'A year may seem like an eternity, but it will soon pass.'

Roger agreed that he must learn to live without Ida, devote himself to his work and let the future look after itself. He felt bound to concede that his painting had suffered in Paris. His obsession with Ida seemed to have paralysed his will. But was this separation to mean he must lose his dear Mrs Widdrington? Her letters had kept his spirits up; they had been the greatest comfort. He hoped she would still write to him. And perhaps, if she was ever in London, they might meet … ? Thus it was agreed.

Ida considered the arrangement to be unduly harsh. Moreover she believed that 'wretch' Roger Fry had ganged up with her mother, which was deeply unfair. Could there not be one final exchange of letters before the ban was imposed? Her mother thought that was acceptable.

Determined to get the most out of this important letter Ida departed from her customary uninhibited scrawl and succeeded in covering 12 closely packed pages in a neat hand. Burning much midnight oil it took her two days to complete her missive, which she headed with a quotation from her favourite poet Lord Byron. Below are some extracts. (Since she ignored paragraphs and was sparing with her punctuation Roger cannot have found the letter an easy read.)

> One more glimpse of the sun,
> One more breath of the sea,
> One more kiss from my dearest
> Then comes Eternity!

Am I to write you only one more letter? Only to tell you once more all about what I think and feel and am? And then write those dreary long pages of rant for the flames to burn? I follow yr lead absolutely in this matter as I see you judge 50 per cent better than I do, no not that because I don't judge at all I would let it all slide till it slid to the Devil and be utterly unreasonable and selfish and you, you alone are good and wise and strong and invent means to help a wretched weak creature like me. Oh my dear good Roger what a night to spend* how is it you can be so brave I could never never have settled all that and yet it is

---

* Ida is referring to Roger's stay at the *Station Hotel*.

> the only right course, I'm afraid I should have been headstrong and helpless and spoilt it all, but I always told you you were worth 50 of me, Mamma said I was not worth one of yr hands and its quite true.

Ida's recollections of how she and Roger met in Venice follow. The pages quoted below refer, among other things, to a watercolour Roger had sent her.

> I went out today with my dog and came to a wild sloping bank all a mass of yellow primroses and bluebells and a very cold rain was soaking through my clothes and my dog stood close to me and wondered why I stood so long in the wet, he will stand by me for ever. I thought the cold primroses and me were about alike, both sound such happy sunny things and all the time we have our troubles too … Your sunset picture is glowing so in the firelight, I have looked at it so much since you sent it and have learned to love it … Oh oh it sounds so scoldy to say our letters must be very different to what they have been, I mustn't tell you my feelings I must reserve everything, now don't think I'm growling I know its right and remember I'm holding your hand very tight all the time to make you understand that whatever I may say now my feelings are just the same …

But what exactly were these feelings? Did she love Roger? The answer is probably yes, but as a 'perfect friend', not as a lover. She admitted that she was too selfish to change her spoilt existence with its dogs and hunting and endless entertainments for a life in some suburban villa, although:

> Mamma says you're the strongest and best man she ever came across and that I'm lucky to have fallen in such good hands … I suppose because I half love you it will be desperation hard [sic] not writing to you for a year or seeing you but I will keep to it for your sake … its so awfully late but you see this is the last letter so I don't care a jot … To say truth it puzzles me to know why I am thus ruthlessly casting aside your dear dear love for me, why we are to live thus far apart and be miserable when I want to have you say you'd be happier if you had me, but whether I love them or not I just can't marry anybody, I'm afraid of them, its too near, I know nothing about it and it affrights me … I'd rather marry you than anybody I ever met but I don't want ever to marry at all or have a home or be peaceful at all and certainly not have any children …

Before they parted in London Roger must have told Ida that he would like to give her a present, for she wrote next:

> oh you funny boy, why do you want to send me something so awfully, of course you must if you really want to but its much too nice of you to want to. Send me one wee blue stone in a finger ring … and I'll be like a naughty girl in a story book and only wear it when I'm alone, when I go out with Barri and the little mare and the falcon, and nobody need ever know, tell me the day you send it and I'll stay by the post and be beautifully deceitful.

There followed a long passage in which Ida returned to a recurrent topic: her love-hate relationship with Willy Lawson. (How sick and tired Roger must have become of references to that obnoxious man, whom he feared – despite her protestations to the contrary – that Ida still loved.)

By this time it was 2 a.m. and time for Ida to lay down her pen. The following day (a Saturday) she took it up to complete her marathon letter. Lawson was still much on her mind.

> I must try to be unsleepy enough to finish this, my last explanation of anything to you. I've written a bit about Willie … because it is the last question you ask me and will be on my mind most. You're very bad to have asked it and very unseeing, how many times have I said 'I am ashamed thro' all my being to have loved so slight a thing' … But you must allow a slight portion of romance to cling around it, like the light fumes of his cigarette which floated about us that night in the conservatory at that wildly happy dance, the trace of them were still in my hair when I pulled it down, tho' he and the cigarette were gone, they are doubly gone now, but still you are growling at the cigarette smoke in my hair. Patience Roger, I am gradually brushing it all out, with much brushing it goes, may you brush yours out better and quicker than I have done.

Ida attempted to explain that it was the 'bad' bit of her that allowed her to fall for Willie: 'and I suppose you are righteously disgusted with it … you have put me on the level of the lowest scum'. She wrote that she was getting tired of being alive, that she wished she could find a big wood and rail it round and live in it: 'but even then I should be haunted with my memories … Roger, Roger I'm so miserable, I don't know what to do.' Finally, squeezing her writing so that she did not have to begin a fresh page, she concluded: 'I think this is about the end of the letter so goodbye for a year. Yours affecty [sic] to the end of it – Idonea.'

What was Roger Fry to make of this self-dramatising and contradictory young woman who 'half-loved' him and admitted to being thrilled at the thought of wearing his ring, but whose obsession with Lawson was still very much alive? Although none of his letters to Ida have survived, included in the Fry archive at King's College, Cambridge, is one he must have started to write to Ida, but then abandoned. It makes poignant reading:

> But now, how do matters stand? What is it you want? Even now, you don't feel, if I read you right, the sort of love which can give up everything, luxury, hunting, sport, flattery and all the things which make life tolerable or less intolerable for you – it isn't the love, is it that could step down and come into a more humdrum life and a lower society – because you know as well as I do that it would be a descent for you – you have blood and breeding, which makes me feel as your sister said (tho' not of me) like 'an underbred carthorse' compared to you, and a villa somewhere near London, which is all I'm ever to be likely to reach to, would be an awful change and in the end that would surely tell against us unless you have a much bigger love for me than I dare believe …
>
> Well I think you want from me a friendship tinged with romance wch was what you thought you had until I told you I loved you … I will write again as of old only you must give me time – you must let me wait till it isn't quite at the awful tearing pitch it is at present … A word from you sets me in such a state that I can't hold a brush to any purpose all day long – so we must wait - you know you have my love, you know that you are everything to me except my art and my friends … that I've never reproached you or blamed you for anything and don't believe I ever shall … So my dear we must wait – the real big love may turn up for you and then you won't want me and my letters any more and seriously I think I could be almost happy to think

of it I think I shd never be jealous of you … and anyhow don't make yourself any more unhappy by thinking I'm a careless absent stranger quite heartless and indifferent to you and if I go about the world just as usual it's because I wear a mask, but it's mighty difficult always to keep it on and it's often very suffocating – but it must give you more pain that pleasure to know about my feelings … so I don't think its worth while to enlarge on them … I know I'm not big enough to love you as you should be loved … but I'm not quite so brutal as you seem to have thought. I know all this will make you think I'm awfully prosaic …

The draft breaks off at this point. It establishes that Roger had not entirely given up hope of winning Ida's hand at some future date. In the last resort, like disappointed lovers before and since, he had succeeded in persuading himself that 'a crumb from the rich man's table' was preferable to starving; and that there was no reason why he and Ida should not remain friends.

14 *Ida in full bloom.*

Meanwhile Cecilia – freed from the fear that she might lose her place in Roger Fry's heart – put her own heart and mind into finding a husband for Ida. Lord Warkworth, a personable young man with a Border castle and a respectable income, came of age that summer and held a great ball; at which both he and Lord Morpeth, heir to the Earl of Carlisle, were observed by Cecilia to be 'very talky' with Ida; 'I thought with a sigh how well you wd have adorned either of their big houses', she recorded. The Yeomanry Ball came and went, and there was the usual round of tennis tournaments, garden parties and cricket matches, with golf (a relatively new diversion) at Alnmouth; the summer season culminating in September with a grand fancy dress ball. Ida went as a 'green and red Vivandiere', her elaborate costume a generous gift from Lady Cust.* 'Very handsome but never suited you', Cecilia commented. 'Stiff and accentuated all yr worst points.'

An unending stream of guests continued to flow through the Widdrington's hospitable house. Yet though Ida was never short of admirers her heart remained obstinately whole. But all was not well with the daughter of the house. Ida had begun to suffer from recurrent stomach pains. Medical advice had been sought, but no physical explanation for the pains could be identified. Cecilia put them down to 'troubles and worries of mind'. However, an

---

* The querulous invalid was by now almost a permanent fixture at Newton, where she tried her hostess's patience to the limits.

eminent Edinburgh doctor whom they consulted was probably closer to the mark when he suggested that marriage might provide a cure. Though sexual frustration could not be decently mentioned, it is likely that Ida had indulged in heavy petting with Lawson (and possibly with others) stopping just short of intercourse; and that by the time she was 22 the stresses of her prolonged virginity were at the root of her mysterious illness.

While Ida's stomach pains and her mother's manoeuvrings to find her a husband were taking centre stage in the Widdrington household, in the wider world the Tory Party, which had held power for the past six years, had finally run out of steam. In midsummer 1892 the Tory Prime Minister, Lord Salisbury, had advised the Queen to dissolve Parliament. The result of the General Election, held in July, had given the Liberals and the Irish Nationalists combined a majority of 40 in the House of Commons. Lord Rosebery, a popular peer, went to the Foreign Office, and to everyone's surprise (not least his own) Sir Edward Grey was selected to serve as his Parliamentary Under Secretary.

Replying to a letter of congratulation from Mandell Creighton, now Bishop of Peterborough, Dorothy Grey wrote:

> Fallodon, 13 September 1892
> We still look on political life as an experiment and it is a good thing that it can now be tried fully ... And if we find we cannot keep our hearts in towns, nor live rightly crowded up with horrible people, we shall still be young, and other things will be possible to us.[1]

Chapter XXVIII

Sir Edward in Office

Whenever a general election loomed Dorothy nursed the secret hope that Edward would lose. She still regarded Edward's political career as an experiment, which to date could not be said to have met with much success. Over six years had passed since he had first been elected to Parliament, five and a half of which had been spent on the Opposition benches. This in itself was frustrating. What made it worse was that throughout that time the once-great Liberal Party had been torn by internal strife. Indeed, so great were the divisions within the Party that many feared it could not survive.

The chief cause of dissent was Irish Home Rule – a policy passionately espoused by the Party's 83-year-old leader William Gladstone and backed by most of the younger members, including Edward, but which was bitterly opposed by the old aristocratic Whig fraternity and also by the Queen – who loathed Gladstone and was not prepared to countenance any diminution of her powers as Queen-Empress. In addition there was conflict between Anglicans and Nonconformists 'and a host of single-issue fanatics … adopting a large rag-bag of radical proposals … cynically designed to appeal to as many different groups as possible'.[1] Knowing that most of these issues were too remote to concern his unsophisticated electorate, Edward decided to base his campaign on matters closer to home, in particular the reform of local government. Believing that the county councils recently set up by the Tory Party had failed to deliver what he called 'real' local government, he campaigned vigorously for the introduction of parish councils, to be elected by full manhood suffrage and having the authority 'to acquire land compulsorily for public purposes such as providing cottages, stores, reading rooms, libraries, public halls and recreation grounds'.[2]

It is likely that Mandell Creighton, the former incumbent of Edward's parish of Embleton, had a hand in shaping this extremely radical programme, in which Edward was wholeheartedly supported by Dorothy, who had her own distressing memories of visits to the homes of the rural poor in the company of her mother. Privately Edward believed that the Liberal Party had little hope of winning the election in its present divided state; and that if the Party lost he would very likely be out of office for the next 10 years. In his heart of hearts he felt 'almost with a sense of guilt, that the relief of being set free from Parliament would be an irresistible joy'[3] and when he learned that he had won (albeit with a much reduced majority) he hardly knew whether to be pleased or sorry.

Dorothy had no such mixed feelings. 'It was quite a clean fight, I thought', she wrote to her friend Mrs Buxton, but 'I rather wish E. was out of Parliament just now and I rather wish the Liberals had not got a majority. It is all very cowardly I know.'[4]

However, Edward's enthusiasm was rekindled when he learned that he and most of his coterie of like-minded friends had come out well. With the 84-year-old Gladstone back at the helm for his fourth term as Prime Minister, Herbert Asquith had been given the Home Office and Arthur Acton put in charge of Education. He himself had been offered the post of Under Secretary for Foreign Affairs under the new Foreign Minister Lord Rosebery. Only Richard Haldane – the cleverest of them all in Edward's opinion and a particular friend of Dorothy's – had been ignored by the Grand Old Man.

The offer made to Edward had come as a complete surprise. With the exception of his and Dorothy's three-month trip to India (which he felt no urge to repeat) he had never set foot on foreign soil. He knew virtually nothing about foreign affairs and still less about his Party's foreign policy. He would have preferred to have gone to the Local Government Board, where his feet would have found firmer ground. He was aware, however, that an Under Secretaryship was a recognised route to Great Things and since the offer was a great honour for a Member who had barely turned 30 he felt bound to accept. 'Mr G. is very imperious and inclined to chuck us all about by the scruff of our necks',[5] he wrote to Dorothy, who had fled London as soon as it was decently possible to do so and had returned to Fallodon. 'It is a terrible plunge but I am inclined to make it and at any rate purge my soul of the possibility of regret before I go into private life.'[6] And despite Dorothy's misgivings she was pleased at Edward's good fortune. 'I am very proud about it,' she wrote to a colleague of her husband's. 'It is good that E. will get a straight start and have lots of work and responsibility.'[7]

Edward's new boss, the 38-year-old 5th Earl of Rosebery, was by any reckoning a very remarkable man. Of towering intellect and imbued with aristocratic hauteur, he was immensely rich, having married a Rothschild and added her fortune to his own not inconsiderable wealth. He had travelled widely and spoke French and German like a native. 'The least insular of men',[8] he was a close friend of Herbert von Bismarck, son of Germany's 'Iron Chancellor', with whom he corresponded regularly. Rosebery's wife had died young, leaving him permanently bereft, and like Grey he had always been a reluctant politician. Only the personal intervention of Gladstone had persuaded him to leave his family estate at Dalmeny in Peebleshire to travel south to join the old man's Cabinet. For though he was a brilliant speaker with a 'strong melodious voice'[9] and the ability to leave huge crowds spellbound, he was by nature a recluse. Moody and unpredictable, he was abnormally sensitive, hated London and was addicted to solitude. His craving often caused him to shut himself away for days at a time in a tower on his estate 'with only his thoughts and his books for company'.[10] He and Dorothy had much in common and hit it off remarkably well. Soon a strong personal friendship developed between the Foreign Secretary and the two young Greys.

The duties of a Parliamentary Under Secretary whose chief was in the Lords were more onerous than if he had been in the Commons. When decisions were reached in Cabinet it was the Under Secretary's job to explain the views of his master to his associates in the Lower House. 'Everybody says … that Edward has got the most interesting of posts and I suppose they are right,'[11] Dorothy wrote to Bishop Creighton. 'I am trying to remember which of Dizzy's novels* contains a man who prided himself on possessing a gallery of the portraits of Under-Secretaries whose chiefs were in the Lords. They are splendid beings it seems.'[12] Though neither she nor Edward could have known it, his decision to serve as Rosebery's lieutenant had 'decided the destiny of his life'.[13]

Edward's arrival at the Foreign Office happened to coincide with a dispute over the future of Uganda – a landlocked nation three times the size of Britain adjacent to the southern border of the Sudan – and he found himself pitched headlong into a clash between his chief and the Prime Minister.

At that time the hysteria which subsequently became known as the 'Scramble for Africa' was causing Britain and the other major European powers to re-evaluate the nature of their interest in the 'Dark Continent'. The fuse had been laid by the building of the Suez Canal, the work of a brilliant French engineer. Previous to that, Western interest in the vast sub-continent had focused on the trading posts its coasts provided. But with the completion of the 120-mile-long canal the picture changed. The British, who had been sceptical of the feasibility of constructing this 200ft-wide 'ditch' (as Lord Palmerston called it) became its chief beneficiaries, for the canal opened up a new and far shorter route to their Indian Empire by providing a direct link between the Mediterranean and the Red Sea. Initially the Canal had been jointly owned by France and Egypt. But in 1875, at a time when the French government happened to be strapped for cash, Benjamin Disraeli (the Tory Prime Minister) with the backing of Baron Rothschild, talked his government into acquiring a major shareholding from the Khedive of Egypt – a coup which was to rankle with Frenchmen for three-quarters of a century. Britain's next step was to secure the Canal from the threat of falling into hostile hands. At that time Egypt was still a vassal state of the old Ottoman Empire ruled over by the Sultan, and was going through a period of upheaval caused by a mix of financial mismanagement and nationalistic fervour. Both France and Britain had valuable investments in the country and, following an uprising in which a number of British nationals were killed (and over which the Sultan and the French seemed equally disinclined to intervene), the British were obliged to go in and 'protect' Egypt in order to restore order. Thereafter Egypt was officially recognised as being a 'Protectorate of the Crown'.

Disraeli's cunning move had galvanised other European powers into claiming their own pieces of Africa. The Boers and the British had already colonised much of Southern Africa, and the French, who had well-established colonies in Algeria and Senegal, were eager to extend their influence. If the remaining powers did not make haste to stake their own claims some other nation would jump in and beat them to it. Thus the scramble for Africa was on.

At that time virtually the whole of the unexplored interior of that vast continent was regarded by Europeans as being 'up for grabs'; its indigenous inhabitants being regarded as savages who had never emerged from their primeval state of barbarism.

---

*   Benjamin Disraeli, a Tory PM and a prolific novelist.

15   *Dorothy Grey, Edward's 'country wife' (photographed 1890).*

The publication of Charles Darwin's *Origin of Species* had reinforced Western man's belief in the hierarchical structure of mankind, with the Negro races occupying the bottom rung of the evolutionary ladder. Thus it was considered perfectly legitimate for the white man, as the trail-blazer of civilisation, to appropriate this wasteland of tribal wars.

When Edward arrived at the Foreign Office he was immediately faced by a divided Cabinet. The problem that had arisen concerned a trading post in Uganda established by the British East Africa Company which had run into difficulties and from which the Company was threatening to withdraw. Should they or should they not be bailed out by the government? Gladstone was in favour of standing by traditional *laissez-faire* policy, according to which the Company should be left to sink or swim. Showing greater foresight than his chief, his Foreign Secretary disagreed. With African land-grabbing fever now infecting Britain's major European rivals, one or other might have an eye to appropriating Uganda, which might be found to possess valuable mineral reserves, and for that reason Lord Rosebery was urging protection.

After absorbing as much relevant information as his head could hold, Edward came to the conclusion that Lord Rosebery's view was the correct one. But in conveying his master's opinion to the Commons, as a fledgling government spokesman he knew he must tread carefully. In the event he was able to put forward some form of compromise on Lord Rosebery's behalf and this was accepted. His tactful intervention was considered to have been 'deft'. It was agreed that Sir Edward had acquitted himself remarkably well and that he was someone worth watching. Knowing that he had negotiated his first hurdle successfully, the young Under-Secretary had every reason to be pleased.

The first year of Gladstone's fourth premiership was devoted largely to his long-running battle for Home Rule for Ireland. After fierce opposition his Bill was passed by the Commons, only to be thrown out by the Lords, many of whose members had extensive Irish landholdings. Gladstone resigned, to be succeeded at Number 10 by Lord Rosebery. Edward's new chief at the Foreign Office was Lord Kimberley. But Rosebery still took a particular interest in foreign affairs, which was to stand Edward in good stead when he committed a serious gaffe. In February 1895 it was reported in the press that the French were making incursions into the Upper Nile Valley with a view to making territorial claims in a region which the British regarded as coming under their sphere of influence. Without seeking clearance from his chief, Edward informed the French government that any such incursion would be viewed by Britain as an 'unfriendly act'. In diplomatic terms his statement was considered to convey a menacing tone. It caused a furore, since in diplomatic circles it had 'the precise significance of a warning which could only be followed by an ultimatum'.[14] As it turned out, the rumours proved to be baseless. But Edward's words had been timely, serving as 'a public warning to the French that such a mission should not be attempted in the future'.[15] Though there were calls in some quarters for his resignation, Rosebery stuck up for his young friend and in the long term Edward's gaffe did him more good than harm, bringing his name before his fellow members as a man of resolution. The Grey 'declaration' was one of the few acts of a lacklustre government that was to be remembered.

Dorothy knew that as Edward's 'Town Wife' she was doomed to be a failure. She continued to loathe Society, while London's cultural delights held few charms for this dedicated countrywoman. Victorian art bored her, music disturbed, and until the eruption onto the London stage in the mid-1890s of Ibsen's plays with their serious moral purpose, the theatre was 'an institution in which she took not the slightest interest'.[16] As often as she could she escaped to the Cottage or returned to Fallodon, keeping in touch with Edward by a daily exchange of letters. One blustery March day she wrote to her husband from Fallodon:

> I arrived last night in a mighty wind; a pure, rushing wind that took hold of me. All the hollies in the drive were whispering, and the large trees above roared loud. Is it not a noble sound? … The garden is full of the funny small spring flowers – aconites, hepaticas, primulas, much too small to pick, but so nice to look at and stroke … I am getting quite drunk and stupid I love it so. I wish I could talk to the trees in their language … I shall go and roll about in the grass – I am so happy![17]

The French windows in the library were always kept open in summer, allowing robins to fly in and out and tame red squirrels to hop onto Edward's desk, looking for nuts. 'The squirrels are emptying the drawer', she told her husband. 'I grow tired of handing them nuts.' When down at the Cottage most of her time was given to reading and quiet observation: 'I have had a splendid fine and coloured day', she wrote. 'I have looked a goldfinch full in the eye while it sat in its hedge. I have heard a water rail … '[18]

Her letters refer frequently to her loathing of town life and in September 1893 she wrote:

> If our life outside politics was to be muddy and doubtful, the contrast would not be so great. But every bit of purity in us, every little bit of heaven shared, is one more shadow cast on the blackness of town life, with its unworthy aims, mistakes and devilishness.[19]

This was strong stuff. But Edward was content to accept his wife for what she was. At no time was he ever heard to complain or to accuse Dorothy of neglecting him.

She had grown very fond of his younger brother, George, finding they had much in common when he visited them on one of his rare breaks from his adventurous life in Southern Africa. They corresponded regularly, and nowhere is her hatred of town life more forcibly expressed than in a letter she wrote to him from 18 Grosvenor Road in November 1894. 'Well, we have got back to this horrible place', she opened her letter:

> The leaving Fallodon was quite dreadful. We had had such a happy week … planting nice things and walking about with spades and axes. The strongest hate we feel now is of people, any people: they are all horrid and there is no health in them; they are mean and selfish. If they see that one is happy they are jealous and hate one, if they see that one is miserable they feel triumph … Clever people only care for themselves and want to dazzle one; stupid people are even more self-conscious and blame other people for their want of understanding … I can't rest in this London, it falls on one like a black darkness, its impurities, its conventionalities, its crowdedness and its filth. In the old wood we could sit on a tree trunk and listen to starlings on the top part of a beech making their extraordinary imitations of other birds, greenfinches, spring curlews, peewits, jackdaws in rocks, faint thrushes in the distance, all done quite clearly and unmistakably, so much nicer and more mysterious and pure than the jabbering of people … How can we praise God and keep our hearts up?[20]

Later she must have regretted her misanthropic tone, for she added a postscript:

> Its quite dreadful for you to have such a letter written to you … I feel inclined to ask you to pray for me, but I should not know what I meant by it, so I will only say go on being fond of me.

It is easy to be hard on Dorothy and to label her selfish. Yet Society has always been a theatre of the absurd – a platform for one-upmanship. Dorothy recognised this. And with her demand for absolute truth and clarity in relationships, the cant and hypocrisy of the 'great and the good' was as loathsome to her as was the sheer press of faceless people thronging the London streets.

In summer the city stank. Though a new and superior drainage system had taken care of the 'Great Stink' of 1849 (when the Thames had been no better than an open sewer and its stench had closed down Parliament), even in the West End the reek of dung deposited on the streets by horse-drawn traffic of every description – plus the mixed odours of unrefrigerated foodstuffs and unwashed humanity – must have been offensive to anyone of a sensitive nature; the more so to a young woman reared in the bracing air of Northumberland.

But the winters were the worst. In the 1890s the heat for cooking and warming the dwellings of over five million Londoners was provided almost exclusively by coal, much of it burnt on open fires. The metropolis was also home to thousands of workshops and manufactories, great and small, 'the bulk of which pumped out smoke and soot (and in all too many cases noxious fumes) into the atmosphere.'[21] As temperatures dropped, 'vast quantities of soot-laden smoke would be released … creating a murky pall over the city'. On windy days much of this could be dispersed, but in calm weather the smoke would turn swiftly into the familiar 'pea-souper' fog immortalised by Arthur Conan Doyle. There were, besides, many winter days 'that were so dark as to reduce the city to a perpetual twilight, as if the sun had forgotten to rise.'[22]

Was it to be wondered at that both the Greys, but more especially Dorothy, echoing their favourite poet Wordsworth, should find a correlation between the filth and muck of cities and the darkness to be found in the hearts of those people who were compelled to live completely out of touch with the rhythms of the natural world?

All his life Lord Rosebery had been plagued by insomnia. It afflicted him most when he was under stress, impairing his judgement. By the summer of 1895 it had become plain that he was losing his grip on his Party, which in June was defeated by a Tory stratagem, and Parliament was dissolved. Edward, judging (rightly) that the Liberals would be out of office for some time, saw this as the perfect moment for giving up the 'experiment' of politics. But when word got round in his constituency that he was thinking of retiring there was an outcry. Touched by the loyalty of his supporters (and almost certain that he would be beaten at the polls) Edward agreed to stand one last time. To his astonishment 300 votes were added to his majority – a success against the tide. Once again, fate had intervened to point him towards his destiny. Dorothy made no attempt to hide her dismay.

Chapter XXIX

Gerard as Go-Between

There is a book in the Newton library written by Dr Henry Maudsley, the founder of the famous London hospital for the treatment of mental disorders which still bears his name. *Body and Mind* was first published in 1875 and it is likely that the book was purchased by the Widdringtons and consulted by them in the hope that it might provide answers to Gerard's problems. At that time, however, a serious stigma was attached to mental illness and there is no evidence that specialist treatment for Gerard was ever sought.

And in any case, though Gerard was undoubtedly odd, out of step with the world and occasionally bizarre in his behaviour, there was nothing to suggest that he was mentally impaired. When at the age of nine he was packed off to boarding school he did well enough to pass the entrance examination to Winchester College, which was no walkover. During his schooldays Cecilia's greatest worry was her boy's solitariness; the fact that he never seemed to make a friend.

Yet sooner or later it had to be faced that Gerard was not growing out of his peculiarities. On the contrary, with adolescence his queerness was growing more marked. Tall for his age, the teenage boy did not seem to know how to cope with his gangling frame; and Cecilia was grieved to see that his social ineptitude and odd way of speaking were becoming an embarrassment to his siblings.

'You are in a strange dumb state', she wrote when Gerard was 16, 'and Father is most concerned. I think you shrink from speaking partly because you speak so indistinctly no one can half understand you … You are terribly inert and unwilling to move much or use yr great strength ever.'

Cecilia believed that Gerard had 'a great sense of religion' from one or two of his remarks, 'but on this subject I never speak to my children as my views are peculiar'. He was 'a pure-minded boy'. She had told him 'many details wch many mothers shrink from but I think it better you should know and hear reverently from me the facts of nature rather than from the jeers and jokes of companions'.

> You are of a saving nature – careful not to have 2 candles burning unnecessarily – and never ask for money or spend much – I fear you are no favourite – how could you be and

dear knows how it will end. You talk a little to me – but to Father and B. utter silence. You are argumentative in an odd pertinacious sort of way when out with Ida – but I am convinced you are of very late mental development – tho' huge in body – you have the face and thoughts of a child of 12 – we must have patience – and wait.

Cecilia refused to abandon hope.

Yet all the patience in the world was never going to turn her ugly duckling into a swan. The boy struggled on and, following a term's coaching at a tutorial establishment in Windsor, he was offered a place at Oriel, one of the smaller Oxford colleges. His parents settled him into his college rooms, supplying him with furniture and pictures, and before long they were encouraged to learn that he had made some friends. This could be a breakthrough and when Gerard invited two of them to stay at Newton during the Long Vacation Cecilia was determined to make the young men feel welcome.

Bell arrived first: 'A small meek fellow, shy and not much to say'. It was soon evident that he was overawed by the unfamiliar mores of a large country house. Oliver, Gerard's second friend, appeared to be equally out of his depth. 'A poor delicate thing, but harmless', was the best that Cecilia could find to say about him.

In his second year his parents learned that Gerard had taken lodgings with the two young men. Cecilia and Ida decided to pay him a visit. 'Yr rooms looked nice and all yr pictures hung about', Cecilia commented. But on closer acquaintance his new friends were revealed to be 'dreadfully commonplace' and no more than a couple of scroungers. However, Ida, whose troupe was short of a man for one of their plays, on the spur of the moment invited Bell to Newton for a second visit. Gerard demurred; and one look at her son's face was enough to tell Cecilia that Ida's invitation had been ill-judged. 'And we ought to have listened and not had him', she recorded in her *Gerard Diary*:

> For he was an awful Bounder, supercilious and thinking to flirt with Ida, was bad for knowing his part and had to be reduced to great order – Ida refusing even to address him … We had a large party in the house who all hated and snubbed him and I fear it was very painful – so I put Bell always by me and was good to him … Bertram hated him badly and altogether it was unfortunate. I was terribly afraid you would never dare to bring yr friends here again.

It was plain that Gerard was becoming alienated from his brother and sister and that his so-called friends were only out for what they could get – though they lacked the wit to see that in accepting invitations to Newton they were entering a minefield. The laws governing the lives of the landed gentry were full of traps for the unwary; and though Ida and Bertram would have been indignant at being called snobs they retained all the innate prejudices of their class and could be merciless to outsiders. It was a hard lesson for Gerard. He returned to Oxford feeling neither flesh nor fowl. He belonged nowhere.

He had managed to pass in 'Mods', the examination sat by undergraduates at the end of their first year. But in his second year his commitment to his studies lapsed and he left the University without obtaining a degree. He returned home and moped about or took himself off on long solitary walks. Cecilia tried to find jobs for him: 'I had to howke

16   *Evelyn (Evie) Lloyd Price.*

weed out of the pond with you and try to be young.' Sometimes he went out with a gun 'but seldom brought anything in'. Cecilia wondered at his perseverance.

The previous summer Fitz and Cecilia, along with Ida, had taken the two boys to their first ball. Bertram enjoyed himself immensely and proved a great hit with the young women. Gerard loathed it. 'Very wretched and shy', he could only be persuaded to dance with Ida, or his mother. Soon Bertram was being asked everywhere and Cecilia saw that Gerard was feeling it bitterly. 'But what is the good of you going? You are far too shy and know no one … We had a heap of people staying and it did pain Father to see you striding aimlessly about with no manners and enjoying nothing.'

What was to become of him? Mr Golightly, their vicar, thought Gerard might be inclined to take Orders:

> such is the gravity of yr mind, the kindness of a great heart … but when I asked you I was met with a very decided no. I am glad – a good quiet-lived squire in my opinion has a far wider field for influence and for doing good than the best of parsons, where good labours under the disadvantage of being professionally good.

Yet if she was honest, could Cecilia see her boy taking on the role of squire? How would he cope? A miracle would be needed. Perhaps (as is the way of mothers) she was hoping for just that.

She took him off with her to Hopwood to get him away for a while. Her widowed mother, Susan, though shrunken and frail, was still a force to be reckoned with. Smoke from the cotton mills built on Hopwood land was now threatening the whole of the estate and the old lady was campaigning vigorously for its abatement. Cecilia's brother Edward, now the squire, was of the opinion that the damage had already gone too far. All his talk was of selling up and moving to Yorkshire. The old lady fumed. Gerard was asked for his opinion. It appeared he had none. His grandmother thought him a poor thing. Edward tried to persuade him to dine with some of his rowdy friends. Cecilia was thankful when he declined.

> Yr old evening clothes were a sight and too small for you and you never would get new ones though I begged you to … I knew quite well they would only make games of you and probably make you drunk.

Cecilia's one relief at this trying time was provided by writing long letters to Roger Fry and receiving his engaging replies. Life in his parents' gloomy Bayswater house was reducing him, so he said, to a 'strange jelly-like mass with about as much consciousness as a chloroformed amoeba'[1] and eventually he had succeeded in moving out. The little house in Beaufort Street, Chelsea, which he now shared with a Cambridge friend, had a studio in the back garden where he could paint with no fear of being disturbed. 'A great mulberry tree hung its branches over the garden wall'[2] and the river Thames which ran at the end of the street was an endless source of fascination, with 'barges passing and the silhouettes of factory chimneys and the yellow lights opening in the evening'.[3]

Rather to his surprise, Roger had discovered that, freed from the confines of the family home he was gregarious. The two young friends started to entertain and soon the house began to fill up with their friends. Unfortunately the detailed and painstaking painting style Roger had adopted at this time was unfashionable, and his work was meeting with little success. He felt his failure chiefly for the pain it was causing his parents, who still supported him. Increasingly he found himself turning for moral support to Mrs Widdrington. In contrast to his mother (whom he loved dearly but felt unable to confide in) she was entirely unjudgemental and unshockable. No subject was barred, no philosophical speculation too wild to be seriously examined; and when he was plunged into temporary despair she would use her native common sense to fish him out.

Of course he continued to miss Ida. Merely to recall that deep throaty voice was to open up a wound. But Mrs Widdrington had assured him that given time it would heal, and he knew he must try to believe her.

An undated letter from Cecilia written from 40 Clarges Street, Mayfair and addressed to 'Dear Mr Fry' invited him to dinner. Gerard, who had accompanied his mother to London, was to make a third. 'We dined with F at a restaurant', Cecilia recorded in the *Gerard Diary*. 'I had feared it wd be dull for you with us two, because F's talk is very above average philosophic, but you assured me you "liked to hear it" so we enjoyed ourselves.'

This was the first of many London outings at which Gerard was destined to play 'gooseberry', his unobtrusive presence serving to throw a smokescreen over a ripening friendship between his mother and Mr Fry, which otherwise might have aroused comment. But in time these occasional lunches and dinners were found not to be enough to satisfy the needs of this oddly matched couple. Cecilia sensed there were whole areas of Roger's personal life which were too confused and far too intimate to be discussed before a third party over a dinner table. She and he needed privacy. But how was it to be obtained?

Eventually she hatched a plan. She had seen that Roger had a flair for capturing likenesses. An early oil painting of his sister Margery she considered very fine, and she had persuaded some of her friends to sit for him. Now she wrote to her sister Evie, hinting at her situation and asking her to commission a portrait.

She and Evie, the youngest and also the prettiest of the Hopwood girls, had always been very close. Evie had married Dick Price, the scion of one of the oldest and most distinguished families in Wales. His principal seat at Rhiwlas – a grandiose mock-Tudor mansion sited among the hills of Merioneth – was set in a vast acreage which its present owner seemed intent on gambling away. In early middle age Evie was still remarkably pretty. Sensing that perhaps there was more to her sister's request than met the eye, she replied that she would be happy to have her portrait painted providing that Cecilia agreed to accompany her protégé to Rhiwlas. Thus it was arranged. And to forestall any hint of a raised eyebrow it was agreed that Gerard was also to have his portrait painted, and with that in view would accompany his mother.

As the setting for a romantic rendezvous Cecilia's choice of Rhiwlas was inspired. The place was only a few miles from Aberhirnant, the lodge which in earlier days her father, Edward Hopwood, had taken each summer for the sport. Cecilia had spent the happiest days of a rather dismal childhood at Aberhirnant, with its tumbling streams and rock-strewn mountain walks, and she had loved that part of Wales ever since.

She and Gerard arrived at Rhiwlas early in April. Roger Fry came by train and was met at Rhuabon. The weather was fine and drifts of daffodils nodded under the trees, which were just breaking into bud. The first few days proved awkward, since Roger could find little to say to his host, who in any case rated artists as little better than tradesmen. Writing to a friend who had met Cecilia, he gave a witty account of Rhiwlas and its owners:

> Her sister's place is an enormous sort of sham Gothic castle furnished in an extravagant Ouida-esque way with things brought from Algeria and every conceivable luxury but kept in curiously bad repair – the whole tone of the place is something utterly unlike anything I ever saw before. Her husband is a vicious man* who gathered round him every kind of boon companion and the place was once famous for its extravagance and recklessness. But Mrs Price is rather a fine character, she manages the whole of their enormous estates, has learnt Welsh in order to do so and is simply worshipped by all her dependents.[4]

Although Roger found Evie 'quite illiterate and common in her views and tastes', he believed she was 'saved by an extraordinarily kindly and benevolent nature and a keen mother wit from being dull or uninteresting'.[5]

The sittings were begun. Roger's 'first attempt' at Gerard 'was really pretty good – he didn't seize your idiosyncrasies … you were a most patient sitter but thankful when it was over but the fact of having to be looked at so long did you good'.†

The river was drawn for salmon and between Roger's painting sessions the party fished and walked. The finished portrait of Evie was voted 'a great success'. Roger

---

* 'Vicious' is too harsh a word to attach to Dick Price. Though he was an inveterate gambler – reputed to have reduced the size of his estates from 180,000 acres to a mere 10,000 – and was the despair of his wife, he was much loved by his friends and though undoubtedly reckless and eccentric was a charmer.

† Painted in oils, the picture turned up recently, propped up against a wall in one of the damp upstairs rooms at Newton among a miscellany of unframed paintings and sketches, mostly the work of Fitz. It is a sensitive study, capturing the dilemma of a young man caught in a world he would never come to terms with; the deep brown eyes seeking a reassurance he was destined never to find.

himself believed it to be 'a better likeness than any I've done yet and quite interesting as a picture'.*

As days turned into weeks the frisson between Cecilia and her protégé intensified. But it was proving difficult for them to find time to be alone, with Gerard always dogging their footsteps. He even 'went out by moonlight with me and R. Fry' – taking an intelligent interest, as his mother recorded 'in all the different talk ... time and space and such like'. However, she must have found his presence very frustrating. Finally Gerard was persuaded to leave Rhiwlas some days ahead of his mother; and with the help of Evie all was resolved.

But if we look to Cecilia's diaries to tell us how this resolution came about we shall find no answers there. For she tells us just as much as she wishes us to know, leaving the rest unsaid. To arrive at the truth we must turn to other sources; notably to a letter Roger Fry wrote to his Cambridge friend, Goldsworthy Lowes Dickinson, known to his intimates as Goldie.

While an undergraduate at Cambridge Fry had been elected to the Apostles, a secret society which, being restricted to six members, considered itself very select. To be elected was 'a priding thing', as Roger admitted to his mother. What he did not tell her (and may not have realised himself) was that the majority of the Society's members were homosexual. An innocent in sexual matters, the truth only began to dawn when he realised that his friend Goldie, who had been elected to the Apostles just prior to himself, loved him in a way which he did not feel it would be possible for him to return. However, as Fry was still a virgin, Goldie believed his friend could not yet be aware of his true sexual orientation, and he continued to hope.

Drawing on what she had learned about Roger's repressed Quaker upbringing Cecilia must have guessed (even if he had not told her) that his unexplored sexuality had left him with many unanswered questions. And since she thought she could supply the answers, and had been made a little light-headed by the power of love, with the connivance of her sister she undertook to instruct him.

She was confident that she could rely on dear Evie's discretion. And assuredly it must have been Evie who had put a cottage at her disposal and provided her with transport and the services of a maid ... In a letter he cannot have found easy to write, Roger outlined to Goldie what had happened:

> My dearest Goldie, ... I want much to see you and talk to you, but I fear to do so by letter for fear I may hurt you – suffice it to say that I think I was right, there was no reaction of disgust or shame – at the end of the time we escaped to a lovely Welsh valley which was wonderfully beautiful and stayed for two days.
>
> I must tell you some things about her past life wch will make you admire her still more, she is very great and generous and I think can only do me good not harm and I am sure I do her good. But enough ...

With his usual sensitivity Roger ended his letter with words designed to reassure his friend that 'all that has happened only draws me nearer to you', signing himself 'Yr Podg'.[6]

---

* Unfortunately it disappeared and has never been found.

Knowledge of this unusual couple's brief idyll was confined to a small number of their intimate friends, until in 1940 Virginia Woolf was invited to write Roger Fry's biography. Cecilia Widdrington was not long dead and out of respect for her family her name does not appear. But there is no mistaking the identity of the woman of whom Mrs Woolf wrote:

> Among those fleeting attachments to young and lovely faces there was a more serious relationship with a lady who was neither young nor beautiful, but old enough to be his mother. She it was who undertook to educate him in the art of love … Endowed, he said, 'with enough fire to stock all the devils in Hell', she stormed at his stupidity, laughed at his timidity and ended by falling in love with him herself. He profited by the lesson and was profoundly grateful to his teacher. Had she not taught him what was far more important than … discriminating between a genuine Botticelli and a sham? So he thought at least, and to the end of life pupil and mistress remained the best of friends.[7]

CHAPTER XXX

Between Two Loves

Cecilia's love for Roger Fry opened her eyes to a world that was to enrich her life until the end of her days. As a child she had been hungry for facts. Painfully aware of her own ignorance she had crept into her father's library in search of information. Facts, she believed, were the basic building blocks upon which knowledge of the world – leading hopefully to understanding – ultimately depended. But the panelled library with its dusty leather-bound tomes and shelf upon shelf filled with the works of Voltaire, many of them in the original French, had dismayed her. Picking out a few books at random she attempted to make sense of them, but to little avail. Eventually Fitz, responding to her unspoken cry for 'light, more light!' had offered her marriage. Thereafter travel, motherhood, and the run of her husband's well-stocked library, all made their contribution to her education and in the quarter-century that had elapsed since she became mistress of Newton her horizons had been immeasurably enlarged. However, the exigencies of running a large country house and raising a family had called for practical skills which did not leave much time for intellectualising. It was not until she met Roger Fry that with him she began to explore the world of ideas.

Roger had 'very luminous eyes with a curious power of observation in them.'[1] How attentively he would look at some inanimate object! Behind the owl-like spectacles his eyes seemed to bore into its very essence. Nothing escaped his scrutiny, even homely household items: the arrangement of a row of jugs upon a shelf ... And he was endlessly asking questions. When you look at a picture, what does it communicate? Do you respond to its form, or to its content? Is landscape painting an imitative or a creative art? How important is 'atmosphere'? Should the artist paint what he sees, or like Turner chose a scene which embodies many individual scenes, harmonising the details so as to create one single intense impression? What is the connection between art and morality? Can we speak of a morality of aesthetics?

When Fitz set up his easel he left theorising behind. Sometimes he would paint what he saw, at others he might fill his canvas with some scene conjured out of his head. In either case he did not discuss with Cecilia (or with anyone else) what his intentions were. He simply did. As an amateur (albeit an unusually gifted one) he had never been swayed by fashion or by the need to find a market for his art (though he acknowledged a debt to the great Venetian painter Canaletto, and to the delicate landscapes of his first teacher, the shy and whimsical tutor Edward Lear).* Fitz's painting was a private passion; he had little communication with fellow artists, and if he chose to vary his style it was only to please himself. Roger Fry, on the other hand, saw himself as a professional artist whose aim was to live by his work. Always willing to experiment, he sought out the work of other artists, different 'schools', attempting to form judgements while striving to find a style of his own and to separate the true from the false.

As a means of supplementing the allowance he received from his father he had begun to contribute short articles and reviews of art shows he had attended to the weekly and monthly magazines. But he was only paid a pittance. Then he was asked to give a series of lectures and after he had gained a little confidence he found lecturing was more congenial to him. 'He had a beautiful speaking voice and the power, whatever its origin, to transmit emotion while transmitting facts'.[2] His live audiences stimulated him and he found himself speaking with assurance and authority. More lecture engagements followed. When Cecilia was in town she sometimes managed to attend them: 'It was good to get up to London once in a while – to blow away the cobwebs and meet new people who cared not a jot for who you were, only being interested in what you thought.' She and Roger had discovered a shared love of music and would sometimes attend concerts together: Bach, Monteverdi, Gluck … ('I suppose Gluck isn't a very great musician, but Lord what a gift for melody and how right in feeling he is!'). Sometimes Gerard would accompany them. At other times, rather daringly, they would go on their own.

Poetry formed another bond, though Roger considered Cecilia's tastes a little old-fashioned. The great Lord Tennyson had recently died – but did not Cecilia agree that the poems of Gerard Manley Hopkins (a poet of whom she had never heard) were infinitely superior? Ideas fizzed around him like firecrackers, though in worldly matters he was still naive. And in the act of love she found he still needed constant reassurance.

Roger had made an oil sketch of Cecilia during their stay at Rhiwlas and now he decided to attempt a full-length portrait. Cecilia had chosen to be painted in a magnificent 18th-century ball gown, once the property of a Hopwood ancestor and preserved at Hopwood Hall. The first sittings for the portrait were to be done at Hopwood. (Whether Susan Gregge-Hopwood – or Fitz, for that matter – knew or guessed that the artist and his sitter were lovers, is impossible to say.)

Cecilia took the uncompleted painting home to be inspected by her family. They approved, but she herself did not like the way Roger had done her eyes and the painting was returned to his studio for further work. Apparently it was never finished and like his portrait of Evie Price it has since disappeared.†

Roger was so entranced by Cecilia's uninhibited personality that he was determined his parents should meet her. By this time Sir Edward had retired and the couple had moved

---

* As a young man Lear had been tutor to Lord Derby's children at Knowsley Hall in Lancashire, which was within visiting distance of Fitz's home and where the two must have met.

† Roger must have hung on to it, for years later he found it when moving house, as he explained in a letter to his friend Vanessa Bell: 'I turned out among other things a vast portrait I did ages ago of Mrs Widdrington in a fancy dress costume of a sort of eighteenth-century idea, coming down a flight of stairs … rather terrible wasn't it, but in spite of horrible lapses not altogether bad, rather raw in colour but not quite hopeless.' The portrait was probably destroyed.

to Failand, their country house in the village of Frenchay, near Bristol. Initially Cecilia had demurred, feeling that the meeting could be awkward, but eventually that autumn she agreed to spend a few days with Sir Edward and Lady Fry. She soon established an easy rapport with Sir Edward, making him laugh and talk 'and discuss metaphysics and religion and politics in a way I haven't heard him do for ages'.[3] Roger wrote to his friend Goldie. Mrs Widdrington and Lady Fry found little to say to one another, and Roger drew an unfavourable comparison between the two women: 'One seems to lead on to further possibilities, to fresh life even, though with fresh suffering, and the other seems to have killed art, all pleasure, all love, all real emotions.'

He admitted the ambiguity of his position had put a great strain on him 'and I sometimes feel tempted when I am in a cowardly mood to think I have cut off a bigger chunk of life than I can chew, but then perhaps that's better than cutting off less'.

Indeed that turned out to be true. Seeing his mother through Cecilia's eyes served to emphasise the narrowness of his parents' vision and the chilling nature of the regime he had suffered under as their child. (When in later life he developed a better understanding of the forces that had shaped his parents, his attitude softened.)

Returning home, caught up in sensations she had never expected to feel again, Cecilia was relieved to find that Ida – with her proclivity for jumping from one love to another – seemed to have put Roger completely out of her mind. She was wrong.

After listening with very mixed feelings to her mother's account of her visit, Ida reached for her pen. 'I have been so interested hearing all about Mamma and your own people,' she wrote to Roger, ignoring her promise.

> She's awfully fond of your father now and keeps quoting him, and says you're all so beautifully clever. She's fearfully bored with us now and calls us all sorts of rude names. My Dad is so amused, he waxes most witty on the subject and chaffs Mother and says he feels awfully out of it now.

It was clear that Fitz was not the only one feeling 'awfully out of it'. And what harm could it do to write to Roger again? His regard for Mamma made it plain he had entirely got over his 'silliness'. So why could they not return to being friends? Ida had missed her 'dearest pen pal in all the world' quite dreadfully, for since parting with Roger she had been through a difficult time – the worst few months she could remember. Bereft of his wise counsel, before she knew what was happening she had allowed Willy Lawson to creep back into her life – though how the situation had developed so rapidly she was at a loss to explain.

The truth was that her mother's preoccupation with Roger had caused her to take her eye off the ball, and Lawson, turning up at one of Ida's singing engagements, had seized his chance to corner her. He lost no time in declaring his unshakeable love, urging Ida to flee with him, leaving wife, family and home. Initially Ida had agreed. But later she changed her mind, retaining just enough common sense to refuse him. 'It was a heavy time for you, poor little passionate thing, and a sore tug,' Cecilia commented when she discovered what had been going on. 'For for no doubt you loved him and had for years, try as you might to tear him from yr heart.'

Her concern for her daughter is notable for its lack of blame or reproach. As she herself had discovered, physical passion is an elemental force well-nigh impossible to resist and, though Fitz was furious, she saw Ida's indiscretion as a small thing when weighed against her courageous decision to put duty before love.

After that searing experience Ida had sworn she would never marry. But what then was she to do with the rest of her life?

The previous summer, when Lady Cust, now a permanent invalid, had been at Newton on one of her interminable visits, Ida had struck up a friendship with her attendant, Nurse Budge. According to the nurse, once you had completed your training you could be sent abroad to one of the far-flung outposts of Empire. Egypt, perhaps, or India, combining the drama of saving lives with the thrill of foreign travel.

Now Ida announced to her astonished parents that she intended to turn round her life and train as a nurse. Cecilia was sceptical. Had not Dolly come up with the same mad idea at a time when she was unhappy and at odds with the world? Fortunately she had met Edward, which put nursing out of her head. Ida was still in shock, her stomach pains had returned, and what she needed was a holiday. Cecilia decided to whisk her off to Paris. She had a double motive, for she knew that Roger Fry planned to be there.

It was, she recorded, 'a very nice visit', with Roger taking them everywhere about – to the *Chat Noir* and Fontainebleau and to the opera, where Wagner's *Valkyrie* was playing. However, there had been times when Ida's flirtatious behaviour had seriously upset her mother. 'Strange captious rather capricious mortal that you are,' she wrote,

> I observed that RF totally banished WL from yr mind for the time! You were more than half in love with him and almost told him so – as I overheard sometimes – its incredible and I couldn't help reproaching you with yr very unfaith to WL, thus taking the side of the impossible – but either love – or not love – you can't understand a middle – you can love a number of men at once for totally opposed qualities – <u>no one</u> man can ever content you.

Roger left Paris and returned home. But Ida's stomach pains still bothered her and Cecilia consulted a French doctor. He recommended 'expensive and futile douches' and when these failed to bring relief sent them off to try the waters at Plombières-les-Bains, a fashionable spa near Nancy. Out of season, it was the most dreary place imaginable: 'V. terrible time – terrible place – no soul was there', Cecilia reported.

Seeking relief from the unutterable boredom of hot baths and dreary walks, Ida once more took up her pen. Her letter to Roger makes it evident that during their *tête-à-têtes* in Paris she told him she would like to resume their correspondence and that he had tried to dissuade her. Plainly, he was in a fix. He could not write openly and frankly to one woman without betraying the other. Ida had no idea that the man who had proposed to her not so very long ago had since become her mother's lover. And Roger could not bear that she should know it. For no sooner had they met than the old impossible anguish started up again. Nothing had changed. He was convinced that the only cure was to put Ida out of his life completely and make up his mind never to see her.

Ida, however, had other ideas. Nursing a badly bruised heart, she had been delighted to see Roger again – her one true friend – the only man she could trust. Never had she needed a confidant more urgently. This time she had no intention of letting him go. She wrote:

Sunday. Plombières. So – may I lift a corner of the sluice and let one small thin particle of stream trickle soberly from Plombières to London? Yes, well, look out because its coming ... But what a duffer you are – because I write to you thats no reason why you need write to me – its only Jews, Turks, infidels, Germans, women & similar indecencies that have time to waste on so frivolous an occupation as forming vague and misty thoughts into words; it had become such a habit with me for years and years, in fact nearly all of my life to write either half the day or half the night that somebody has to suffer.

In a letter covering eight closely written pages, Ida explained that where formerly she had confided her thoughts to a black ledger, she far preferred to write to him. She begged Roger to tell her really candidly if her letters (which she did not expect him to answer) upset his work? She assured him that since they last met she had become a different person; benefiting from his reproaches on her aimless life, she had made up her mind to take up nursing. 'I'm the right age – just for Kings* and may get in but there's awful competition.'

In Paris Ida must have confessed how close she had come to running off with Willie Lawson and now she could not keep off the subject of her doomed love affair. 'I'm sorry I love him so badly, quite sorry, but if ever he gets free I'll make his life decent for him again and help him not to bungle things so ... Please don't say its horrid of me (to write)', she concluded, 'I'm sure its quite a dull impersonal letter and I only want the shortest of answers.' She signed herself 'Apologetically, Idonea.' It is not known whether Roger replied.

When Ida returned home she applied formally to be considered for a place as a trainee nurse at King's College Hospital. That summer Bertram had passed out of Sandhurst, the elite army officer training college, and he was given six months' leave while waiting for his commission. It would be his last taste of freedom before the Army claimed him and he decided to spend it at Newton.

By this time his relationship with Gerard had completely broken down. Exasperated incomprehension on his side was met by a stoic withdrawal on the part of his brother. But at least there would be Ida to keep her brother company. She and Bertram had always been close and their parents decided 'not to mind a little extra expense' but to give them 'a real good time' before they embarked on their respective careers.

In October cubbing began and as it was a mild winter sister and brother got plenty of hunting. Seeing the colour return to her daughter's cheeks, Cecilia doubted whether Ida, with her love of outdoor sports and frivolous grasshopper nature, would be capable of submitting to the discipline required of a nurse. She would have far preferred Ida to be looking for a husband! She consoled herself with the reflection that a nurse's training could only do Ida good and might even tame her a little.

Meanwhile both brother and sister were having a whirl. But in November, Ida's hectic social life was curtailed by her need to rehearse for the season of plays and concerts which now filled her winter months, taking her all over the county. She had just returned from one of her acting engagements when a wire was received from King's College Hospital, requesting her to report for duty at 24 hours' notice.

* King's College Hospital in London.

The household was thrown into confusion. How should Ida respond? There was no doubt in her mother's mind: family must come first. 'Bertram being at home all these months thought he wd be very dull without Ida, that she ought to devote herself to him.' A wire was sent requesting postponement to which King's consented. Yet obviously Ida felt guilty, fearing what Roger would have to say. In a long letter to her 'dearest of all human pals' she confessed she felt 'a coward and a defaulter and a low down skunk', but that 'poor little Mamma is worried to death and looking ill and perfectly wretched, she says she dreads the winter alone with Bertram about the place being bored and no one to help'.

Anticipating that Roger would not easily be convinced of her altruistic motive for postponing her training she continued to lay it on with a trowel:

> Mamma nearly died of this week without me [i.e., when Ida had been away with her theatre troupe], what with Auntie T[*] being so ill and Gerard's friend Hughes being so utterly out of key, and Lady Cust having gone so entirely to the bad again, worse than ever and the Father getting rampant with low spirits and me leaving them all in the lurch. When I got home she was looking like a half boiled ghost and its not fair on her.

Ida's description of her mother was intended no doubt to make Roger smile, though by the time he had read to the end of Ida's 14-page missive, the mixed messages she was sending him must have driven him close to despair. For once embarked on a letter to her unwilling confidant, Ida's need to unburden herself proved impossible to resist. Still pining for Lawson, she insisted (not for the first time) that the affair was now over: 'So utterly utterly gone that its only folly to bring it up again, why remember, why regret, when Time is tearing on at this awful rate, hurrying one into every sort of new phase and experience.'

It is plain from this letter that Ida and Roger had met briefly in London. It would have been their first meeting since Paris and she had found his manner stiff and somewhat strained. 'You'll never believe how much I care for you,' she insisted:

> You always speak as if you were indifferent to me and unless you are chatting it pains me, Roger … it does hurt so to go away from you always, but there, I won't say any more, what's the good, and I shan't see you for ages now … I'll never be alone with you at a station again, it's more than one's life's worth, how funny we were walking round miserable Hans Place in the dark, I couldn't <u>help</u> taking your arm Roger, I dare say it was bad of me … the tears got into my throat and it must have been too beastly for you, I'm so sorry for behaving like a weary idiot.

Following this highly emotional passage Ida switched to news of her pet tortoise. And after promising to knit Roger another pair of stockings (like her mother and sister she was an expert knitter) she must have compounded his confusion by signing herself his 'lovingest Idonea'. What was Roger supposed to make of that?

During the early months of 1894 Ida's concert schedule became increasingly frenetic, her charity concerts drawing enthusiastic audiences wherever she went. Her grandmother

---

[*]   Fitz's sister Lady de Tabley, formerly Smith-Barry.

Susan came up from Hopwood for the Newton village concert on 12 January and was 'astounded at Ida's 'talent and cleverness and fine voice'. She gave her granddaughter a turquoise ring. 'It was a real grand time and triumph for you', Cecilia recorded, 'real awful excitement and adulation … and why you don't take to it, and not nursing, I can't see.'

The downside was that having postponed her entry into nursing for Bertram's sake, Ida was now too busy to spare much time for her brother and on the rare occasions when they were at home together 'there had got to be a sort of coldness … yr talk bores him, its so personal to yrself'. In truth, Bertram's madcap sister was beginning to embarrass her highly conventional younger brother. The close companionship of earlier days was starting to unravel. It was the first sign of the bitter enmity which in later years was to poison their relationship.

In the last week of January 1894 Bertram learned that he been commissioned into the 60th Rifles and was being posted to India. Though the regiment had not been his first choice (he had been hoping for the Horseguards) it was considered 'a great prize and an advantage by everyone'. Last-minute shopping was now urgent and, after a tearful farewell to his mother, Fitz and Ida accompanied Bertram to London, where they were to spend a week with Dorothy and Edward. On 24 February the 20-year-old set off for India to join his regiment and Fitz returned to Newton, Ida having received permission from her sister to stay on for another week.

At that time the sisters' relationship was better than it had been for some time. Dorothy knew about Ida's friendship with Roger Fry, of which she thoroughly approved. Though abysmally ignorant of the art world she perceived that Mr Fry was a man of integrity, who was besides both witty and kind. She believed that he had been good for her sister, and told her so. Ida was delighted. She had never ceased to worship at her older sister's shrine, believing her sexless marriage to be an ideal state of utter blessedness. How fortunate she and Edward were to be capable of living lives untainted by the earthly passions that had come so close to ruining hers!

What happened during that week has been endlessly debated. Yet, however finely the evidence is sifted, the lack of verifiable documentation, coupled with the passage of time, makes it unlikely that a definitive conclusion will ever be reached.

Chapter XXXI

May

At some time during the early months of the year 1895 a smart horse-drawn equipage drew up outside a cottage in Riverwood Road in the village of Frenchay. The village was some six miles from Bristol, on the north bank of the River Frome. Watched by a handful of villagers, a groom climbed down from the box and opened the carriage door. A plainly dressed woman emerged, carrying a baby. The infant, who was reckoned to be about three months old, wore a pretty bonnet trimmed with swansdown and was wrapped in a fine cashmere shawl.

A woman came out from the cottage accompanied by four little girls, the eldest about eight years old, the youngest still a toddler. The groom asked her if she was Mrs Mann and when she had confirmed that she was he unloaded a single small trunk (very new and shiny) which between them the two elder girls carried into the cottage. The plainly dressed woman (who was judged to be a nursemaid) handed the baby over to Mrs Mann, who was observed to take a good look at it – jigging the infant up and down and making clucking noises.

'May, isn't it?' she asked the woman, who nodded.

'Any other names?'

'Not as I know of,' the woman replied.

She passed an envelope to Mrs Mann and was heard to explain that it contained details of the baby's birth weight and vaccination and so forth and some notes on how the child was accustomed to be fed. Mrs Mann asked the woman if she would care to step inside for some refreshment and offered to bring something out for the coachman and groom. All three declined. The woman got back into the carriage and was driven away.

In those days Frenchay was a pretty place, having a good-sized village green and a common that reached to its outskirts. The commodious Georgian houses at its upper end were mostly the property of Quaker families, who had their own Friends' Meeting House and a burial ground within the purlieus of the village.

It emerged that Mrs Mann – a capable woman who before her marriage had been a midwife – was being paid ten shillings a week for fostering little May. Noted for her discretion, she never divulged the source of the money. Mr Mann was employed as gardener to one of the Quakers, a Mr Ward, who was a barrister-at-law.

The Manns made no distinction between May and their own four daughters. A striking child, tall for her age, with fair hair and piercing blue eyes, May grew up to have a passion for animals and loved to be out of doors. But by her fourth birthday she had become headstrong and obstinate, refusing to curtsy to the gentry when they passed in their carriages. (The village of Frenchay at that time was almost feudal.)

May had never been formally adopted. Nevertheless when she started lessons at the village school she was registered as May Mann. However, when she began her confirmation classes some busybody pointed out to the rector that Mann was not, strictly speaking, the child's correct name. Most of the village knew the story of May's arrival, and drawing their own conclusions they were content to let matters rest. At least the father (who it was assumed was a gentleman with local connections) had not shirked his responsibilities.

When May discovered that the couple she had always looked on as her mum and dad were not her parents she took the news very badly. Whose child was she then? She badgered Mrs Mann to tell her who her real parents were. She particularly wanted to know the identity of her mother. 'Your mother was a very wicked woman, you don't need to know – don't ask me again,' her foster mother replied. Though Mrs Mann was not a hard woman she thought she knew right from wrong and she was not to be argued with. May never dared to question her again and Mrs Mann kept the secret till the end of her days, leaving May with an ache in her heart which never quite went away.

At the other end of the village, in one of the large houses bordering the common, there lived a certain Mrs Tuckett. She was a Quaker and a first cousin to Mariabella Fry, Roger Fry's mother. The Quakers were a very close-knit band, most of them were inter-related and they never discussed personal matters with anyone outside their own circle. Mrs Tuckett was known to take a great interest in the Mann children and was very good to them. For example Edith, the eldest, had been profoundly deaf since birth and Mrs Tuckett had insisted on paying for her to be sent to a special school for the deaf in Bristol, where she had learned Braille and lip-reading.

Edith was never to leave home, but when the three younger Mann girls reached the statutory school-leaving age of 14 they were sent into service. This was seen as a better option than the only alternative for local working-class girls, which was to work in the unhealthy atmosphere of the flock mills. However, when May reached her 14th birthday she received better treatment. She was a beautiful needlewoman and money was found for her to be apprenticed to Brights of Bristol as a seamstress, opening up the possibility of a career. Whether Mrs Tuckett had any hand in this was not disclosed. May grew into an attractive, outgoing young woman and collected a string of admirers. In 1915, at the age of 20, she was married to a Mr Frederick Bartlett. Her maiden name on the marriage certificate was given as Mann. Mrs Tuckett presented the young couple with a bedroom suite and a handsome table with a central pedestal and clawed feet. She also gave May a brooch set with 20 garnets.

In 1920 the Bartlett's first child was born: a girl, whom they named Margaret. Five years later she was joined by a sister – Edith. During these years May had made one or two abortive efforts to discover more about her parents. But in the years immediately following the First World War times were hard for young working-class couples and her husband was not anxious to begin stirring up trouble.

Some years earlier Mr Mann had left the employment of Mr Ward to become gardener to a Mr Cecil Fry, a cousin of Sir Edward Fry and an employee in the family chocolate firm. Mr Cecil had been exceptionally generous to the Mann family and in particular to May, raising questions in some minds. But Fred Bartlett thought it was best to let sleeping dogs lie and May had gone to her grave at the age of 84 as ignorant about her parentage as she had been as a child. There the matter might have rested if the Bartlett's elder daughter Margaret had not been of an enquiring mind.

One evening when Margaret was still a child and had been walking home with her father after seeing her grandparents, Fred Bartlett had blurted out: 'Your gran is not your real gran, you know.'

'Who is, then?' Margaret asked, somewhat taken aback.

'Your granddad was an artist who travelled the world a lot,' her father replied. Mr Bartlett had refused to say more – warning Margaret not to repeat to her mother what he had said.

Years later, pressed for more information, he had admitted to his daughter how one evening 'over a few glasses of beer with Mr Mann at the *White Lion*' he had been emboldened to ask his father-in-law who May's father was. 'One of the Frys', Mr Mann had growled back. Then realising he had broken a confidence the old man had shut up like a clam and the subject had never been raised again.

Putting these two pieces of information together Margaret concluded that the artist who travelled the world a lot and was one of the Frys must be Roger Fry, an artist and a notable art critic in his day. Her heart swelled with pride at the thought of having such a distinguished grandparent! Roger Fry must have had a mistress who had borne him a child. And concealment being the common currency of those much-intermarried Quaker families they had obviously banded together to put up a smoke screen around the miscreant. That was the reason, Margaret told herself, why May had been fostered at Frenchay rather than at nearby Failand which was where Roger's parents had settled in their retirement. It all seemed to make perfect sense.

However, one piece of the jigsaw was still missing: the identity of that 'very wicked woman' who had been Margaret's grandmother. Time passed.

In 1946 Margaret married Ken Turner, who after war service in the army had joined the Fire Service. Rising steadily, his promotions had involved frequent moves, and what with that and raising a family Margaret had put her quest for her grandmother to one side.

A biography of Fry written by Virginia Woolf and published in 1940[*] had revealed that in his youth the artist had an affair with a much older woman. As the woman concerned had only recently died Woolf did not name her. But in the 1980s a new biography by Frances Spalding[†] disclosed that the woman had been Cecilia Widdrington. After reading Spalding's book Margaret worked out that Mrs Widdrington must have been

---

[*] Virginia Woolf, *Roger Fry*, Hogarth Press, 1940.
[†] Frances Spalding, *Roger Fry, Art and Life*, Granada Publishing, 1980.

53 when the affair began. Was she too old to have conceived a child? Margaret wrote to the medical correspondent of the *Daily Telegraph* to check. Quoting the *Guinness Book of Records* he replied that a woman of 63 had been known to conceive and give birth to a healthy child.

Margaret now became convinced that she had solved the puzzle and that Cecilia Widdrington was her grandmother. She wrote to Spalding setting out her theory, asking the author whether she had any information that would support it. Spalding's reply was circumspect. She suggested that Margaret get in touch with Mrs Widdrington's grandson, Captain Francis Widdrington, who had been helpful to her when she was researching her book. This plainly was a sensible idea, but Margaret hesitated. It was a tall order for a woman of 65 to write to a complete stranger with a theory which on the face of it appeared so far fetched. All too likely she would be taken for a madwoman or some small-time crook looking for money. Her letter would be destroyed and that would be the end of it. She decided her best tactic would be to call on Captain Widdrington unannounced, trusting to an honest face to see her over the threshold. Once inside she knew she would have to play it by ear.

Margaret and her husband, now retired, lived at Ottery St Mary in Devon. In September 1985 she made the long rail journey to Alnwick, stopping overnight at York. After some difficulty she managed to locate a taxi and to persuade the driver to take her to Newton Hall and wait for her there. Refusing to be intimidated at the sight of the imposing stone mansion, she found a pedimented door at the side of the house and rang the bell. When no one answered she walked round to the back of the house and tried the tradesmen's bell, which after what seemed an interminable wait was answered by a young woman. Margaret explained that she had come to see Captain Widdrington and eventually a tall tweed-jacketed man appeared, accompanied by half a dozen small yapping dogs. It was difficult to make herself heard above the din but somehow or other she managed to stammer out the purpose of her visit and at her mention of Mrs Widdrington and Roger Fry Captain Widdrington's manner changed. Shooing the dogs inside he began to fire questions at her. Who did she say she was? Where had her information come from? Towering over Margaret on the doorstep he rapidly dismissed her theory, insisting that she had got it all wrong. The woman she was after must be his Aunt Ida – and to be frank with her, he was not at all surprised. There was no end to the stories he could tell Mrs Norman about his aunt and her scandalous youth!

Margaret hoped that Captain Widdrington would invite her to come indoors, but just then her taxi driver appeared, grumbling at being kept waiting. Feeling confused, she scribbled down her address, handed it to the Captain, and thanking him for giving her his time (which could only have been counted in minutes) she left. Had her long journey been worth it? Back at home, she hardly knew.

Two days later she received a letter from Captain Widdrington. Apologising for his rudeness in keeping her talking outside his back door, he was writing to say how interested he had been in what Mrs Norman had told him and was anxious to hear more. He had indeed attempted to go after her taxi, but had been too late to stop it. Would she be willing to pay him another visit? He would be happy to meet her train

17 *May.*

and put her up at the Hall if she would care to name a day.

When Margaret repeated her visit to Newton some months later everything seemed to fall into place quite naturally. To her delight it soon became clear that Captain Widdrington was prepared to accept her theory and so apparently was his wife, Gay. Their only reservation (and it was a big one) was over the identity of the woman who had borne Fry's child. At 53, they insisted, Cecilia had been well past the age for child-bearing. Obviously the woman in question had been Ida, she had always been the prodigal – wild as a hawk, as she said of herself.

After listening to Captain Widdrington's account of his infamous aunt, Margaret was won over to his view of the matter. She rather liked the sound of this madcap young woman who had been prepared to fly in the face of convention. Had not her own mother been something of a rebel? Everything seemed to fit: Ida Widdrington was her grandmother.

In the hall at Newton, propped on an easel, was a portrait of Ida as a young woman. To Margaret's intense joy Captain Widdrington said he would like her to have it. She was overwhelmed with gratitude. It was the ultimate confirmation that he believed her story. Margaret was convinced she had discovered her roots. Now all that remained was to find the evidence that would support her conviction. She was to spend the next fifteen years searching for clues.

Captain Widdrington had told her that there were diaries. He promised to hunt them out and let her read them. (She was, after all, one of the family now.) Margaret seized on them eagerly. But they proved hard to decipher – a thorough perusal of the contents would occupy her for weeks. Never mind, Captain Widdrington said – Mrs Norman must come again – come as often as she liked. And they must drop the formalities. He and Mrs Widdrington – Francis and Gay – were both so kind …

Margaret learned that a Fry Archive existed and was kept at King's College, Cambridge. The city was a long way from Ottery St Mary, but no matter. Regardless of time and expense she paid a number of visits to King's, obtaining copies of letters written to Roger by Ida and Cecilia and reading and re-reading letters he had sent to friends. She was hunting for clues, though they appeared to her to be brimful of meaningful hints she found nothing that could be seized on as evidence.

But what had she been hoping to find? If she was looking for proof of the existence of a child was it not unthinkable that a scandal of such epic proportions would have found its way into the archive? Without doubt all the evidence would have been suppressed.

Nevertheless Margaret began to build up a picture of how things might have been. Returning to the diaries she discovered that Cecilia had abandoned all the records she had been keeping for her children in April 1894. The date jumped off the page: that must have been the time when Ida's pregnancy had been confirmed. It all fitted. Ida's distress. Her mother's anguish. No wonder those diaries, faithfully kept up from the time of each child's birth, had been cast aside, neglected for 35 years until in her old age Cecilia had added postscripts.

It occurred to Margaret that in order to conceal her pregnancy Ida would have needed to disappear. Where would she have gone? France seemed the obvious destination. In France there had apparently been no law obliging you to register a birth.

Turning to Cecilia's diary written in old age, Margaret learned that mother and daughter had indeed spent several months in France at around that time. To be sure the dates given by Cecilia did not perfectly fit with such facts as were known. Yet the coincidence seemed too great to be ignored.

There was besides the question of her mother's name. Why had she been called May? One piece of information that Margaret had unearthed was that Roger Fry had a Pease cousin called May. A woman in her mid-30s, May was at that time warden of

18a and b *Margaret Norman (left) and Cecilia Widdrington (right): is there a likeness?*

a women's hostel in London, and she was single. Was it possible that she had a part to play in the story?

Margaret reasoned that Roger would have been adamant that even if Ida refused to marry him he must take responsibility for his child. But he couldn't have managed alone – some trustworthy woman would have been needed to work out a strategy – take the infant from its mother and engage a temporary nurse and find it a foster home. To whom could he turn? There must be no hint of gossip, for Ida's sake. Would not his cousin May – a woman of the world – be the ideal choice for such a delicate commission? Margaret thought it highly probable that May Pease had been taken into Roger's confidence and that she had agreed to take on the role of go-between. The more she thought about it the more everything seemed to fit.

Next, driven by curiosity about Ida's wider family, Margaret travelled to Middleton near Manchester to see what she could discover about the Hopwoods. She found an extensive Hopwood archive in Middleton library. And what a hornet's nest she had uncovered! Evidently the Hopwoods had been a quarrelsome lot. In the 1850s there had been a notorious family lawsuit over a will, which had been reported in all the national newspapers and had apparently rocked the nation. The history of her family was turning out to have been anything but dull.

By the close of the century Margaret's single-minded quest for proof of her mother's ancestry had taken her down many paths and she had amassed an impressive portfolio. Yet though she had uncovered a heap of circumstantial evidence the proof she sought continued to elude her.

Chapter XXXII

A Question Without an Answer

On 4 April 1894 Cecilia took up her *Idonea Diary*, which she had not touched since Christmas, to bring it up to date. The first three months of 1894 had been outstandingly successful ones for Ida. Her acting had been applauded by no other person than young Mr Cochran,* then aged 22, who had written a play 'on purpose for you, in wch yr dog is to appear – yr very words are reproduced, it is most flattering and a tremendous excitement getting it up'. It was 'a real grand time' and a triumph for Ida. No wonder she would not listen to a word of reproof from her parents!

In February she had gone to London with her father to see Bertram off to India to join his regiment. They were all staying with Dorothy and Edward. After Bertram's departure Fitz left for a painting holiday at Hyères. Ida stayed on for a few days and during that time Cecilia learned (she doesn't mention from whom) that her daughter had seen more than was perhaps wise of Roger Fry.

Addressing Ida she wrote:

> I think you tried him a good deal – you will not see that a man must either become a friend or be a lover but not both and you meant him to be both – and its hard on him – why can't you let him go in peace when you have so many?

It was one of the rare occasions when she allowed her heartache to show. And who could blame her for being vexed with Ida, 'for he would only be a victim if you married him and he doesn't want to marry you, it would disorganise all his life and he is too good to be a victim'.

When her daughter got home Cecilia saw at once that Ida had worked herself up into a high old state.

> You went on the moors and walked barefoot in the snow which is a folly full [*sic*] thing to do anyhow, and you got yr toe wounded and frost-bitten ... Dr Welsh came it was seriously bad and you had to lay up ten days and in great pain. I was away part of it and you were cross and miserable when I got back.

---

* Charles Cochran (1872-1951) was to bring Diaghilev's *Ballet Russes* to London and to launch a famous dancing troupe known as 'Cochran's Young Ladies'.

Cecilia omitted to disclose that she, too, had been seeing Roger in London. It must have been he who had told her about Ida's earlier visit. Once her wayward child had recovered from her foot injury there had been more acting engagements, more balls, and a number of bracing days out with the hounds, all of which Cecilia recorded. Finally she wrote: 'Father went to Hyères and you came home for 2 nights to see Gerard's 3 Oxford friends and now 6 April you are gone to Orde House to rehearse and for a ball till the 16th.' Those are her last words in the *Idonea Diary*, which lay abandoned for 35 years until Cecilia took it up again in order to add a postscript. At the same time her *Gerard Diary* came to an equally abrupt end.

During March some of Gerard's Oxford friends had been staying at Newton, including Cecilia's abomination, Hughes, to whom she had been obliged to be 'very curt' when she found him helping himself to Fitz's whisky. She and Gerard had taken the young men about: 'to Hauxley and Warkworth among other places – so I hope it wasn't quite an unhappy time, but you are very sad and silent.'

That was all. Cecilia's *Bertram Diary* was broken off even more abruptly: 'On 24th Feb you joined yr regiment at Parkhurst with all yr new things wch you really enjoyed having … You are far ahead of anyone with rifle shooting still – April …' She never finished the sentence. Why?

From that April day in 1894, until Cecilia took up her pen again in her 90th year and began to set down the story of her own life, none of her written records have survived. She left nothing that would give her descendants a clue to the cause of her sudden abandonment of a long-kept habit. Nor did she give any hint of what had caused the rift with Dorothy which took place at the same time – a sundering so fundamental that their friends were forced into taking sides. ('You must choose between us', Cecilia would say with a wry smile. 'For you cannot be friends to both.') Yet it seems safe to assume that these two occurrences were in some sense connected. And if they were, we are driven to look for some event within the family of such traumatic significance that it must never be written down.

It was a mystery that had passed into oblivion; until some ninety years later a woman quite unknown to the Widdrington family presented herself at Newton Hall with a startling theory. Had Margaret Norman stumbled on the truth of what had happened all those years ago? Certainly Francis Widdrington was prepared to believe that she had. He and his wife Gay thought it all too believable that Aunt Ida, with her rackety reputation, had kicked over the traces – to find herself disastrously pregnant with Roger Fry's child.

But were Francis and Gay Widdrington perhaps being a little naive? It was of course established that there had been a child, who was fostered by the Manns. An infant whose father, according to hearsay, was one of the Frys – the finger pointed at Roger. Nothing more was known; all else was conjecture.

Yet if Margaret Norman had guessed correctly, who can doubt that Ida's pregnancy would have torn Cecilia apart? It was almost past belief and yet it had happened and she was the one who was going to have to cope with it. Faced with a calamity of such shattering proportions, should we be surprised that she had abandoned the diaries? For the truth could never be recorded; nothing that would hint at the scandalous event could ever be written down.

In all probability, if Margaret Norman had guessed correctly, Ida would have been whisked off to France on an extended 'holiday'. Dorothy meanwhile, deeply shocked and determined to protect her husband's reputation, could well have decided to fence herself off from her parents and sister.

Everything could be made to hang together – except that the dates recorded in Cecilia's *Diary* do not quite fit. According to the *Diary* Ida had begun her nurse's training in October 1894, which would have been impossible if she had been eight months' pregnant with Roger Fry's child. The extended holiday in France had come later. But diary-writers have the advantage of being able to select, and when it suits them are not always honest. Cecilia's *Diary* was written for the edification of her descendants, and in the interest of propriety and to protect the family name she may well have decided to doctor the facts a little. They did not need to know all. May had been reared in an atmosphere of concealment, with only a whisper of rumour to link her to Roger Fry and an impenetrable wall of silence between herself and the 'very wicked woman' who was her mother. So far as Cecilia was concerned, whatever the truth of the matter, she would have intended that wall of silence to remain. Thus precisely when Ida embarked on her short-lived nursing career must remain uncertain.

If Ida had imagined that she would be stepping into the shoes of some latter-day Florence Nightingale, she was to be swiftly disillusioned. At that time King's College Hospital, one of the finest and most up-to-date teaching hospitals of its day, was situated close to the Law Courts in the City of London. It backed onto narrow streets and alleyways which to Ida looked both threatening and mean. Her knowledge of the metropolis was confined to the West End where the poor were seldom seen. In the City the 'great unwashed', as she was accustomed to think of them, jostled her on every side. The men in their threadbare jackets and cloth caps, the women clutching their shawls, all seemed to exhibit a weary resignation rarely seen among the rural poor of Northumberland. And while there were plenty of ragamuffin children to be found in her native county, by and large their sturdy frames and weather-bronzed cheeks gave them a cheerful look. The sight of the pinched white faces and skinny limbs of the urchins who roamed the city streets filled her with dismay.

And when seen from the standpoint of a young and inexperienced probationer, the great hospital lacked the smallest vestige of glamour. Ida found she was the lowest of the low and under strict supervision. The incorrect tucking-in of a bedsheet was liable to draw down as much wrath from her superiors as if she had committed some major crime. And she was shocked by the reality of having to cope with the patients' most intimate needs, in particular their bodily functions. All the most unpleasant tasks seemed to be reserved for the wretched probationers – the more experienced nurses taking a gleeful delight in the girls' distress as they handed out bedpans and swabs.

Drawn together by these trials, Ida succeeded in making friends with some of the other young nurses. When they were off duty she would entertain them with popular songs accompanying herself on her guitar.

It was plain to Cecilia that Ida was finding hospital life irksome and, in a constant fret over her daughter's well-being, Cecilia made several trips to London to cheer her up with 'lunch or tea at a good café'. But London had never suited Ida. And as Cecilia had all along predicted, the 'long hours of indoor work and not near enough exercise' soon began to take their toll. Too spoilt and too accustomed to a life of freedom to buckle down to hospital routine, it was only a matter of months before Ida's nursing career was given up.

Yet whether it was the shock of hospital life (or the effect of some deeper hurt that could never be spoken of) after she returned home it became apparent to Fitz and Cecilia that Ida had changed. A new and more serious-minded young woman seemed to have emerged from the confines of the hospital – an Ida with an ambition to tackle something useful; to get stuck in to some work that would show a return. To her parents' surprise she announced that she intended to learn about dairying, with a view to taking over the management of the Newton home farm. Fitz and Cecilia thought this a capital idea. A Dorset farmer was contacted who was willing to take on Ida as a pupil. It was not long before she began to win prizes for her butter-making at the local county show, and after a year's instruction she declared that she was ready to come home and begin farming in earnest. Gerard, who was at a loose end, was enrolled to assist her in the enterprise and with one man (appropriately named Hogg) to help her she took over the farm and was soon selling her own butter and cream.

A year slipped by. Fitz and Cecilia settled down to enjoy a period of calm. Then, when all seemed well, tragedy struck. For some time Fitz had been having trouble with his eyes. His vision was becoming blurred, interfering with his painting. He had sought advice from specialists in London, but had not received much help. Then one morning he made a horrifying discovery: he found he could no longer read his daily newspaper. All he could make out were a few dim shapes. The rest was a hazy blur. Overnight it appeared that Fitz had gone blind.

It was a devastating shock. Cecilia took him to Edinburgh for a consultation with her old friend and adviser Dr Grainger Stewart. His news was not encouraging.

> He said alas that a blood vessel had burst on the retina and nothing could be done – poor Fitz was in terrible despair – all his pleasure in life came thro his eyes – I heard him pray <u>Please</u> God don't make me blind – but it had to be and all his beloved drawing and painting given up … He could see light from dark for many months after this, but no features in a face, nor could he read, but he went to Alnwick for his Magistrate work every fortnight and could grope his way to the village and garden and about the house, being very sensitive to sound and touch.

Cecilia, however, was not prepared to give up hope without a struggle. She took Fitz to Germany to see the foremost eye specialist of his day at Wiesbaden. The great doctor was blunt. Fitz was informed 'very curtly' that nothing could be done.

He was now 70 years of age and the disappointing news coming from such an eminent source almost broke his spirit. What made things worse was that the split which had developed between the Greys and the Widdringtons was such that Dorothy never came to see her 'poor blind father'. 'She was never very sympathetic', Cecilia recorded, adding that she 'never knew why'.

Did she in point of fact have a perfectly clear understanding of the cause of Dorothy's coldness? Some knowledge that she was not prepared to commit to her *Diary*? It is a question without an answer and in all probability must remain so.

CHAPTER XXXIII

A Providential Illness?

> And I was taught to feel, perhaps too much
> The self-sufficing power of Solitude.
> William Wordsworth, *The Prelude*, Book II

Before the 1895 General Election which was to put the Liberal Party out of office for the next eleven years, Edward Grey, anticipating his Party's defeat (and what was likely to be his own) wrote in *The Cottage Book*: 'I shall never be in office again and the days of my stay in the House of Commons are probably numbered. We are both very glad and relieved.'[1] But his loyal constituents were in no mood to let Sir Edward go and after his unexpected re-election had forced him back into the saddle Edward was surprised to find he was not as unhappy as he had expected to be. His work at the Foreign Office had given him an appetite for foreign affairs, and though in many ways it was a relief to be free of the responsibilities of office, it was clear that an abiding interest in the interaction of nation with nation had been kindled in Edward; an absorption which would sometimes find him at loggerheads with Dorothy – and with himself.

In the meantime Edward could only watch from the Opposition benches as the ruling Tory Government battled with one crisis after another on the international front. A long-standing dispute over boundaries between British Guiana and Venezuela was propelling the United States to protest against 'British Imperialism' and for a time the squabble looked ominously like a prelude to war.

And while a diplomatic solution was still being hammered out at the Foreign Office, Britain was gripped by news of a conspiracy in Southern Africa, which became known as the 'Jameson Raid'. Covertly supported by the Tory government, a raiding party of some five hundred men of British stock, led by a Dr Jameson, had attempted to wrest Johannesburg from the Boers, as a preliminary to driving them out of the Transvaal. However, when it became clear that the conspirators had failed, the government chose to disavow them. Since entering Parliament, Edward had taken a keen interest in Southern African affairs, for a number of his relations, including his younger brothers George and Charlie, had chosen to seek their fortune there, and two of his cousins had been wounded while taking part in the abortive raid.

The whole reckless affair and the severity of the punishment meted out to the raiders drove Edward close to despair. There seemed no way he could turn his back on politics, yet while he sat on the Opposition benches he was powerless to influence policy. Perhaps after all he should seek the first opportunity to free himself from the mire of political intrigue – escaping once and for all with Dorothy to the 'perpetual benediction of the English countryside'.

In the summer of '96 a crisis of conscience blew up in the Liberal Party over the lack of action being taken by Britain to stem the massacre of its Armenian citizens by Turkey. Lord Salisbury, the Tory Prime Minister, cynically defended his government's inaction 'on the grounds that from Archangel to Cadiz there was not a soul who cared whether the Armenians were exterminated or not.'[2] Lord Rosebery, the Liberal leader, pressed for intervention – but only on condition that the other European powers agreed to join in. Gladstone – at 85 still breathing righteous indignation – was incensed by this mealy-mouthed approach to a humanitarian disaster, proposing that Great Britain should 'go it alone'. At which point Rosebery retired to his Scottish fastness at Dalmeny, where he brooded for a fortnight before announcing his resignation from the Liberal leadership – not, as might have been expected, to his Party, but to readers of *The Times*. The Liberal Party was still deeply split and this quixotic method of going about things caused a flurry in the Liberal ranks over who was to succeed him. Though Parliament was in recess, Liberal MPs broke off their holidays and hurried to London.

But Edward was far removed from all knowledge of these grave events. He and Dorothy had been enjoying a month's fishing holiday in the Shetland Isles, until Dorothy, quite uncharacteristically, had been overcome by a feeling of lethargy and exhaustion. A bicycling expedition in Scotland on their way home had made matters worse and by the time they reached Edinburgh it was clear that something was seriously amiss. Delaying their return to London they consulted an eminent physician, who after a thorough examination informed Dorothy that she was suffering from Graves Disease, a condition caused by a thyroid deficiency. He advised her to 'abstain from any excitement or fatigue and live as quiet and simple a life as possible'.[3]

Back in the capital, Dorothy began to suffer from palpitations and her condition deteriorated. By now thoroughly alarmed, Edward insisted she should be examined by two prominent London doctors, one of whom put them both in a panic by diagnosing 'advanced heart disease'. Fortunately his diagnosis proved to be wrong; while it seems likely that the physician who diagnosed Graves Disease had been equally mistaken. Dorothy had been reassured by his advice that no medication was necessary. She would eventually recover, she was told, though it might take some time. Yet it is now known that recovery from Graves Disease can never occur spontaneously. Caused by a hormone deficiency,* unless the hormones are replaced artificially the condition will persist. Moreover, in addition to lethargy of body and mind, typical symptoms of the disease include a coarsening of the skin, obesity, hair loss and cold hands. Yet during the course of her long illness Dorothy kept both her looks and her figure, and while her physical frailty persisted, her mind remained needle-sharp. A more likely explanation is that she

---

* The action of hormones was not known in the 19th century.

was suffering from myalgic encephalomyelitis or ME, a condition that went unrecognised until the late 20th century and which is still not thoroughly understood.

Some of the doctors' 'do's and don'ts' strike the modern reader as bizarre. 'Do what you enjoy and forget the rest', they appeared to be prescribing. For example, while mixing in society was discouraged, riding to hounds was thought to be good for Dorothy. 'I had a perfect day's hunting', she wrote to a friend from Scotland that autumn. 'We ran nearly all day and the jumping was very big, but I got to tea at Kelso at four, so wasn't one bit tired.'[4] Could any illness have proved more delightful to its sufferer?

Dorothy now shunned London as often as she could, provoking an acid comment from Lady Monkswell, a noted political hostess, that 'for a very pretty and admired woman she looks as displeased as anyone I know'.[5] And after meeting Dorothy in November 1896 the peeress added: 'Lady Grey ... is a very handsome, delightful & clever woman ... but could anyone be more "madly with her blessedness at strife?" If Sir Edward Grey goes on he is bound to be Foreign Minister when the Liberals come in; there is no one else in the running.'[6]

But would Edward 'go on'? With his friend Rosebery now replaced by Lord Kimberley in the Lords and Sir William Harcourt leading the Liberals in the Commons, the prospect looked far from enticing. However, at this point Edward was invited by Joseph Chamberlain, the Colonial Minister, to join a Royal Commission with a brief to enquire into the parlous state of the sugar industry in the British West Indies. The islands had been brought close to bankruptcy by the emergence onto the market of sugar beet, most of it grown in Germany. Considerably cheaper to grow than cane sugar, it was flooding the European markets. The task of the Commissioners would be to travel among the sugar-producing colonies to assess their economic problems and attempt to come up with remedies. However, as there was talk of a possible subsidy (anathema to Liberal Free Traders) some of Edward's colleagues had attempted to warn him off, arguing that the Commission's work would keep him out of Westminster for several months and could, moreover, turn out to be politically damaging.

'Exactly where are the West Indies?', Dorothy asked her husband when she learned of the invitation.

Edward produced an atlas, pointing to what looked like a string of beads threaded between the Atlantic Ocean and the Caribbean Sea.

'If you decide to go then I shall come too,' Dorothy said.

Her doctors, when consulted, gave it out that the journey would do her no harm. The warm climate might even prove beneficial. Had that been the deciding factor? 'The job is one which is worth putting one's back into and I don't think I should have been justified in refusing,' Edward wrote to one of the doubters, Monro Ferguson.[7] For – unusually for such a dedicated stay-at-home – he had made up his mind to go.

The four Commissioners (chaired by Sir Henry Norman, a former Governor of Jamaica) set off early in the New Year. They had planned to be away for around four months. Dorothy was the only female member of the party, for she did not take a maid. Their first port of call was Barbados, where they were put up by the Governor, who did not object to Dorothy sitting in while evidence was given regarding the dire plight of the islanders. 'The different accounts of things given by different sets of people are

The Widdrington Women

very curious,' she wrote to Mrs Francis Buxton. 'A good deal of it is the same as in England, gentlemen trying to make fortunes out of land without learning their profession, landlords struggling to keep rents high (which they have been remarkably successful in) and workmen wanting higher wages.'[8]

She expressed pity for the plight of the 'niggers', though it was the struggles of her countrymen to maintain their privileged way of life that drew most of her sympathy. 'If something isn't done to help the planters quite soon, there won't be a white man left in the islands', her letter continued. 'And it seems a pity, because the islands are so very beautiful and the niggers are so very ugly.' (Unacceptable today, Dorothy's words reflected the sentiments of the majority of her contemporaries, to whom 'niggers' were not simply a race apart, but were barely considered human.)

Dorothy accompanied the Commissioners on some of their island visits, where the pace was often hectic. 'I have been very sociable and have gone to all the balls and parties',[9] she wrote to a friend while staying in Jamaica. Responding to the informality of the planters and their wives she had loosened up and lost much of her shyness. Her illness was not mentioned at all.

Then a miracle occurred. A 'nice man', who had got to hear of Dorothy's need for complete rest and her wish to see more of the flora and fauna of the islands, offered her the use of his hideaway – a retreat high up in the hills on the small island of Dominica. It was a five-hour trek from the nearest white people, her new friend explained. Dorothy accepted at once. Arriving on the island she was provided with a pony and a maid and a boy to look after the pack animals and set off into the unknown on what was to be a life-changing adventure.

The hideaway proved to be a three-roomed wooden bungalow raised on legs and fitting snugly into a plantation of limes. It was her Hampshire Cottage in another guise – the river bank exchanged for lush tropical forest bursting with exotic plant life and haunted by strange whistling bird-calls. Dorothy instantly fell in love with this unspoilt Paradise. 'Far the most beautiful of all the islands,' she wrote to Constance Herbert. 'Uncultivated, mountainous and altogether splendid. I did not expect it to be nearly as grand as it is. It is far more than picturesque.'[10] Apart from the 'dear black woman' who cooked for her and the boy who attended to the animals Dorothy was completely alone and this novel experience seemed to satisfy a hitherto unacknowledged need. Their Hampshire Cottage had never given her this sense of uniqueness – this Wordsworthian 'bliss of solitude' – for even when Edward was in London she would be conscious of his presence. His being seemed to inhabit the very fabric of the place. Now there was no 'other' to come between herself and the awesome, mystical one-ness of the natural world.

She wrote to Edward daily, reporting on what she had seen and the books she had been reading. She was still striving to educate herself – ploughing through Carlyle's biographies of Voltaire, Burns and Goethe. Her letters bubble over with enthusiasm.

> My things and servant all came in a boat to within two hours walk and two men arrived carrying loads on their heads, and with flaming cocoa-nut torches in the dark last night. Its a fearful steep climb up here, 1000 feet above the sea … I feel more than ever adventurous

and independent now that I am in the real wild. I have summoned green coconuts and shall drink nothing but them and tea.

She felt no sense of fear. 'The night noises are splendid and there are strange whistling birds which will have to be identified. I had a bird in at breakfast which was the size of a sparrow and all black except a patch of red on its throat.' She read or wrote letters for part of each day, she explained to a friend, 'and just wander slowly about in the early mornings and at sunset. The birds, fireflies and vegetation are splendid and I am happier than I have ever been. It is a real luxury to be alone.'

During the weeks spent on Dominica Dorothy seems to have enjoyed perfect health. The climate obviously suited her – constant at around 85 degrees Fahrenheit. 'I go on being very well, so it was right to come out,' she wrote to Constance. 'The most heavenly breeze always blows and keeps one cool ... I ride slowly about the two or three little paths that there are, and gaze on palms and long-shaped mosses and trailers, and one comes to wonderful rushing burns with perhaps two white herons feeding in them.'

In a sense Dorothy's 'ideal life' could be seen as one of supreme selfishness. Though her independence might run to managing without a lady's maid, she expected at all times to be attended by menials. For as we have seen even at the Cottage, the simple life she and Edward set such store by would not have been possible without the daily ministrations of Susan Drover, their housekeeper and cook.

Yet one should not be too hard on Dorothy, who was reared in an age and a society in which service was taken for granted and familiarity with the 'lower orders' frowned upon. She was in fact an exemplary employer, whom the ordinary people of Northumberland (not always easy to please) loved for her directness and her fearlessness in speaking her mind.

To most members of her own class she remained an enigma. Her manner could be abrupt – even sarcastic – and many would echo Lady Monkswell in finding her haughty and cold. Yet the few who succeeded in penetrating her icy reserve could find themselves amply rewarded.

One such was Captain Barton, a young army officer whom Dorothy met in Barbados while she and the Commissioners were guests of the Governor. Discovering that they shared a love of birds the two struck up a friendship. Captain Barton was happy to share his knowledge of local birds with Sir Edward Grey's charming wife and the friendship forged at that time (which soon came to include Edward) continued for many years. Barton was one of the small number of their friends who were invited to stay at the Cottage and after Dorothy's death he and Edward continued to meet and to exchange bird news. Probably the young Captain had been more than a little in love, for when asked by Louise Creighton to contribute to her *Memoir of Dorothy* he provided the following moving tribute:

> The first thing which drew us together was the discovery that we were both fond of birds ... We soon found that we had other affinities – likings for, and intolerance of, certain books: impatience of certain conventionalities. I remember too that we felt alike as to what things were laughable and what were not ... There was a total absence of affectation in her manner and in her conversation. One could see that she held in contempt cant, vulgarity and posing

for effect ... Human passion in all its various phases was a subject she delighted to analyse. She possessed an extraordinarily keen sense of humour. But for this quality I think she might have seemed to be rather austere, so independent were her views, and so philosophic was her mind ... Her perception, too, of the ridiculous was delightful ... I think that at times she took delight in startling ultra-conventionalised people by a sudden unexpected sally, remark or criticism, never for the sake of effect, but probably to divert some hollow drift of the conversation which made her impatient.

She was not the easiest guest, then, to have at one's table. What would Lady Grey decide to say next? Was anyone safe (society hostesses must have asked themselves) from that supercilious manner and sharp tongue? Only her intimate friends were spared, of whom Captain Barton was one. He concluded his tribute to Dorothy with the following words:

I have not known any woman for whom I felt so profound a regard and such free and cordial friendship as I felt for Lady Grey. It gave one an uplift, a knightly feeling to know that one was regarded as a friend by her ... It was a fellowship established in the first instance by common interests. That on my part it did not in the least diminish during the seven years I have been in New Guinea is due to the deep impression her personality made on me. The receipt of a letter from her had the effect of keeping me in buoyant spirits for days.[12]

After completing their inspection of the islands the Commissioners came to the conclusion that there was little the British Government could do to alleviate the plight of the planters. In the long term a subsidy (which they could not recommend) was unlikely to save them. Unless America agreed to take their sugar the plantation owners appeared to be doomed – a conclusion which Edward found deeply depressing.

On their return to Britain in May, Dorothy was more than willing to heed her doctors' advice and give London a wide berth, and she and Edward made straight for the Cottage. 'I am not to be in London at all this year, as I have started an illness and am told to be quiet for perhaps two years',[13] she wrote to her friend Angela Kay-Shuttleworth. 'I am quite happy and comfortable and delight in the idea of doing nothing ... I shall have lots of time for reading and shall get a little education.' To Constance Herbert she confided: 'I am rather looking forward to the quiet time I am to have. It will be an excuse for not doing many things I don't like.'[14] And in a letter to her old friend Mandell Creighton (now Bishop of London) she allowed herself to be even more frank: 'I am quite priggish about being ill. I rather like it, but I find it is very bad for me. I shirk seeing people who have troubles and want sympathy. I want only to see people who do well for themselves and make me feel nice.'[15]

Since Dorothy's parents were judged to have failed miserably in their efforts to 'make her feel nice' it is likely that she felt justified in cutting them out of her life and that Edward supported her. How fortunate she was to have contracted an illness that chimed so perfectly with her needs and her disposition!

She was, however, disappointed at having to give up the Sunday bicycle rides which had given both of them so much pleasure. But not for long, for Edward managed to fit a trailer onto the back of his bicycle in which his wife could sit and be 'trailed' round the Hampshire lanes – 'changing my life', as Dorothy said. They must have made a comical pair, but neither of them cared for appearances. The contraption even accompanied them to Scotland, where Dorothy was 'trailed' over the Highlands on Edward's fishing trips.

There were times when Dorothy's condition seemed to improve, but these false dawns were invariably followed by relapses. Sometimes she was so prostrated by her 'odd illness' that she had to take to her bed. As she always seemed to do better at the Cottage it made sense for her to spend as much time as possible there, even when Edward's Parliamentary duties obliged him to stay in London. Having developed a taste for solitude, if she could not have her husband's company she was quite happy with her own. During those years they began to open up the Cottage as early as March and to delay their last visit until halfway through November.

The small number of her friends permitted to visit Dorothy at the Cottage during her illness felt greatly privileged. One friend recalled 'the delicious sensation of being a naughty child':

> I never went without Sir Edward's leave, but that did not prevent my feeling wicked. I would turn off a Hampshire road in June, down a track almost lost in the meadows ripe for hay, under a beautiful avenue of old lime trees … to find her lying on a low couch surrounded with roses, watching the goldfinches' nest, with the scent of the lime trees in the air and the trout stream not far away.[16]

Dorothy in her invalid guise plays the Victorian heroine par excellence – though unlike many of her fictional counterparts, she was eventually to recover.

In the rarefied social and political circles in which the Greys moved it was common knowledge that their marriage was *un marriage blanc*. In some quarters it was rumoured that Edward was 'not a full man'.* This rumour was almost certainly false. More credible is the opposite view, namely that Edward was able to sustain his unusual marriage because over a long period of time he had had a mistress.

In her gossipy memoir *A Passing World* Mrs Belloc Lowndes wrote of Grey that 'after he and Dorothy had been married a considerable number of years she suddenly suggested that they should lead a normal married life. He demurred, giving the reason that they were both happy and satisfied with the life they had both agreed on leading.'

If it is true that Dorothy had made this proposal it suggests that she may have had cause to suspect that she had a rival. And if such was the case, the woman she had in mind would almost certainly have been Pamela Tennant, the wife of one of Edward's closest friends, the Hon. Eddie Tennant, son and heir of the self-made Glasgow multi-millionaire Lord Glennconner.

Pamela Tennant was one of the three famously beautiful Wyndham sisters whose family, although they had royal connections, were not rich. As a young woman she had fallen deeply in love with Harry Cust, the younger brother of Lord Brownlow and a cousin of the Custs, who were old family friends of the Widdringtons. Harry Cust had

---

* The German Ambassador evidently believed so, reporting on Sir Edward's supposed impotence to his masters in Berlin as a sign of Great Britain's degeneracy.

been endowed by nature with a super-abundance of good looks, wit and charm. Half the women in London were reputed to have been in love with him.* But as a younger son Cust had no prospects and in order to remove Pamela from his orbit her parents took her on a tour of India. While on their way home Pamela met Eddie Tennant in Florence. He fell deeply in love with her and when he proposed Pamela felt it her duty to accept him. Though the marriage yielded six children, Eddie, who adored her, probably knew that on his wife's side it had been a marriage of convenience, for he appears to have taken a generous view of her infidelities. On the authority of her granddaughter† the most enduring among her lovers was Edward Grey, whom she was eventually to marry.

Indeed it has been hinted that the Tennant's second son, baptised Christopher Grey Tennant, was Edward's child. Be that as it may, Dorothy may have felt she had cause to be alarmed, though Edward must have been able to reassure her. ('Passion is attractive', he had once written to his wife, 'but there is a love which is larger and stronger and has a fuller life.') Thus, even if he had been driven to seek physical fulfilment elsewhere, the love he bore Dorothy – a pure and constant flame – could never be eclipsed.

Yet Dorothy's illness, with her doctors' stipulation that she must have rest and seclusion, meant that husband and wife were forced to spend an increasing amount of time apart; and when Edward was alone in London he began to treat the Tennants' comfortable house in Queen Anne's Gate almost as a second home. Whether he committed adultery with the wife of one of his best friends while enjoying his hospitality is one of the great unknowables. All that can be said is that the two Edwards succeeded in remaining friends.

---

* In her old age, Lady Diana Cooper, supposedly a daughter of the Duke of Devonshire, publicly acknowledged that Harry Cust was her real father. While a story going the rounds of Whitehall in the 1980s had it that Margaret Thatcher was Cust's granddaughter – he having exercised his *droit de seigneur* by impregnating the Prime Minister's grandmother while she was employed as a housemaid at Belton House, the Brownlow family seat near Grantham. 'So you see – she's actually one of us', the mandarins congratulated themselves happily.

† The writer Emma Tennant.

Chapter XXXIV

Two Inauspicious Marriages

As the years passed Ida's enthusiasm for farming began to wane. Her determination to lead a useful and productive life was at odds with her essentially frivolous nature. Cows needed to be milked and butter churned on a regular basis, and it was soon evident that Ida was incapable of sticking to a routine.

As the unmarried daughter of the house she continued to live under her parents' roof, where she began to relapse into her former wild ways. In summer she scandalised the neighbourhood by pitching a tent up on the moors, sleeping out for nights at a time with only her big Newfoundland dog Bari for company, sending out carrier pigeons when she wanted food – and even having a visitor to stay with her now and then.

Was this sequestered camping 'with its heather and bracken and little streams and now and then a spring of the most wonderfully clear water' as innocent as it seemed? Cecilia evidently thought so. But was she perhaps being a little naive? All kinds of rumours were flying about, gathering substance with time, and whatever the truth, Ida's escapades did little to improve her already tarnished reputation.

September 1898 marked Ida's 29th birthday and her parents were beginning to despair of her ever finding a husband. That autumn, determined to follow up every lead in their quest to restore Fitz's sight, the Widdringtons travelled to Leeds after hearing of a doctor practising there who had developed a wonderful new cure for blindness. They took rooms in the doctor's 'rather uncomfortable' nursing home, where Fitz submitted himself to his 'revolutionary' treatment, which involved the use of electricity. After some weeks had passed, the doctor (who was almost certainly a quack) told Fitz that 'he had some hopes' and persuaded him to buy one of his 'machines'. Needless to say it proved useless. The couple returned home, to be greeted by some 'very bad news'. They learned that while they had been away Ida had been seeing a great deal of a certain Addy Baker-Cresswell, and the two announced that they were engaged. Fitz and Cecilia arrived on the scene too late to do anything about it, though 'we knew he was quite unscrupulous … and with heavy hearts we had to consent'.

On the face of it Ida had pulled off a brilliant coup, for Addison Baker-Cresswell was one of the richest men in the county. The rent roll from his two Northumbrian properties – Cresswell, situated on a bleak stretch of coast near Acklington, and Harehope, a

19   Addison Baker-Cresswell boasted he wore the tallest collars in London.

splendid sporting estate near Alnwick – was said to be second only to that of the Duke of Northumberland. A forebear's advantageous marriage to a London heiress (a Miss Baker of Baker Street) had contributed her share to the family's immense wealth, in recognition of which her name had been appended to that of Cresswell. It was mining interests, however, which were responsible for the bulk of his annual income, derived from the rich coal deposits which underlay the Cresswell estate. At the time of Addy's engagement Cresswell Hall was leased to his self-indulgent and twice-widowed mother, who had been born Sophia Denman and in her youth was a notable beauty. Her first marriage, to Addy's father, had been brief. Oswin Baker-Cresswell was a drunkard and a wastrel, who had died (it was rumoured by his own hand) at the age of forty-two. Two years later his widow had been briefly married to the elderly Earl of Ravensworth, who when he died had left her little besides his name.

By an odd coincidence Addison Baker-Cresswell and Edward Grey had both lost their father at the age of twelve. But in no other way did the two men bear the slightest resemblance to each other. Edward Grey, raised after his father's death by a timid mother and an evangelical grandfather, passed his formative years in an ambience governed by firm moral principles and shaped by an uncompromising sense of duty. Addison was raised by a fluffy-headed socialite, happy to indulge his every whim. By the time he was enrolled at Eton Addy was already a spoiled dandy, who failed to distinguish himself either academically or on the playing field. Strikingly tall and excessively vain, as a young man-about-town it was his boast that he wore the highest collars in London. A first-rate horseman, at the time of his engagement to Ida he was Master of the Percy Foxhounds, but he played no other part in local affairs, choosing to spend his time hunting, shooting, fishing and womanising. Despite the advantages to Ida of his ancient lineage and great wealth, Fitz and Cecilia were horrified to learn of their daughter's engagement to this dissolute man. 'Two great estates and heaps of money,' Cecilia observed witheringly, 'but he bore the worst of characters as regards women and was cruel and overbearing.'

But while the flurry arising from her younger daughter's forthcoming marriage was being enacted centre stage, Cecilia was beset by further worries. Her dearest friend Roger Fry was in serious trouble, for he too had recently entered into what was proving to be a disastrous marriage.

After closing the door on his tangled involvement with Ida, Roger's relationship with Cecilia had miraculously survived, mellowing on both sides into a warm regard. They still corresponded regularly and contrived to meet whenever they could.

It was through Roger that Cecilia had first met the Dolmetsches, a family of musicians destined to play a significant part in Roger Fry's life. Monsieur Dolmetsch, a designer of harpsichords, had created a fashion for playing on old musical instruments and, when Cecilia heard that the Dolmetsch family were going to Edinburgh to give a concert, she invited them all to come and play at Newton. 'We emptied the drawing room and put in all their instruments and we gave a concert and asked about 40 people from all over the county … It was a great success and a novelty to most of them.' The Dolmetsches stayed on at Newton for two or three days and Madame Dolmetsch and Cecilia struck up a friendship and began to correspond.

At that time Monsieur Dolmetsch was having a harpsichord made in London to his own specifications, and was eager to have it decorated in the Arts and Crafts style which was then all the rage. A young artist named Helen Coombe was commissioned to carry out the work. Unsure how to set about it she turned for advice to Roger Fry whom she had met through a friend. Helen, one of a family of 12, was a tall and graceful woman of 28 with a fey type of beauty and a quick wit. She made an instant impression on Roger who fell passionately in love and made up his mind he must marry her. His parents were dismayed. Not only was Helen penniless, but even at that time rumours concerning her mental stability had begun to circulate. Kept in touch with the progress of the affair by her new friend Madame Dolmetsch, Cecilia became seriously alarmed for Roger, doing all she could to caution him against making a hasty decision. Roger refused to listen. Not for the first time the promptings of his heart had overruled his head and after a short courtship the pair were married during the winter of 1897. A brief period of happiness followed, much of which the couple spent travelling abroad. Yet within a year Cecilia's

20 *Addy, Master of the Percy Foxhounds.*

forebodings started to be fulfilled. Helen began to suffer bouts of extreme agitation, diagnosed as 'nervous excitability'. These bouts gradually became worse, causing Roger almost unbearable anguish. Anxious to keep the severity of his wife's condition from his parents, he unburdened himself to Cecilia in a series of heartrending letters. Though there was little she could do to help him, the long newsy letters she dashed off in her distinctive scrawl (most of which Roger kept) at least brought him some comfort, and when she was in town she always tried to find time to visit this unhappy couple.

Ida's wedding took place at Shilbottle Church on 2 February 1899 and almost from the outset it ran into difficulties. The bride's first problem was that she and her new husband were without a proper home. As a bachelor Addy had not wished to be encumbered with the management of his two great houses and both were let – Harehope to a friend and Cresswell to his mother; the latter arrangement suiting him very well since he could keep his hounds in the kennels there and have the run of the stables for his hunters. Retaining only his London house, he had been in the habit of renting a place at Alnmouth for the hunting season. And after a brief honeymoon it was to this modest establishment that he and Ida went.

But Addy was incurably restless and soon it became all too obvious that marriage had not tamed him. Since he was not prepared to give up his bachelor ways, Ida was obliged to live a peripatetic life, which did little to cement the marriage. Much of the couple's time was spent in London where Addy treated his house as if it was his club, 'staying out all day and half the night and only using it for sleeping'. Ida, who had become pregnant almost at once and loathed town life, pined for the hills of home and fretted for an establishment of her own. 'Even in those early days there were signs of unhappiness and unkindness on Addy's part', Cecilia recorded.

The trouble was that Addy and Ida had far too much in common. Each was as narcisstic as the other while both were reckless and accustomed to getting their own way. A self-centred woman such as Ida should have sought out an easy-going husband, willing to indulge her and to turn a blind eye to her shortcomings. Addy was not that man.

She had first caught the attention of the Master of the Percy Hounds on the hunting field. Flaunting her red coat as she urged her steed over obstacles a more prudent horsewoman would have avoided, she must have impressed Addy with her skilful handling of her horse, and her reckless disregard for her own safety. Four years his senior, he guessed she was a woman of the world and made plans to seduce her. Whether he succeeded is unknowable, but Ida must have succeeded in getting under his skin. Was it possible that Addy was in love? It does not seem likely. But like an unbroken thoroughbred Ida represented a challenge and he was determined to master her.

For her part Ida must have been flattered by the attentions of a young blade with access to untold wealth, who seemed to have the world at his feet. And though there were ugly rumours concerning his treatment of women, she too must have seen him as a thoroughbred who would respond to her skilful handling. Once married, Ida felt confident of her power to rein him in. She was wrong.

The couple's first child (a boy, who was baptised John) was born at Newton to great family rejoicing. Addy was gratified to have a son and heir, but took little interest in the child and steered well clear of the nursery. Ida had always been ready to admit that she preferred animals to humans, though like most Victorian wives she saw children as an inevitable consequence of marriage. (The pleasures of the bedchamber came at a price, as Queen Victoria had been displeased to discover.)

Her second pregnancy was well advanced by the time Addy's tenants were ready to vacate Harehope, allowing him to take possession of the fine Tudor-style house built 50 years earlier by his grandfather as a shooting box. Ida was settled at last. But when the time for her confinement drew near her husband insisted on dragging her off to London, making it clear that he did not intend to put a brake on his own pleasures while his wife was indisposed. Ida was miserable, complaining to her parents that Addy 'only came home to dine and sleep' and begging them to come up to London to provide her with some support. This they did. And thus it was that Cecilia was on hand to witness one of the grandest and most impressive processions that had ever passed through the capital. A few days earlier the Queen Empress had died at Osborne House, her retreat on the Isle of Wight, and on 2 February her funeral cortège (which included most of the crowned heads of Europe, accompanied by a vast concourse of colonial and foreign dignitaries) made their way to Westminster Abbey, passing close to Addy's house. Fitz (to whom the procession was only a blur) wanted to open a window to hear the muffled drums, but the day was cold and Cecilia would not permit it. It was on that momentous day that Ida's second son, Addison Joe, was born. It was also his parents' second wedding anniversary.

Ida made a good recovery. Her parents, however, had been 'much troubled by little John's nurse, who was harsh and rough with him'. They persuaded Ida to get rid of her and a young girl from the Orkney Isles, one of the northernmost parts of Britain, was engaged to fill her place. John's new nurse (who eventually was to become known as Nana) was destined to take on a significant role in the lives of the Baker-Cresswell family.

The move into Harehope provided Ida with an interlude of comparative content. Much work was needed on the house to bring it up to a standard befitting its owners' wealth and station. Addy particularly disliked the gloomy portraits of his ancestors which decorated his walls, and he and Ida set about looking for some more cheerful replacements.

When considering the purchase of pictures, to whom should they turn for advice? The obvious person was Roger Fry, and from Ida's letters we know that he acquired paintings on their behalf, including a much-loved landscape by Richard Wilson which took pride of place in their hall.

This raises the question of how much Addy knew (or guessed) regarding his wife's past? When he married Ida he must have been aware that she was not a virgin. But did he know more? (Indeed, was there more to know?) Are we to suppose that Ida sought the advice of a man who had been not merely been her lover, but was the father of her child? Such an act would have required a colossal nerve. Was Ida capable of it? Like a jigsaw with some of the pieces missing, the question must remain unanswered.

What we do know is that from the day Addy made Ida his wife he showed her scant respect, frequently treating her as if she were no better than one of his mistresses: a whore to be used and then discarded. For, barely a year after he and Ida were settled at Harehope, his utter disregard for his wife's feelings led Addy into a disastrous escapade, which left Ida with no other option than to accept another woman's child.

Chapter XXXV

'O the Misery the Tears the Trouble'

For the long period of time covering Dorothy's illness the Liberals had been out of office and while sitting on the Opposition benches Edward had considerable freedom to set his own agenda. To his fellow Liberal David Lloyd George he was a slacker, since he never took any part in the 'toil and unpleasantness of Opposition' and 'rarely appeared on the platform at Liberal gatherings up and down the country.'[1]

While it is true that Edward had none of the fiery little Welshman's burning zeal for the cut and thrust of politics, and that he succeeded in maintaining a deeply satisfying parallel life far removed from the turmoil of Westminster, he was not without ambitions of his own, though he and his friends Herbert Asquith and Richard Haldane had often despaired of seeing them realised.

In 1899, following the failure of the Jameson Raid into the Transvaal – which aimed to precipitate a revolt against Kruger, the Transvaal President – what became known as the Boer War broke out, causing a deep split within the Liberal ranks. Up till then the British, with their colonies in the Cape and in Natal, had been the most powerful force in Southern Africa. But the discovery of gold in the Transvaal, which had been settled by the Boers, threatened to change all that. With a new source of virtually unlimited African wealth opening up, thousands of Britain's colonial citizens (who were known to the Boers as Uitlanders) trekked north, hoping to make their fortune in the new goldfields. The newly appointed Governor of the Cape Colony, Sir Alfred Milner, had insisted that all British citizens in the Transvaal should be given equal voting rights with the Boers. But President Kruger was proving troublesome, demanding that the Uitlanders serve a seven-year waiting period. The British government considered this to be unreasonable. Not least among their objections was the breeding pattern of the Boers, whose numbers were swelling alarmingly. They felt their position of supremacy was being threatened and were determined to take a stand.

Edward had grave doubts about the legitimacy of the war. On the other hand he had strong family connections with Southern Africa, where two of his younger brothers were pursuing an adventurous life of big game hunting and skirmishes with the natives. Eventually family feeling proved stronger than his misgivings and he came out on the side of a 'firm stand' being taken by Her Majesty's government.

To Dorothy the Empire had always seemed faintly absurd.* Yet she stood by Edward. 'What is to be done while people will go on making this devastating torrent of children and expecting them to be fed?' she wrote to Mandell Creighton (apparently overlooking the fact that the new Bishop of London had quite a 'torrent' of children of his own!).

The split within the Liberal Party – with Lloyd George giving a vigorous lead to the anti-war faction – was echoed by the nation at large, although a majority sided with the Government and the 'Liberal Imperialists' as the pro-war Liberal faction styled themselves. Eventually Edward became sickened by the barbarity of the tactics on both sides, though he continued to maintain that the war was justified. However the infighting did little for his Party's reputation and when the war was finally concluded in 1902 the Tory Party – still wedded to its policy of protectionism – seemed to be firmly entrenched. In April 1903 Edward wrote to his friend Katharine Lyttleton that he saw 'no prospects of Liberals coming in before 1910 and have no more thoughts of office than for the last several years.'[2]

In view of the poor prospects for his Party, we might ask what force it was that drove Edward to perpetuate the struggle? A deep loyalty to his constituents – who time and again had demonstrated their loyalty towards him – must provide part of the answer. But not all. Throughout his life Edward had 'hung suspended' between his private and his public lives; the call of the natural world constantly at odds with his determination to get on and leave a mark. Dorothy was his soul's companion – his muse. But she did not command the whole of him. Success in politics demanded contrivance: a degree of cunning. Politicians seldom rise to the top without getting their hands dirty. It is possible that Pamela Tennant – mistress of a large household and surrounded by a brood of children with their incessant demands – may have had a better understanding of Edward's political self than did Dorothy. Pamela in a sense was his 'town wife', her more earthy persona providing a counterbalance to Dorothy's high-minded disdain for scheming and artifice.

With the coming of the new century Dorothy's health began to improve, though her recovery was to be slow and erratic. At the Cottage she continued to revel in her solitude, caring not a jot for her isolation. The autumn of 1902 was unseasonably wet, blighted by 'unconventional' thunderstorms. It remained mild, however, and the Greys set about a major alteration to their garden 'bringing new soil by railway from a distance and digging and planting very boldly'. Dorothy remained at the Cottage until the end of November and most 'Fridays to Monday' Edward would join her, staying on for longer when he could be spared. Given the flimsy construction of the Cottage (with the only heating provided by a single closed stove) this must have required considerable hardiness. Yet both were sorry when the time came to shut the place up. On 28 November of that year Dorothy wrote in the Cottage Book:

> Going away on a fine grey day, very grateful for my cottage cure. The month has been full of beauty and meadow colours and soft days of wintry sun. Thrushes have sung well since

---

* When Edward's brother George turned up in Bulawayo after a trip into the heart of the Zambezi country, Dorothy commented wryly: 'He seems to have been annexing territory or making spheres of influence of some sort. I am glad he should enjoy himself, but I daresay there will be a horrid little war about it someday.' (Letter to H. Paul, quoted by Robbins.)

the first week of November. The curl* has been about every day and many kinds of wagtails go flitting by the river. There is a little hoarse-throated owl which we have loved very much. Once it flew over the valley hooting all the time as it went … Five months is far too long to be away from cottage joys, and I am very homesick.[3]

On Dorothy's return to Fallodon she must have heard rumours that her sister's marriage was in crisis, but she made no attempt to go over and see her, or to contact their mother. In her fragile state of health the last thing she needed was to get mixed up with her troublesome sister. Her determination to keep her distance from Ida, for Edward's sake as well as her own, was as unbending as ever.

In a long letter to Roger Fry, Cecilia gave an account of what had happened.

> A terrible disaster has befallen us … Addy Cresswell has left his home and wife and children and eloped with a Mrs Forrester, sending Ida a cold and cruel letter to tell her so, and that he loved her no longer – two months ago they were a loving and devoted couple … The end of May they went to London and became acquainted with a Capt. and Mrs Forrester, dined with them and saw them a few times and suddenly one morning Addy told Ida he'd had enough and they must go home – she was very much surprised and disappointed – yet made no difficulties – she never did – and home they went. Two days after he said he couldn't stand the cursed country and solitude and must go back to London, but without Ida. 'It's bad form to have one's wife always tied to one' and so on. So he went and all thro' June and July stayed 10 days at a time there coming back only now and then very wearied and discontented, hating and refusing even to see the children … I went to her several times and consulted and we made up our minds to be patient – and that when the hunting began he wd be all right again … 20th July he met her at N'castle to go to a great puppy judging of his hounds and stay with some friends near who had asked this Mrs F. among their large house party. Here Ida's Hell began – the two were inseparable, wandering together, driving, riding and not even speaking to Ida, so that she was positively forced in this abominable and public manner to see what was going on.

Always at pains to defend her younger daughter, Cecilia insisted that Ida had 'behaved admirably and said never a word'. At the end of four days' torment she and Addy returned home and 'at her earnest request he told her the truth, and that they were going to elope together as soon as Capt. F. could be got out of the way'. Ida was told that she was at liberty to stay at Harehope for the present and that Addy's agent would be instructed to give her such money as could be spared, 'but that he'd want a great deal for Aline', which was Mrs Forrester's name. Then he issued a threat. He said, 'I know your mother is capable of anything – tell her this from me – if she stirs a finger to prevent me I shall cut off little John without a farthing.' This was the message the 'poor heartbroken thing' took back to her parents, as she fled to Newton the next morning, taking her children with her.

While these dramatic events were unfolding in far-off Northumberland the recipient of Cecilia's indignant letter, Roger Fry, had been enjoying a rare spell of marital happiness. Following Helen's breakdown in the early days of their marriage her health had remained

* Curlew.

reasonably stable and with the coming of the new century her doctors' opinion was that she was well enough to risk the birth of a child. In March 1901 their son Julian was born, followed a year later by their daughter Pamela.

Roger must have been acutely aware of the contrast between his happy domestic hearth and the maelstrom that had overtaken Ida and he wrote to her at once. His letter has not survived, but Cecilia reported from Newton that 'you wrote just right to Ida, she liked yr letter exceedingly' – before bringing Roger up to date with the unfolding drama. Addy, she told him, had left Harehope at the end of July to join his mistress in Scotland and Captain Forrester had retaliated by initiating divorce proceedings. This had come as a terrible blow to Ida, for in those days divorce spelled social ostracism. Even as the innocent party you were banned from all Court functions (including the Royal Enclosure at Ascot) while many London hostesses would refuse to receive you. Fortunately 'before any formalities could be completed he applied for leave to withdraw it – wch was granted to him … you can scarcely grasp the enormous relief to Ida and to us all'.

Cecilia's advice to Ida was to sit tight and remain hopeful that given time the culprit would return. 'No doubt that is the only way to mend up her poor life, so we also must hope for it, tho one can but feel that life with such a brute is life at the edge of a precipice and that far the best would be to get rid of him.'

Addy spared his wife nothing, sending orders for her to superintend the parcelling-up of the clothes he would need for Scotland 'and his and <u>her</u> fishing rods'. Bills from Harrods for every kind of luxury came into Ida's hands. Cecilia's letter went on:

> He is a quite inconceivable man, insensible to every feeling of delicacy … I think I told you his father died mad and an aunt – and no doubt many signs in the past 6 months of alternate silence, moroseness, passion and violence – point to this new passion having upset his brain.

Cecilia concluded her letter by dwelling yet again on her daughter's nobleness of character and her 'capacity for absolute Love – all wasted on a half-mad brute'. Yet should she herself have accepted some of the blame for what had happened? Addy may have felt a genuine sense of grievance at the way Cecilia leapt to her daughter's defence at the slightest sign of trouble. Four years younger than his wife and accustomed to getting his own way, the last thing Addy needed was a powerful older woman swooping down like an avenging fury to protect her innocent child.

And was Ida always the innocent victim? Hearsay had it that even in the early years of her marriage she gave Addy tit for tat – reacting to his neglect and recurrent infidelities with affairs of her own. Whatever the truth it seems likely that she would have shared her mother's realistic view of her situation: even if her marriage was a mockery there were solid advantages in attempting to salvage what she could – thus retaining her position in society and protecting her sons from the threat of disinheritance.

Events were to prove her right – at least, in the short term. On 21 February 1903 Cecilia wrote to Roger:

> Addy Cresswell came back to Harehope to Ida last Tuesday evening – you will understand that I cannot now enter into any details, but he is heartbroken and repentant and says all his

> life's devotion will not be enough to atone for what he has done … We gather that both he and Mrs F are sick of it – but her punishment will be swift and sad – the man always gets off cheap … Anyway this is my news and very big news too.

After signing the letter with her initials Cecilia added a postscript: 'This madness has lasted just 17 weeks … and he says he couldn't have come back to any other woman in the world – but O the misery the tears the trouble the futile journeys for such a feeble feeling as it has proved.'

By this time Aline Forrester was well advanced in pregnancy with her lover's child. But now that the culprit had repented and returned to his home, Cecilia was minded to take a more forgiving line 'in justice even to "criminals"'. She reported to Roger that Addy was 'heartbroken and almost dangerously depressed'. He seemed to believe he was being pursued by demons and while Ida had to be away he asked his mother-in-law to stay with him:

> He won't see a soul – not even his own mother – but he asked for me almost as soon as he got here … This has been a very trying 10 days, you may imagine it is not very congenial to be here alone with him … and I am thankful for my good dull sons.

Unfortunately Addy's show of repentance was short-lived. Soon he was making it obvious that he was pining for his lost love. 'I get here whenever I can be spared,' Cecilia wrote to Roger from Harehope:

> It's a comfort to Ida to at least talk – at times he doesn't utter the day long and it's so trying, only less trying than when he is weeping or raving over her [Mrs F's] perfections – or as lately blaspheming – for as you and I judged his religion is but a shallow new-fledged <u>emotion</u> and I fear will fade – I fear because it seems the <u>only thread</u> to keep him here, and when that breaks I cannot prophesy.

During this trying time Cecilia's 'only thread' – her lifeline – was Roger Fry, their correspondence enabling her to cope with the unfolding drama and the sheer mess her daughter had got herself into. Roger kept all the letters from his 'dear friend'. They provide a running commentary as the catastrophe unfolded.

By this time Cecilia had become convinced that her son-in-law was exhibiting positive signs of madness – 'especially after much drink … its quite awful'. Addy was crazy about his and Aline's coming child: 'So proud of having created it and you can't get the idea into him of the injury he has done it and the shame it will feel some day for its mother – but O what can you get into him save utter self? – Selfish, selfish beast!'

It is at this point that Margaret Norman's theory relating to the parentage of her grandmother begins to unravel. When Cecilia set out to write the story of her life she had her descendants in mind and was capable of dissembling when it suited her, to protect the family honour. Yet the comfort of writing to Roger lay in the fact that she could be frank – she wrote exactly as she felt. And in the letter quoted above, what she felt was moral outrage at the selfishness of a man who could father a child out of wedlock. Would she – could she – have written to Roger in those terms if she knew he had been equally guilty? It seems highly unlikely. Yet the mystery remains.

The one individual who appears to have shown some nobleness of character during this difficult time is 'that strange enigma Capt. F – who still stands on the brink of asking Mrs F back'. Just then, however, to Cecilia's dismay the Captain fell seriously ill and for a while it was believed he could not recover. Thankfully he did, and it began to seem that he was genuinely prepared to forgive his wife and allow her to come home. But he baulked at accepting the child. 'I'll take my wife, but not the brat', was how he put it.

It was now that Addy struck an extraordinary bargain with his wife. He was prepared to stay with Ida and resume marital relations on condition that she agreed to take his child, who he insisted must be brought up at Harehope alongside his two sons. Faced with the alternative of losing husband, home and children, Ida felt she had little choice but to comply.

According to Cecilia, the wretched Aline Forrester never set eyes on her child. Her grandmother Lady Millbank had made herself responsible for the reinstatement of her granddaughter into society and on her ladyship's advice the infant (a girl) was whisked away the moment she was born and given into the care of a wet nurse.

When his daughter was brought to Harehope Addy was over the moon. She was baptised Rosemary Cresswell. However, the scandal had not passed unnoticed. It rocked the county and the Baker-Cresswells found themselves ostracised. Ida, deeply humiliated, could not bear to show her face, and Addy – feeling it would be wise to put some distance between himself and his neighbours – looked about for a temporary refuge.

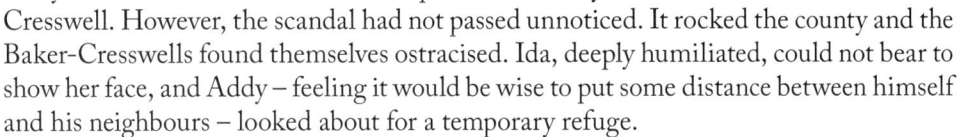

It transpired that Lord Lorne, husband to Queen Victoria's youngest daughter, Princess Louise, and heir to the Duke of Argyle, was looking for a tenant for the family seat, Inverary Castle, since he was unable to afford its upkeep. He was quite happy to lease it to Mr Baker-Cresswell – remarking to a friend that 'it would be all right since there is nobody for him to elope with round these parts'. Addy took it on a seven-year lease – an expensive arrangement as things turned out. Cecilia helped Ida with the move and the summer of 1903 was passed happily enough. She described to Roger the pleasures to be had from living in such ducal splendour: 'A perfect kingdom rather than an estate.' Two salmon rivers ran through the grounds, the sea was at the end of the lawn, while fallow deer grazed 'at the very door'. She could 'hardly find time for writing in this heavenly place' with its glorious views and ever-changing colours. Best of all was the sight of her two little grandsons 'flitting about barefoot in their little green and white quaintness of dress and glorious colour of cheeks and hair'. Peace reigned, with 'Addy unrecognisable in amiability and thoughtfulness – it seeming quite natural to see a baby once more in

21 *Rosemary Cresswell, aged five.*

22 *Cynthia Baker-Cresswell.*

the nurse's arms and Ida saying she must indeed be wicked and ungrateful to murmur at such a small speck in her rich blessedness.'

Yet Cecilia's sunny letter concluded on a darker note, for Roger had not written for some weeks and she was becoming anxious for a word 'and do give it to me – but not here ... I did not like Helen's looks and manner when I saw you lately and when you don't write I fear calamity.'

In fact her friend had been exceptionally busy that summer, preparing for his first one-man show. Held at the prestigious Carfax Gallery, to everyone's surprise (including his own) it proved a tremendous success. Nevertheless Cecilia's premonition proved to be well founded, for Helen was becoming increasingly disturbed and later that year suffered a serious relapse 'under which her mind fell apart and she was reduced to incoherent ramblings, or long periods of silence broken only by requests to see her children'.[4]

But that was yet to come. Meanwhile the Baker-Creswells' summer at Inverary seemed to promise a new beginning and by September Ida knew that she was pregnant again. The coming of autumn, however, was to show up the disadvantages of living in a turreted castle, no matter how grand, that lacked any proper system of heating and was open to the westerly gales. The glamour of the place rapidly wore thin and, scandal or no scandal, the Cresswells decided to pack up and head for home. They were never to stay at Inverary again.

On 29 May 1904 Ida and Addy's third child was born. A girl, she was baptised Cynthia May.

Ninety years later, following in the tradition of her mother and her grandmother, Cynthia took up her pen and embarked on writing her own autobiography. Her birth, she began, 'was not an auspicious occasion or one that called for any rejoicing or pleasure – the reason being that there was already a girl in the family born exactly a year and a day previously'. The girl Cynthia referred to was, of course, Rosemary. Not only was she her father's eldest daughter – she was, and would always remain, his clear favourite – a fact my mother resented until her dying day.

Chapter XXXVI

A Horse that Shied

By 1905 it was becoming clear that the Conservative government, which had held power for almost 11 years, was finally running out of steam. But once again the Liberals were split, on this occasion between factions holding opposing views over foreign policy. The 'Old Guard', headed by their former leader Lord Rosebery, favoured strengthening Great Britain's ties with Germany. Since Germany was the most powerful nation on the European continent, with an army of four million men and the second-largest navy after Great Britain, Rosebery and his supporters believed it was essential to retain the Germans as allies. The Liberal imperialist wing of the Party (which included Grey) did not agree. It was their belief that over-close ties with Germany would alienate France, thereby upsetting the 'balance of power' upon which Europe depended for the maintenance of peace. Grey and his supporters were eager to strengthen the *Entente Cordiale* recently negotiated by Balfour, which sought to draw a line under Great Britain's age-old rivalry with the French.

The Conservative government was eventually brought down by a dispute over its decision to bring in indentured Chinese labour to work in the South African mines. But in September 1905, with a general election imminent and his Party's differences still unresolved, Edward escaped to the Highlands, where he and Dorothy had taken a fishing lodge, called Relugas, above a wooded gorge on the River Findhorn, overlooking 'the most beautiful and various river in Scotland', according to Dorothy: 'I can hardly believe it is a real place, it is so dream-like and lovely.' The place was a veritable Paradise. 'We catch salmon in deep dark brown pools with a line of white foam curling down the middle, and steep green rocks leading up to birch trees against the blue,' Dorothy wrote to her friend Captain Barton.

Their peace, however, was soon to be interrupted by the arrival of two of Edward's friends and close political allies – Richard Haldane and Herbert Asquith; the latter having taken a fishing lodge close by. It was by now a foregone conclusion that the Liberals would win the forthcoming election and after years in the political wilderness the friends were eager to assume power. All three were united in their belief that the present leader of the Party, Henry Campbell-Bannerman, would not make a good Prime Minister and they agreed that they would be reluctant to serve under him. In what later became known as the 'Relugas Compact' Asquith and Haldane now proposed to Edward that Campbell-Bannerman, while nominally retaining the Premiership, should be persuaded to accept a peerage. He could then be 'kicked upstairs', as the saying went, to the House of Lords, leaving the effective leadership of the Commons to Asquith, as Chancellor of the Exchequer. If their plan succeeded Edward was to be appointed Foreign Secretary and Haldane would become the Leader of the House. If it did not, Asquith and Haldane persuaded Edward to join ranks with them in refusing to serve in a Campbell-Bannerman Cabinet.

But their plot misfired when even before the election had taken place it became clear that the Liberal Leader had no intention of being sidelined. After a discussion between themselves Asquith and Haldane reneged on the compact, leaving Edward isolated. He was now in an awkward position. Since 1896 he had been a Director of the North-Eastern Railway – its main line from King's Cross to Edinburgh having the advantage of a Halt stop within walking distance from Fallodon. In 1904 he had been elected chairman, with a salary of £2,000 a year. Edward enjoyed the work, and his chairman's salary would have enabled him, had he so wished, to live the life of a country gentleman, freed from all financial restraints. After Campbell-Bannerman had proved immovable, Dorothy felt as if a door of opportunity had been thrown open and until the very last minute she pleaded with Edward to stick to his guns and resign. Knowing that after so many years in Opposition he would never consent to return to the back benches, his resignation would effectively mark the end of his political career and they would both be free.

At one point Edward seemed ready to take Dorothy's advice. But this proved more difficult than he had anticipated. On the day Balfour, the Conservative Prime Minister, resigned Edward arrived at Campbell-Bannerman's office and repeated his terms. Campbell-Bannerman replied that he had no intention of quitting the Commons. But as he was convinced that Edward was the best man for the job of Foreign Secretary he was prepared to hold the position open.

At this point Edward wrote to Dorothy, who had escaped to Fallodon:

> It is harassing beyond all experience. I held out all yesterday ... which was peculiarly difficult, especially as by this I was wrecking Asquith ... If it had not been for me there would have been no difficulty. I am afraid they must think me a beast ... Now don't form any opinion on this till you see me. It has put me on short rations of sleep for two nights. If I go on, you mustn't judge me till you have heard. If I stay out ... no explanation to you will be necessary.

In the event, after the pleading of his friends and political allies, Edward gave in and agreed to serve as Foreign Secretary, a position he was destined to fill for the next 11 years. The die was cast. By such slender threads hang the fates of men and of nations. It had been touch and go.

After that events moved rapidly. A general election was called, involving all the usual speech-making and travelling. Mercifully Dorothy seemed fitter than she had been for many years and she did all she could to support her husband. However, she confessed to her old friend Ella Pease: 'This last fortnight has been quite the most horrid we have ever had ... We shan't be able to judge for a long time whether he was right to go in or not, but as he has, I am very glad that he has work that interests him so much. There is a lot of flummery about the Foreign Office and I try not to think how badly I shall do my small part of the work, but I shall try very hard.'[1]

Electioneering got under way at the beginning of January. Some time earlier Louise Creighton, who was by this time a widow,* had been invited to stay at Fallodon, but when she suggested that under the circumstances her visit should be postponed, Dorothy would not hear of it. The company of her dear friend Louise, she said, would be one of the few good things she had to look forward to in that weary time.

Mrs Creighton's account of the days she spent with her friend provides a moving picture of Dorothy in what were destined to be the final weeks of her life.

> The days we spent at Fallodon were beautiful quiet winter days. In the evening they had to motor out to some village for an election meeting. Dorothy loved the motoring on those fine moonlit nights. She was bright and well, quite calm and unfussed by what would have been to others the turmoil of entering on a new life of such importance ... We fed the ducks, we wandered about the woods and fields as usual. In the mornings before breakfast I used to see her walking with her decided springy step on the gravel path before the windows without hat or cloak, to taste the morning air ... She was very full of talk in those days. I have never known her talk so much ... I think she was a little interested at the prospect of having to mix with men and women of many varied kinds, though absolutely humble about her capacity to do her social duties well, and very afraid lest her blunders might in any way harm Edward's career ... one felt that whatever part she had to play would be played with the same fearless, sincere desire to do her best, and to use her opportunities as a means to help other lives.[2]

The election was handsomely won by the Liberals, who came out of it with an absolute majority of 84. When Edward's poll was declared he was found to have achieved his greatest electoral success, having a majority of 2,240 over his Conservative opponent. After years in the political wilderness he had made it to the top. Letters of congratulation piled up on Dorothy's desk. To one friend she replied: 'People write and ask me if I am not very proud. It seems to me that the time has hardly come yet. One will be proud enough to look back on work well done if that be possible some day.'[3]

The 'flummery' Dorothy had dreaded began almost at once. One of Edward's first duties as the new Foreign Secretary was to attend a royal banquet at Windsor Castle, accompanied by his wife. No record exists of what Dorothy wore for this grand occasion, but according to Mrs Creighton (admittedly a partial witness) 'All who saw her there were struck with her radiance, her wonderful charm. Improved health had brought back all the old beauty ... She sat next to the King at dinner and it was easy to see how much she interested him. He spoke afterwards of his great appreciation of her charm and her ability.'[4]

Dorothy had passed her first test in her new role with flying colours. But the ordeal of having to play the Cabinet Minister's wife and being so publicly on display had taken its toll and following the royal banquet she fled to Fallodon, leaving Edward to cope with his new duties alone.

---

* Bishop Creighton had died of cancer in 1901.

And should we not level some censure at Dorothy for abandoning her husband at this critical time? For immediately after taking office Edward had been flung into a crisis over Anglo-French relations, after the Kaiser had paid a deliberately provocative visit to Tangier – steaming into the harbour of the French protectorate in his royal yacht in a deliberate attempt to challenge French hegemony in the area and to foment trouble between the signatories of the *Entente Cordiale*. Faced so early in his tenure of the Foreign Office with a situation which might conceivably have led to war, who can doubt that Edward would have derived strength and comfort from having his wife at his side?

But Dorothy went to Fallodon, where, with the exception of the domestic staff, she was quite alone. On Thursday 1 February she was observed going into the garden, where 'the last thing she was seen to do in her dear home was to go and pick a bunch of lilies of the valley which had just come up in the greenhouse, and walk up and down the path outside the drawing-room window smelling them.'[5] Had she intended to take the flowers to a neighbour? Who can say? After luncheon Dorothy ordered her dog-cart to be got ready and without informing any of the staff where she was going she set off down the lanes.

A dog-cart is a horse-drawn two-wheeled open carriage with two seats back-to-back, the rear one made to shut up as a box for sportsmen's dogs. It is lightly constructed and not particularly stable and in those days it was frequently used by the lady of the house for making short trips or paying calls.

A few weeks earlier Dorothy had driven Mrs Creighton 'in that high dogcart with a swift poney [*sic*] which she seemed only just able to manage. I remember it kicked up a lot of mud into her face and she could not find a handkerchief to wipe it off and had borrowed mine.'[6] Though Dorothy was an experienced horsewoman she lacked that natural affinity with the equine order which characterised her younger sister and when the pony shied she was not able to control it. The dog-cart was overturned and she was thrown out onto her head.

The accident occurred three miles from Fallodon, just outside the schoolmaster's cottage at Ellingham. Dorothy was picked up and carried unconscious into the cottage. The schoolmaster, her friend Mr McGonigle, was there and her doctor, Dr Waterson, was immediately summoned. He arrived within the hour and after examining her declared that nothing could be done except to watch and wait. A telegram was despatched to Edward which he received while attending a meeting of the Committee of Imperial Defence. He left at once, setting off for Fallodon by train and arriving that same night. Dr Waterson advised that Dorothy should not be moved in her dangerous condition and for the following three days she lay unconscious at the schoolmaster's cottage. She died in the early hours of Sunday 4 February without regaining consciousness. She was just forty-two.

Before the advent of X-rays and sophisticated brain surgery there was little that could have been done and no specialist advice had been sought. Dorothy's body was carried back to Fallodon and laid in the library – the couple's favourite room. 'The sun streamed in through the open windows and the squirrel came in as usual to fetch its nuts from the box. The first snowdrops from the garden were laid upon her breast.'[7]

Dorothy had previously made it known to Edward that after her death she wished to be cremated. As a means of disposing of a human body cremation had only been legalised in

23   Edward Grey, 'awakened from his dream of happiness'.

England in 1885 and the practice was still rare. Despite the disapproval of her family Edward was determined that his wife's wish should be honoured. The nearest crematorium was at Darlington, an industrial town some forty miles south of Newcastle upon Tyne. On the day of the funeral Edward set off from Fallodon with his wife's coffin in a train hired specially for the occasion. Apart from the Fallodon servants only five close friends accompanied him. These were Mr McGonigle, Ella Pease, Constance Herbert, Alice Graves and Louise Creighton. No member of Dorothy's or Edward's family were invited to be present. Afterwards Mrs Creighton sent the following account to her son Oswin who was in Canada:

> I had never been at a cremation and felt rather a dread of it, but it was all very nice. The cemetery at Darlington is right out of the town among the fields and it was a beautiful sunny day, with the snowdrops coming up in the grass. First we had a bit of a service in the little bare cemetery chapel ... Then we followed the coffin on a bier a long way through the cemetery where the crematorium stands, and there we had the rest of the service, and the coffin was just slid away through some curtains, when the words committing it 'to be consumed' came ... And then we all came away.[8]

Many of Edward's friends assumed that the shock of his wife's death would persuade him to retire from politics. But his bereavement was to have the opposite effect. Mrs Creighton was invited to stay on at Fallodon after the funeral and her letter to her son continued:

> It is a very wonderful time because he is so unlike anyone I have ever known in a great sorrow; there is no repining, no murmuring. He loves to talk about her and to go over again all the memory of their past happiness. It has been a very wonderful married happiness and I think that he is going to build on its memory a splendid life of service.

And that is what Edward did. G.M. Trevelyan, in his biography *Grey of Fallodon*, wrote this of his fellow Northumbrian:

> He had been awakened from his dream of happiness with Dorothy amid the woods and the birds ... Yet it had not been a dream; for long it had been a reality on earth and it lived in his retentive and practised memory. On these terms he was left alone, to face for eleven years a task as grim as any British statesman has ever had to face. His eyes were grave to sadness, as men saw who looked on him, but the well-springs within were not dry.

Chapter XXXVII

Broken Lives

Though Fitz and Cecilia were deeply shocked by the death of Dorothy, it was Ida who was the most 'distressed and enervated' by the loss of her sister. As the crow flies Harehope lies only about 12 miles south of Fallodon, yet the scandal attached to the name of Baker-Cresswell and Ida's rackety life had resulted in the Greys cutting the couple and their children clean out of their lives. Thus when Ida learned that Dolly lay mortally injured in the schoolmaster's house, fearing that she would not be admitted, she stayed away.

Yet she had never ceased to idolise her elder sister, whom she believed to be her superior in every conceivable way: cleverer, wiser and more beautiful, who after capturing the heart of one of the most brilliant statesmen of the age had succeeded in creating a perfect marriage, free of the tyranny of the flesh and the curse of sexual passion. Unlike her mother, Ida had always had the greatest respect for Ed and Dolly's 'union of souls' – a state of blessedness which her own nature had denied her. Now she was married to a monster of selfishness whose nature was even more ungovernable than her own; and whom she had failed to tame. Yet while Dolly was alive she could still hope for an eventual reconciliation. With her death, that hope was extinguished.

Ida's misery was so extreme that she had given way to hysteria, infuriating Addy. Fearing for her sanity her parents took her abroad. At Arcachon, a coastal resort south of Bordeaux, she went riding on the sands and took long walks with her mother in the pine woods, their pungent resiny scent reminding them both of happier times.

Yet rest and relaxation were never going to provide a cure for the root cause of Ida's unhappiness which was the parlous state of her marriage. The peaceful interludes were few and were growing shorter. Addy, having come out to join them, took Ida off to fashionable Baden-Baden where she 'had a horrid time'. It was all too evident that the couple were happiest when apart.

Later that year Bertram came home from India on leave. Aline Cust was staying at Newton and she and Bertram got very close and before his leave was up they had announced that they were engaged. 'We didn't like it,' Cecilia admitted, 'her whole mind was set on vetting and we felt sure that would never suit Bertram, he knew she wouldn't be tolerated in India and by the regiment – strongly preferring feminine women as they did.'

Bertram had even talked about leaving the army and he and Aline doing up a house on the Newton estate. What may have prompted him to think that way was that some months previously 'Gerard had disclosed his intention of leaving his inheritance of Newton to Bertram.' Naturally his proposal had caused a lot of discussion, 'for it couldn't be settled in a hurry, but it was understood to be so'.

Gerard had always felt an outsider, never being comfortable with his family's values, or the way they lived. His slurred speech (which elocution lessons had failed to improve) was a continuing embarrassment to himself and to everyone else and as he grew to manhood even his fond mother must have realised that he was quite unfit to fill his father's shoes. His decision, therefore, sounded perfectly reasonable. Why then do doubts persist?

Ever since Gerard's birth it had been rumoured that he was not Fitz's child; that he had been fathered by Fitz's nephew Jem Smith-Barry. Why else had he been baptised plain Gerard Widdrington? Eventually, according to Cecilia's *Diary*, Gerard and his parents 'all 3 went to Newcastle … and the Deed was signed, Gibson being the lawyer on his side, and he had thoroughly examined G in a previous visit as to whether it was his own unbiased wish for his own disinheritance, so that was settled and G was to have 300£ or 400£ a year of the estate for his life.' Whether that was a truthful account of what had happened and why, or whether it was a cover-up devised by Cecilia to spare Fitz's honour, we shall never know.

Life went on. At Newton Fitz had a stone balustrade erected at the end of the lawn, a new stone summerhouse built and two stone lions secured on plinths outside the conservatory door. The pond was cleared of weeds and enlarged. In September 1907 Cecilia's mother, the redoubtable Susan Hopwood, died at the age of eighty-seven. Only the once-despised Rose was with her in her last illness. 'She wd. have no one else. Gerard and I went to the funeral wch was in the Mausoleum where my father also was laid in his tomb.' Ida's second daughter, Diana, was born at Newton that October. And Addy's mother, the Dowager Countess of Ravensworth, caused a storm of gossip by marrying her groom.* (By Cecilia's account 'they only lived a few weeks together when she pensioned him off!') Then Bertram got more leave and came home again, shot five blackcock and broke off his engagement.

In 1908 Gerard set off on an epic journey encompassing Paris, Athens, Constantinople, Cairo, Alexandria, Sardinia and Corsica. He was accompanied by Mr Golightly, the former vicar of Shilbottle, and though Gerald does not appear to have enjoyed the trip very much he and the parson became friends. Shortly afterwards Mr Golightly was installed as rector of North Shields, a bleak mining and industrial town in the north-

---

* Joe Baker-Cresswell, Addy's younger son, gave the following account of his grandmother's short-lived third marriage:

> My grandfather died of typhoid caught in Alnwick in 1886. My grandmother married the Earl of Ravensworth and when he died proceeded to marry the groom. Shortly afterwards my father returned home from a long tour abroad and to his astonishment was met on the steps of Cresswell by the groom dressed in plus-fours with a gun under his arm. When asked why he had married my grandmother, he answered: 'Because her ladyship wished it.' My father very quickly had him sent to Canada from whence he never returned.

east of England. Seeing Gerard once more at a loose end, Cecilia suggested that he might go to North Shields and help Mr Golightly in the parish; Gerard 'seemed to like the idea' and in the event stayed at the rectory for a number of years, getting to know and help the poor of the parish. He seemed much happier there, forming a friendship with one of the lay readers, a Captain Pike of the Church Army 'and they two worked much together'.

It was about that time that Fitz had both his eyes taken out. The pressure on his eyeballs caused by glaucoma had been giving him excruciating pain and Cecilia took him to London where an ophthalmic surgeon advised their removal. In those days surgical procedures were frequently carried out in the patient's home. 'End of Oct. Dr Wardle of N'Castle came, he took the eyes out in our nursery wch was the best light,' Cecilia recorded. 'The relief from pain was instantaneous – he had a nurse and was only in bed a few days.'

In 1910 after only nine years on the throne Edward VII died, bringing to a close an age of conspicuous consumption among the upper and middle classes of Great Britain that has never been equalled and is unlikely ever to be surpassed. He had been a popular monarch whose death was mourned by the nation. For despite his reputation for serial womanising Edward had possessed an inestimable gift: a rare love of life and an ability to spread the 'feel good' factor among his subjects. He had moreover proved to be a skilful diplomat. His bonhomie and charm had played a useful role in oiling the wheels of the diplomatic machinery, bringing about the *Entente Cordiale* with France of 1904 and the Anglo-Russian agreement three years later; both these compacts having been created in order to maintain the 'balance of power' upon which Europe's peace was believed to depend. He had succeeded in seeing through these tricky manoeuvres without alienating his irascible and half-mad cousin the German Emperor, Kaiser Wilhelm II. With Edward VII's passing a close-knit family of cousins – which included the three powerful monarchs of Great Britain, Russia and Germany – had been broken up. For since the three had maintained regular contact and were, more or less, on friendly terms, a useful brand of informal diplomacy had existed, which Edward VII's untimely death at the age of 69 had brought to an end. His passing can be seen as one of the precursors of that 'war that was to end all wars'. Had he lived, matters might – just might – have turned out differently, and war have been averted.

But war and rumours of war were far from the minds of the Cresswells and the Widdringtons, who had troubles much closer to home. For 1910 was to see the final collapse of Ida's disastrous marriage. During its closing years Addy had been much from home and Ida's response to his continuing infidelities had been to plunge recklessly into affairs of her own. According to her mother, Ida had gone out to India 'about 1910' to visit Bertram, whose regiment was stationed in Calcutta. Apparently she had gone with her husband's blessing for Addy had provided her with money for the trip. Bertram had been 'very pleased to have her and showed her the chief beautiful buildings and towns', exerting himself to give his sister 'a splendid time'.

No doubt that was true so far as it went. But reports began to reach Addy which suggested that his wife's 'splendid time' had been more in the nature of a wild fling. Though Ida was now a matron past 40 she still had her captivating eyes and curvaceous figure, and finding herself the toast of a mess full of sex-starved young officers it seems likely that her conduct got rapidly out of control. Addy was furious. So far as he was concerned, the day of reckoning had arrived. He wired his wife to come home immediately, informing her that their marriage was over and that Harehope was to be sold.

In those days an erring wife had little recourse to the law. When Ida returned to Harehope Addy only permitted her to remain in the house long enough to pack up her belongings and those of their daughters (who she was determined should stay with her) before turning her out of the house. Having nowhere else to go she returned to Newton, throwing herself on the mercy of her parents.

On the advice of his solicitor Addy did not sue for divorce, fearing that Ida might decide to contest the case and that the ensuing scandal could be as damaging to himself as to her. He was nevertheless determined to punish his wife with all the force which the law permitted. Ida, determined to fight back, hinted that Addy had molested his daughters and had all four children put in Chancery and held as wards of court. Addy

24   *Ida before the deluge, with John, Joe, Cynthia and Diana.*

vehemently denied her accusation, retaliating with a list of Ida's sexual improprieties and declaring she was not fit to be a mother. In a highly acrimonious atmosphere a great deal of mud was thrown by both sides. Eventually, advised by Sir Walter Trower, the Widdringtons' family solicitor, Ida was persuaded to accept extremely harsh terms. Though Addison Baker-Cresswell was one of the wealthiest men in the county, under the Deed of Separation his wife was to receive an annual sum of £1,500 and to have custody of the two girls, whom their father was not permitted to contact and for whom no financial provision was made. Custody of John and Joe was given to their father and Addy's daughter Rosemary continued to live with him.

Thus Ida, returning from India with trunks full of finery (jewels and gossamer-fine shawls and bolts of embroidered silk intended for ball gowns) found herself and her daughters without a home and, by the standards she was accustomed to, virtually penniless. What was to become of them?

For the next four years mother and daughters led a vagabond life. It was the bleakest of times. Fitz, profoundly affected by his daughter's disgrace, fell into depression. Always a bad sleeper, he would spend wakeful nights pacing the silent house until Cecilia found him and led him back to his bed, perhaps throwing open a window so that he could hear the dawn chorus. She herself was in a state of utter misery, refusing to believe the scandalous tales Addy Cresswell was throwing about.

Meanwhile the final collapse of the marriage of her dear friend Roger Fry, though long foreseen, was heartrending when it came, adding another tier to Cecilia's unhappiness. After Helen Fry's relapse during the winter of 1904 she had made a reasonable recovery, good enough to give Roger grounds for hope. Yet the state of his finances was still far from secure. Though his paintings were beginning to sell, the main part of his income was derived from journalism and fees for his lectures which, though becoming immensely popular, were ill paid. Then on a visit to New York, quite out of the blue, he was offered the post of Curator of Paintings at the Metropolitan Museum at a salary of £1,600 a year, plus an allowance to enable him to travel in Europe to acquire paintings for the museum. His anxiety over Helen's health made him hesitate at first, but ultimately both of them agreed it was an offer he could not refuse.

Roger's five-year tenure of this post, which required him to spend three or four months of every year in New York, was destined to be plagued by worries over his wife, who remained in their Hampstead house with their two children. Eventually he fell out with the President of the Museum and was sacked.* Roger returned to a wife who doctors advised him was unlikely to recover. And in the following year he was forced to acknowledge that Helen was now permanently insane. With a heavy heart he accepted that she must be certified and confined to an asylum. 'I've given up even regretting the callus that had to form to let me go through with things', he wrote to his friend Lowes Dickinson. 'Now and again it gives and I could cry for the utter pity and wastefulness, but life is too urgent.'[1] As matters stood it was a blessing that the Society of Friends – whose members, on account of their frequent intermarriages, were no strangers to

* The President was the larger-than-life railroad multi-millionaire and art collector J. Pierpoint Morgan, who Roger described as 'the most repulsively ugly man with a great strawberry nose, who behaved like a crowned head'.

25 *Cynthia and Diana at Hyères, oil sketch by Roger Fry.*

mental instability – had established their own private asylum. It was to this establishment that Helen Fry was committed, leaving her husband to care for their children and to attempt to get on with the rest of his life.

Though the collapse of his marriage was to leave him permanently scarred, Roger had received huge support from his family and friends. His sister Joan stepped in to run his household and help him care for his children, and he and Cecilia Widdrington remained in close touch. His busy life left him little time to brood on what might have been. And that year he had more than ever before to occupy him.

While travelling in France on behalf of the Metropolitan Museum, Roger had been bewitched by the work of an artist who was completely unknown in Britain. His name was Paul Cézanne. His style was revolutionary: a reduction of form, with no attempt made to hide the brushstrokes. And he had a 'quite extraordinary feeling for light ... never rendered before in landscape art.'[2] Roger was convinced of Cézanne's genius. Equally unknown and equally radical was the work of two of his contemporaries, Henri Matisse and Vincent Van Gogh. Entranced by their boldness and striking use of bright colours, Roger was determined to make their work known to the British public. Thus it came about that in November 1910, the year that had begun so tragically, Roger mounted an exhibition at the fashionable Grafton Gallery that was to become the talk of London. The first Post-Impressionist exhibition (a term Roger had coined at the very last minute) was to change the face of art in Britain. Among the exhibits on display were works now regarded as some of the finest in the history of art: Cézanne's *La Veille au Chapelet,* Matisse's *Femme aux Yeux Verts* and Van Gogh's *Crows in a Cornfield.* Though the exhibition drew vitriolic abuse from most of the critics* it was destined to establish Roger's reputation as a major arbiter of taste and the foremost art critic and art historian of his day. Almost overnight, and somewhat to his dismay, Roger discovered that he had become a public figure. The exhibition showed a handsome profit and a second Post-Impressionist show was held the following year.

Was Cecilia among the crowds who poured into the Grafton Gallery that November to witness Roger Fry's *succès de scandale*? Since her *Diary* contains no mention of the exhibition the question must remain unanswered. If she had made the effort to take the train to London in order to support Roger, what message would she have carried home to Fitz? It would be interesting to learn how she reacted to her friend's attempt to drive a coach and horses through the Art Establishment of his day.

---

* An entry in the diary of the poet Wilfred Scawen Blunt summed up the feelings of many: 'The drawing is on the level of that of an untaught child of seven or eight years old, the sense of colour that of a tray painter, the method that of a schoolboy who wipes his fingers on a slate after spitting on them.'[3]

Chapter XXXVIII

A Fresh Start

Once the deed of separation had been signed, Ida's most pressing need was to find a home for herself and her daughters, six-year-old Cynthia and Diana, almost three. Northumbrian society had turned its back on her as a disgraced wife. She believed that she would have to look outside the county for a house and lowland Scotland seemed the most suitable option. Her one stipulation was that she must live within sight of the sea. Her parents put out feelers, eventually finding a house for her at Saltburn, a seaside town in Fife, putting 100 miles between their daughter and the scene of her disgrace.

Cynthia's abiding memory of that house was that it was perishingly cold. It must have been a miserable time for the two little girls, caught up in the tears and recriminations and the flurry of packing and unpacking, with no one to explain to them what was happening – or indeed why.

Ida did not stay long at Saltburn and for the next four years she and her daughters seem to have lived like gypsies, repeatedly on the move. Cecilia's *Diary* mentions that for a while they lived at Monks House, 'a queer house almost in the sea', within sight of the Farne islands. But that could not have suited either, for shortly afterwards they moved a few miles south, taking lodgings at Beadnell Bay.

Little Diana, a stoical child with a capacity for remaining unsurprised by whatever life threw at her, seems to have come through these years relatively unscathed. But Cynthia suffered. She became fractious and ungovernable; at times hysterical. Deeply unhappy and at odds with her mother, she retreated into a make-believe world of fairies and princesses, watched over by the father she had lost. 'It was not surprising that I wanted to go to my father', she wrote years later, recalling the fantasies she had woven round the man who (though she did not know it) she was never to see again. 'The refrain of my childhood was that my father was the most evil man in the world and I was exactly like him.'[1]

Addy meanwhile had taken Rosemary and the boys to live in his London house, where they were cared for by 'Nana', their former nurse who was now Addy's housekeeper. Since by this time the sturdy little Highlander was also his mistress she had been given the courtesy title of 'Mrs Cumming'. At some stage she had given birth to Addy's child, whom he insisted should be named Aline, after his erstwhile mistress. In contrast to his

211

beloved Rosemary, Nana's infant received little love from her father, who had her boarded out with one of his gamekeepers.*

Addy's son John was determined to enter the Royal Navy and when he was 13 his father sent him to Osborne, the naval training college. Joe was eager to follow him, but there was a problem. At 12 years old he was still bed-wetting occasionally and seemed generally out of sorts. His affliction did not endear him to his father, who had no time for a son who was less than perfect. Addy decided to hand the problem over to Ida and Joe was packed off to join his mother and sisters, who welcomed him with rapturous delight.

Ida, however, was still without a proper home and she and her children had perforce to spend long spells at Newton, 'wearied after constant changes of lodging'. In the end it was Fitz, now over 80, who came up with a solution.

The Widdrington property of Hauxley, some ten miles from Newton and six miles south of Alnwick, comprised a few tenanted farms and a pitmen's village of low stone cottages adjacent to a small working pit. Hugging the coast was a second village occupied by fishermen and their wives, their main catch being salmon netted at the mouth of the River Coquet. Hauxley Hall, a substantial stone house of indeterminate age which had been partially gentrified in the 18th century, was situated at the centre of the property, about a mile from the sea. It had been occupied for some years by a tenant farmer, but it was settled between Fitz and Bertram that a new farmhouse was to be built and Hauxley Hall made over to Ida for her lifetime.

'It was almost a ruin then', Cecilia recalled, though the house still retained some good features, 'especially a lovely staircase winding up out of the hall'. This beautiful 18th-century stair with its wrought-iron twist balusters was the most striking feature of the house.† Fitz was advised that no structural alterations would be necessary in order to bring the house up to an acceptable standard. By the time central heating and acetylene gas lighting had been installed he judged that Hauxley would make Ida and her family a comfortable home in which they could feel settled at last.

Meanwhile Joe, who had been receiving lessons at home from a tutor, was plainly still far from well. Ida took him to Edinburgh to see the famous Dr Milan who had successfully treated the ailing Duke of York. The doctor, who diagnosed a urinary infection, suspected that Joe might also be suffering from incipient tuberculosis. He recommended that the boy be taken to a warm climate, with complete rest. Ida jumped at the chance of going abroad. Since several months' work was still needed before Hauxley could be considered habitable the waiting time could be spent in the South of France. It was decided that Diana should go with them to keep Joe company, but that 10-year-old Cynthia, 'who was very tiresome just now and disturbed all the family', would stay behind with her grandparents.

So in the spring of 1914 Ida and the children set off for Cavalière, a modest resort on the French Riviera not far from Nice, putting up at the *Grand Hotel*. In common with the

---

* Aline Cresswell's eventful and ultimate tragic life falls outside the scope of this narrative. Strikingly pretty, she was to marry four times. One of her grandchildren is the novelist and biographer Cressida Connolly.

† 'A delightful surprise', according to Nikolaus Pevsner; see *The Buildings of England: Northumberland*.

26 *Aline Cresswell, Addy's daughter by his housekeeper, Mrs Cumming.*

bulk of her countrymen, Ida had not the slightest suspicion that their carefree holiday was to mark the end of an era.

The following month saw the celebration of Fitz and Cecilia's Golden Wedding. Their tenants put up a fountain in the village to commemorate the event and 'Ed Grey sent us a real gold cup' – a token of the fact that by that time relations between the Grays and the Widdringtons had eased.

In the previous year Bertram had finally found himself a wife, a young woman named Enid Rivière, whom he had met on board ship while returning from India on leave. Enid was the daughter of an artist, well-known in his day but now forgotten, called Rudolph Onslow Ford. 'We were quite pleased at this artistic talent coming into the family', Cecilia commented. And great was the Widdrington's delight when, in their anniversary year, Enid gave birth to a son, thereby securing the Widdrington succession. The boy was named Anthony.

The renovation of Hauxley Hall for the benefit of his favourite child was to be Fitz's swan song. When Ida and her children took possession of the house her father knew that he had given her back a life. No longer the humiliated cast-off wife, Ida could begin to regain her place in society. Dropping the hyphenated 'Baker', as plain Mrs Cresswell of Hauxley Hall she was now free to reinvent herself. Of course, the war (which changed so many lives) was also to help.

Chapter XXXIX

At War

'The lamps are going out all over Europe.' Edward Grey famously observed on the evening of 4 August 1914, as he looked down on the lamplighters from a window in the Foreign Office. 'We shall not see them lit again in our lifetime.'

On the previous day, which was August Bank Holiday Monday, Grey had gone down to the House of Commons to face what his biographer G.M. Trevelyan called 'the greatest and most tragic occasion of his life'. As His Majesty's Foreign Secretary he believed it was his duty to persuade the House that, in the event of the small nation of Belgium being attacked by Germany, Great Britain was left with no honourable alternative but to go to war in her defence. He knew his task would not be easy. No European nation had wanted war. The assassination five weeks earlier of the Archduke Ferdinand of Austria and his wife by a Serbian patriot, in the remote Bosnian town of Sarajevo, had created little more than a ripple. Even the German Kaiser, for all his sabre-rattling and paranoid fear of 'encirclement', had seemed unwilling to step over the brink. At least half the British Cabinet were opposed to armed intervention on the European mainland. Just over a week ago no less a figure than the Chancellor of the Exchequer Mr Lloyd George had delivered a strong speech to the House advocating cost-cutting in the Navy. He had, moreover, gone so far as to inform the Members that 'our relations with Germany are better than they have been for years' and that in consequence the next budget ought to show a cut in expenditure on armaments.

However, a week can be a long time in politics. And just as a small fire, carelessly fanned, can swiftly develop into an inferno, the Bosnian atrocity had set in train a series of events which ultimately were to prove unstoppable. Unbeknownst to the rest of the world the German High Command had issued a 'blank cheque' to Austria – her partner, together with Italy, in the 'Triple Alliance'* – authorising the tottering Hapsburg Empire to take whatever reprisals it wished against the Serbs and guaranteeing Germany's full support. Austria had responded by sending an ultimatum to Belgrade,

---

* A pact designed to counterbalance Britain's *Entente* with France and in the event of war her likely decision to form an alliance with Russia.

couched in such belligerent terms that when Grey eventually learned of it he believed Austria's demands to be so unreasonable as to amount to a virtual declaration of war. The Foreign Secretary was appalled. While Britain and the rest of Western Europe sweltered in the longest heatwave anyone could remember, in a last ditch attempt to avoid catastrophe, Grey had proposed a Conference of Ambassadors to take place in London, at which he would be the mediator. Scornfully, Germany had refused to attend. And in the meantime Austria, confident of Germany's backing, had declared war on Serbia, while Russia had instigated mobilisation in defence of its fellow Serbs. On 2 August Germany had presented Belgium with an ultimatum, demanding a safe passage for its armies. Following Belgium's rejection of that ultimatum Grey felt it was his duty, on that scorching Bank Holiday Monday, to persuade the House that war was now inevitable.

As an arbiter for peace the Foreign Secretary had failed. So how had it happened? It is now generally accepted that it was the German Military High Command which triggered the war. Among a number of factors prompting them to act, the most significant was the growing strength of Russia. That slumbering bear – sprawled across the vast landmass of northern Europe with its hind paws resting in Asia – had begun to stir, and with alarming speed was seen to be getting on its feet. Slowly but inexorably Russia was emerging from centuries of feudalism and beginning to modernise. As yet its road and rail systems were rudimentary, but the situation was changing rapidly. Given a few more years the Russian Empire could pose a serious threat to the West; to Germany in particular. Determined to seize the initiative while the odds were still in their favour, the German High Command resolved to act. First, though, they had to deal with the Kaiser, always a loose cannon, who as supreme Head of State could if he wished scupper their plans. In July they packed him off for his annual summer cruise in the Baltic, assuring him that no crisis was pending.

The Field Marshals' plan was simple. First their armies would knock out the French, taking the easiest route to Paris by storming through Belgium. In a repeat of 1870 Germany would achieve a swift victory over France before turning eastward to engage her principal foe, which was Russia. Meanwhile their ally, Austria-Hungary, after dealing decisively with the Serbs, would add its military strength to theirs by attacking the Russian underbelly. Poring over their maps it all looked so clear, so logical! It would be a great land war which Germany, with four million well-trained men under arms, could not fail to win.

There was, however, one potential stumbling block and that was Great Britain. If the British decided to enter the fray the picture would look very different. But was this likely? The Field Marshals had taken note that Britain's *Entente Cordiale* with France, while pledging friendship and co-operation between the two nations, lacked the force of a legally binding treaty. However, the British Government had a 60-year-old treaty with Belgium, which guaranteed to uphold its neutrality in the event of war. When it came to the crunch, how likely was it that the British would take up arms in support of this small and insignificant nation, they asked themselves. Though Great Britain had the largest navy in the world and an Empire covering a quarter of the globe, it was widely believed that its people had no stomach for war. A nation of shopkeepers – was it not true that they were governed by incompetent nincompoops, of whom Sir Edward Grey, their Foreign Secretary, was one of the worst?

Truth to tell, the German High Command had a poor opinion of Great Britain's Foreign Secretary. Famous for his insularity, Sir Edward's beaked nose and high forehead gave him an air of patrician superiority which stuck in their craw. They regarded him as degenerate: an aristocratic ditherer. (Had it not been rumoured by no less an authority than their own Ambassador that Grey was 'not a proper man'?) Was it likely that a man of his stamp would be willing to commit his nation to war? On balance, they thought not.

As the German Field Marshals finalised their preparations for a lightening strike through Belgium (which by their calculations would see their armies in Paris in a matter of weeks) they knew they would be taking a gamble. Edward Grey knew this too, and was convinced that a word in time might yet serve to avert catastrophe.

Yet with half the Cabinet firmly opposed to war he felt powerless to issue a warning that would commit his country to hostilities. Playing it by the book, he believed he had no authority to act without bringing the matter before Parliament. And Parliament, up to the very last minute, could not make up its mind.

By the time Grey entered the House on 3 August to make what many regarded as the finest speech of his career – setting out the nation's moral commitment under the *Entente* to come to the aid of France and her obligation towards Belgium – it was too late for diplomacy. On the morning of 4 August, after waves of German troops had poured across the Belgium border, Edward Grey was finally authorised to telegraph an ultimatum to Berlin, protesting against the violation of Belgium territory and requiring a satisfactory reply by midnight. When the hour struck, with no response forthcoming from Berlin, Grey had to accept that Great Britain was at war.

The nation's first response to the outbreak of hostilities was one of patriotic fervour. Crowds poured onto the streets, cheering and waving flags, men and boys queued up to enlist, and everyone seemed to agree that the war would be over by Christmas. But when the first casualty lists began to come in the mood changed. Women whose menfolk were at the front were gripped with fear, only learning to cope by turning their minds to practical matters. 'Carbide was scarce and we lessened all lights and everyone declared what beds they could offer for wounded soldiers,' Cecilia recalled. 'We cut up sheets for shirts and 12 women came to sew and later 14 more.'

Bertram, returned from India in October with Enid and their 'nice fat baby', barely had time to see his wife and child settled at Newton – which was now his property – before being recalled for duty and setting off with his regiment for the 'Front' as the battle zone was becoming known. For thanks in part to Britain's rapid response to the German onslaught the Field Marshals' hopes for a quick victory had been frustrated, leaving the armies of both sides bogged down in hastily prepared trenches, facing each other across a wasteland of mud.

Ida had narrowly escaped being trapped in France, having delayed her departure to the very last minute. On the day war broke out she was forced to beat a hasty retreat and Joe's first intimation of the war was being thrilled by the sight of Zouave soldiers with their baggy red trousers, standing by the side of the railway. Before leaving Cavalière

Ida had acquired an extra child. She had made friends with a Lady Elliot, whose granddaughter, Mary, had been parked on the elderly woman after her ne'er-do-well son and his wife were banished to Australia. Seeing her new friend at a loss how to cope with a lively seven-year-old, Ida had offered to take the child until some permanent arrangement could be made for her. Back at Hauxley Mary Elliot and Diana quickly struck up a friendship which left Cynthia feeling isolated. The 10-year-old also had a new governess to contend with, a sharp-witted little woman with protruding eyes called Miss Waller.* The governess set Joe and Cynthia the same lessons, which were too advanced for Cynthia to follow. Still at odds with her mother, who dubbed her stupid, she would tag along after her brother, making herself useful by digging lug-worms to bait the lines he laid along the foreshore.

Though Ida would always be grateful to her father for providing her with a home, with war raging across the Channel and casualties mounting at an alarming rate, she felt she could find better ways to help the war effort than by caring for a gaggle of children. Ida yearned for the heroic. To be on the front line, within range of the guns. If only she had born a man!

She knew nurses were needed, but her few months training as a probationer hardly qualified her to minister to severely wounded men. Dora Waller, on the other hand, was a fully trained nurse. Why should not the two of them go out to France together and chance their luck? Ida was prepared to do anything to get into the war. She spoke French like a native, which must be to her advantage. She floated the idea to the governess, who readily agreed to accompany her. That left the problem of the children. Ida solved it by packing Joe and Cynthia off to boarding school† and hiring a new governess for Mary and Diana, having decided they should remain at Hauxley.

After disposing of these practical difficulties, in January 1915 Ida and Dora Waller set off for France. Despite the restrictions of war, civilian traffic across the English Channel was still possible. Once on French soil Ida presented herself at the headquarters of the British Red Cross and applied to join. She was turned down on the grounds of age. She was forty-four. Mortified, she applied to the French equivalent, who were happy to make use of her driving ability and her perfect command of their language. Dora's nursing skills were at a premium and the pair were directed to a large military hospital at Wimereux, near Boulogne, where Dora was enrolled as a nurse and Ida's time was divided between driving ambulances and working in the canteen. While her work fell some way short of the heroic, at least Ida was serving the gallant young men who were fighting for King and Country and the preservation of the Empire, and when the wind blew from the north she could hear the deadly, monotonous, pounding of the guns.

---

* Dora Waller was a parson's daughter from North Shields who had never met anyone like Ida and rapidly fell under her spell. The two women became inseparable and were to remain together for the next 40 years.

† By this time Joe was too old to apply for Osborne and on the advice of Edward Grey, who had two nephews there, he was sent to Gresham's School in Norfolk. Cynthia went to St Margaret's, a girls' public school based at Scarborough, which after the east coast was bombarded by enemy shells early in the war had been evacuated to the *Atholl Palace Hotel* at Pitlochry, Perthshire.

27   *Roger Fry, self-portrait. Oil on canvas. (National Portrait Gallery)*

Meanwhile on the Home Front things were not going exactly according to plan. When hiring Miss MacPherson as governess Ida had neglected to mention that in addition to her duties in the schoolroom she would be expected to keep an eye on the servants and pay their wages. She was an elderly woman whom Ida seems to have employed without bothering to obtain references. All these extra duties, compounded by the fact that she did not get on with her young charges, who made fun of her, came to a head after Joe and Cynthia came home to Hauxley for their school holidays. When Cecilia drove over to see how Miss MacPherson was getting on, it became obvious that the wretched woman was finding it impossible to cope; in fact she had already handed in her notice. Scooping up the children, Cecilia took them all back to Newton, where she set the three girls to knitting comforts for the troops while she read to them, otherwise allowing them all to run wild.

For Cecilia, as for so many women whose menfolk faced mortal danger, the onset of war had not presented itself as a field for the display of personal heroics. Her role had been more prosaic and more practical. Although the Newton and Hauxley estates were now the property of Bertram, with their son away on active service in France it was left to his parents to keep an eye on his two properties. There was in addition Cecilia's Cheshire property at Moore. She had decided to let the house, keeping a smaller place, Moore Manor Farm, for her own use. At 75 she was still fit and active, making little of the awkward journeys by coach and train* between Newton and Moore. Fitz, however, blind and frail now and in his 90th year, must have found the frequent to-ing and fro-ing extremely trying, though he never complained.

And now, added to all these duties, it became obvious that if she did not make herself responsible for Ida's brood, no one else would – least of all Ida. So for the two years that Ida spent in France Cecilia had perforce to take charge of Mary Elliot and her grandchildren.

By the time war broke out both Cecilia's parents were long dead, but while her mother Susan was still alive Cecilia's only brother Edward, a keen sportsman, had decided to

---

*   Fitz and Cecilia never owned a motorcar.

give up Hopwood in favour of a Yorkshire property, where the sport was superior and the air blessedly free from industrial pollution. His decision to abandon the property that had been in Hopwood hands since the time of King John had caused a bitter feud to break out between himself and his mother, with his three surviving sisters taking their mother's side. Consequently Edward and Cecilia were completely out of touch for the war years, during which Edward suffered a double tragedy. 'My brother's two sons both killed in the war', Cecilia noted laconically in her *Diary*, without supplying details. The facts were that Edward's younger son, Captain Robert Gerald Hopwood, died at Flanders in August 1916; the death of his elder brother, Colonel Edward Byng George Hopwood, Edward's heir, taking place on that same bloody battlefield 18 months later. As neither of Edward's sons had married, their deaths marked the extinction of the ancient Hopwood line.

One friendship that was badly dented by the war was the close bond that had existed for many years between Cecilia and Roger Fry. By conviction most of the Bloomsbury set of which Roger was a leading member were pacifists. So too were the Quakers. And though Roger Fry had long ago separated himself from his Quaker roots he shared his friends' and his family's belief that to take up arms against your fellows was barbarous and in all circumstances inexcusable.

In 1913 Roger had been left a small legacy which he resolved to use to set up a workshop in which struggling young artists could find employment. For years he had been sickened by the tawdry design of so many of the mass-produced objects in daily use. After sitting in a railway restaurant one day, contemplating the 'dismal catalogue' before him, he wrote: 'The window was half-filled with stained glass; the stained glass was covered by a lace curtain; the lace curtain was covered with patterns, the walls were covered with lincrusta; the tables were covered with ornate cotton cloths.'[1] Every object that his eye rested upon was covered by what he called an 'eczematous eruption'. And 'not one of these objects', he fumed, 'had been made because the makers enjoyed the making; not one had been bought because its contemplation would give anyone pleasure.'[2] Roger reasoned that if half his poverty-stricken young artists' time could be employed, for a basic wage of 30 shillings a week, in the design and construction of everyday objects combining utility with good taste, the time that remained could be devoted to their own creative work. Having acquired premises in Fitzroy Square, in the heart of Bloomsbury, in July 1913 the Omega Workshops opened for business.

It was an idiosyncratic and highly idealistic scheme, promising 'Original Modern Designs by British artists, including printed textiles, loom carpets, hand knotted rugs, furniture, lampshades, stained glass windows, hand-dyed silks etc' and advertising 'wall decoration in various mediums'. In addition to putting his own money up front Roger himself was no mean contributor, making furniture and learning how to throw pots at a pottery in Poole. Intrigued, the *beau monde* came, first to look and then to buy* and during its early days the Workshop showed promise of proving a financial as well as an artistic success.

---

* One of Roger's beds with striking hand-painted headboards, commissioned by a certain Madame Vandervelde, may be seen today in the Victoria and Albert Museum.

But when the First World War broke out everything changed. Although conscription was not brought in until 1916, all able-bodied men were under enormous moral pressure to enlist. 'Your Country Needs You', the fierce stare and accusing finger of Britain's most illustrious soldier Lord Kitchener, berated them from huge posters up and down the land and those men who refused the call to arms were branded as cowards. As a pacifist Roger was sickened at the idea of young officers having to lead their men on suicidal missions 'over the top' to face almost certain death or serious injury and he used every means he could think of to prevent his young workforce from having to enlist.

But Roger's ethos was out of tune with the times and he found himself fundamentally at odds with Cecilia, his long-time friend and mentor. For Cecilia was fiercely patriotic – and indeed how could she and thousands like her have withstood the horror of that war without seeing it in heroic terms?* With her son risking his life in Flanders and her grandson John serving as a naval cadet on the dreadnought *Thunderer*,† the war had to be seen as a fight between good and evil or it was nothing. And though Roger was himself, at 50, too old to enlist, Cecilia saw his support for the 'Conchies' (conscientious objectors who would explore every avenue in order to escape conscription) as being little short of treason.

Ida and Dora Waller spent nearly two years working in the hospital at Wimereux. According to Ida's son Joe (who after he grew up seldom had a good word to say for his mother), 'she was finally flung out by the French' who eventually rebelled against the flamboyant Englishwoman and her overbearing ways. Be that as it may, she and Dora returned to Hauxley sometime in 1917. But before they left the two women had a chance meeting which was destined to have lasting repercussions. Below is Cynthia's account of how it happened:

> Mother and Dora were called downstairs one night by someone asking in a rather pathetic voice if anyone was about. There they found a very young army padre looking completely worn out and obviously needing some care and attention. He was a Welshman called Davies and he did indeed speak with a very Welsh accent. Well of course they gave him food and refreshment and were able to put him up for the night. He was a very nice friendly young man, good looking with curly black hair. He came to see them at their canteen as often as he could and having got my mother's home address promised to go and see the two women when the war was over.[3]

True to form, Ida seemed to have made another conquest. Yet when 'Davy' (as she and Dora had taken to calling the young padre from South Wales) eventually fulfilled his wartime promise and came to call on them at Hauxley Hall, the consequences of his visit (as we shall see) were entirely unforeseen.

---

* In 1914 Arthur Winnington-Ingram, Bishop of London, had declared that the nation was fighting a 'Holy War'. Bishop Diggle of Carlisle had gone even further, suggesting that Satan was openly backing Germany.

† The *Thunderer* was part of Admiral Jellicoe's battle fleet. The 16-year-old served in her at the Battle of Jutland.

Chapter XL

The Death of Fitz

The war dragged on. Late in 1916 Ida and Dora Waller (who were now inseparable) returned from France, Hauxley Hall was put under wraps and the pair moved into a house in Newcastle, having found work at the military hospital. Diana and Mary went with them and were sent to the local high school.

But with her daughter back home Cecilia was faced with a fresh problem. For whenever Ida could escape from her duties at the hospital she would head straight for Newton, only to find that an alien presence had usurped her place as the daughter of the house. Her brother's wife Enid, adopting, as Ida saw it, a patronising air, was already acting as if she owned the place – which in point of fact she did. Or at least Bertram did, seeing that their father had signed away Newton – handing it over to her brother, lock stock and barrel, in a bid to escape death duties.

Ida believed that Enid was getting above herself and found her presence intolerable. So also was that of her wretched child, who instead of being confined to the nursery was everywhere to be seen, trotting after his mother like a little crown prince!

It was not long before a state of open warfare was declared between the two sisters-in-law, manifesting itself in slammed doors and shrill bitter voices.

'I can't have Enid and Ida together now – so tiresome,' Cecilia complained, her patience tried to the limits as she surveyed the comforts spread out on the dining room table, waiting to be parcelled up for despatch by the Red Cross. For in addition to caring for Fitz she had her team of local women to consider, whom she had employed in knitting socks and mittens for the mounting number of prisoners of war incarcerated behind German lines. Surely, she thought, when thousands of men were risking their lives on the Western Front, personal differences ought to be set on one side.

Of course it was perfectly obvious what was at the bottom of it. Ever since Bertram was a baby Ida had come first in his affections and she could not bear to feel she had been supplanted. Certainly not by this *southerner* – this townee wife who spent hours at her dressing table, flinched at the sight of an unplucked bird and scarcely knew one end of a horse from the other. Ida's scorn for Enid was made all too plain: she mocked her sister-in-law's pretentions to be thought *artistic* and her boring interest in what she chose to call *interior design*. Flouncing around her old home as if she was still the unchallenged favourite, Ida did her very best to make her sister-in-law feel like an interloper.

28 *Fitz.*

Though Enid got on well with her mother-in-law there were times when the wretched young woman felt that she and little Tony had been dumped among savages; condemned to live in a cold, bleak, windswept house looking out upon the desolate moors. And we may guess that she would have let Bertram know of the insults she was forced to endure from his sister.

Then Ida went too far. At the hospital where she and Dora worked were a number of young officers who were convalescent. Ida felt sorry for them, cut off from their families. Thinking to cheer them up she roped in some of her male friends and organised a shooting party at Hauxley.

Ida never did anything by halves. Scrounging where she could, she prepared a lavish picnic for the 'guns' and since she had no wine, which was hard to come by on account of the German blockade of the ports, she asked her father if she might help herself to a few bottles from the Newton wine cellar. Strictly speaking the contents of that cellar, like everything else at Newton, was now the property of Bertram. However, since Fitz had paid for the wine he saw no harm in Ida having a few bottles.

The Hauxley shoot was a tremendous success. Ida had gone about it in the old way, with no effort spared. The sun shone benignly, the air was crisp and dry and despite the wartime shortage of keepers the 'bag' was judged to have been pretty fair. Ida glowed. 'I have pulled off a triumph' she reported to her parents, who agreed that she had.

The only trouble was that the shoot had taken place over land which was now the property of Bertram. And not only had Ida failed to seek her brother's permission, Bertram had been left in complete ignorance of what was afoot. When word got to him at the Front (doubtless relayed by Enid, who had watched Ida's plundering of the Newton cellar with a mordant eye) Bertram exploded with righteous indignation. Nor was his wrath merely directed at Ida. He blamed his over-fond father, who had no business to collude with Ida in what amounted to barefaced robbery. 'Horrid letters from Bertram about Ida's friends going for a day's shooting,' Cecilia reported miserably.

Worse was to follow. Bertram was due home on embarkation leave, his regiment having been posted to Salonika in northern Greece to do battle against the Bulgarians. When he arrived at Newton shortly after Christmas a 'terrible wrangle' developed

29   Bertram Widdrington.

between himself and his father. The gist of it was that Fitz, having made over the estate to his son, was treating the place as if he still owned it and 'not keeping to the bargain'.

It seems likely that Bertram's outburst was fuelled in part by the hideous strain of having spent more than two years fighting on the Western Front in an insane campaign of pointless slaughter. (How many men had survived those terrible years unscathed?) Added to that Bertram must have felt he had ample cause for complaint over the behaviour of his sister. Time and again Ida had brought disgrace upon the family; yet despite a string of indiscretions, their parents, against all reason, had continued to offer her their unqualified support. And now – to add insult to injury – Ida seemed intent on persecuting his wife!

It had all been too much for Bertram, a man of exceedingly conservative views whose temper had got the better of him, causing him to descend to levels of abuse against his old blind father which were to prove unforgivable.

Cecilia was appalled. 'B. so insolent,' she recorded, 'that we left the house and went to Ida in N'castle.' When Bertram set off for Salonika a few days later Cecilia went to the station to say goodbye, 'but Fitz and Bertram never met again'. The old couple 'went sadly back to Newton in deep snow and cold'. They had decided that after Bertram's words they could no longer live in the house that had been home to them for over 50 years 'and would go off and live at Moore'.

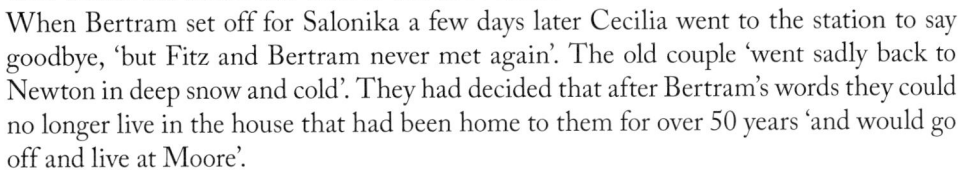

It must have been a heartbreaking decision and from a distance it seems extraordinary that the quarrel could not have been patched up. Perhaps if Ida and Enid had been on better terms they might have intervened to pour oil on troubled waters, but as matters stood no one was prepared to make a conciliatory move and events took their sad course.

Cecilia began the daunting task of sorting out what needed to be taken to Moore. The work made for a miserable winter. Gerard, who had spent most of the war years helping in the parish at North Shields, came home to help and Ida came over 'on her last sad visit', choosing a time when Enid was away. To add to their troubles their excellent butler, Short, began 'behaving very badly and we found he was drinking hard and had to go.'

By this time Cecilia was having to 'dress and do all for Fitz'. However, she was determined to leave everything 'as settled and easy as possible for Enid' by the time they left. 'We cleaned the cellar (in a dreadful state) and improved the oldest part of the house over the pantry, putting in windows and floors and letting in light and air.'

By the July of 1917 they were ready to leave. 'Fitz and I drove to Hauxley and said goodbye there – all very sad. On the morning of 17 July all the schoolchildren and villagers and people about assembled round the front door for a last handshake and farewell to the old squire – many tears and a trying scene.'

The following day they were driven to Newcastle, accompanied by Gerard. Through the good offices of Edward Grey, who was by then Chairman of the London North Eastern Railway Company, a special saloon carriage had been added to the train, which was to convey them by a branch line to Daresbury, a halt within two miles of Moore.

In those days Moore Hall was not the medium-sized Georgian country house that we see today. Some Victorian 'improver' had doubled the number of bedrooms and extended the back quarters, converting the original house into something of a rabbit warren.* However, there was a pleasant walled garden at the back with fruiting and ornamental trees and shrubs and beds of late summer flowers, which provided them with somewhere to walk about and sit. And set into the east wall was a little wooden gate giving access onto the Bridgewater Canal. It was a very hot summer and sometimes after dinner if Fitz was not too tired they would go out and take a stroll along the towpath.

However, since the removal of his eyes Fitz had lived without a glimmer of light to guide his way. At Newton he had learned to manage – the echo his voice threw, the familiar feel of a chair back or squeak of a door serving to tell him where he was, so that he was able to move about unaided. At Moore he had none of these familiar props and thus had become a helpless prisoner, entirely dependent on his wife. By now he could no longer manage stairs and Cecilia converted the dining room into a bedroom for them both. 'But Fitz got ill and the Dr ordered that a nurse must sleep in his room, and I felt sadder than ever at having to go to my own room, but doubtless was safer.'

It soon became plain that Fitz was in terminal decline. 'Very disturbed nights', Cecilia recalled, 'He got some sleep in the daytime now, and often my reading sent him off – He rested a great deal both by day and night and he made quite nice wool scarves which many were glad to have in memory of him.'

They had a succession of visitors, staying 'just for a night'. One of these was Aline Cust, who by this time was running her own successful veterinary practice in Ireland. Aline had never forgotten the support she had received from Fitz when, ostracised by her family, she had been helped by him during the difficult student years.

As the days shortened Fitz developed a 'bad weary cough' and their doctor ordered a second nurse as he now needed round-the-clock nursing. Gerard was a great support during those weeks and Ida came twice to see her father. On her last visit, speaking with difficulty, 'he said to her "So you've crept in little thing" and seemed pleased … ' On 22 December nurse signalled to Gerard not to go out and he gave his last sigh as I was sitting by him, quite gently, we hardly knew when he passed away … Now I had to go to my lonely room, most forlorn.'

When she looked back on those last sad and difficult months Cecilia often wondered if she had done the right thing in agreeing to leave Newton.

---

* In 1932 Cecilia had extensive modifications made to Moore Hall: 'Six bedrooms kitchen dairy larders and Housekeeper's Room taken down, thus reducing it to its former size and shape of little square Dutch House, a great improvement.'

> I think Fitz had felt the leaving of his home most keenly – but after we had settled to go it seemed impossible to change and stay on. Many blamed me for it and said that the move had killed him, I think perhaps it did hasten his end – but there was very little of happiness left in his life. Dolly's unkindness had hurt him badly and Bertram's still more and Ida's unhappy marriage was a constant sorrow and Gerard a disappointment – so I think our best days were over and he was happier gone and at peace and I felt this all the time and it did console me somewhat … I now have to live my life on a different level and no one can help me.

Fitz Widdrington had died in his 92nd year. Cecilia, who was 77 when he died, was to live a further 19 years. During those times of momentous change she was to witness the arrival of women's suffrage, the coming of the radio and cinema entertainment, the birth of the Ford Popular and the modern production line, air travel and the horror of aerial bombardment, and the rise to power of two of the most heinous tyrants the world has ever known.

Meanwhile daily life had to go on, and the Great War (as the first major conflict of the 20th century came to be known) had still to be won. Laying her grief on one side, Cecilia summoned Gerard and together mother and son set to work with patriotic zeal to 'dig for victory'.

Chapter XLI

Peace at a Price

By January 1917, the third winter of the war, it was becoming plain to the combatants on both sides that despite the ghastly losses sustained on the Somme and at Verdun neither side had succeeded in gaining a strategic advantage. With their armies joined 'like two fighting elks who have locked horns'[1] it seemed that some alternative means would need to be found to bring the conflict to a conclusion.

As early as 1915 the Kaiser's military advisors had been pressing for unrestricted submarine warfare against neutral merchant shipping as a way of starving Great Britain into surrender. Bethmann, the German chancellor, had counselled against it, fearing that such a barbarous policy 'would inevitably cause America to join our enemies'.[2] The military finally got their way, however, arguing that by cutting Britain's supply lines the war could be brought to a swift end before America had time to mobilise. On 1 February 1917 the German submarine fleet set in motion an all-out attack on civilian shipping. As Bethmann had prophesied, this barbaric action duly brought America into the war. Yet it has to be said that this murderous policy very nearly succeeded.

On the home front lawns were ploughed up and put down to potatoes and farmers were urged to redouble their efforts, using every means to step up production. With so many men away at the war, however, farms were suffering from an acute shortage of labour. What was to be done? As familiar items began to disappear from the nation's shelves girls and young women were recruited to serve in a new 'Women's Land Army'. Ida, who was becoming bored with her work as an untrained auxiliary nurse, decided to seize her chance.

Plainly these young women would need some training before being let loose on the nation's farmyards and, realising that her practical knowledge of dairying could be put to good use, Ida offered her services to the Ministry of Food and was accepted. She discovered she had a talent for organisation, and with her abundant energy and natural air of command she was popular with the 'land girls', as they came to be known, refusing to be daunted by the filthy conditions on many of the farms and the sneers of some of the farmers. 'Never forget we are pioneers,' she lectured her students. 'What we lack in strength we shall make up for by our humanity.'

For Ida had noticed that many of the farm workers were unnecessarily cruel in their handling of their animals. The conditions in the slaughterhouses, moreover, were a disgrace. All too often terrified beasts would be despatched in the most heartless way and Ida vowed that once the war was over she would fight for more humane treatment for Britain's farm animals. Thus the foundations were laid for the work that would occupy Ida during her middle years: her long and ultimately successful campaign for a complete overhaul of Britain's slaughter houses.

As Ida's work took her all over the place and Dora Waller was now resident at the hospital there seemed no point in hanging on to the Newcastle house. So Ida appealed to her mother to find boarding school places for Diana and Mary Elliot and the house was given up. The welfare of the girls had never rated highly on Ida's list of priorities and more and more Cecilia found herself taking responsibility for the children's welfare and providing a home for them at Moore during the school holidays.

She found that keeping active was the best remedy for grief. She and Gerard grew potatoes, reared pigs, kept chickens, 'cut wood and chopped sticks' and in addition she would walk into Warrington twice a week* to pack up food parcels for prisoners of war. 'It was quite hard work standing for 6 or 7 hours a day but I liked doing it.'

On 7 October 1918 news came from Salonika that Bulgaria had surrendered. 'So Bertram scored first Pax!' Cecilia recorded proudly, temporarily forgetting the bitter quarrel that had driven her and Fitz from their home. A month later, on 11 November, the war that had caused so much misery and taken so many lives finally came to an end. Ida's family, including her mother, gathered at Hauxley for the first Christmas of peacetime – the last Christmas they would spend together before Joe went off to join the Royal Navy.†

Also included in that Christmas party was 'Davy', the young padre from South Wales who had turned up bedraggled and half-starved at Wimereux when Ida was working in the hospital canteen. True to his promise he had come to Hauxley to call on his benefactress. Ida was thrilled by the attentions of her blue-eyed admirer with his mop of raven curls, though to be honest it was the three pretty girls, Cynthia, Mary and Diana, who had taken Davy's fancy and he was only too happy to join in their boisterous games.

In March Bertram retired from the army with the rank of Brigadier-General and he and Enid set up house at Newton. A year later their second son, Francis, was born. Enid's 'bitter enmity to Ida' precluded any possibility of the quarrel between Bertram and his sister being made up and it persisted to the end of their days.

However, Cecilia eventually succeeded in patching up the quarrel with her son, though she confessed she 'couldn't endure the sight of Newton for many years after, with the crowd of sorrows and remembrance of happier days'. When staying with Ida at Hauxley she used sometimes to meet Bertram and his little family on the beach at Alnmouth, and they in turn visited her at Moore. She had always liked Enid, whom she considered to be a good wife and mother, while she and her grandson, Tony, 'were always good pals'.

As Ida's life expanded during the post-war years – a variety of interests steering her into the public eye as she became an indefatigable champion of a variety of good causes

---

* A distance of some five miles.

† In 1918 Joe passed the Special Entry exam set by the Civil Service, enabling him to join the Navy straight from school as a Midshipman.

– Cecilia's world continued to contract. She missed the bracing air of Northumberland, finding the climate at Moore enervating, and was frequently obliged to take to her bed with heavy colds. Though family and friends came to visit, she knew that the old busy life – when a full calendar of events required her constant supervision and the doors of Newton always stood open – could never return.

Yet the duties incumbent upon a woman in her position were still observed and every Monday she went to the workhouse in Warrington 'and read out or recited to the old women … they looked forward to it greatly in their dull lives'. Sometimes Gerard would accompany her, bringing 'baccy' for the old men.

After a year or two she saw there was nothing to be gained by burdening herself with the expense of a sizable country house and resolved to let Moore. Tenants were found who agreed to take it on a 12-year lease.*

To the surprise of her children she had decided to make a complete break with the past. Her sister Rose, by this time a lame and rather querulous widow, lived at Donhead St Mary in Wiltshire. Rose, who was childless, had been left very comfortably off by her late husband, Sir James Pender. She had a comfortable home, a motorcar and a chauffeur. Cecilia had decided to look for a house on the south coast within motoring distance of her sister and after 'terrible farewells' to her loyal staff at Moore she and Gerard set off for Budleigh Salterton, settling themselves into the *Rosemullion Hotel* in order to begin house-hunting. They had not been there long, however, before a family tragedy sent them hurrying back to Northumberland.

Since the severing of her marriage to Addison Baker-Cresswell, Ida had had very little contact with her elder son, John. The last time she had seen him was in 1916, when after passing successfully through Osborne John had been posted as a cadet to the battleship *Thunderer*. While on embarkation leave he had been permitted to pay a brief visit to his mother at Hauxley and that was her last memory of him.

In October 1920 John was at Dartmouth, attending a gunnery course. He was now a midshipman and one of his duties was to take his turn as officer in charge, patrolling round the lines of ships laid up in reserve in Portsmouth Harbour. One night the young officer whose turn of duty it was fell sick, and John was ordered to take his place. His brother Joe has given an account of what happened:

30 *John Baker-Cresswell as a cadet with his half-sister, Rosemary.*

---

* 'As the tenants didn't need the large attics they were quite willing I shd stick my furniture in them … but what a work it was – pulling and hauling up the very narrow steep stairs and G and I did it all with very little help.' Cecilia was indeed an extraordinary woman!

It was a cold night and they set off as usual. At the end of a line the coxswain turned round and asked 'Shall we turn sir?' John replied 'Yes' and they went down the next line. That was the last time he was seen alive. Why he should have fallen overboard and without being heard on a quiet night was never discovered. Eventually his body was recovered and he was buried in the churchyard at Cresswell. The mystery was never solved.

Various theories have been advanced to explain this tragic event, none of which have proved entirely satisfactory. In order to understand the circumstances which form the background to the tragedy we must return to Addy at the time of the legal separation. Under its terms, which made Cynthia and Diana Wards in Chancery, it would have been perfectly possible for Addy to have had controlled access to his daughters if he had wished it. He never tried. Rosemary was the only one of his daughters he cared for. So far as he was concerned the younger two, together with his housekeeper's child, could go to the devil.

In the early days following the separation he had been happy enough to have his two sons, together with Rosemary, living with him in London at 28 Hyde Park Gate* and by Joe's account there had been good times while he was living with his father. In 1912 Addy had bought one of the largest yachts then afloat, the schooner *Adela*, which had previously been owned by the Kaiser, and that summer John and Joe had been permitted to join their father and a party of his friends at Cowes, sailing to Dieppe and Ostend. Yet once Joe had fallen from grace by becoming ill and had been banished to live with his mother, Addy seems to have lost all interest in his younger son, leaving Joe feeling immensely bitter.†

When war broke out Addy had been commissioned into the 60th Rifles and sent out to serve in France. But his wartime military career had been ignominiously brief. By that time he was drinking heavily and alcoholism had affected his liver. He was rapidly relieved of his commission and invalided out. For the years that remained to him Addy was a sick man. Cared for by 'Mrs Cumming', most of his time was spent in London where he is believed to have entertained a succession of mistresses.

John would almost certainly have kept in touch with his father during those years although there is no evidence to confirm this. Yet something seems to have gone disastrously wrong between father and son at that time, leading Addy to cut John out of his will.

One theory which has been raised is that Addy had learned (or been led to suspect) that John was homosexual. No evidence exists to support this allegation, nor to validate the suggestion that John's death was self-inflicted on account of his father's malice. Others have implied that John was drunk at the time of the accident; and yet others that a member (or members) of the crew had a grudge against him and conspired to murder him. John's body was recovered 10 days later and a verdict of accidental death was recorded by the coroner. So far as the Admiralty was concerned that was the end of the matter.

* Addy's commodious flat subsequently became the last London home of Sir Winston Churchill, who died there in 1965.
† In later life Joe laid the blame for his father's neglect squarely at the feet of his mother, maintaining that Ida had made monstrous allegations against her husband and had poisoned his mind.

31 *Ida Cresswell, oil sketch by Roger Fry.*

Whatever the truth, the loss of John devastated Ida, who had always kept a special place in her heart for her elder son. She had kept the hope alive that when he grew to manhood she would tell him her side of the story and there would be reconciliation. She could not live with the bleak fact that John's death was final and, like many mothers who had lost sons in the war, she found very seductive the belief that it was possible to get in touch with loved ones who had 'passed over' through the agency of a medium.* For a while Ida dabbled in spiritualism. But then a friend of hers, Marna Pease – ridiculing the mediums and their fraudulent 'voices' – introduced her to the writings of a persuasive Austrian philosopher. Rudolf Steiner, the founder of a sect to which he gave the Greek name 'Anthroposophy' (the 'Wisdom of Man') claimed that anyone who was prepared to follow his teaching could gain esoteric knowledge of 'higher worlds'. Marna Pease gave Ida some of Steiner's books to read and she made a start on them and was briefly impressed. But finding Steiner's prose (inexpertly translated from the original German) virtually impenetrable, she soon lost interest.

Her daughter Cynthia would turn out to be more persevering. For most of her life the unhappy child had been searching for an idealised father, and at the age of 19 she found him in the person of the Austrian seer. Cynthia was to become one of Steiner's most ardent disciples, never deviating from her belief in the infallibility of her spiritual teacher.†

---

*   After losing her beloved eldest son 'Bim' in the First World War, Pamela Tennant was one of many bereaved mothers who found comfort in spiritualism.

†   When Cynthia wrote the story of her life at the age of 90 she subtitled it: 'Autobiography of a student of Anthroposophy'.

Chapter XLII

A Time for Reconciliation

Cecilia's house-hunting would prove to be a long-drawn-out and frustrating business. At one point she thought she had found a house that seemed just right in Exmouth, a quiet coastal resort on the South Devon coast. There was no garden, but it looked out on a pleasant park which was not too 'towny'. The only snag was that the house had a sitting tenant, though the woman swore she would shortly be moving out, and Cecilia decided to buy it for a very reasonable £400. She called it 'Chance House' because she had found it quite by chance.

Meanwhile a bare year after John's tragic death, Ida was to suffer another shattering blow. In 1921 she learned that Addy Baker-Cresswell was dead and that when his will was read it was discovered that he had left his family nothing.

The circumstances of his death were puzzling. Addy had booked himself into a hotel in the New Forest and the day after his arrival a hotel servant, entering his room, had discovered him dead. Some empty whisky bottles were found in his room. A post-mortem was carried out, the conclusion being that he had died of alcoholic poisoning. Why Addy had gone to the hotel no one knows, and whether his death was self-inflicted and deliberate, or simply an accident, was impossible to say.

It appears that in the last months of his life Addy had taken a mistress who was a distant relative of his, and to his family's consternation he had left his entire fortune to this woman's daughter, a Miss Winkworth. In consequence his estranged wife and three surviving children were left with no money over and above Ida's £1,500 allowance from the separation agreement. Addy's bitterness against Ida was so great that he had been determined to punish not only her, but her children – making no allowance for the fact that they were also his.

Ida was devastated, though in the years to come it was Joe who suffered most. As his father's only surviving son he would have expected to inherit two extensive Northumbrian estates. In the event he was left with nothing. For the rest of his days Joe was to live under the shadow of his father's malice, his bitterness against his mother (whom he considered was largely to blame) poisoning his life.

The tenant in possession of the Exmouth house proved harder to shift than Cecilia had anticipated, rendering her temporarily homeless. Together with Gerard she passed much

The Widdrington Women

32   Cecilia Widdrington in old age.

of the waiting time in travel, taking trips to the Channel Islands and the Lake District and revisiting Hyères (which she found 'much changed'). Eventually she lost patience and put the house back on the market.

Then her luck changed.

> I went back to Exmouth and while sitting in Phear Park … I saw workmen building another house in my row and thought why not buy it before it is built? I went and talked to the workmen, they told me the builder, Mr Greenway might come there – so I sat on a barrow and waited and by <u>Chance</u> he came and I talked to him and offered to buy at <u>once</u> and it was settled … and so I got my 2nd Chance House.

In 1924 Cecilia moved into the brand new terraced house in which she was destined to to spend the last 12 years of her long life.

33   Chance House, Grange Road, Sidmouth, was Cecilia Widdrington's last house.

Chance House suited her very well. She engaged a cook and one maid to look after her and attend to the many guests, both family and friends, who continued to visit her.

It was to be a time of reconciliation. Bertram and Enid and their young family paid her frequent visits, the mild climate of Devon suiting the two little boys, who enjoyed their seaside holidays with 'Grandmama'. 'We dug sandcastles and boated and shopped and basked in warm sunshine', Cecilia recalled. The long-lasting quarrel with her brother Edward over the sale of the Hopwood estate was eventually patched up. After losing both his sons in the war and having recently suffered the death of his wife, Edward was, Cecilia found, 'very forlorn and lonely, nearly blind and very deaf, but still a charming gentleman of the old school and we often deplored the family quarrel which had separated us for so many years'.

One very special relationship which had been fractured by the war was thankfully mended. During the last decade of his life Roger Fry and Cecilia took up the threads of their long friendship and harmony was restored. Roger, by this time a distinguished art critic much courted by the great and the good, chided Cecilia for choosing to live in such a 'horrid place'. How could she prefer Devon to southern France, with its magical combination of balmy climate, romantic landscapes and colours to die for? Yet he came to see her at Chance House and they continued to correspond. His last recorded visit was in 1929: 'Roger Fry came Nov. 9th to 11th', Cecilia noted in her diary. He died in 1933 at the age of 67, outlived by three more years by his old friend and one-time mistress.

'All my old friends are dying', Cecilia lamented as one by one the men and women who had filled her busy life passed away. Her two surviving younger sisters both pre-deceased her. Evie, the youngest (who 40 years earlier had played a vital role in Cecilia's love affair with Roger Fry) died first.

On a visit to Rhiwlas in 1924 Cecilia had found her sister (whose husband Dick had died the previous year) 'very worried and desponding abt money, rents and expenses everything, said her life was just a burden and she shd be glad to lay it down'.

Jack Price, not without a sense of humour, had had the following verse carved over the entrance to the mausoleum which he had erected after one of his rare successes on the racecourse, when Bendigo, the horse he had backed, won the Jubilee Stakes:

> As to my latter end I go
> To seek my Jubilee
> I bless the good horse Bendigo
> Who built this tomb for me.
>
> Richard John Lloyd Price, 1887

Evie died the following year and was buried beside her husband.

By the time Rose died she had lost most of her wits and had taken to her bed. But before her final decline she and Cecilia had enjoyed some good times, sharing 'much talk of old times' and endless games of cards. Her passing had been a sad loss to her sister.

Yet life was not all gloom. In 1925 at the age of 21 Ida's elder daughter Cynthia became engaged to Hugh Chance, a member of a well-respected family of glass manufacturers whose firm had set up lighthouses all over the world and in the previous century had supplied glass for the building of the Crystal Palace. Though not a member of one of the old county families he was well liked by Ida and the engagement received her blessing. Cecilia developed a great respect for this 'business man' – a rare species seldom encountered in her milieu – and Hugh Chance became one of her trustees. The marriage ceremony took place in the fine old church at Alnwick on 20 April 1926 – the 62nd anniversary of Cecilia's marriage to Fitz.

Joe's marriage in the following year was less well received by Ida. After the war Joe had re-established contact with his half-sister Rosemary, now a beautiful young woman with a wide circle of fashionable London friends.* Anti-Semitism was rife in those days among the middle and upper classes and when Rosemary became engaged to Archie Probart, a wealthy 'Jewboy', and asked Joe to give her away, he found himself in a fix. He heartily disapproved of the match, but was in a quandary over how to refuse without offending his half-sister. He appealed to the Second Sea Lord, who obligingly appointed him to a sloop bound for service in the Antipodes – about as far from Archie Probart and St Margaret's Westminster as it was possible to get. The young Sub-Lieutenant sailed away, putting in at Auckland, New Zealand, where he was to meet his own fate in the shape of Rona Vaile, one of three pretty daughters of an Auckland business man.

When Ida learned that Joe was planning to marry the daughter of a 'colonial' she was furious and Rona received a frosty welcome from her mother-in-law. As a young bride attempting to adjust to an ambience governed by snobbery and bristling with traps for the unwary, Rona had a hard time of it at first and Joe was disgusted with his mother. Nevertheless the marriage prospered, with the couple both living well into their nineties.

The marriage of Ida's younger daughter Diana got off to an even less auspicious start. Since leaving school Diana had lived at home, performing the humdrum duties which in those days were expected of an unmarried daughter, arranging the flowers, running the local Girl Guide troop, and generally making herself useful. Financial constraints meant that neither she nor Cynthia had been given a London Season, and her contacts with young people of her own age were few and far between.

Ever since Davy paid his first visit to Hauxley at the end of the war the young padre from South Wales had been a regular visitor. He was always given a warm welcome by Ida, who in modern parlance looked on him as her 'toy boy'. So in 1928, when he and Diana announced that they were in love and wanted to marry, Ida was horrified. And although Cecilia's views were on the whole more liberal, she tended to agree:

> Though he was very nice with the children (when they were children) he was hardly the husband for Diana we had hoped for, he was too old and very poor and we were not pleased at it and I fear we were not very kind about it, for they were very much 'in love'. It was decided to put it off for some months, in hopes it would fade … [But] they only grew more decided.

---

* It must be presumed that Addison Baker-Cresswell had made provision for both his illegitimate daughters, since Rosemary and Aline Cresswell were both 'brought out' and presented at Court. Mrs Cumming must also have been provided for, as she was able to live out the rest of her life in reasonable comfort.

Eventually Ida was obliged to give in, while Cecilia, touched by the couple's obvious devotion, set about sewing underclothes for her granddaughter's trousseau. 'I could sew quite neatly then', she recalled. She was eighty-nine.

The years passed. Great-grandchildren began to appear. Ida, a neglectful mother, was to prove better suited to the less arduous role of grandmother. Yet she had always freely admitted that she preferred animals to humans, and in her middle years she became an indefatigable campaigner for animal welfare. Never afraid to force her way into slaughterhouses to obtain first-hand evidence of cruelty, she travelled all over Britain campaigning for humane slaughter until eventually she succeeded in getting the law changed.

In quite another sphere, observing the restricted lives led by so many women living in the rural parishes, she set up the Northumberland branch of the Women's Institute and became its first President. In addition she sat on her local parish and district councils, served, like her father, as a Justice of the Peace and chaired numerous local committees. Thus the flighty young woman whose scandalous affairs and injudicious marriage had set in train a whole chapter of disasters, successfully remodelled herself as a pillar of society and purveyor of good works.

Yet in contrast to her warm-hearted mother, Ida's taste for mischief was never far below the surface. In common with her Hopwood forebears Ida was a 'stirrer' – seldom able to resist the temptation to cause trouble between her relations.

In old age she and Mrs Cumming – still known as 'Nana' – formed an unlikely alliance. With sharp little Dora making a third, like a coven of superannuated witches they would meet together at Hauxley to inveigh against the wickedness of men. All three lived to a ripe old age. In their different ways they were remarkable women.

As Cecilia entered her 10th decade her thoughts increasingly turned to the generations who would come after her. Since her personal needs were few she resolved to simplify her life by ridding herself of most of her possessions, reasoning that if they were distributed during her lifetime much wrangling would be averted.

She was still the owner of Moore Hall, and by that time it was obvious that Bertram and Enid would never choose to live there. So she decided to embark on a programme of modernisation, reducing the size of the house to its original Georgian dimensions, which she judged would render it more suitable for letting on a long lease.

In June 1932, accompanied by Gerard and her maid Mrs Neat, she travelled to Warrington by train and put up at the *Patton Arms Hotel*, going that same afternoon to inspect the alterations being made at the Hall. She was well pleased. The furniture she and Gerard had hauled laboriously up to the attics had already been distributed. But there was still one more job to be done.

> Next morning we all went to old Parr's Bank where the big Moore plate chest had been kept for me for many years past. I took out some of the silver meaning to get it divided up and sent to my relations but the manager said it was not possible to do it in so short a time and the small space available and that it would be better to send it straight home where I should have plenty of time to think it over and pack properly …

> A couple of days after the box arrived and a job it was to get it lifted into Gerard's room, the driver remarking we must be bringing the Bank of England in it! Mrs Neat cleverly remarked it was a lot of curiosities left to me of great weight! We put them all out on the bed and drawers and tables and chairs and floor, and well it was that the burglars did not get word of it! I divided it up as fairly as I could and she being a splendid packer (having been a great traveller) it all reached its destination without a single break wch 1 think was a great feat ... We took almost a week doing it and glad I was to see the last one go off and I think all were satisfied with their share.

The huge silver-chest was given to a builder who had just turned up to mend the garden wall. 'He said it was capital to hold his wife's blankets – and there was an end of a long-dreaded job.'

It was also (all but a page or two) the end of Cecilia's *Diary*. Her eyesight had been failing for some time and in the following year she was forced to lay down her pen. She lived on for a further three years, still visited by her children and grandchildren, but increasingly coming to depend on her 'dear Gerard' who helped her to sort through photographs and burn papers and accompanied her on the days when she felt well enough to take a short walk.

As has already been observed, Cecilia never had much time for orthodox religion, believing that the Anglican Church of her day was both hypocritical and self-serving. Since she was unable to comfort herself with thoughts of a hereafter in which the meek and the pure in heart would receive their just reward and the wicked be cast down, the *Diary* closes on a rather melancholy note:

> I have had a very happy peaceful sheltered life, far more so than most humans, and yet even so, how little of it seems to have been worth living and how can one be really happy, knowing the miseries and agonies of the lives of far the greatest number around one – nay, the knowledge only intensifies the terrible injustice of creation, for what have I done to merit this happy fate? And if I had a tombstone I should wish these lines carved upon it –
>
> >   We toil thro' pain and wrong
> >   We fight, we fly
> >   We live, we love, and then 'ere long
> >   Stone dead we lie
> >   Oh life, is then all thy song –
> >   Endure and die.
>
> This account must now stop.
> Goodbye to all. CW

In September 1936 Cecilia celebrated her 96th birthday. She was by then very frail and she died that same year at Chance House on 30 December. She had lived for some twelve years in the little seaside resort of Exmouth where, as reported by the *Exmouth Chronicle*, 'her distinguished and somewhat old world figure was familiar to the townspeople'. The same newspaper described her as being 'of a most generous and gracious disposition'.

Cecilia, born in the early days of steam locomotion, lived through Queen Victoria's long reign and the horrors of the First World War, to the dawn of commercial air travel and the rise of the Fascist dictators. When she died the outbreak of the Second World War was less than three years away. On Monday 4 January 1937 her body was taken to Bristol to be cremated, as had been her wish. Later the ashes were conveyed to the parish church at Daresbury, some half a mile from Moore Hall, to be interred in the same grave as her husband. By her request there were no flowers at either ceremony.

Endpiece

In 2004 the historian Andrew Roberts edited a book which he called *What Might Have Been – Leading Historians on Twelve 'What ifs' of History*. In his book he assembled 12 contemporary historians to illustrate his proposition that human existence is not determined (as Marxists and other Determinists would have us believe) by some kind of pre-ordained Destiny, but that world-changing events may frequently hinge on circumstances which may very well have turned out differently. Suppose for a moment that the Gunpowder Plot had succeeded. Or that Gavrilo Princip's gun had missed its targets at Sarajevo. Or that Margaret Thatcher had been killed by the Brighton Bomb. In any of those circumstances Andrew Roberts maintains that the world today would look a very different place.

As we know, on the afternoon of Thursday 1 February 1906 Dorothy Grey was driving her dog-cart along a country lane a few miles from Fallodon when her horse shied, upsetting the dog-cart and throwing her out onto her head, causing injuries from which she died three days later. No one could have foreseen the accident – although with hindsight it could be said that Dorothy had been forewarned. Only a few days previously she had driven out with her friend Louise Creighton 'with a swift poney which she seemed only just able to manage' and in the aftermath of the tragedy Mrs Creighton remembered that it had 'kicked up a lot of mud into her face & she could not find a handkerchief to wipe it off and had to borrow mine.' Though Dorothy had known that the horse was difficult to manage she had gone ahead and taken it out, which was perhaps a trifle rash.

That Dorothy's death was a heavy blow to her husband of 20 years does not need repeating. But can the tragedy be seen to have had wider repercussions? After his wife's funeral Edward Grey wrote to the newly elected Prime Minister, Henry Campbell-Bannerman, saying that he had been very much shaken by Dorothy's death and suggesting that his best course would be to resign. Campbell-Bannerman would have none of it. He had no one else in mind whom he judged capable of filling the post of Foreign Secretary and he encouraged Grey to go on. The grieving widower was persuaded and a week after the funeral the Foreign Office 'pouches' started to arrive at Fallodon. 'The mechanism of the brain began to digest work as that of the body digests food; that is how life continues in such an ordeal', Grey wrote in his autobiography. Work became the antidote to his otherwise unendurable pain and there was no more talk of resignation.

Edward Grey saw his chief task as Foreign Secretary as the preservation of peace at home and among the nations of Europe. Great Britain had been at peace with her European neighbours for almost 100 years and during that time the nation had prospered mightily. When Grey took office the unpopular Boer War was a recent memory and with peace restored the British had no appetite for further military engagements. Few of his countrymen had a notion of the dangerous tensions that were building up on the other side of the Channel, while the majority of his fellow Cabinet Members were equally ill-informed.

Nor were they aware of the increasingly heavy burden that these tensions were placing upon the shoulders of their Foreign Secretary. For the truth was that as the years passed Edward Grey's magnificent constitution was being subjected to strains beyond anything he had previously been asked to bear and his health was suffering.

When her husband's appointment as Foreign Secretary was announced Dorothy had seemed well on the road to recovery from her mysterious illness. Yet her health was still an issue. In January 1906 she had written to a friend:

> I have got spoilt by living in a small way and being rather ill and just seeing either people I liked very much or nobody at all. And now I've just got to come out of that and we have properly to try and like it. *It won't last long though, and I shall go back.* [Author's italics]

Dorothy had been proud to see Edward elected to the Cabinet and was pleased that he had been given work that interested him, though 'she felt that, for both of them, it was a very real and great sacrifice of personal happiness, and that there was very little personal satisfaction to be got out of the "glory"'.[1] She did not, however, anticipate that her husband's tenure of the post of Foreign Secretary would last long. After a year or two in the corridors of power (which she would try to avoid as much as she could, but otherwise do her best to endure) she felt sure that Edward would have had his fill of public life and be ready to retire. No one, least of all herself, could have foreseen that he would remain at his post for 10½ years, becoming Britain's longest-serving Foreign Secretary.

G.M. Trevelyan, Edward's first biographer and a fellow Northumbrian who knew both the Greys well, was of the opinion that if Dorothy had lived she would have had her husband out of the government well before the outbreak of war in 1914:

> One can hardly imagine it going on ... For she hated ceremony. There is little doubt that if she had lived, the mere fact that she was there, even if not her direct advice, would always have been a pull to draw him back out of office.[2]

But Dorothy was not there. And in the meantime the war clouds were gathering.

Edward's eyes had been troubling him for some time and by the spring of 1914 he was forced to acknowledge that his eyesight was failing. His father-in-law, Fitz Widdrington, had gone blind. Was it possible that he too – the passionately keen fisherman and bird-watcher – was heading the same way? That summer he had made arrangements to see the eminent German eye specialist at Wiesbaden whom the Widdringtons had consulted. But the pressure of work had forced him to cancel the visit.

The Widdrington Women

Thus it came about that Edward, who by this time was having to use a magnifying glass to go through his papers, was still manning his post at the Foreign Office when the German armies invaded Belgium, plunging half the world into war.

Among those who were to criticise Grey's handling of the crisis, no one was more damning than David Lloyd George; the man who as Chancellor of the Exchequer had proposed cutting expenditure on armaments and right up to the eleventh hour had turned a blind eye on the impending conflagration. In his *War Memoirs*, published in 1933 (the year Grey died), Lloyd George gave what he described as a 'frank estimate' of Edward's qualities as Foreign Secretary. He wrote:

> His tenure of the crucial office of Foreign Secretary constituted an essential part of what happened, and his personality was distinctly one of the elements that contributed to the great catastrophe ... He had qualities, largely of appearance, manner and restraint, which gave the impression of the 'strong silent man' whom the generations brought up on Carlyle earnestly sought, and when they thought they had discovered him, fervently adored. His striking physiognomy, with the thin lips, the firmly closed mouth and the chiselled features, gave the impression of cold, hammered steel ... [But] I am inclined to believe that the verdict of posterity will be adverse to his handling of the situation ...
>
> Of one thing there can be no doubt: he failed calamitously in his endeavours to avert the Great War ... [He was] a pilot whose hand trembled in a palsy of apprehension, unable to grip the levers and manipulate them with a firm and clear purpose. He was pursuing his avowed policy of waiting for public opinion to decide his direction for him ... Had he warned Germany in time of the point at which Britain would declare war – and wage it with her whole strength – the issue would have been different. [He could] in the name of a united people, have intimated to the German Government that if they put into operation their plan of marching through Belgium they would encounter the active hostility of the British Empire ... And he could have uttered the warning in sufficient time to leave the German military authorities without any excuse for not changing their dust-laden plans. When the ultimatum was actually delivered war had already broken out between Germany and her neighbours, and the German staff were able with some show of reason to inform the Kaiser that it was then too late to alter their arrangements without jeopardising the German chance of victory ... It was a temperamental failure. Grey's mind was not made for prompt action ... He altogether lacked that quality of audacity which makes a great Minister .. Throughout, Grey mistook correctitude for rectitude ... He was the most insular of our statesmen and knew less of foreigners through contact with them than any Minister in the government. He rarely if ever crossed the seas. Northumberland was good enough for him, and if he could not get there and needed a change, there was his fishing lodge in Hampshire. This was a weakness ... which accounted for some of his most conspicuous failures ... He lacked the vision, imagination, breadth of mind and that high courage, bordering on audacity, which his immense task demanded.

The thought behind Lloyd George's passage of high rhetoric is transparent: 'If only I had been at the helm things would have turned out differently.' A nagging suspicion suggests that he may have been right. 'Audacity' (a word he uses twice) had never been lacking in the fiery little Welshman, who as a schoolboy had stood against the authority of

Endpiece

the Established Church and as a young man had succeeded in toppling his own landlord in order to gain a seat in the House of Commons.

In 1910 Edward Grey had tendered his resignation over a matter of internal policy concerning the right of the House of Commons to veto obstruction by the Lords. After a compromise had been reached Grey yielded to pressure and withdrew his resignation. It is highly unlikely that he would have yielded if Dorothy had still been at his side. His eyesight was deteriorating. Would she not have said that 'enough was enough' and pulled him back from the political maelstrom, to enjoy with her the quiet flow of the Itchen river and their beloved wildfowl at Fallodon? On the other hand it is equally unlikely that if Grey had resigned, Lloyd George, who had never shown much interest in foreign affairs, would have been chosen to succeed him.

However, since a week (so it is said) can be a long time in politics, in the space of a year or two the political scene may change radically. So let us suppose that Grey had resigned and that by some unforeseen sequence of events Lloyd George had found himself in Grey's shoes in those last critical days before Great Britain was plunged into war. Might the 'Welsh Wizard' have succeeded in keeping the peace where Grey failed?

The entire success of Germany's plan for the conquest of France depended on speed.

Field Marshal Count Moltke and his generals had planned a short but devastating campaign that would deliver Paris, and hence France, to the German forces within a matter of weeks, if not days. Great Britain's only hope of stopping them was to issue an ultimatum: if German troops invade neutral Belgium Great Britain will immediately declare war on the Second Reich. Grey was perfectly well aware that this was the position. His tragedy was that he believed (correctly) that without the consent of Parliament his hands were tied.

Faced with the same predicament, would Lloyd George have been equally particular? Might he not rather have torn up the rule-book, leapt on a train to Berlin, confronted the German High Command with the threat of instant retaliation, bombarded the Kaiser with telegrams and harangued the German union officials (whose pledge to support the war had been given with considerable reluctance) – forcing Moltke and his fellow conspirators to draw back from the brink?

Of course, none of this happened. War came. But there are many who will continue to argue that the catastrophe of 1914 with its tragic repercussions was not inevitable. Lloyd George believed that Grey was the wrong man in the wrong place at the wrong time. And perhaps he was right. For with the dawn of the 20th century the world had entered a new and lawless phase, in which the old-fashioned gentlemanly diplomacy of checks and balances was to find no place. If this is held to be true, could there be another answer (not altogether fanciful) to that hoary old question: who (or what) was responsible for the outbreak of the First World War?

Was it a horse that shied?

Notes

PREFACE
1. Cynthia Chance, *My Life as a Student of Anthroposophy*
2. Nikolaus Pevsner, *Buildings of England: Northumberland*
3. Mrs Belloc Lowndes, *A Passing World*
4. David Lloyd George, *War Memoirs*

I EARLY DAYS
1. A.M. Macdonald, *Hopwood Hall 1250-1963*
2. The Hopwood Archive, Middleton Library

II THE GREAT WILL CASE
1. A.M. Macdonald, *Hopwood Hall*
2. Ibid.
3. Ibid.
4. Ibid.

VIII EXEMPLARY WIFE - TROUBLED MOTHER
1. Nikolaus Pevsner, *Buildings of England: Northumberland*

XI THE GOVERNESS YEARS
1. Louise Creighton, *Dorothy Grey*
2. Connie Ford, *Aleen* Cust, Veterinary Surgeon - Britain's First Woman Vet*
3. Ibid.

XII MANDELL CREIGHTON
1. James Covert (ed.), *Memoir of a Victorian Woman*
2. Louise Creighton, *Dorothy Grey*

XVI 'I HATE ALL THE MEN I MEET'
1. Louise Creighton, *Dorothy Grey*
2. Ibid.
3. Ibid.
4. Ibid.

XVII 'THE SUPREME GOOD EFFECT OF LOVE'
1. Louise Creighton, *Dorothy Grey*
2. Ibid.
3. Ibid.
4. Ibid.

XVIII EDWARD GREY
1. G.M. Trevelyan, *Grey of Fallodon*
2. Viscount Grey, *Twenty-Five Years*
3. Keith Robbins, *Sir Edward Grey*
4. Ibid.
5. Ibid.
6. Ibid.
7. James Covert, *A Victorian Marriage*

XX AN ELECTION
1. Janet Browne, *The Power of Place*
2. Louise Creighton, *Dorothy Grey*
3. Keith Robbins, *Sir Edward Grey*

XXI 17 HEREFORD SQUARE
1. Louise Creighton, *Dorothy Grey*
2. Ibid.
3. Ibid.
4. Keith Robbins, *Sir Edward Grey*
5. Louise Creighton, *Dorothy Grey*
6. G.M. Trevelyan, *Grey of Fallodon*
7. Keith Robbins, *Sir Edward Grey*
8. Louise Creighton, *Dorothy Grey*
9. Ibid.
10. Ibid.
11. Ibid.
12. Ibid.

XXII THE 'TIN HOUSE'
1. Viscount Grey, *Twenty-Five Years*
2. G.M. Trevelyan, *Grey of Fallodon*

* Always spelled 'Aline' in the Diaries.

242

Notes

    3. *Ibid.*
    4. *Ibid.*

XXIII   'A Very Strange Little Soul'
    1. Louise Creighton

XXIV   Two Friends
    1. Connie Ford, *Aleen Cust, Veterinary Surgeon: - Britain's First Woman Vet*

XXV   A Fateful Encounter
    1. Frances Spalding, *Roger Fry, Art and Life*

XXVI   'Dear Mr Fry'
    1. Frances Spalding, *Roger Fry, Art and Life*

XXVII   'A Friendship Tinged with Romance'
    1. Louise Creighton, *Dorothy Grey*

XVIII   Sir Edward in Office
    1. Leo McKinstry, *Rosebery: Statesman in Turmoil*
    2. Keith Robbins, *Sir Edward Grey*
    3. Viscount Grey, *Twenty-Five Years*
    4. Louise Creighton, *Dorothy Grey*
    5. Keith Robbins, *Sir Edward Grey*
    6. *Ibid.*
    7. Louise Creighton, *Dorothy Grey*
    8. Leo McKinstry, *Rosebery: Statesman in Turmoil*
    9. *Ibid.*
    10. *Ibid.*
    11. Louise Creighton, *Dorothy Grey*
    12. *Ibid.*
    13. G.M. Trevelyan, *Grey of Fallodon*
    14. Keith Robbins, *Sir Edward Grey*
    15. *Ibid.*
    16. Louise Creighton, *Dorothy Grey*
    17. *Ibid.*
    18. *Ibid.*
    19. *Ibid.*
    20. *Ibid.*
    21. Stephen Inwood, *The Birth of Modern London*
    22. *Ibid.*

XXIX   Gerard as Go-Between
    1. Frances Spalding, *Roger Fry, Art and Life*
    2. Virginia Woolf, *Roger Fry*
    3. *Ibid.*
    4. Frances Spalding, *Roger Fry, Art and Life*
    5. *Ibid.*
    6. The Fry Archive, King's College, Cambridge
    7. Virginia Woolf, *Roger Fry, Art and Life*

XXX   Between Two Loves
    1. Virginia Woolf, *Roger Fry, Art and Life*
    2. *Ibid.*
    3. The Fry Archive, King's College, Cambridge

XXXIII   A Providential Illness?
    1. Louise Creighton, *Dorothy Grey*
    2. Keith Robbins, *Sir Edward Grey*
    3. Louise Creighton, *Dorothy Grey*
    4. *Ibid.*
    5. Keith Robbins, *Sir Edward Grey*
    6. *Ibid.*
    7. G.M. Trevelyan, *Grey of Fallodon*
    8. Louise Creighton, *Dorothy Grey*
    9. *Ibid.*
    10. *Ibid.*
    11. *Ibid.*
    12. *Ibid.*
    13. *Ibid.*
    14. *Ibid.*
    15. *Ibid.*
    16. *Ibid.*

XXXV   'O The Misery the Tears the Trouble'
    1. David Lloyd George, *War Memoirs*
    2. Keith Robbins, *Sir Edward Grey*
    3. Michael Waterhouse, *The Cottage Book: The Undiscovered Country Diary Of An Edwardian Statesman Sir Edward Grey*
    4. Frances Spalding, *Roger Fry, Art and Life*

XXVI   A Horse that Shied
    1. Louise Creighton, *Dorothy Grey*
    2. *Ibid.*
    3. *Ibid.*
    4. *Ibid.*
    5. *Ibid.*
    6. *Ibid.*
    7. *Ibid.*
    8. James Covert, *A Victorian Marriage*

XXVII   Broken Lives
    1. Frances Spalding, *Roger Fry, Art and Life*
    2. *Ibid.*
    3. *Ibid.*

XXXVIII   A Fresh Start
    1. Cynthia Chance, *My Life as a Student of Anthroposophy*

XXXIX   At War
    1. Frances Spalding, *Roger Fry, Art and Life*
    2. *Ibid.*
    3. Cynthia Chance, *My Life as a Student of Anthroposophy*

XLI   Peace at a Price
    1. Barbara Tuchman, *The Zimmermann Telegram*
    2. *Ibid.*

    Endpiece
    1. G.M. Trevelyan, *Grey of Fallodon*
    2. *Ibid.*

Bibliography

THE DIARIES
Cecilia Widdrington, *My Diary*, 1840-1928, 1929-1930
   Frances Dorothy Widdrington, 1865
   Idonea Widdrington, 1869
   Gerard Widdrington, 1871
   Bertram Fitzherbert Widdrington, 1873
Idonea Cresswell *née* Widdrington, *The Events, Experiences etc. of Idonea Widdrington My Life*, 1869-1965

UNPUBLISHED MANUSCRIPT
Cynthia Chance, *My Life as a Student of Anthroposophy*

ARCHIVAL SOURCES
The Roger Fry Archive, King's College Library, Cambridge
The Hopwood Archive, Middleton Public Library, Greater Manchester

NEWSPAPER
The *Northumberland Gazette*. In 20 weekend issues running from 22 January 1993, Captain Joe Baker-Cresswell recounted his life to his grandson John.

BOOKS
Arnold, Ralph, *Northern Lights, The story of Lord Derwentwater*, Constable and Company Ltd, London (1959)
Belloc Lowndes, Mrs, *A Passing World*, Macmillan & Co., London (1848)
Browne, Janet, *Charles Darwin, The Power of Place* Jonathan Cape, London (2002)
Chamberlain, M.E., *The Scramble for Africa*, Longman Group, London (1974)
Covert, James, *A Victorian Marriage*, Hambledon & London (2000)
Covert, James (ed.), *Memoir of a Victorian Woman*, Indiana University Press (1994)
Creighton, Louise, *Dorothy Grey*, Spottiswoode & Co. Ltd, London (1907)

Cronin, Eileen, *A Sprinkling of Fota*, Carraig Print, Cork
Debrett's Peerage, Baronetage and Knightage, 1881 edition
Ford, Connie, *Aleen Cust, Veterinary Surgeon - Britain's First Woman Vet*, Biopress Ltd, Bristol (1990)
Inwood, Stephen, *The Birth of Modern London*, Macmillan and Co., London (2005)
Lloyd George, David, *War Memoirs* (6 vols), Ivor Nicholson & Watson, London (1933)
Lloyd George, Robert, *David and Winston*, John Murray, London (2005)
Macdonald, A.M., *Hopwood Hall 1250-1963*, Waldegrave, London (1953)
McKinstry, Leo, *Rosebery: Statesman in Turmoil*, John Murray, London (2005)
Pevsner, Nikolaus, *The Buildings of England: Northumberland*, Yale University Press, (2002)
Roberts, Andrew, *What Might Have Been*, Weidenfeld & Nicolson (2004)
Robbins, Keith, *Sir Edward Grey*, Cassell, London (1971)
Smith, Margaret, *Collected Articles on the History of Middleton*, Edward Pilling
Spalding, Frances, *Roger Fry, Art and Life*, Granada Publishing, London (1980)
Trevelyan, G.M., *Grey of Fallodon*, Longmans, Green and Co., London (1937)
Tuchman, Barbara, *The Zimmermann Telegram*, Ballantine Books (1985)
Viscount Grey of Fallodon, *Twenty-Five Years, 1892-1916* (2 vols), Frederick A. Stokes Company, New York (1925)
Viscount Grey of Fallodon, KC, *Fallodon Papers*, Constable and Company Ltd, London (1926)
Waterhouse, Michael, *The Cottage Book: The Undiscovered Country Diary of an Edwardian Statesman: Sir Edward Grey*, Victor Gollancz, London (1999)
Woolf, Virginia, *Roger Fry*, Hogarth Press (1940)

Index

Please note: page numbers in **bold** refer to illustrations

Aberhinant (estate), 4-5, 7, 8
Acland, Arthur, 111
Acton, Arthur, 148
Adelphi hotel, Liverpool, 12, 15
Africa
    Scramble for, 149-50
    Southern, 149, 179, 192
Algeria, 63
Alnmouth, 35, 49, 227
Alnwick
    Bench, 35
    Castle, 48-9
    Church, 234
    Workmen's Sociables, 127
Anglo-Russian agreement, 206
Ann family, 136
Anthroposophy, 230
anti-semitism, 234
Antwerp, 133
Apostles (Cambridge), 159
Armenian massacre, 180
Asolo, 133
Asquith, Herbert, 111, 148, 192, 199, 200
Athens, 44
Austria, 214-15

Baalbek (ruined city), 43
Baker, Miss, 188
Baker-Cresswell, Addison Francis (Addy), **188**
    character, 188
    death and will, 231
    family properties, 187-8
    Ida, relationship with, 187, 190
        reunion with, 196, 197-8
        separation from, 206-8
    leaves wife, 191, 194-7
    Master of Percy Foxhounds, 188, **189**, 190
    wartime career, 229
Baker-Cresswell, Addison Joe, 191, 205*n*, **207**
    anti-semitism, 234
    childhood illness, 212-13
    disinherited by Addy, 231
    father's custody of, 208
    Ida, relationship with, 220, 231, 234
    joins Royal Navy, 227
    marriage to Rona, 234
    schooling, 217, 218
Baker-Cresswell, Charles, xiv
Baker-Cresswell, Idonea (Ida) (formerly

Widdrington), **145**, **207**, **230**
Addison Joe, birth of, 191
Addy, marriage to, 190
    relationship with, 187-8, 190, 194-6
    reunion with, 196, 197-8
    separation from, 206-8
Bertram, relationship with, 54, 56, 221, 227
birth, 46-7, 52, 54
campaigns and good works, xix, 235
    against slaughter-houses, xix, 226-7, 235
camping on the moors, xix, 187
childhood/teenage years, 68-72, 118-19
coming-out, 119-20
Cresswell, changes surname to, 213
Cynthia, birth of, 198
    marriage of, 234
dairy farmer, 178, 187
Diana, birth of, 205
Dorothy, relationship with, 121-2, 123-4, 139, 167
    distressed by death of, 204
Enid, rift with, xvii, 221-3, 227
Events, Adventures, Experiences ... in the life of (self-portrait), xxi, 68-71
friendships, 125-7
Gerard, relationship with, 155
Greys, estrangement from, 178, 184, 204
hawking, 136, 137
holiday at Riviera, 212-13
hunting, 119, 124
illness, 145-6, 164
India, travels to, 206
John, birth of, 190-1
    death of, 228, 230
knitting skills, 166
love affairs, early, 119-21, 126, 127, 136, 138, 140, 143, 163
    in Italy, 128, 129
Fry, Roger:
    meeting, 129, 131-2
    mother (possibly) of his daughter, xvi, 171-4
    relationship with, 135-9, 140-1, 142-5, 157, 163, 175-7
Ministry of Food work, 226
mountaineering feat, 80-1
moving house, 211, 212
    to Harehope, 191
    to Hauxley Hall, 212, 213
    to Hyères, 76, 77, 81

nurse, trains as, 164, 165-6, 167, 177-8
old age, xiii-xiv
political gossip, 122
runs away from governess, 63
sexuality, 124, 127, 145
singing/acting, 119, 120-1, 122, 127, 165, 166-7, 175-6
spiritualism/Anthroposophy, 230
war work in Newcastle, 221
work behind the Front, 217
Baker-Cresswell, Joe, *see* Baker-Cresswell, Addison Joe
Baker-Cresswell, John, 190-1, **207**
    Addy's custody of, 208
    death, 228-9
    enters naval training college, 212, **228**
    Jutland, 220
Baker-Cresswell, Oswin Cumming, 188
Baker-Cresswell, Rona (formerly Vaile), 234
Bala, 5
Balfour, Arthur, 199
Ballet Russes (Diaghilev), 175
Balliol College, Oxford, 96-7
Barri (dog), 140
Barrymore, Lord, xviii
Bartlett, Edith, 169
Bartlett, Frederick, 169, 170
Bartlett, May (formerly Mann), xvi, 168-74, **172**
    adoption, 168-9
    Fry identified as father, 170
    marriage and family, 169-70
    mother's identity, 169, 170-4
Barton, Captain, 183-4
Baskervyle-Glegg family, reputation, 4
Baskervyle-Glegg, Susan, *see* Gregge-Hopwood, Susan
Beaumont, Mr (best man), 102
Bell (friend of Gerard), 155
Belloc Lowndes, Mrs, xiv, 103
Belton House, 186
Bendigo (racehorse), 233
Bertram Diary, 74, 176
Besant, Annie, 104
bicycles, 115, 184-5
Bishop, Miss (singing teacher), 119
Bismarck, Herbert von, 148
Blunt, Wilfred Scawen, 210
La Boccherini (villa), 81, 83
Boer War, 192-3

246

Index

Boucheron, Isaac de, xvii
Bradlaugh, Charles, 104
Britannia (training ship), 62
British Guiana, 179
Brownlow, Lord, 185
Budge (Nurse), 164
Budleigh Salterton, 228
Buxton, Mrs Francis, 182
Buxton, Mary, 112
Buxton, Sydney, 111
Byng, the Hon. Cecilia, *see* Hopwood, the Hon. Cecilia
Byron, Lord, 3, 142

Cairo, 38-9, 41-2
Cambridge University, 131
Campbell-Bannerman, Henry, 199-200
Canaletto, 161
Carlyle, Thomas, 182
Cavalière, 212-13, 216-17
Cézanne, Paul, 209-10
Chamberlain, Joseph, 181
Chance, Cecilia (author), xiii-xxii
Chance, Cynthia May (formerly Baker-Cresswell), **198**, **207**, **209**
  Anthroposophy, 230
  autobiography, xiii, 230
  birth, 198
  childhood, 211, 212, 217
  Hugh, engagement and marriage to, 233-4
  Rosemary, relationship with, 198
  schooling, 217, 218
  teenage years, 227
Chance Houses, 231-3, **232**
Chance, Hugh (William Hugh Stobart), 233-4
Chance, Idonea, xiv
Chesham Place, No. 26, 45
Childe Harold's Pilgrimage (Byron), 3
Clarence, Duke of, 138
Clowes, Mrs, 138
Cochran, Charles, 175
Cock and Barker (inn), xviii, xx
Connolly, Cressida, 212*n*
conscientious objectors, 220
contraception, 104
Conway, 28
Coombe, Helen, *see* Fry, Helen
Cooper, Lady Diana, 186*n*
Corbett, George, 138, 140
Cottage Book – the Undiscovered Country Diary of an Edwardian Statesman (Grey), 115-17
Cowburn, Sir Alexander, 11, 12, 13
Creighton, Louise, 64, 66, 67, 75, 183
  and Dorothy's death, xv-xvi, 201-2, 203
Creighton, the Rev. Dr Mandell
  career, 65-7, 122, 184
  death, 201
  Dolly/Dorothy, correspondence with, 92-3, 107, 109, 122, 146, 184, 193
    mentor to, 64, 75-6, 77, 85-6, 87-8, 97
  Edward, mentor to, 97-8
  liberalism, 90, 97, 147
Creighton, Oswin, 203
Creighton, Robert, 65
Cresswell, Aline, 211-12, 212*n*, **213**, 234
Cresswell, Rosemary, *see* Probart, Rosemary
Cresswell Hall/estate, 137-8, 187-8
Crossley, Henry, 78
Crossley, Lucy (formerly Gregge-Hopwood), 7, 15, 32
  death, 78

Crows in a Cornfield (Van Gogh), 210
Crystal Palace, 233
Cumming, Mrs (formerly nurse Nana), 191, 211-12, 229, 234*n*, 235
Cust, Aline, 125-6, 127, 204-5
Cust, Amelia, 30
Cust, Sir Charles, Bt (Charley), 30, 62, 92
Cust, Lady Charlotte, 61-2, 73, 125, 126, 145, 164
Cust, Harry, 185-6
Cust, Leo, 73-4, 126
Cust, Sir Leopold, Bt, 27, 28, 55, 61, 62, 125
Cust, Percy, 73-4

Damascus, 43-4
Daresbury church, 237
Darlington, 203
Darwin, Charles
  contraception, views on, 104
  On the Origin of Species, xvii, 104, 150
  servants' wages bill, 48
Davidson, Dorothy, *see* Widdrington, Dorothy
Davies, Diana (formerly Baker-Cresswell), 205, **207**, **209**
  childhood, 211, 217, 221
  Davy, marriage to, 234-5
  schooling, 227
  teenage years, 227
Davies, the Rev. John (Davy)
  Army padre, 220, 221
  visits Hauxley, 227
Davies, W.H., 52
Dene School, 73
Denman, Emma, *see* Ravensworth, Emma Sophia Georgiana, Countess of
Derby, Earl of, 3, 11
Devonshire, Duke of, 186*n*
Diaghilev, Serge, 175*n*
diaries (Cecilia's), xiv-xv, xx-xxii, 47, 51, 173, 236
Dickens, Charles, 60
Dickinson, Goldsworthy Lowes (Goldie), 159, 163, 208
Diggle, Bishop (of Carlisle), 220*n*
Disraeli, Benjamin, 149
Dolgellau, 120
Dolmetsch family, 188-9
domestic service, 47-8
Dominica, 182
Donhead St Mary, 228
Dorothy Diary, 51, 63, 84, 88, 101, 102
Drover, Mrs Susan, 117, 183
Duff Gordon, Lady, 41
Duff Gordon, Sir Marcus, 41
Duke, Miss (governess), 63

Earle, Mr (lawyer), 11, 13
Edoeur, Dr (physician), 79, 80
Edward VII
  death, 206
  Prince of Wales, 96
Egypt
  as Protectorate, 149
  visits, 37, 38-9
Elliott, Lady, 217
Elliott, Mary, 217, 221, 227
Embleton parish, 64, 89, 147
Miss Emmy, *see* Williams, Emma
Entente Cordiale, 199, 206, 215-16
Exmouth Chronicle, 236

Fallodon Hall, 88, 94, 95, 123, 151, 200, 201-2

Felton (builder), 36
Femme aux Yeux Verts (Matisse), 210
Fenton, Mr (headmaster), 74
Ford, Rudolph Onslow, 213
Forrester, Aline, 194-7
Forrester, Captain, 194, 197
Fota House/Island, xviii, 28-9, 35, 37, 52, 55
Foulmart hunting, 5
Frenchay, 168-9
Fry, Sir Edward, 130, 131, 163
Fry, Edward Portsmouth, 131
Fry, Helen (formerly Coombe), 189-90, 198
  insanity, 208-9
Fry, Joan, 209
Fry, Margery, 157
Fry, Lady Mariabella, 163, 169
Fry, Roger, **131**, **218**
  artistic career, 131, 138-9, 161
  background/education, 130-1
  Cecilia, meets, 129-30, 131-2
    relationship with, 133, 135, 136, 139, 141-2, 175-7, 176
    after his marriage, 188-9, 190, 194-6
    lover, 157-60, 161, 162-3
    resumes friendship with, 233
  Cecilia or Ida as possible mother of his daughter, 170-4, 176-7, 196
  curator at Metropolitan Museum, 208, 209
  daughter identified, xvi, 170, 174
  Helen, marriage to, 188-90
    collapse of marriage, 208-9
  Ida, acquires paintings for, 191
  meets, 129-30, 131-2
    relationship with, xvi, 135-9, 140-1, 142-5, 157
  lecturer, 162
  pacifism, 219, 220
  parents, relationship with, 131, 163
  Post-Impressionist exhibitions, 209-10
  visit to Newton, 133, 135-6
  Workshop, 219-20

Garcia, Signor (singing teacher), 16-17
George III, 94
Gerand, Mlle (governess), 7
Gerard Diary, xxi, 74, 155, 157, 205
Germany
  High Command opinion on Edward, 185*n*, 216
  Liberal splits over, 199
  outbreak of First World War, 214-16, 240-1
Gibson (lawyer), 205
Gladstone, Catherine, 122-3
Gladstone, William, 110, 111, 180
  fourth premiership, 147, 148, 150
Glegg, Mrs (Grandma), 33, 34
Glencomer, Lord, 120*n*
Gluck, 162
Golightly, Mr (parson), 73, 156, 205-6
Grafton Gallery (London), 209-10
Grand Hotel, Cavalière, 212
Graves, Alice, 203
Graves Disease, 180
Gregge, Edward, 2-3
Gregge-Hopwood, Cecilia, *see* Widdrington, Cecilia
Gregge-Hopwood, Edward, 1-2, 5, 7, 8
  death, 136
  dispute over will, 7, 8, 9-13, 14
  Hopwood Hall, 17-19, 20-1
  Knutsford, 22
  wealth, 19, 27

247

The Widdrington Women

Gregge-Hopwood, Edward (jnr), 14-15, 52, 102, 156, 219, 232
Gregge-Hopwood, Lady Elinor (formerly Stanley), 3, 7, 8, 10
Gregge-Hopwood, Evelyn, *see* Lloyd Price, Evelyn
Gregge-Hopwood, the Rev. Frank, 3-4, 7-8
   dispute over Hopwood estate, 7-8, 10-11, 13, 14
Gregge-Hopwood, Lt Col Harvey, 9, 10
Gregge-Hopwood, Lucy, *see* Crossley, Lucy
Gregge-Hopwood, Lucy (husband of Harvey), 9
Gregge-Hopwood, Mary Augusta, *see* Sefton, Mary Augusta, Countess of
Gregge-Hopwood, Robert, 1, 2, 8
Gregge-Hopwood, Rose, *see* Pender, Lady Rose
Gregge-Hopwood, Susan Fanny (formerly Baskervyle-Glegg), 1-2, 4, 8, 13, 16-19
   and Cecilia's coming out, 20-2
   death, 205
   illness, 17
   as old lady, 156, 167
Gresham's School, Norfolk, 217*n*
Grey, Charles, 179, 192
Grey, 1st Earl, 94
Grey, 2nd Earl (Edward's cousin), 94, 111
Grey, George (Edward's brother), 151-2, 179, 192
Grey, George (Georgy), 95-6
Grey, Mrs Harriet (formerly Pearson), 64, 95-6, 101, 102
Grey, Lady (Anna Sophia), 64, 95, 100, 123
Grey, Lady, Dorothy (Dolly) (formerly Widdrington), **52**, **101**, 102, **108**, **150**
   accident and death, 116, 202, 238
      consequences for Edward as Foreign Secretary, 238-41
      funeral/cremation, xvi, 203
      last weeks, 201-2
   arts/nature, attitude to, 60, 64, 113, 115-16
   aversion to physical intimacy, 51-2
   beauty, 82
   bicycles, 115, 184-5
   birth, 31, 32-4, 36
   charitable works, 109
   childhood, 45, 51-4
   Creighton, relationship with, *see* Creighton, the Rev. Dr Mandell
   Dominican bungalow, 182-3
   Edward, accompanies to West Indies, 181-3, 184
      engagement to, 91, 92, 93, 99
      helps campaign, 100, 105-6
      marriage, 100-2
      political life, 110, 111, 122-3, 147, 148
      sexual relations with, 103-5, 167
   haughtiness, 181, 183, 184
   Fry, approves of, 167
   Earl of Rosebery, friendship with, 148
   early education, 53-4
   early experience of death, 61
   early illness, 56
   Empire, view on, 193
   Fallodon, stays at, 88
   family reputation, xix
   friendship, 89-90
   governess experience, 59-64
   Grey family, meets, 64
   happiness, 109
   health improves, 193-4
   Hyères, move to, 74, 77-8, 81
   Ida, contrast with, 118
      relationship with, 121-2, 123-4, 167

   illness, 180-1, 184-6
   India, travels to, 112
   introspection, 92-3, 107
   Liberal party, views on, 110-11
   London, dislike for, 151-2
      first season, 83-5
      home, 107
      second season, 90
   memories of, 183-4
   mother, early relationship with, 51-4
   nurse's dismissal, reaction to, 63
   pantheism, 115, 152
   parents, relationship with, 118
   physical courage, 52
   political gatherings, 111-12
   Quaker ethic, 89
   reading, 109, 122
   relationships, demand for clarity and truth in, 152
   reputation, xv-xvi
   tin house, 113-17, 182, 183, 185, 193-4
   Widdringtons, estrangement from, xv-xvi, xix, 178, 184, 194, 204
Grey, Sir Edward, Bt, **95**, 102, **203**
   bicycles, 115, 184-5
   Boer War, 192-3
   'declaration', 150-1
   Dorothy:
      bird expertise, acknowledgement of, 115-16
      death, 203
         consequences for Edward as Foreign Secretary, 238-41
      engagement to, 91, 98
      marriage to, 100-2
   early life, 94-9, 188
   education, 96-7
   eyesight, failing, 239-40
   fishing, 96, 111, 113
   Foreign Secretary, 106, 200-2, 214-16, 238-41
   Foreign Secretary's Parliamentary Under Secretary, 146, 148-51
   German opinion on, 185*n*, 216
   Ida, relationship with, xix, 123
   India, travels to, 112
   London home, 107
   Member of Parliament, 105-7, 111, 147-8, 153, 193
   mistress, (possible), 185-6
   Northumbrian, 94
   opposition interest in foreign affairs, 179-80
   outbreak of war, 214-16
   pantheism, 115
   political career, 109, 109-12, 148, 181, 192, 193, 199-200
      first steps, 92, 98-9, 100
   sexuality, 103-5, 185-6
   tin house, 113-17, 182, 183, 185, 193
   West Indies on Royal Commission, 181-3, 184
   Widdringtons, ease in relations with, 213
   Winchester College, 64
Grey, Sir George, 95
Grosvenor Road, No. 18, 151

Haldane, Richard, 111-12, 192, 199, 200
Harcourt, Sir William, 181
Hard Times (Dickens), 60
Harehope house/estate/Moore, xix, 187-8, 191, 207
Harrup, Mr (businessman), 11

Hauxley Hall, xiii, xiv, xvii, 212, 220
   Fitz's final visit, 224
   wartime shoot, 222-3
Hauxley village/colliery, 35, 50, 218
   elementary school, 119*n*
hawking, 136, 137
Hecht, Mr (piano teacher), 16
Herbert, Constance (governess), 63-4, 80, 84
   Dorothy:
      at funeral of, 203
      letters from, 105-6, 183
   family, 83
   Ida, relationship with, 71, 77-8, 118
Herbert, Doris and Flo, 83
Herbert, Mr and Mrs, 83
Hereford Square, No. 17, 107, 118
Heron, the Rev. George, 25
Heron, Kate, 18, 25-6
Hogg (farmhand), 178
Hopwood, Colonel Edward Byng George, 219
Hopwood, Captain Robert Gerald, 219
Hopwood, Dr Robert, 2-3
Hopwood Cottage, 1, 2, 15, 16
Hopwood family archive, 174; *see also* Gregge-Hopwoods
Hopwood Hall, 1, **3**, 8-9, 10-11, 16, 17-19, 156, 219
Hopwood, the Hon. Cecilia (formerly Byng), 3
Hôtel de l'Hermitage (Hyères), 77
House of Commons, 90
Hudson, W.H., 114
hunting, 5, 49, 119, 124
Hyères, 75-6, 77-82, 138, 139, 175, 176, **209**, 233

Ibsen, Henrik, 151
Idonea Diary, 175
India, 112, 175
Inverary Castle, 197-8
Ireland, 26-7, 28-9
Irish Home Rule, 147, 150
Irish Question, 110
Italy, 128-30

Jacson, Mrs Frances, 24, 31, 34, 45, 46, 52, 61
Jamaica, 182
Jameson Raid, 179, 192
Jellicoe, Admiral, 220
Jenner, Dr (physician), 74-5
Jerusalem, 92
Jervis, the Hon. Ronald (Ronnie), 119-20, 121
John, King, 219
Josephine (nurserymaid), 53-4

Kimberley, Lord, 150, 181
King's College, Cambridge, 131, 172
King's College Hospital, London, 165, 177
Knutsford, 22-3

Lambton, the Hon. F.W., 111
Lawson, William (Willie), 121, 126, 136, 143, 163
Lear, Edward, xvii, 25
Leasowes Castle, 62, 92
Liberal party splits, 110-11, 192-3, 199
Liverpool, 12, 15, 37
Lloyd George, David, xv, 111, 192, 214, 240-1
Lloyd Price, Evelyn (Evie) (formerly Gregge-Hopwood), xviii, 4, 120
   death, 233
   portrait, **156**, 157-9
Lloyd Price, Richard (Dick), xviii, 120, 157-8, 233

Index

London, 152-3
London, Bishop of, *see* Creighton, the Rev. Dr Mandell
Longhurst Hall, 121
Lorne, Lord, 197
Louise, Princess, 197
Lower Berkeley Street, No. 6, 90, 91

McGonigle, Mr (schoolmaster), 202, 203
MacPherson, Miss (governess), 218
Malta, 38
Manchester, 16, 19
    Races, 25
Mann, May, *see* Bartlett, May
Mann, Mr (gardener), 170
Mann, Mrs, 168-9
Marberry (House), 32
Marshall, Miss (governess), 63
Matisse, Henri, 209-10
medical training for women, 125-6
Memoir of Dorothy, 183
Metropolitan Museum, New York, 208, 209
Middleton, 19
    library, 174
Milner, Sir Alfred, 192
Ministry of Food, 226
Monkswell, Lady, 181, 183
Moore Hall (Manor Farm), xvii, 18, 218, 224, 227, 228, 234-5, 236
Morgan, J. Pierpoint, 208
Morgins les Bains, 79-81
myalgic encephalomyelitis (ME), 181

Nana (nurse), 191
Neat, Mrs (maid), 235, 236
New York, 121, 208, 209
Newcastle, 221
Newton Hall, 31, 32, **33**, 35, 218
    Bertram settles at, 227
    changes to grounds, 205
    Christmases at, 48, 50, 118
    conservatory, **134**, 135
    Dolly's wedding, 102
    holidays at, 61, 62, 85
    shooting at, 49
    visited by author, xvi-xvii, xx
    visits by Margaret Norman, 171-2
Newton-on-the-Moor, 35, 45-6, 50
    elementary school, 119*n*, 120
Nile trip, 38-41
Norman, Sir Henry, 181
Norman, Margaret (formerly Bartlett), xvi, 169-74, 176-7, 196
    likeness to Cecilia, **173**
North Shields, 206, 223
Northbrook, Lord, 113
Northumberland, Duke of, 52-3, 188
Northumbrian Gazette, 75

Oliver (Gerard's friend), 155
Omega Workshops, 219-20
On the Origin of Species (Darwin), xvii, 104, 150
Orde, Reginald, 126-7
Orde family, 50
Orde House, 46
Oriel College, Oxford, 155
Orinoco (steamer), 37-8
Osborne naval training college, 212

Palestine, 42-3
Palmerston, Lord, 149

Paris, Monsieur (dancing master), 20
Past Friends (play), 120
Pearson, Harriet, *see* Grey, Harriet
Pease, Ella, 89-90, 91, 107, 128, 129, 200, 203
Pease, Marna, 230
Pease, May, 173-4
Pender, Sir James, 34, 228
Pender, Lady Rose (formerly Gregge-Hopwood), 7, 15, 32, 34, 120, 205, 228, 233
Percy Foxhounds, 188, **189**, 190
Percy, Lord, 106
Peterborough, Bishop of, *see* Creighton, the Rev. Dr Mandell
Pevsner, Nikolaus, xiv
Pike, Captain, 206
Plombières-les-Bains, 164
Post-Impressionist exhibitions, 209-10
Poulson, Mlle (governess), 63
The Prelude, 115
Price, *see* Lloyd Price
Prince of Wales (later Edward VII), 96
Princips, Gavrilo, 238
Probart, Archie, 234
Probart, Rosemary (formerly Cresswell), 197, **197**, 198, **228**
    lives with father, 208, 211-12
    marriage and inheritance, 234, 243*n*
Puck (horse), 118

Quaker community (Society of Friends), 89, 130, 131, 168-9, 208, 219
Qui Vive (horse), 89

Rabbits for Profit and Pleasure (Lloyd Price), xviii
Rachel (nurse), 2
Ravensworth, Earl of, 138, 188, 205*n*
Ravensworth, Emma Sophia Georgiana, Countess of (formerly Denman; Mrs Baker-Cresswell; later Mrs Wadsworth), 138, 188, 205
Reis (Nile boat captain), 39-40, 41-2
Relugas Compact, 199-200
Rhiwlas estate, xviii, 120, 158
Riddle of Alnwick (cake-maker), 102
Rifle Brigade, 126-7
Rivière, Enid, *see* Widdrington, Enid
Roberts, Andrew, 238
Rosebud Dinner Parties, 123
Rosebery, Earl of, 147, 148, 150-1, 153
Rothschild, Baron, 149
Royal College of Physicians, 3
RSPCA, xix
Ruskin, John, 66
Ruthven, Lord, 41, 42

St Margaret's School, Scarborough, 217*n*
St Vincent, 4th Viscount, 120
Salisbury, Lord, 146, 180
Saltburn, 211
Sandringham, 96
Sarajevo, 238
Scarborough, 58
Schopenhauer, Arthur, 109
Scots Guards, xix
Scramble for Africa, 149
sea bathing, 6
Sefton, Earl of, 4, 7, 8, 10-11
Sefton, Mary Augusta, Countess of (formerly Gregge-Hopwood, Mary Augusta), 3-4, 8
Shepherds Hotel, 38
Short (butler), 223

Shotton (coachman), 75, 118, 135
Sidmouth, 232
Simpson, Dr, 33
Singer sewing machine, 46
slaughter-houses campaign, xix, 226-7, 235
Smith-Barry, Arthur Hugh, 26, 32
Smith-Barry, Elizabeth, 26, 29, 31, 32, 36-7, 102
    London residence, 45
Smith-Barry, James, 29
Smith-Barry, James Hugh (Jem/Jim), xviii, 32, 34, 55, 56, 205
Smith-Barry, Geraldine, *see* Willoughby de Broke, Geraldine, Lady
Smith-Barry family, 31-2, 52
Smoke Abatement Society, 19
Society of Friends (Quaker community), 89, 130, 131, 168-9, 208, 219
Southern Africa, 149, 179, 192
Spalding, Francis, 170, 171
spiritualism, 230
Stanley, Lady Elinor, *see* Gregge-Hopwood, Lady Elinor
Steiner, Rudolf, 230
Stewart, Dr Grainger, 178
Sudan, 149
Suez Canal, 149
sugar industry in British West Indies, 181-2
Switzerland, 79-81

Taubman, Sir Goldie, 40-1
Tennant, 'Bim', 230*n*
Tennant, Christopher Grey, 186
Tennant, Eddie, 186
Tennant, Edward (Eddie), 120*n*, 122
Tennant, Emma, 186
Tennant, Margot, 123, 126
Tennant, Pamela, 120, 123, 185-6, 193, 230*n*
Thatcher, Margaret, 186*n*
Thessiger, Sir Frederick, 11
Thunderer, HMS, 220
tin house, 113-17, 182, 183, 185
Tipperary Free Press, 62
Torrington, Lord, 3
Trevelyan, G.M., 94, 106, 203, 214, 239
Trosset, Eva, 78
Trower, Sir Walter, 208
Tuckett, Mrs (a Quaker), 169
Turner, Ken, 170

Uganda, 149, 150

Valkyrie (Wagner), 164
Van Gogh, Vincent, 209-10
La Veille au Chapelet (Cézanne), 210
Venezuela, 179
Venice, 128-30, 143
Veterinary Record, 126
veterinary training for women, 126
Victoria, Queen
    court, 126
    funeral, 191
    Golden Jubilee, 119
von Glehn, Louise, *see* Creighton, Louise

Wadsworth, James William, 205
Wadsworth, Mrs, *see* Ravensworth, Emma Sophia Georgiana, Countess of
Wagner, Richard, 164
Waller, Dora, xiii, xix, 217, 220, 227
War, First World
    continuance, 221-5

effect on Home Front, 226
  ending, 227-30
  outbreak, 214-20
  preventability, 238, 240-1
War, Second World, xvii-xviii
Ward, Mr (a Quaker), 168, 170
Ward (nurse), 32, 34, 36
  dismissal, 62-3
  Dolly's illness, 55-6
  relationship with family, 47, 51, 53-4, 60-1
  relationship with governess, 59
Wardle, Dr (opthalmic surgeon), 206
Warrington, 227
  Infirmary Ball, 25-6
  Pattons Arms Hotel, 235
  workhouse, 228
Waterhouse, Michael, 116
Waterson, Dr (physician), 202
weekend, 109
Welsh Guards, xviii
West Indies, 12, 181-3, 184
Widdrington, 3rd Lord, 24
  still-born son, 34
Widdrington, Anthony
  birth, 213, 216
  childhood, 222, 227
  death, xvii
Widdrington, Aunt, 27
Widdrington, Brigadier-General Bertram, **223**
  Aline, engagement to, 204-5
  army career, xviii, 165, 167, 175, 206
  birth and early childhood, 57-8
  Cecilia, reconciliation with, 227, 233
  conservatism, xviii
  death, xvii
  Dolly's wedding, 102
  Enid, marriage to, 213
  Fitz, rift with, 223
  Gerard, relationship with, 155
  holiday in Italy, 133
  Ida, wife's rift with, xix, 221, 222, 227
  illness, 74-6, 77, 78-9
  Salonika, 223, 227
  schooling, 119
  Western Front, 216, 218, 220, 223
Widdrington, Cecilia (born Gregge-Hopwood), **26**, **232**
  acquires two Chance Houses, 231-3, **232**
  attractiveness to men, 42
  Bertram, heals rift with, 227
    relationship with, 74-5
  birth, 1
  childhood holidays, 4-6
  coming out, 20-3
  Creighton, disquiet about, 87-8
  Cust family, helps, 61, 62
  Dolly:
    birth of, 31, 32-4
    distressed by death of, 204
    first season, 83-4
    relationship with, 51-4, 90, 123-4
    wedding, 101-2
  diaries to record children's development, xiv-xv, xx-xxii, 47, 51, 173, 236
  dismissal of nurse, 62-3
  early married life, 31-6
  early motherhood, 45-50
  education deficiencies, 7, 14, 24, 53, 161
  Edward, reconciled with, 233

Fitz, courtship, 24-7
  death of, 224-5
  overseas travels with, 37-44, 63, 121, 123, 128-30, 132-3
Fry, after his marriage, 188-9, 190, 209
  friendship with, 219, 220
  lover, 157-60, 161, 162-3
  meeting, 128-32
  mother (possibly) of his daughter, 170-1, 196
  relationship with, 133, 135, 136, 139, 141-2, 175, 188
family reputation, xviii
Gerard, relationship with, 73, 74, 154-6, 227, 228, 235
Golden Wedding anniversary, 213
Greys, estrangement from, 178, 184
horsewoman, 49
Ida:
  birth of, 46-7
  difficulties between Ida and Enid, 221, 223
  on engagement of, 188
  on marriage of, 188, 190, 194-6
  relationship with, 69-70, 119, 120-1, 123, 124, 127, 128-9, 163-4, 177-8
Jem Smith-Barry, relationship with, xviii, 32, 34, 55, 56, 205
last years and death, 236-7
likeness to Margaret Norman, **173**
Moore Hall (Manor Farm), 18, 218, 224, 228
mother, memories of, 1-2, 4-5
mountaineering feat, 80-1
move to Hyères, 75-6, 77-82
move to Switzerland, 79-81
music lessons, 16-17, 21
relationships with staff/people, 47-8, 51
religion, attitude to, 236
sexual side of marriage, 101
shyness, 21-2, 51
sons, birth of, 55-8
teenage years, 15-19
visits to poor, 49
and war, 216, 218-19, 220, 227
wedding, 27-8
will dispute, 11-13
and women of her own class, 50
Widdrington, Dorothy (Aunt Dorothy) (formerly Davidson), 31, 32, 35
Widdrington, Dorothy (Dolly), *see* Grey, Lady, Dorothy
Widdrington, Enid (formerly Rivière), 213, 216
  reconciliation with Cecilia, 227, 233
  rift with Ida, xvii, xix, 221-3, 227
Widdrington family forbears, 24
Widdrington, Captain Francis
  birth, 227
  meetings with author, xiv-xxii
  meetings with Margaret Norman, xvi, 171-2, 176
  Second World War, xvii-xviii
Widdrington, Gay, xiv, xx, xxi, 172, 176
Widdrington, Gerard, **58**, 158
  birth, 54, 56
  Cecilia:
    accompanies her and Fry, 157-9, 162
    with her at Moore Hall, 225
    helps her, 227, 228, 235
  disinherits himself, 205
  family legends about, xv

family reputation, xviii-xix
Fitz, death of, 224
future role, 156
holidays in Hyères, 78
Ida, helps on farm, 178
North Shields, 206
Oxford friends, 155, 176
paternity, xviii-xix, xxii, 55, 56
returns home, 223
schooling 72, 73-4, 75, 76, 119
teenager, 154-5
travels abroad, 204
unmanliness, 57, 58, 73
Widdrington, Idonea (Ida), *see* Baker-Cresswell, Idonea
Widdrington, Shalcross Fitzherbert (Fitz), **4**, **222**
  artist, xvii, xx, 25, 161-2, 175, 176
  Bertram, rift with, 223
  blindness, 178, 187, 206, 239
  Cecilia, courtship, 24-7
    first meeting with, 23
    marriage, 27-30, 31-6, 45-50
    overseas travels with, 37-44, 63, 121, 123, 128-30, 133
  Christmas entertainment, 118
  Cust family, helps, 61-2
  Dorothy, distressed by death of, 204
    relationship with, 84, 89
  forbears, 24
  Gerard, relationship with, 73, 74, 224
  Golden Wedding anniversary, 213
  hunting, 49, 119
  Ida, relationship with, 70-1, 119, 121, 129, 164, 208, 213, 224
  Irish business affairs, 26-7, 28-9
  Jem Smith-Barry, wife's relationship with, 55, 56-7
  last years and death, 218, 224-5
  militia command, 49-50
  move to Hyères, 75, 78, 81
  move to Switzerland, 79-80
  old age, 64
  travel, love of, 35-6, 121
Wilhelm II, Kaiser, 206, 214
William (footman), 61
Williams, Emma (Miss Emmy) (nurse-governess), 2, 4, 6-7, 16
Williams, the Rev. J., 15
Willoughby de Broke, Geraldine, Lady (formerly Smith-Barry), 24, 31-2, 34, 55, 58
Willoughby de Broke, Lord, 34
Wilson, Dr (physician), 56, 59-60
Wimereux hospital, 217, 220, 227
Winchester College, 64, 73, 96, 119
Winkworth, Miss, 231
Winnington-Ingram, Arthur, Bishop of London, 220*n*
Withington, 22-3
Women's Institute, xix, 235
Women's Land Army, 226
Woolf, Virginia, 160, 170
Wordsworth, Dorothy, 105
Wordsworth, William, 104-5, 115, 152
Wuthering Heights (Brönte), 135

Yates, Miss (governess), 59-63
York, Duke of, 212